Other Books by Jacob D. Eppinga:

The Soul of the City

For Sinners Only

Cabbages and Kings

More Cabbages and Kings

A CENTURY OF GRACE

Psalm 90:1 and 17

Lord, thou hast been our dwelling place in all generations.

And let the beauty of the Lord our God be upon us: and establish thou the work of our hands upon us; yea, the work of our hands establish thou it.

A CENTURY OF

Published by the LaGrave Avenue Christian Reformed Church
Edited by Nancy Peters
Printed by Hoekstra Printing
Bound by John H. Dekker and Sons
Grand Rapids, Michigan

Second printing, 2019
Funding provided by the LaGrave Benefactors Trust Fund
Printed by Pageworks
Bound by Dekker Bookbinders

Jacob D. Eppinga

GRACE

Acknowledgments

The responses to requests by the Centennial Committee, chaired by Dr. Gerald VanderWall, for assistance in the production of this book were overwhelming. It would be difficult to estimate the hours contributed to its creation by many willing workers. Nancy Peters as editor and Ruth Snoek as church secretary, typist, and proofreader, are just two who have much time invested in making this book a reality. There are many more, including James Hoekstra, printer, and Howard Dekker, bookbinder. For all, it has been a labor of love, carried out with the prayer that the combined efforts would result in a worthwhile contribution to the life and spirit of the LaGrave Church — and to the glory of God.

Library of Congress Catalogue Card Number: 86-93353

Copyright© 1987 by LaGrave Avenue Christian Reformed Church

A DEDICATION

TO: **THE LAGRAVE AVENUE CHRISTIAN REFORMED CHURCH**

"Let the favor of the Lord our
God be upon us, and establish
thou the work of our hands upon
us, yea, the work of our hands
establish thou it"

Psalm 90:17

ITS MEMBERS IN THE PAST

"Lord, thou hast been our dwelling place in all generations"

"Make us glad as many days as
thou hast afflicted us, and as
many years as we have seen evil"

Psalm 90:1 and 15

ITS MEMBERS IN THE PRESENT

AND, IF CHRIST TARRIES,

ITS MEMBERS IN THE FUTURE.

"Let thy work be manifest to
thy servants, and thy glorious
power to their children."

Psalm 90:16

TABLE OF CONTENTS

Preface

This book is offered to commemorate a Century of Grace at the LaGrave Avenue Christian Reformed Church and represents an earnest effort to capture not only the facts of LaGrave's history but also the flavor of its days. To accomplish this, it was necessary to consider LaGrave in the context of world, national, and denominational developments. Intertwined with these separate strains there is also the mythical Troon family, binding the generations.

The Rose window, appearing at the beginning of each chapter — an integral feature of both the old and new sanctuaries — is used as an ongoing symbol. The newspaper notices in the earlier chapters are presented exactly as they appeared originally, and the translations from the Holland language are rendered in such a way by the translators as to retain the idiom and nuance of the language in which they were written. An addendum at the end of the book includes as much material as was deemed pertinent and a limited budget permitted.

Deficiencies and inaccuracies may appear and names which should, may not. Where this is true and certain facts are overlooked, the reader's understanding is solicited. No effort, however considerable, can tell it all exactly as it was. It is hoped that a look backward by way of this book will inspire a look forward to another Century of Grace.

Chapter 1

"GRACE BE UNTO YOU..."

It is any Sunday morning. The place is 107 LaGrave Avenue, South East, Grand Rapids, Michigan. There is nothing lacking. Everything needful is there for a celebration — a meeting between a covenant God and His people. There is —

- a beautiful sanctuary with open doors, and enough room for all;
- a book, open, authored by God himself, proclaiming His love and the way of salvation;
- a minister who, through study, is prepared to speak in Christ-centered words of life;
- a choir that has rehearsed and is ready to offer musical praise, with talent and dedication;
- a hymnbook containing psalms and spiritual songs composed through the years and useful as a vehicle for expressing God's glory and lifting His people;
- a gathering of worshippers who assemble for praise and prayer in a communion of believers;
- above all, the Lord Himself, who is always where His people gather.

It is thus on any Sunday morning — Sunday evenings too. All the ingredients are there for an-other blessed encounter. Where do these ingredients come from? Who made and developed them? They are traced to one ultimate source —

The grace of God!
At the LaGrave Avenue Christian Reformed Church!
A whole century of it!
One hundred years!

Consider:

What has kept these weekly celebrations of praise through all the changing years? What has kept the people coming? Wars and depressions? Trouble and death? Is it true that afflictions often turn human hearts heavenward? But, reversals and disillusionments can, as easily, exact spiritual toll. How many hospital calls were made, across the years, by LaGrave's pastors? How much comfort and guidance was given? How many funerals did they conduct? Most, if not all forms of human misery to which mankind is heir have been seen and experienced within the LaGrave family — ills of body and ills of soul. Even so, each Lord's Day the members gather to sing, "Praise God from whom all blessings flow." Why?

There is an ancient parallel in the Old Testament Book of Psalms. In it, every human cry known to man is heard, yet everything issues, finally, into that last cry of that last Psalm wherein all are called upon to "Praise the Lord." For Christians, that is always the end of the matter.

Across one hundred years, LaGrave's parishioners, too, have not always seen blue skies. The gamut of human emotion has been experienced. They have often been lifted to the heights through the worship hour, and, many times, brought low by adversities. They have often cried in the language of Psalm 42, "Why art thou cast down, O my soul . . . why go I mourning because of oppression?"; or in the tones of Psalm 73, "My steps had well nigh slipped." Nevertheless, they went on to that final Psalm 150, to sing, "Praise the Lord, O my soul." Why is this?

It is true that, over the years, there were those who, like Demas, forsook and departed. For Satan, too, has been at LaGrave for a century. But more remained, and remain. How? Why? Thus, on Sunday morning, any Sunday morning, and Sunday evening too, the people gather. And they rise. And the minister says, "Our help is in the name of the Lord."

It's all the grace of God, you see.

That's what one of the LaGrave members said so simply and so beautifully, just before he transferred from LaGrave to the Church above. William Harry Jellema was renowned as a philosopher. He taught in a number of centers of learning — some prestigious. For many years he was chairman of the Department of Philosophy at Calvin College.

For all his erudition, however, Dr. Jellema was a man of simple faith. That is why the last person he quoted, just before his death, was not Plato, but someone else. For, after a final prayer with his pastor, he summoned what strength remained to review his eighty-nine years with one short sentence: "As my grandmother used to say, 'Everything is grace.

It's all the grace of God.'"

A review of one hundred years of LaGrave Church's history leads us to the same conclusion. A century of grace! LaGrave's membership, covering ten decades, adds up to quite a list. There were those who were on it for only a brief time. Others for a lifetime. They varied in occupation and in dedication. They were ministered to by preachers diverse in their strengths and weaknesses. LaGrave Church could not have survived without its dedicated clergy and laity. Yet, at the same time, it must also be said that LaGrave not only survived, but flourished — not because of, but in spite of its membership. For, ultimately, it was only grace.

It's all the grace of God!

LaGrave was blessed to have existed for a hundred years in a free land. No soldiers ever appeared to lock its doors. No sermons were ever stilled or censored by the local constabulary. There were times of war. They claimed some of her sons. Yet no tanks levelled LaGrave's buildings, and no enemies scattered her people. There were many churches which suffered from earthquake, pestilence, hunger, persecution, and more. Yet, not any of these plagues came near LaGrave's doors. This was not because the church was so deserving. It was, instead, all grace.

A century of grace!

From the day of LaGrave's birth, and even before, Satan tried to control. Sometimes he made progress, yet his victories were minor. Some churches capitulated before various winds of doctrine. Modernism, as it was called in the earlier days, made astonishing inroads here and there. Yet, through all the years, the LaGrave Church has remained faithful to its confession. It was sometimes accused, but falsely. The creeds and the standards were maintained. The Heidelberg Catechism is still taught. The Bible, inspired, infallible, remains central. The Gospel of Jesus Christ is still proclaimed, and received, and believed. In a period of human history which has seen more change and challenge than any other, the LaGrave Church yet holds fast the Christ, who is the same today as He was yesterday when LaGrave was born. But this, too, is not so much the result of human dedication as it is the result of divine preservation. The perserverance of the saints is really the perseverance of the Holy Spirit.

And so, viewed from whatever angle, LaGrave's history can be captured in four words —

A century of grace!

Without that grace, LaGrave would not have lived to its present age. Without that grace, it could not see tomorrow. It is fitting, therefore, that LaGrave seize its Centennial as an occasion for witness —

A witness to the grace!
A century of grace!
The grace of God!

The early Christian Reformed congregations sang only The Psalms and only in Dutch. A great favorite was Psalm 42. It appears here as it did in an 1875 Dutch edition of The New Testament which included the 150 Psalms. Interestingly enough, this book also included, set to music, The Ten Commandments, The Song of Mary, The Song of Zacharias, The Song of Simeon, The Beatitudes, The Lord's Prayer, The Apostles' Creed, Prayer for the Minister, Morning Song, Song Before Meals, Song After Meals, Thanksgiving After Meals, and Evening Song.

The pages following trace this grace. It comes to a more visible expression any Sunday morning — and Sunday evening, too — at 107 LaGrave Avenue, South East, Grand Rapids, Michigan.

Where there is nothing lacking, where everything needful — and more — is there for a cele-bration between a covenant God and His people; and the minister, after saying, "Our help is in the name of the Lord," continues as God's spokesman and says, as his predecessors for a hundred years have said,

"Grace be unto you."

Chapter 2

"WHAT LANGUAGE SHALL I BORROW ... ?"

God has a noisy family. That was evident already in the Upper Room, and before. In Corinth, they differed on Christian liberty (I Corinthians 8), developed factions (I Corinthians 1), and polarized as rich and poor around the communion table. Even Peter and Paul, apostles, had an issue between them (Galatians 2). All of Church History, from beginning to the present, reflects differences of opinions and convictions, at times sifted and resolved, and at other times rushing forward headlong on disastrous collision courses. The issues varied from very small to large, even though they were *always* seen as very large by those who were involved. In its one hundred years, LaGrave has lived through a variety of such issues, both major and minor, and survived, although not always unscathed. A listing of them covers widely disparate items and provides occasional insights into the spirit of the decades:

The common grace question
The millennial question
The matter of worldly amusements
Bobbed hair for women
Infralapsarianism and supralapsarianism (Was the divine plan in any way conditioned by the human response?)

The common cup versus the individual cup in serving communion
Joyriding on the Lord's Day and the use of Sunday radio
Women in church office
Ecumenism
World Council membership
Liturgics
Mission policies
Hermeneutics
The love of God controversy

These, mentioned in no particular order and more denominational than congregational in scope, raised blood pressures and caused rifts which, for some, became ruts.

Klaas and Anna Troon and their growing children, Dirk, Anna, and Pieter, lived before any of these issues surfaced. Inhabitants of the latter half of the nineteenth century and involved with their church and denomination, they were preoccupied with other questions, no less burning, in their recently formed denomination, born in 1857 and known today as the Christian Reformed Church in North America.

It was an exciting period of history in which to be alive. The Civil War had ended. Mark Twain said of his childhood days that it was a time when everybody was poor and didn't know it; and everybody was comfortable and did know it. But his wasn't quite the story of the latter half of the 1800s. The more thoughtful were worried about poverty. Indeed, Joseph Pulitzer, a Hungarian, purchased the *New York World* (1893) and articulated what had been a growing social conscience. Others, however, went from good gray to yellow journalism. With garish articles, they reported that by 1880 no fewer than 100 Americans claimed an income of more than one million dollars per annum. Many others, a few in Grand Rapids, too — mostly lumber barons — were nearly as rich and falling victim to "culture" and their own bad tastes. Some hired architects who designed frilly houses, examples of which can still be found in Grand Rapids. Nothing succeeded like excess.

It was a bonanza time for news: The great Chicago fire (1871); the most famous blizzard in American history (1873); Custer's last stand (1876); the assassination of President Garfield (1881); Buffalo Bill's greatest shows on earth (1883ff.); the Johnstown flood (1889); and the Spanish American War (1898). In 1875, the bicycle was an idea whose time had come, and sermons were preached warning how young people could now fly unchaperoned to far distant places. The hazards of new elevator travel (circa 1880 — called death traps), made many take the stairs instead. Meanwhile, pianos so dominated the scene that by 1890, within a population of seventy-five million Americans, there were one million pianos. It was a shame that they were replacing parlor organs. An even greater shame was that they were finding their way into some churches.

In 1869, Horace Greeley said that not all people could live in the cities. Yet many determined to do so. Urban centers swelled! Detroit's population leaped from 80,000 to 285,000. Los Angeles from 5,800 to 103,000. Philadelphia grew from 675,000 in 1870 to 1,300,000 in 1890, a period which coincided with the greatest influx of immigrants in American history.

There were two events which especially summed up the exhilarating state of America in the last third of the nineteenth century. The first was the opening of direct coast-to-coast service on the first transcontinental railway (1870). The second was the centennial celebration of the nation's founding. The Barnum Circus of 1876 was a "surpassing event." There were many more

events that celebrated 100 years of a nation fast being recognized as one of the industrial giants of the world. However, not everyone lavished unmeasured praise. The Suffragettes, for one, said that the government was not a republic but a hateful oligarchy of sex.

In the headlong rush to the future, Grand Rapids did not lag. It was, indeed, a thriving place in the closing decades of the last century. More than eighty-five furniture manufacturers launched themselves. The Nelson Company was the largest. The Widdicomb Companies, Berkey and Gay — where Klaas Troon was employed for a time — and the Grand Rapids Chair Company, were included among the leaders. In the '70s, local manufacturers sent samples of "elegant chamber furniture" to the Centennial Exposition in Philadelphia, which resulted in buyers coming from everywhere to the valley of the "Grand." It sparked the city's first furniture market in 1878.

Other businesses, too, were prospering. Limestone was quarried from the riverbed. The Alabastine Company successfully marketed a wall coating, with high quality gypsum being the principal ingredient. The clay in the area of the present Fulton Cemetery was used in a new and successful process of brick-making. The area became known as The Brick Yard. Anna Troon, whose sixteen-year-old son, Dirk, worked there, referred to it in her Dutch accent as "De Brick Yaat." Belknap's Wagon and Sleigh Company was organized in 1884. There were six bicycle factories. Iceboxes were made by the Leonard Refrigerator Company, established in 1881. There were fifty cigar factories. The Troons could buy "Perfection," the finest flour in the world, produced by Valley City Milling Company which advertised its product as being "Lily White."

Z.Z. Lydens, in his history of Grand Rapids, observed that "Christianity is the greatest force in two-thousand years of Western civilization." Indeed, it had arrived in Western Michigan long before the Troons had "come off the boat." St. Mark's Episcopal Church opened its doors for worship in its present building in 1848. Park Congregational Church was the fruit of a Congregational and Presbyterian outreach before mid-century. St. Andrew's Cathedral was under construction in 1874. Baptists and other groups were active. The Troons kept their distance from these, as well as other "outside" influences, notably the arts. The first fully equipped "modern opera house" in Western Michigan opened its doors in

1874. The Redmon Grand Opera House was built in 1882. Smith's Opera House opened in 1885. It was described as one of the handsomest in the country. But Klaas called it worldly and sinful. (Ironically, at the turn of the century, it began to serve as the Mel Trotter Rescue Mission.) The Ladies Literary Club built its clubhouse on Sheldon Avenue in 1887. It was the first structure of its kind in the United States. This organization worked hard to establish a city library. The St. Cecilia Music Society, established in 1883 by nine women devoted to improving and developing the music program of Grand Rapids, erected its Italian Renaissance building on Ransom N.E., in 1894. This organization was instrumental in establishing the Grand Rapids Symphony, the Grand Rapids Youth Symphony, Community Concerts, and the Opera Association of Michigan.

This, and more, constituted the world of Klaas Troon and family a century ago. Yet, there was a sense in which this wasn't his world at all, for his attentions were riveted elsewhere. With roots in The Netherlands and having deeply religious beliefs, he had affiliated with the Reformed Church in America, which had begun in New Amsterdam (New York) early in the seventeenth century. But, it was a church which, in the eyes of some, Klaas included, fell short on several counts. It did not

exclude Masons and members of similar organizations, and it was weak in the matter of Christian education. There were other criticisms, but for Klaas Troon, these were the serious issues — an opinion in which he was supported by his wife Anna. And so it was inevitable that the Troons, with their three children, eventually affiliated with a smaller and much younger Christian Reformed denomination, born in 1857. Here they found kindred spirits who felt as they did about such matters as Christian schools and secret societies.

Their move, however, was accompanied by all the by-products such situations can evoke among the fallen children of a fallen Adam and Eve. They were Christians, just as their neighbors who remained in the church they left, and with whom they had been such good friends. But now, there was a wall. Anna had to separate her ten-year-old Pieter from her neighbor's eleven-year-old. The children had fought — with fists — over their respective churches, and over issues neither understood. And Anna's eldest, Dirk, who worked in "De Brick Yaat" was told to terminate his growing friendship with their neighbor's daughter. The girl had received a similar order from her father.

Klaas, in warning his son, even murmured about such a thing as being "unequally yoked." There would be those, a hundred years later, who would

Valley City Milling Company, Grand Rapids, Michigan, produced the world's finest "lily white" flour.

Last Edition. | GRAND RAPIDS HERALD | Last Edtiion.

FIFTEENTH YEAR. | GRAND RAPIDS, MICH, MONDAY MORNING, MAY 2, 1808. | NUMBER 4877.

Big Naval Battle of the War Was Won by the American Fleet at Manila Sunday and the Spanish Fleet Practically Annihilated.

FLEET NEARLY ANNIHILATED

American Asiatic Squadron Attacked the Spanish Fleet in the Inner Harbor of Manila.

SPANISH FLAGSHIP COMPLETELY BURNE

As Was the Cruiser Castilla, and the Don Juan de A

CRUSHING DEFEAT

Rear Admiral Dewey Won a Victory Over Spanish Squadron.

DID NOT CAPTURE CITY OF MANILA

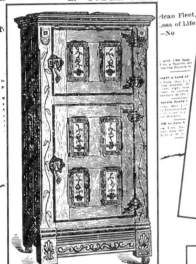

Newsworthy items of the late 1800s.

judge Klaas and Anna adversely. But how can one century judge another? The truth is that the Troons were good people and a credit to their adopted country. And so, too, were their neighbors with whom they no longer visited.

Mr. and Mrs. Troon, happier in their new denominational affiliation, soon discovered there were battles to fight there as well. They were satisfied with its position on secret societies and Christian education. But there were some, at least a few, of their fellow church members who favored the holding of worship services in the English language. The Troons were totally opposed to this. They were grateful to be in America. Yet, they made a distinction between America — a good word — and Americanization — a bad word. Such Americanization had not proved a blessing in the church they had recently left. Maintaining Dutch services of worship was an aid in keeping the world out of the church. Furthermore, their native tongue lent itself far more readily to spiritual expression. Introducing English into the Sunday services was certainly a step in the wrong direction. And so Klaas, who for all his lack of education was an articulate man, found himself, once again, involved in an issue of the gravest sort.

It is thought-provoking when one considers how much energy God's people expend through all the years opposing each other on matters intramural. A hundred years later, there would be those who would decry all the effort put into the "women-in-office" debate when there was the Gospel to proclaim and the devil to fight. So now also, there were those who insisted that there were more important things to do than to resist Americanization and the introduction of English into the worship services. Such comments, however, fail to consider that church history, too, is a process in which new days bring new questions — all of which need much prayer and careful sifting.

There were many who agreed with the Troons. Indeed, the language question would remain in many Christian Reformed Churches even after the introduction of English. In the 1920s, for example, there were churches which held three services on Sundays, the afternoon hour being conducted in the English language. When the shift began to English in the morning and evening, with Dutch in the afternoon, it took place with considerable difficulty and opposition.

The Troons were clearly with the majority in opposing the introduction of a "foreign" (!) tongue into the Sunday services of worship. But, there

was that minority! Their son Dirk was a part of it. Indeed, a growing number of young people, increasingly conversant with English and increasingly unfamiliar with the language of their parents, wanted a change. And so, alas, new hard feelings developed — this time within the Christian Reformed Church, and even within some family circles. Dirk, as stubborn as his father, joined the Methodist Church when he was twenty-two. The resultant estrangement within the Troon family brought tensions which were not soon to dissipate. During the struggle, in which time the first English-speaking Christian Reformed Church — LaGrave — was to see the light of day, the Troons and others were part of a prolonged crisis in the denomination. Not only was there the continuing challenge of adjustment to a new culture, and the temptation to materialism, but also the question of:

"What language shall I borrow
To thank Thee, dearest friend?"

Some felt that the faith of the fathers was inextricably wound around the Dutch language. Others wondered how they could hold their children with a tongue increasingly foreign to their new environment. And so, there were those who came together on September 16, 1886, to discuss the matter.

Klaas Troon was not among them.

Chapter 3

"IN THE BEGINNING ... "

In 1937, LaGrave celebrated its fiftieth birthday. To mark the occasion, one of its members, B.K. Kuiper (seminary professor, author, editor), wrote a brief historical sketch. In it he observed, and with typical insight, that,

> If the life of the church appears at times unintersting and dull, it does so not because it really is dull, but because we are dull, unseeing, without vision. It is for that reason that it may be well for us, in viewing the life of our LaGrave Avenue Church, to climb to a higher plane whence we shall enjoy wider horizons and a deeper background.

Alas, we seldom pause to do this! Seeing the church today, and attending its services, it is easy to overlook the drama of its beginnings. But heeding Kuiper, we shall ask who were those men who gathered on the evening of September 16, 1886, in Grand Rapids, Michigan, to found, if possible, the first English-speaking Christian Reformed Church? Seeing the "wider horizons" and the "deeper background," as Kuiper suggests, we shall view them, together with Klaas Troon who opposed them, as children of a historic revival.

Today, revivals connote organized campaigns with high powered advertising, music, and a "big name" evangelist. The revival of 1834, however,

in the Netherlands, was not premeditated or planned or organized from the top down. Indeed, at first, it was not organized at all but was a true revival that originated from the people's renewed interest in religion, following a period of indifference and spiritual decline. It was a reawakening. J. Edwin Orr, who has written extensively on revivals in the history of the worldwide church, has correctly identified ecclesiastical vitality as dependent on the reanimating influence of the Holy Spirit. The Great Awakening of 1834 in this country was of this sort. So was the revival of 1857—1859, which began with a prayer meeting in New York with just a few in attendance, but through which the Holy Spirit stirred the stagnant waters like the angel at Bethesda. So, too, in the years prior to 1834, a secession took place from the State Church in the Netherlands, and a new church came into being. Men like H. DeCock, H.P. Scholte, A. Brummelkamp, S. Van Velzen, and A.C. Van Raalte were used of God, as were others in various European countries. Their preaching reflected a groundswell return from dead orthodoxy and liberal theology. It was a bit like Ezekiel's valley of dry bones coming back to life. There was a rediscovery of the doctrines of man's depravity and God's sovereignty and sovereign grace. This Gospel was opposed by the official church, and its followers were persecuted and prosecuted by the authorities. It was under these difficult circumstances that the secession of 1834 took place. And with economic weather hardly more favorable than the religious climate, it was inevitable that there would be a migration. Thus there came about Van Raalte and his followers.

They landed in a strange country; but not as strangers. More than 200 years before, their countrymen had arrived and founded the Reformed Church in America, in what was then New Amsterdam and is today New York. This denomination befriended Van Raalte and his followers who had plunged into the wilds of Western Michigan, and who were invited into ecclesiastical unity by this established church. It was a strange relationship, and it would not last; for in the East, there was an established and cultured church speaking one language, and in Michigan, an enclave in a wilderness — whose occupants were preoccupied with survival — speaking another language.

In the previous chapter, several of the issues that made for a short-lived association on the part of some with this well-established Reformed Church in the East have already been cited. It is necessary, however, in tracing the history of the LaGrave Church, to cite a schism which occurred in the Reformed Church in America a little more than twenty years before Van Raalte and his followers arrived. This schism resulted in the formation of a small group which called itself "The True Reformed Protestant Dutch Church," a communion in New Jersey from which LaGrave would eventually recruit its first pastor, Rev. John Y. De-Baun. Dead orthodoxy and Arminianism were said to have found their way into the established Reformed Church, resulting in the formation of

this new denomination which was never large, and which, eventually, joined the Christian Reformed Church as Classis Hackensack. Its ministers and members, unhappy with the news that the immigrants in Western Michigan were associating with the established Reformed Church, alerted the newcomers to its doctrinal laxity.

One of these newcomers was Gysbert Haan. He was a man of intellect and possessed leadership ability. He was also a rug manufacturer. His products had won prizes at various international fairs, giving his home town of Hilversum some standing. He came to Michigan, briefly settling in Vriesland before moving to Grand Rapids where he joined the Second Reformed Church. But, together with a few others, he became increasingly restless, not with the local congregation but with the denominational affiliation. Haan frequently repeated what he had heard from ministers and members of the separated group in New Jersey. And so, he and some others, organized a new congregation on March 19, 1857. Gysbert Haan, Jan Gelock, and Johannes Gezon served as its first elders. B. DeGraaf, H. Moerman, and A. Pleune served as the first deacons. Some of these names were to figure prominently, thirty years later, in the beginnings of the LaGrave Church. Thus the first Christian Reformed Church came into being. On April 8, 1857, it united with churches in Noordeloos, Polkton, and Graafschap. And so the Christian Reformed denomination was born.

These, then, were the roots and spiritual heritage of those men who gathered on the evening of September 16, 1886, to found, if possible an English-speaking Christian Reformed Church. In a sermon entitled "Thinking on God's Lovingkindness," delivered February 22, 1912, by the Rev. Henry Beets at the Quarter Centennial Celebration of the LaGrave Church, there is a further description of these committed men and their sense of mission:

... They saw more and more that their children were unable to understand Holland preaching. They noticed how several of their youth had already joined other denominations. Procrastination appeared to them, not only as a thief of time, but also as a robber of the children of the church. And so a meeting was arranged to discuss in a formal way the cause so dear to their hearts, so necessary for the future of the church they loved. It was held September 16, 1886, at the residence of Mr. John Scheffer, 407 South Lafayette Street. The following were present: Messrs., John Benjamin, J. Scheffer, B. DeGraaf Sr., Cornelius Borrendamme, W.H. Doran, L. Schuitema, L. Drukker, G. Zeilstra, C. Koetsier, and Jacob Wierenga. Mr. John Benjamin was chosen chairman, and Mr. Scheffer, secretary.

There had been earlier attempts in a similar vein in the 1870s. There was the effort to get the pastors of Classis Hackensack (The True Reformed Protestant Dutch Church) to come to preach an occasional English sermon, but this was blocked. Rev. J.H. Vos, pastor from 1881—1900 of the First Christian Reformed Church (often called "Bates Street" today), said it was not desirable. In 1882, Synod decided to do this, but nothing came of it. In 1884, the increase of the use of English among the young people was discussed at the synodical level, but no action was taken. A synodical attempt in 1886 was likewise sidetracked. There was some understandable frustration, therefore, which came to expression in many ways, including that historical meeting of September 16, 1886. The minutes of that meeting, written in Dutch, have been preserved and translated as follows:*

The members are informed by J. Scheffer of the purpose of the meeting, namely to make attempts to organize an English congregation in view of the fact that there appears to be a need for this. This matter is of the utmost importance to our meeting, and everything should therefore be done decently and in good order. The speaker thus proposed that a president be appointed, and suggested the name of Mr. J. Benjamin in this connection. This proposal was seconded by Mr. C. Borrendamme and accepted unanimously. Mr. Benjamin then considered it his duty once more to announce the purpose of the meeting, explaining with examples why an English church in our denomination has become necessary, namely in order not to lose our youthful generation which is now breaking up into organizations whose principles do not agree with ours.

In order to test the opinions of the members on this matter, it was suggested that everyone freely express his thoughts whether these be for or against. Everybody was in favor of establishing an English congregation, although a few considered that an answer from candidate Mr. Vos, who had been called,† be received first. The majority agreed that care should indeed be taken but considered it to be in the interest of the matter, not to wait for Mr. Vos because he, if he should come, would not be

able to perform the function of minister in addition to teaching the students anyhow. The general feeling was then expressed that when the activities were to be continued in reaching the goal, all should act in agreement with moral and church rules. It was judged necessary that all interested members of the four Dutch Christian Reformed congregations in this city be allowed to express their opinions on this matter. It was decided to appoint a committee which would address a petition to the consistories of the four Dutch congregations, requesting them to consider the matter which would be explained to them. If they would be prepared to do so, a general meeting would be announced from the pulpit, informing the congregations also of the place and time of such a meeting.

After some deliberation, such a committee was appointed: J. Scheffer, G. Zeilstra, and J. Benjamin, after having decided that another meeting would be held on Monday, September 20, at the home of J. Scheffer. On that occasion, the petition which the committee had to compose would be considered. The petition would then be put before the consistory meetings which would take place on Tuesday. The meeting was closed with prayer by Mr. B. DeGraaf, Sr.

Carried and passed in the meeting
of September 30, 1886.

† Mr. Vos had been called to teach in the Theological School; he was also willing to preach an occasional "English" sermon.

* Translated by Professor Martinus A. Bakker of Calvin College.

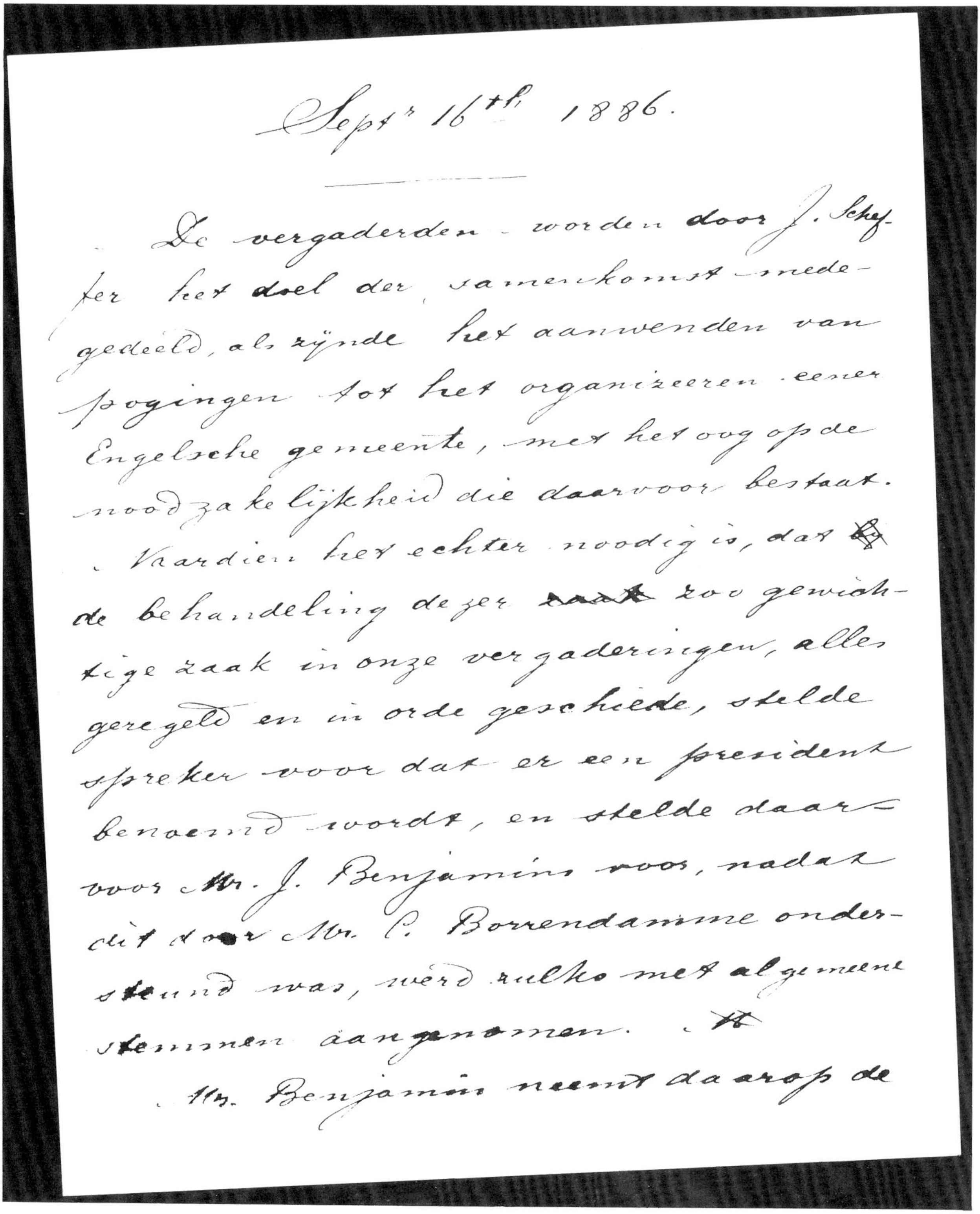

Sept.r 16th. 1886.

———

De vergaderden worden door J. Scheffer het doel der samenkomst mede-
gedeeld, als zijnde het aanwenden van
pogingen tot het organizeeren eener
Engelsche gemeente, met het oog op de
noodzakelijkheid die daarvoor bestaat.

Vaardien het echter noodig is, dat
de behandeling dezer zoo gewich-
tige zaak in onze vergaderingen, alles
geregeld en in orde geschiede, stelde
spreker voor dat er een president
benoemd wordt, en stelde daarvoor Mr. J. Benjamins voor, nadat
dit door Mr. C. Borrendamme onder-
steund was, werd zulks met algemeene
stemmen aangenomen.

Mr. Benjamin neemt daarop de

A page from the original minutes of the first meeting held in Grand Rapids, Michigan, regarding the organization of an
English-speaking Christian Reformed Church.

Between this meeting and the birth of LaGrave Church on February 24, 1887, over thirteen gatherings took place. The determination at the outset to seek the help and cooperation of the four Dutch Christian Reformed Churches in the city brought a discouraging response:

Coldbrook Church:
"We cannot give cooperation because this would be acting ahead of the decision of Synod."

Spring Street Church:
"Synod has dealt with this matter to which you refer. Let us therefore, esteemed brethren, not act rashly but rather wait prayerfully."

East Church (Eastern Avenue):
"We will agree with whatever decision is made by Spring Street."

Alpine Avenue:
No reply.

Synod had discussed English-preaching services as occasional events, but the group that met sought the formation of an English language congregation. Lacking the support they had sought from the other churches, and finding the Synod more given to debate than action on this issue, the group, at their meeting of October 28, 1886, decided to address the following letter (translated from the minutes) to the Classis of Grand Rapids:

To the Esteemed Classical Meeting,

Highly Esteemed Brethren of the Classis, Greetings!

The undersigned are submitting to the honorable meeting their opinion that, here in Grand Rapids there is a serious demand for English preaching in order to prevent great loss of young people of whom large numbers have withdrawn from their own church hearths to go to the (English) Reformed Church or Baptists, Methodists, etc., as they prefer to listen to preaching in the language of the country, and they also understand it better. Since the undersigned also deeply appreciate the feelings of the last Synod of the church concerning preaching in English; and since we also prefer to remain under one roof together with the Christian Reformed Church, and in that way maintain the same doctrine, discipline and service, but in the English language, the petitioners urgently request you to support them in this matter and to appoint a committee which will cooperate with people who are interested in realizing our objective to combine into an association of mission post or establish a congregation, if justified by a reasonable number of interested persons, and to obtain the service of a brother from the East who would preach on Sundays, and should catechize during the week if catechism in English also should be necessary.

These actions could be taken in preparation of discussions regarding the future, to be held upon arrival of the new lecturer in September 1887.

The undersigned, and many others along with them, trust that many young people will stay in our church, and also that some dispersed ones will return who would otherwise be lost for the church, wherefore we submit this document for your serious consideration.

This attempt met with success. Seventeen voted in favor of the request, and nine (one of whom was Klaas Troon) voted to turn it down. The Classis appointed a committee (Rev. T.M. VandenBosch, Rev. P. Schutt, and Rev. P. Ekster), over against strong opposition, notably the Spring Street consistory, to assist the group in its further explorations. The exhilaration of the petitioners, pioneers towards the establishment of an English-speaking congregation, is captured in the minutes of their subsequent meeting (November 25, 1886), in which the chairman, in an expansive mood, offered to buy 100 postcards at his expense ($1.00) to send out 100 invitations to their next meeting. After some debate, in which his offer was accepted, it was deemed prudent that the announcements on the cards should be written in the Dutch and not the English language. There was fear of unnecessary offense.

With the guidance of the classical advisors, Rev. J.Y. DeBaun, of Hackensack, New Jersey, was asked to come to Grand Rapids to preach. This would give opportunity to test the general interest, and to determine further action, if any. For the sake of a cause he loved, Rev. DeBaun came to deliver the first sermon on January 9, 1887, in the Metropolitan Hall (no longer in existence) on Pearl Street. There was a surprising audience of over 200 in attendance. This minister remained for two weeks. The Rev. John C. Voorhis of Englewood, New Jersey, was the second preacher to come. He also served for two weeks. The next minister, Rev. J.A. Westervelt, of New York City, remained five weeks.

The good attendance at the services of worship encouraged the committee. On January 17, 1887, with the aid of their advisors, they formulated a letter to be sent to the Classis. It was a petition for permission to organize. The first draft read as follows (translated from the Dutch):

To the Honorable Classis of Grand Rapids, of the Holland Christian Reformed Church

Dear Brethren:

With the support of the Reverend Brethren T.M. VandenBosch, P. Schut, and P. Ekster, appointed by you at the last classical convention, to aid us, a committee conformable with our petition, in which our objective was also presented to your Honorable body, being the establishment of an English-speaking congregation, we have, with the Lord's blessing, been laboring preparatory.

For two Sabbaths, and once during the week, we were granted the privilege of having Rev. J.Y. DeBaun of Hackensack, N.J., preach for us. The exceedingly large number of hearers present was entirely above our expectations, which may be accepted as a convincing proof of the general interest taken in English preaching. It was also gratifying to us to see so many of our young people present at the different services.

Having earnestly considered this very important matter, dear brethren, we, the undersigned, do hereby declare that we desire preaching of the Gospel in the English language, and the organization of an English-speaking congregation of the Holland Christian Reformed Church at Grand Rapids, Michigan, under the care of Classis Grand Rapids, and promise to aid in its establishment, or support, or by becoming a member thereof, and trying our own power, we shall thankfully receive the aid, which may be extended to us from outside.

Hoping, dear brethren, that you may give this petition your earnest consideration and to grant us our request as your petitioners we will ever pray.

At the next meeting, held February 1, 1887, a month which would see the birth of the LaGrave Church, the letter to the Classis, which had been drafted at the previous meeting, was revised with great care. After this arduous task had been completed, another matter which was to keep the meeting going into the late hours of the evening occupied everyone's attention. It was the question of how this letter should be signed. It was decided that there would be three categories of signatories: members by confession with families, baptized members with families, and supporters. At the conclusion of what had been an evening of hard concentration for all, the treasurer made his report, entered into the minutes as follows:

Received by subscription $72.00
Collected in the halls and
    Spring Church 74.78
        Total $146.78

Disbursements for postal cards,
    printing, and telegram 3.11
Paid to Rev. DeBaun 65.00
Donation to the poor fund of
    Spring Church 5.00
Rent for hall — 3 weeks @ $8 per week . . . 24.00
        Total $97.11

Which leaves a balance in the
    treasury of 48.67
Received this evening 1.00
        Total in treasury $49.67

The meeting of the Classis which received the formal request for the organization of an English-speaking congregation was a stormy one. The matter was considered in hot debate for three and one-half hours. The end vote favored the petitioners sixteen votes to nine. The committee for advice was continued and charged with assisting the group in their organization and in the extension of a call to a minister. When the matter of finances surfaced at the very end of the Classis meeting, it was explained that the group "would stand for $800." At this announcement, those who had opposed their formation shrugged their shoulders.

The committee, under the leadership of Mr. Benjamin, met on February 9, 1887, to consider, with gratitude, the favorable action of the Classis. Exhilarated, they were also sobered by the responsibilities that would now be thrust upon

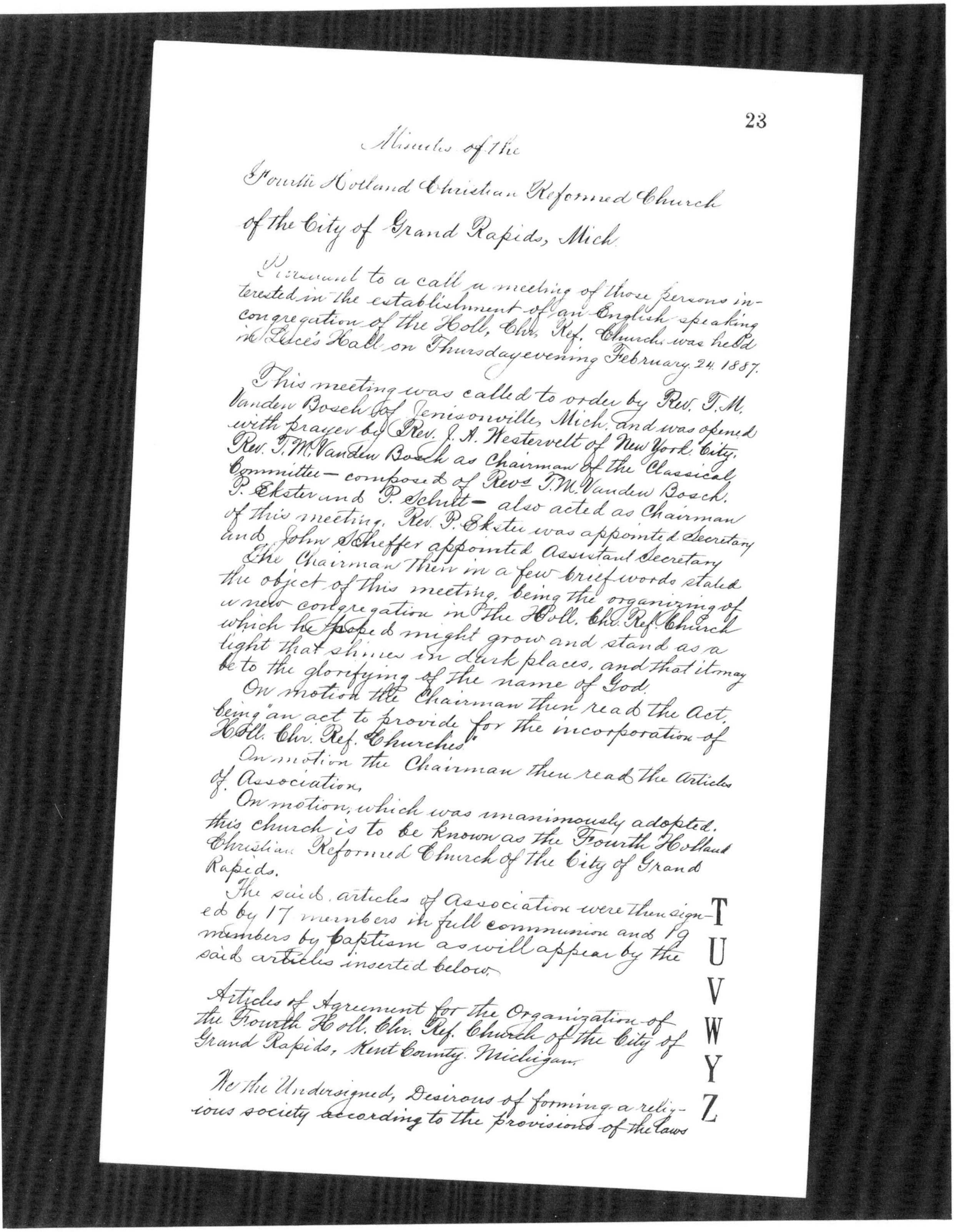

Minutes of the

Fourth Holland Christian Reformed Church

of the City of Grand Rapids, Mich.

Pursuant to a call a meeting of those persons interested in the establishment of an English speaking
congregation of the Holl. Chr. Ref. Church was held
in Luce's Hall on Thursday evening February 24. 1887.

This meeting was called to order by Rev. T. M.
Vanden Bosch of Jenisonville, Mich. and was opened
with prayer by Rev. J. A. Westervelt of New York City.
Rev. T. M. Vanden Bosch as Chairman of the Classical
Committee — composed of Revs. T. M. Vanden Bosch.
P. Ekster and P. Schut — also acted as Chairman
of this meeting. Rev. P. Ekster was appointed Secretary
and John Scheffer appointed Assistant Secretary

The Chairman then in a few brief words stated
the object of this meeting. being the organizing of
a new congregation in the Holl. Chr. Ref. Church
which he hoped might grow and stand as a
light that shines in dark places, and that it may
be to the glorifying of the name of God.

On motion the Chairman then read the Act,
being an act to provide for the incorporation of
Holl. Chr. Ref. Churches

On motion the Chairman then read the Articles
of Association,

On motion, which was unanimously adopted.
this church is to be known as the Fourth Holland
Christian Reformed Church of the City of Grand
Rapids.

The said articles of Association were then signed by 17 members in full communion and 19
members by baptism as will appear by the
said articles inserted below.

T
U
V
W
Y
Z

Articles of Agreement for the Organization of
the Fourth Holl. Chr. Ref. Church of the City of
Grand Rapids, Kent County, Michigan.

We the Undersigned, Desirous of forming a reli-
ious society according to the provisions of the laws

An excerpt from the original meeting finalizing the official organization of the Fourth Holland Christian Reformed Church, Grand Rapids, Michigan.

them. Mr. B. DeGraaf, Sr., urged all present to go home and discuss with their wives how much they could pledge in financial support. During a recess of five minutes, it was announced that forty dollars had already been subscribed. Those who had not pledged were urged to bring their money or commitment to J. Benjamin's store before the next meeting. On such a small amount, but great faith, a sub-committee was appointed (Messrs., J. Gezon, B. DeGraaf Jr., and A. VanSledright), to hire a hall. Mr. R. VanderWerp volunteered to commandeer a small organ. Mr. B. DeGraaf Sr., said he would make a pulpit. Mr. R. VanderWerp would see to it that there was a big Bible to put on the pulpit. Mr. Gerhard Zeilstra was commissioned to invite the Classical Advisory Committee to meet with them in two weeks to organize them in proper ecclesiastical fashion. Mr. A.J. Welmers, B. DeGraaf, Sr., and J. Scheffer were appointed a sub-committee on arrangements. Then they went home. None of them could sleep that night. It was an exciting time.

And so, on Thursday evening, February 24, 1887, the organizing took place in Luce Hall (a meeting place erected in 1856 containing a stage and used for various cultural events, now a parking lot) at the southwest corner of Monroe and Ottawa. This meeting place was rented for $300 per year. The name chosen was Fourth Holland Christian Reformed Church. The word "Holland" was a necessary legality. Furthermore, changing it to "American" or "English" might confuse some into believing that they were a new denomination. Seventeen members in full communion and nineteen members by baptism signed the Articles of Incorporation, their names going down into history as charter members.

Mr. B. DeGraaf, Sr. and Mr. A.J. Welmers were chosen as elders; Mr. J.C. VanHeulen and Mr. L. Drukker as deacons.

A future pastor-historian, Henry Beets, with the perspective of twenty-five years of the new church's history, delineated four motives that lay behind this movement launched in a turbulent decade:

1. To provide our young people with the means of grace administered in a language they understand;
2. To keep them in our denomination, that its growth may not be retarded, its best lifeblood not transfused into other ecclesiastical bodies;
3. That in generations to come we may preserve the old Reformed principles of our fathers, though clothed in the dress of a new language;
4. To remove the language barrier that we may be able to spread our Calvinistic principles in ever widening circles and thus carry out God's great purpose in bringing our ancestors to these shores — to be a salt and leaven to our nation.

CHARTER MEMBERS OF THE FOURTH HOLLAND CHRISTIAN REFORMED CHURCH

Berend De Graaf, Sr.	Lucas Drukker
John Gezon, Jr.	John Quartel
Martin Gelock	John Scheffer
Cornelius Scherphorn	Cornelius Koetsier
Arend Jan Welmers	Jacob Haan
Hermanus Gezon	B. De Graaf, Jr.
John Benjamin	Dennis Schram
J. Wierenga	Jacob Trompen
A. J. Benjamin	J. C. Van Heulen
F. C. Benjamin	L. Semeyn
G. Nyburg	Gerhard Zeilstra
J. Van Oeveren	Louis Schuitema
A. Van Sledright	W. H. Doren
D. Nyburg	C. Borrendamme
John Vis	N. Rosema
John D. Van Wyck	L. Lamberts
C. Schram	C. Semeyn
R. Van der Werp	Henry Kievit

THE ANSWER TO A CONUNDRUM

Have you been wondering how or why LaGrave was first called The Fourth Holland Christian Reformed Church? Perhaps this will help:

The first daughter of Spring Street (First, Bates) Christian Reformed Church was Kelloggsville (not in Grand Rapids), born in 1875. The second daughter, also born in 1875, was Jenison (also not in Grand Rapids). The third daughter was Eastern Avenue, born in 1879. It was the second Christian Reformed church in Grand Rapids. The fourth daughter (Alpine), born in 1881, was the third Christian Reformed church in Grand Rapids. LaGrave, born in 1887, was the fifth daughter and became known as the Fourth Holland Christian Reformed Church of Grand Rapids. Franklin Street Christian Reformed Church was the sixth daughter.

But what about Coldbrook Christian Reformed Church? When the Coldbrook church was organized in 1873, it was known as the Fourth Reformed Church. In 1881, it became known as the Holland Reformed Congregation of Coldbrook. December 12, 1882, this church became the Coldbrook Christian Reformed Church. Having come out of the Reformed tradition, Coldbrook was not a daughter of the Christian Reformed denomination.

Spring Street Church (First, Bates) was the mother of the LaGrave Church. She had other children: Kelloggsville, Jenison, Eastern Avenue, Alpine Avenue, and Franklin Street. But in her own words, LaGrave was an unwanted child. There were many who, like Klaas Troon, viewed the birth of the Fourth Holland Christian Reformed Church with less than enthusiasm. The spirit of separatism of 1834 was still alive and well, and these people viewed the language breakthrough with alarm. The Calvinism of Abraham Kuyper (b.1837—d.1920), attributed to LaGrave's founders by Henry Beets in his fourth motive, was more a reflection of his own enthusiasm for Kuyperianism. The fact is that many of the founders of LaGrave were as separatist as their spiritual fathers. They were as separatist as Troon and others. Indeed, it was their separatism and pietism (both in the good sense) that dictated for them the embrace of the English language, for it provided a means whereby the young people could be kept from other churches. Klaas and Anna Troon might well have kept their son Dirk within the fold had they aided and abetted LaGrave's beginnings. On the other hand, without any opposition at all, the new idea of an English-speaking Christian Reformed Church might not have had the testing, nor its proponents driven to such self-examination and prayer.

Chapter 4

I WILL COME OVER AND HELP YOU

Washington Irving (b.1783—d.1859) was the first American writer to gain fame abroad, as well as at home. His characters, Rip VanWinkle, Ichabod Crane, and others, bring chuckles to every generation. His stories about the Dutch in the East reflect Irving's sense of humor, natural charm, and pleasant disposition. Dutchmen in wide trousers, big hats, wide boots, and puffing on long pipes, walk through his pages with their wives and daughters in voluminous petticoats. They had names like Ten-Broek, VanKortland, Oosthout, VanTwilk, VanWyck, VanDyke, and VanEyck. Their ways made Irving chuckle.

The people he wrote about, however, in *Knickerbocker's History of New York,* simply could not be captured by the word "quaint." Had Washington Irving's portraits been more complete, he would also have sketched their business acumen, their religious commitment, and their love for freedom. Taken altogether, they were a people who contributed well to the fibre and future of a new nation. Indeed, one of their descendants, John Yeury DeBaun, would emerge, for one, as a dedicated and talented minister of the Gospel.

Joast DeBaun came to New Amsterdam from France in 1684 as a schoolmaster. Several generations later, around 1800, Isaac DeBaun saw the light of day. In time, he married Elizabeth Yeury. Together, they settled on a farm near Monsey, New York. There, a son, John Yeury, was born to them on August 22, 1827.

Early in his youth, John showed a spiritual sensitivity. His pastor's (Rev. J. D. Demarest) sermons found ready soil in his heart. Soon after his profession of faith, John Yeury felt an inclination towards the Gospel ministry as a life's work. He had already settled down in the cigar-making trade, and had married Margaret Iserman of Spring Valley, New York. These factors alone might have deterred him. Instead, he borrowed his pastor's copy of *Brown's System of Divinity,* and read it. Rev. Demarest also agreed to launch him into the study of languages. It was not long before John was accepted as a ministerial student at a meeting of Classis Hackensack of The True Reformed Protestant Dutch Church.

John DeBaun proved to be an apt scholar and a hard worker. In two-and-one-half years, he finished his prescribed course and in April of 1855, was declared eligible for a call. He was as a prophet with honor in his own country, for his church of Monsey, New York, together with a neighboring church, chose him to be their pastor.

In 1860, he began a fruitful twenty-seven-year ministry in the combined churches of Hackensack and Leonia, New Jersey.

J.Y. DeBaun had attended neither high school, college, nor seminary. His formal training, under tutelage, had been thin as compared with those who followed the more usual route. Nevertheless, he became a man of considerable erudition. Pursuing his studies alone, while tending his countless ministerial tasks, he became remarkably proficient, mastering Greek, Hebrew, Latin, and the various theological disciplines. He was a talented teacher as well, and eight men received their ministerial training in his parsonage in Hackensack.

During these years, Rev. DeBaun also founded *The Banner of Truth,* a sixteen-page monthly, which added greatly to his workload inasmuch as very few able men among them contributed material for what was known as "DeBaun's baby." Later, looking back on this project, he wrote, "For eleven years we were alone with the responsibility, and almost alone to provide matter, and bearing the financial burden myself, none concerned themselves whether the expenses were met or not — a few friends excepted, who occasionally sent a few dollars as an encouragement to continue." Upon its transfer to Grand Rapids in 1903, *The Banner of Truth* soon became a weekly publication. In 1906, the words *"of Truth"* were eliminated

THOU HAST GIVEN A BANNER TO THEM THAT FEAR THE ?, THAT IT MAY BE DISPLAYED BECAUSE OF THE TRUTH. SELAH!—Psalms 60 : 4.

VOL. 1.   HACKENSACK, JULY 1, 1866.   NO. 1.

PROSPECTUS.

UNTO THE CHURCH OF GOD IN HER MILITANT STATE

"To them that are sanctified in Christ Jesus, called to be saints, with all that in every place call upon the name of Jesus Christ our Lord, both theirs and ours."

Dearly beloved: We propose in the fear of God, and with humble dependence upon the Divine blessing, to commence the publication of a Religious Periodical monthly, to be called THE BANNER OF TRUTH, designed to establish, confirm and build up the heritage of the Lord in the most precious fundamental truths of the Gospel, to show what fruit those truths bear in those who receive them in love, and what a true Godly experience is, as distinguished from the merely common operations of the Spirit in many who have a name to live and are dead.

We have been moved hereunto by the consideration that those truths, once esteemed as the foundation of all True Religion, are being sadly undermined, and their Glory eclipsed by specious errors in doctrine and practice in these days of formality, these perilous times.

Against the floods of Socinian, Arminian, Hopkinsinian, Antimonian, and such like errors, for their names and forms are Legion — We propose to raise a Standard: *"When the enemy comes in like a flood,*

the Spirit of the Lord shall lift up a standard against him." Isai 59:19. Lest all be swept away by it, and this should be so. *For if the foundations be destroyed, what can the righteous do."* Psa. 11:3.

Laboring to maintain the Truth in its Purity, Savour, and Unction, will then be our earnest endeavour.

We propose to take as our standards, first — the *Bible,* then The Heidelberg Catechism, the confession of Faith, and the heads of doctrine established by the Synod of Dort, &c. With such approved authors, whose writings have ever by the pious been considered safe guides in exposition and illustration, we shall quote from such authors as Owen, Flavel, Toplady, Brakel, &c., of the purer days of the Reformed Church: and also from time to time select sermons of those faithful men whose praise is still in the churches. We shall also endeavor to give the news of the churches, as may be interesting and important; so that all who feel an interest in the things pertaining to Zion, may know of the dealings of the Most High, in providence and grace with us.

With a deep feeling of our unfitness for the work, yet with earnest desire to further the Master's cause, and maintain the truths we love, and with ardent prayer for his blessing, we remain yours to serve, with such as we have,

THE EDITOR.

THE BANNER OF TRUTH.

By consent of the general Synod of the True Reformed Dutch Church, will be published on or about the first of every month.

The size will be uniform; so that persons wishing to have their numbers bound, will at the end of the year be in possession of a volume intended to be made worthy of preservation.

Communications from the friends of truth are affectionately solicited; and those who feel friendly to the undertaking will oblige by acting as agents to procure and forward the names of subscribers, &c.

Articles intended for publication, except marriage and obituary notices, must be received by the 15th of the month previous to publication.

TERMS, IN ADVANCE:

Single copy for one year. - - $1.00
single copy for Six months, - - .60
single copies 10 cents.

Subscriptions commence at any time.

Friends in Hackensack and vicinity, will much oblige us, if they will call for their papers at E. E. Vreeland's Book and Stationery Store, who will also receive subscriptions.

All communications, remittances, and subscriptions, together with all business letters for the BANNER, should be addressed to

REV. JOHN Y. DeBAUN
Hackensack, P.O.,
Bergen Co., N.J.

The first page of the first Banner of Truth *states Rev. DeBaun's purpose for beginning such a publication.*

All the practical matters were stated on the back page.

for the sake of brevity and convenience. The first twenty-one years of the life of this periodical rested solely in DeBaun's hands. The magazine still exists today as an official publication of the Christian Reformed Church in North America.

It was this denomination which held DeBaun's interest, as well as that of others in his church. Already in 1869, DeBaun travelled all the way from New Jersey to Michigan to attend the Christian Reformed Denomination's General Assembly (Synod) in a city called Grand Rapids, for the purpose of learning more about it and introducing his own denomination to it.

On a subsequent visit, DeBaun sounded a warning to the brethren in Grand Rapids that unless preaching in English was introduced, many would be lost to the church. As a visitor, and as a gentleman, he was circumspect in his advice, knowing that there were powerful forces opposed to such an innovation. There was Rev. J.H. Vos, for example, of the Spring Street Christian Reformed Church; and another, Rev. L.J. Hulst of the Cold-

Rev. DeBaun's letter indicating his interest in the establishment of an English-speaking Christian Reformed Church.

brook Christian Reformed Church. He met an elder, too, a certain Mr. Klaas Troon, who did not at all welcome DeBaun's observations. Indeed, Mr. Troon almost gave Rev. DeBaun the impression that God was a Hollander.

Meanwhile, DeBaun continued his labors in his successful pastorate in the East, but with a continuing and ever deepening interest in the fortunes of the church in the Midwest. His sympathy with this struggling group was great. When he learned of its difficulties in training ministers because of a lack of books, he personally dispatched a large box filled with theological volumes to Graafschap, Michigan, for the use of the few theological students who were there. This gave the pastor at Graafschap, Rev. D.J. VanderWerp, the occasion to make an appeal in the Dutch denominational periodical for more books to be added to this nucleus. Therefore, today, Rev. DeBaun can be viewed not only as the founder of *The Banner* but also as the founder of the Calvin College and Seminary libraries.

And so, J.Y. DeBaun reached his sixtieth year. After twenty-seven years in one church, his popularity in his congregation had not waned, while his influence outside his church and denomination had increased. During his ministry, his congregation grew to number sixty-six families — the largest in The True Reformed Protestant Dutch Church. It was at this juncture in his career, when many a clergyman would have thought in terms of slowing his pace and enjoying the fruits of his labors, that John Yeury DeBaun received, in God's providence, a challenge that might well have tested the strength and endurance of a man much younger in years. The newly-formed Fourth Holland Christian Reformed Church of Grand Rapids, Michigan, extended a call to him to serve as the first pastor of the first English-speaking Christian Reformed Church in the new denomination's brief history.

Rev. DeBaun prayed earnestly for guidance from above. It was most difficult to avoid those human considerations and priorities that argued for his continuing stay in New Jersey. Only God knew the struggle that went on in his soul. His people wanted him to remain at his post. Had the Lord not signally blessed his ministry among them? The Midwest, when all was said and done, was a "foreign" land, even if it was in the same country! Furthermore, he would meet much opposition there. Not all would welcome him. There would be strong influences, sincere but ill-advised, that would be arrayed against him.

Rev. DeBaun knew all this. He had preached for the people who were calling him. That helped him to decide. He felt it was God's will for him to cast in his lot with this pioneering congregation. It meant separation from a region he loved and where he had received abundant blessings for sixty years. It meant separation, as an older man, from the place of his roots, where his friends and his relatives and his children lived. It meant additional hardship for his wife, whom he loved. But, in view of his qualifications, by the grace of God, and in view of the needs of the newly-born Fourth Holland Christian Reformed Church of Grand Rapids, Michigan, with its seventeen members in full communion and nineteen members by baptism, had he not come to the kingdom for such a time as this?

Years later, Professor J.G. VandenBosch, professor at Calvin College, and a member of the LaGrave Church, would write that it was a gracious Providence that sent the right man to the right place at the right time. And so it was! Rev. DeBaun sent his letter of acceptance.

In Acts 16:9, a vision appeared to Paul in the night: a man of Macedonia was standing, beseeching him, and saying, "Come over to Macedonia and help us." Often, through the years, calling Christian Reformed Churches borrowed this language. Ministers, accepting calls, sent letters saying, "I will come over and help you."

Rev. DeBaun's letter of acceptance has been lost. We do not know today what specific form it took. Whether he wrote, "I will come over and help you," as so many others through the years have written, is not known. What is known, however, for it is a matter of record, is that he did come over to Michigan from the East.

And he did help.

Immensely!

REVEREND AND MRS. JOHN Y. DEBAUN 1887–1892

An experienced pastor from the East Coast guides a new congregation of English-speaking Dutch Americans

See Addendum for key to all portraits.

Chapter 5

HISTORY IS BUT THE LENGTHENED SHADOW OF ITS PEOPLE

In the decade of the 1880s, Grand Rapids grew in population from 32,000 to 60,000. Part of the increase was due to the trainloads of Dutch immigrants walking through its depot and into its streets on wooden shoes. With such increasing congestion everywhere, bicycles and tricycles were banned in the business district. A smallpox scare more effectively cleared the streets — streets that were lighted by eleven electric lights, one-hundred-seventy-six gas lights, and four-hundred-thirty naphtha lamps. The electric ones were the least favored and deemed to be the most temporary.

The triangle of Monroe, Fulton, and Division Streets was dedicated to the memory of fallen Civil War heroes. The city charter was amended, giving women the vote in school elections. In 1887, the year the Fourth Holland Christian Reformed Church (LaGrave) was born, the State of Michigan proposed prohibition. It failed to pass. Grand Rapids was so opposed, its politicians extended the closing hours of its one-hundred-forty saloons from 10 P.M. to 11 P.M., and then to midnight.

It was in this decade that Klaas Troon reached his fifty-fifth year. His wife was five years younger. Their children, Dirk, Anna, and Pieter were now parents themselves, each having two children of their own. Dirk was thirty-four and a deacon in the Methodist Church. Anna, thirty-one, and Pieter, twenty-seven, still attended Spring Street, the church of their parents. Dirk's children had American names. This didn't sit at all well with Grandpa Klaas, but Grandma (Opoe) Anna urged her husband to "Not tink about it."

For those grandchildren, life in Grand Rapids in the 1880s was fun. Skating and coasting were great winter sports. Bridge Street (now Michigan Street) was closed to all traffic on Saturdays so the children could slide down the hill on home-made sleds. In the summer, they played pom-pom-pullaway, snap-the-whip, hide-and-seek, duck-on-the-rock, and baseball with a ball made of store cord or rag strips. Making kites with newspapers and sticks gathered from the waste of the saw mills, or rolling hoops from old barrels was a pleasure. And there was Reeds Lake for fishing, swimming, and picnicking. Victorian prudishness had not yet dawned, and so the boys went skinny dipping in Plaster Creek.

Life for Klaas and his sons was entirely different. A cacophony of factory whistles called them to work early every morning. The city council members voted to silence what they called a "rooster racket," but the mayor vetoed their decision. Shoe leather was cheaper than nickel carfare, and so Klaas walked to work, where long days were the rule. His sons, being of the softer generation, according to their father, rode bicycles. Meals were complete with Bible reading and opening and closing prayers. Often there were church meetings to attend in the evenings. Summer evenings were more relaxed. There were fewer church meetings. Porch sitting and talking to the neighbors was popular when the air was warm.

The lot of mother and housewife was the hardest. There were few labor saving devices. There were endless washings in a copper oblong boiler on the wood burning kitchen stove. Clothes were boiled and thereafter rubbed on a washboard. There were carpets to beat and windows to wash. Children's fingers and knees were always getting bloodied. And there were those never ending epidemics of colds, measles, mumps, and scarlet fever. Quarantine signs tacked to front doors by the health authorities were often seen, designating those houses as off limits. Then, too, there were those endless hours of patching, mending, darning, knitting, sewing, canning, lunches to pack, and meals to prepare. Saturday nights were busy. There were shoes to polish and baths to schedule. Sunday mornings were no less a strain in getting everyone ready for church. Anna enjoyed the Sunday services because, as she said in an unguarded moment of candor, "The hour of worship is 'en rest. I can yust sit for en while."

There were breaks in the everyday routine for harried housewives. The milkman came. The iceman too. The fruit wagon, the vegetable wagon, and the kerosene wagon made their daily rounds. The butter and egg man called once a week. There was small talk with all of them. But wives and mothers had to go to meetings too. Every church had its Ladies Aid, the counterpart to the Mens Society.

It was to this world of Grand Rapids that Rev. and Mrs. J.Y. DeBaun came in 1887 to throw in their lot with the members of the first English-speaking Christian Reformed Church. The salary was $800. Coming from a more sophisticated eastern lifestyle, they had to adjust to ways somewhat less cultured. This situation provided all the ingredients for an incompatible union between pastor and flock. But the DeBauns were gracious people who were anxious to accommodate themselves to the ways of the West. The parishioners,

Reverend John Yeury DeBaun

in turn, were eager to learn. They provided their minister and "juffrouw"* with a hearty reception, given at the residence of Mr. and Mrs. John Benjamin. The following Sunday, May 15, 1887, Rev. P. Ekster of the Alpine Avenue Christian Reformed Church, presided at the installation service. It was the first time Rev. Ekster had ever attempted a sermon in English. A reporter from *The Eagle,* a local newspaper, wrote that his effort was "most satisfactory and pleasing to all." That same reporter returned for the evening service and reported his impressions of DeBaun's inaugural message as follows:

> In the evening the Rev. Mr. DeBaun preached his introduction sermon to his congregation. The body of the hall was thoroughly filled, and many of the seats in the gallery were occupied. He read the sixteenth chapter of the Acts of the Apostles, taking his text from the ninth and tenth verses, enlarging upon the duties of a minister to his congregation and of the congregation toward its members, its pastor and the community. He was especially touching as he addressed his consistory, G.E. Boer and G. Hemkes of the Theological School, the Revs. Vanden Bosch and P. Ekster of the Classien Committee, and the students of the Theological School. His appeals to the congregation and to all present, were most eloquent and tender. He closed with an invitation to his congregation to visit him frequently, and with a promise to meet its members in their own homes and places of business. The day was a most important one, one that will never be forgotten by the present members of the new church.

The article went on to state that the new pastor, who had been so loved in New Jersey, would, no doubt, gain a host of admirers in Grand Rapids as well. This prophecy proved to be true. Rev. and Mrs. DeBaun were heartened by the many tokens of friendship they received. Indeed, not long after their arrival, the following article appeared in *The Eagle*:

THEY SURPRISED THEM.

Last night about eighty of the parishioners of the Rev. J.Y. DeBaun of the Fourth Reformed church, invaded his home on State Street and gave them a surprise visit. They had induced Mr. and Mrs. DeBaun to go out early in the evening, and when the worthy dominee and his wife returned they found it full to overflowing with happy friends who had come to spend the evening, and to leave with them substantial tokens of their esteem and affection, which included a most beautiful parlor coal stove and furniture, a hearth rug for it, etc. They had provided refreshments, and what with discussing them, music, vocal and instrumental, and social pleasurers, midnight came all too soon.

Worship services began at Luce Hall and continued at that location. The building had been designed to serve a city of 6,000. With so many more added to the population, a balcony was constructed to more adequately house political and other civic affairs. The result did not enhance what little worshipful atmosphere existed. Rev. DeBaun and his congregation increasingly felt the need for a more ecclesiastical setting.

There were visitors at every service, and many joined. Indeed, before Rev. DeBaun would depart for the East again, his church would grow from its charter membership of seventeen communicants and nineteen members by baptism, to 100 families and 455 souls. Rev. DeBaun found his days filled with much to do, including some part-time teaching in The Theological School.

With the increasing dissatisfaction with Luce Hall as a place of worship (the congregation had to ascend two flights of stairs), a business meeting was called. This resulted in the purchase of a piece of property at the southeast corner of Sheldon and Oakes Streets. The local residents were upset with the prospect of a church building

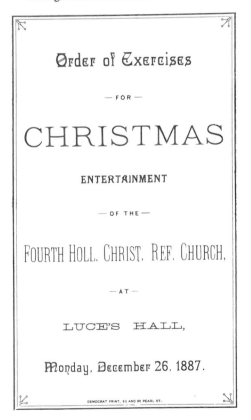

Order of Exercises

— FOR —

CHRISTMAS

ENTERTAINMENT

— OF THE —

FOURTH HOLL. CHRIST. REF. CHURCH,

— AT —

LUCE'S HALL,

Monday, December 26, 1887.

DEMOCRAT PRINT, 93 AND 95 PEARL ST.

Officers of Sunday School.

Rev. J. Y. De Baun,	-	Superintendent.
Mr. J. Trompen,	-	Ass't Superintendent.
Mr. C. Borrendamme,	-	Sec. and Treas.

Committee on Arrangements.

C. A. Benjamin,	Chairman.
G. J. Haan,	Secretary.

Miss Anna De Baun,	Mr. Jas. Van Heulen,
" Jennie Johnson,	" Jno. Scheffer,
" Anna Pell,	" C. Borrendamme,
" Mary De Baun,	" Frank Van Houten,
" Anna Benjamin,	" John Benjamin,
" Anna Lubach,	" B. H. Boer,

Miss Cornelia Benjamin,

" Annie Johnson,

" Anna Lanninga.

This was the first and only Christmas program held in Luce Hall. The new sanctuary of the Fourth Holland Christian Reformed Church was dedicated June 17, 1888.

at that location and offered the congregation a bonus of $2,300 to induce it to give up that site. It was thought best to accept the offer. Another piece of property (the present location of the La-Grave Church) was acquired. This, too, was met with some opposition by people living on La-Grave Street, but the congregation held firm. The total cost of real estate was $7,800. The cost for a worship edifice and parsonage was estimated at an additional $12,200. Money was subscribed. Loans were made, and Mr. S.J. Osgood, an architect, was engaged to draw the plans — his sixty-sixth set created by him since he had become a resident of Grand Rapids. *The Eagle* reported that the congregation, financially poor, had, neverthe-

less, undertaken this "noble work." It was not long before the paper would headline:

NEW HOUSE OF WORSHIP
The Fourth Holland Christian Reformed Church Edifice. A Handsome Structure. The Cornerstone to be Laid Tomorrow. Brief Description of the Building, and a Short History of the Society.

The order of service for the cornerstone laying was arranged by the pastor.

Prayer — by the pastor	J.Y. DeBaun
Singing of Psalm 137	By the Choir
Reading of History	By J. Scheffer
Singing of Anthem	By the Choir
Laying Cornerstone	By the Pastor
Addresses	
Doxology	By the Choir
Benediction	

LaGrave Street, circa 1886, looking north from Cherry Street. LaGrave Street was changed to LaGrave Avenue in 1912.

The ceremony was well attended. *The Democrat,* another paper in the city, described the details of the cornerstone laying at considerable length. The anthem, "I Love Thy Kingdom, Lord," was chosen and sung by the choir. The history, given by Mr. J. Scheffer, was long and detailed. The addresses were delivered by Professor G. E. Boer (in the Holland language) and Professor G.K. Hemkes (in the English language). Both speeches were congratulatory in nature. The remarks by the pastor, Rev. DeBaun, were appropriate. He said that it was his hope that the church would be an honor to its members, the neighborhood, and the city, and that it would redound to the best welfare of the church-at-large, and to the advancement of the Kingdom of God. "A year ago," he

Architect's drawing framed and given to Rev. DeBaun by an early consistory member, C. Borrendamme.

said, "no one would have thought that the work would have reached its present stage so soon," and he could not help but quote the line: "'What hath God wrought!'" "The church," he added, "was not designed to advocate any of the new and untried doctrines which, like Jonah's gourd, had sprung up in a day. It was being built to proclaim the truths of God and the salvation of souls."

When the foundation was viewed, Rev. DeBaun said, "He who builds on the foundation laid by the Apostles, of which Christ was the chief cornerstone, is heir to the grace of life." He closed his remarks by observing that the church was built, "not to destroy the Christian Reformed Church, but that Americans of Holland descent might worship in the language of their new country." Thus did he seek to relax tensions on the part of those who viewed LaGrave's growth with misgivings.

The November 8, 1887, edition of *The Eagle* reported the contents of the cornerstone as follows:

> A copy of the history of the church, a copy of yesterday's *Eagle*, a copy of Rev. J.Y. DeBaun's sermon when he entered upon his pastoral work, and other papers.

As the stone was laid in place, no one noticed, not even the pastor, that the word "architect" was misspelled. Today it can be seen in the area adjacent to the chapel in the present LaGrave Church. It says "Archetect."

The cornerstone laying was a great event for pastor and flock. This is not to say that this period was not without its difficulties. The church from which most of LaGrave's charter members had come (Spring Street), lodged a protest at Classis alleging that the organization of the new English-speaking congregation had been carried forward illegally. For this reason, Spring Street Church did not transfer memberships to this new church. This same consistory also charged that the Heidelberg Catechism was not faithfully proclaimed by Rev. DeBaun — an allegation that was not proven. Others accused DeBaun of unorthodoxy — an assertion that was discredited when Rev. DeBaun, exerting great personal effort in mastering the Holland language, preached some sermons in Dutch, to assure his critics. Gradually, the notion that orthodoxy depended on the Holland language abated in part; and prejudice diminished to a degree, although it did not disappear.

Three years after the DeBauns came to Grand Rapids, the small denomination in the East, The True Reformed Protestant Dutch Church, from which they had come, united with the churches in Michigan. This filled Rev. DeBaun's heart with joy. In contrast, the death of his wife filled his heart with great sadness. It was not the first time death had entered his house. Indeed, five of his nine children died young. Grief and sadness added new dimensions to his ministry, giving him a deeper understanding of the sorrows of others.

And so, the church, under DeBaun's ministry, grew and prospered. A Sunday School (Sabbath School) was organized on March 20, 1887. Catechism classes were organized in May. The Central Ladies Aid was born March 14, 1888, at the home of Mrs. Quartell. A Sewing Circle was begun in 1889. A choir, to aid the congregation in the singing of English hymns, was organized at the very beginning of the church's life, in a day when choirs were not approved of in the denomination. It was another argument in a long list Klaas Troon had against the organization and existence of an English-speaking church. No one had anticipated all the implications and ramifications of introducing English into the official worship services. English hymns, in place of Dutch Psalms, opened doors for the entrance of unsound doctrines — so

From its very beginning, the Fourth Holland Christian Reformed Church had a choir. This choir picture is circa 1892.

it was said. Thus, Rev. DeBaun chose them with extra care. Indeed, only those which had been approved and used by the True Reformed Protestant Dutch Churches of Classis Hackensack were used. Even so, they were viewed by Klaas Troon, and many others, as unwelcome; they were another step downhill.

After a five-year ministry, the time came when Rev. DeBaun would depart for the East again. He received a call from the Christian Reformed Church of Leonia, New Jersey. When he received it, his announcement filled the congregation with apprehension, and with regret when he accepted it. Something of its feelings for its pastor, and something of his character, was captured by *The Democrat* in an article entitled:

DEEP IN THEIR HEARTS

In their pastor the people of the English Christian Reform church have a man of a million, and they appreciate the fact. There are few clergymen of any denomination who will leave a church of which he has been pastor for 28 years on a salary of $1,300 to come to a place where they offer him $800 and ask him to build them the church. It is small wonder that all his congregation love him and say, "Put it as strong as you can when you write it for the paper, and it will be all too weak for this noble man." In 1888 they raised their pastor's salary to $1,000. He protested, saying that the church had still a large debt, and that all they had promised him was $800, and the Lord had promised nothing but bread and water and had given him all these things. This endeared him more than ever to his congregation, but they made him take $1,000. In May, 1889, Rev. DeBaun received a call from a New York church offering him $3,000. He declined and told his people that he would not leave Grand Rapids until his work was done and when the Lord called him elsewhere all the money in the city could not keep him.

And so, for the first five years of LaGrave's existence, the lives of pastor and flock were inextricably bound. The Lord sent LaGrave another pastor. Rev. DeBaun moved out of its life. What happened to him? Although this record purports to be a history of LaGrave, it would seem altogether proper to trace the remainder of his days. In *The Banner* of July 1, 1966, his great-grandson, Willis P. DeBoer, Professor of Bible at Calvin College, wrote an article in the paper his great-grandfather founded, entitled: "First Editor — My Great-Grandfather." The conclusion of this article reads as follows:

In five year's time the LaGrave Avenue congregation grew from seventeen members in full communion and nineteen members by baptism to one hundred families and four hundred and fifty-five souls. For several of these years Rev. DeBaun also taught part time in the Theological School. But soon he felt the work becoming too taxing for him, and at the age of sixty-five he accepted the call of the Leonia church which he had served part time earlier in his ministry. Back in New Jersey among his lifelong friends and relatives he ministered for two and one-half years. Then in February, 1895, after a brief illness, he passed away.

Truly, as Professor J.G. VandenBosch of Calvin College, and member of LaGrave, had written in *The Reformed Journal* of April 1957: "Had he, DeBaun, not come to the Kingdom for just such a time as this?" The Grand Rapids *Eagle* edition of February 3, 1895, contained this news item:

C.A. Benjamin and wife have been summoned to the sick bed of Mrs. Benjamin's father, the Rev. J. Y. DeBaun, in New Jersey. The Rev. Mr. DeBaun was formerly pastor of the LaGrave Street Christian Reformed Church of this city. He has many friends in this city who will hear with regret of his illness. His old age and feeble condition render his recovery impossible.

The February 7 edition carried the final notice:

> The Rev. J.Y. DeBaun died yesterday at 4:45 P.M., at Leonia, New Jersey. Rev. DeBaun was pastor of the LaGrave Street Christian Reformed Church and it was during his pastorate that the new church was erected.

His son, the Rev. John A. DeBaun, D.D., wrote an "In Memoriam" in *The Banner (Of Truth)*. He concluded as follows:

> Earth is the poorer, nay — earth is the richer, for his influence and his works do follow him — I was going to say, earth is the poorer for the stilling of his great, tender, affectionate heart, and for the ceasing of his voice of testimony for Jesus and His grace.

Rev. and Mrs. DeBaun with family members in front of the original LaGrave Church parsonage.

REVEREND AND MRS. SAMUEL I. VANDERBEEK 1892–1898

Spiritual and financial hardship confronts the second pastor as LaGrave struggles to survive

Chapter 6

A DARK PERIOD OF TRIAL

Klaas Troon's worst fears were being realized. The older he became the more often he said, "I told you so." He had taken a dim view of the organization of an English-speaking congregation. "Before you know it, we will maybe have two — maybe tree." The fact was that there would soon be more than three, and they were not long in coming. By 1907, the year of Klaas Troon's death, there were eight English-speaking churches. Besides LaGrave, there were Third Church, Kalamazoo; Sherman Street, Grand Rapids; Third Church, Roseland, Illinois; Broadway, Grand Rapids; Bethany, Muskegon; Second Church, Englewood, New Jersey; and Burton Heights, Grand Rapids, daughter of LaGrave. Also, in 1890, the Christian Reformed Synod had gone ecumenical, uniting with the True Reformed Protestant Dutch Church (TRPDC) in the East. The president of the synod, Rev. L.J. Hulst, had extended the right hand of fellowship to the representative of the Dutch Church in the East, in the person of Rev. S.I. VanderBeek. It was this man that the Lord would send, two years later, to serve as LaGrave's second pastor. Thus, in some ways, LaGrave's beginnings were more closely linked with Classis Hackensack (TRPDC) than with the local scene, which may have been one factor, among others, for viewing LaGrave as "different."

Samuel I. VanderBeek had served a church in Ramsey, New Jersey, from 1875 to 1888, at which time he transferred to his home church (TRPDC). There he assisted the venerable and ailing Rev. J. Berden, who died in 1889, having served his church for an astonishing length of fifty-nine years. It was Rev. Berden who had warned Gysbert Haan and others about the immigrants in the West uniting with the Reformed Church in America. Following Rev. Berden's death, Samuel Vander-Beek took his place but only succeeded his long tenure with a brief three-year stay. A man of varied talents, Rev. VanderBeek drew up the plans for a new church for his congregation. It was built in 1890, the same year he and his flock united with the Christian Reformed Church. While serving as Berden's successor, he also initiated a Sunday School which met before the afternoon service. He wrote about it later as "a maiden effort." It is worthy of note in this chronicle because among the seven or eight who were present for the first session in October 1889 there was a widow, Mrs. Jane VanHouten, who a few years

Reverend Samuel I. VanderBeek

later would become the second Mrs. J.Y. DeBaun. VanderBeek was enterprising, capable, and dedicated. He had a good command of the English language. Already acquainted with this man, it is no wonder that LaGrave called him. On May 8, 1892, Rev. S.I. VanderBeek was installed as the second pastor of the LaGrave Street congregation. His inaugural sermon was based on Hebrews 10:23, 24:

Let us hold fast the confession of our hope that it waver not; for He is faithful that promised; and let us consider one another to provoke unto love and good works.

Rev. VanderBeek divided his message into two points:

I. The exhortation given to the church — "To hold fast its profession."

II. The ground upon which it is urged — "That God is faithful who has promised."

Considering the length of sermons in that day, it was short. There was a good attendance. The congregation now numbered 121 families, 143 communicants, and 575 souls. His message, too, was well received. But, little did anyone realize that night how soon the new minister's exhortation would be put to the test and how nearly all would fail. The past had been almost too bright and easy. In His providence, the Lord would lead His new church into deep waters.

Rev. VanderBeek could not have had a better reception or beginning. A local newspaper called it "A Happy Reception" and reported that:

In spite of the stormy weather there was a large and very happy social gathering at the home of Mr. and Mrs. John Benjamin last night to welcome the Rev. Samuel I. VanderBeek, the new pastor of the Christian Reformed Church on LaGrave Street, and his wife. The young people of the congregation gave some musical and literary selections and the evening was devoted to social pleasure. Rev. VanderBeek and his family will reside for the coming six months at 323 Cherry Street. The church society will build a parsonage on a site adjoining the church this summer and when completed will be occupied by the pastor and his family.

Scarcely six months later, the congregation had completed the parsonage. The pastor and his family moved in. The event was heralded in the local press on November 4, 1892, with the following article:

A BEAUTIFUL PARSONAGE.

THE HOME OF REV. S.I. VANDERBEEK ON LAGRAVE STREET.

The Lagrave Street Christian Reformed Church Parsonage Opened with a House-warming and Festival — What an Energetic Pastor and His Flock are Doing — Other Church News.

Last Friday evening the handsome new parsonage of the Lagrave Street Christian Reformed Church was formally opened and turned over to the church by the building committee. The parsonage is a new frame building with all modern conveniences, erected just north of the church at a cost of $3,000. The older people of the church assembled in the afternoon, and in the evening 200 young and old members of the congregation assembled at the house-warming. Alderman Gezon in behalf of the building committee formally presented the building to the church and its pastor. Rev. S.I. VanderBeek responded for the church in his usual graceful style. The Ladies Sewing Circle presented the pastor with an elegant quarter-sawed parlor suite. Musical selections by various young people of the church and from the recently organized male chorus, whiled the time pleasantly away and were agreeably varied by literary selections

from several students from the Theological Seminary. This intellectual feast was supplemented very acceptably by light refreshments served under the auspices of the Ladies Sewing Circle.

Rev. S.I. VanderBeek was installed as pastor of the church last May, and the congregation has prospered mightily and is daily growing in grace and .strength under his ministrations. The church was heavily burdened with debt when Mr. VanderBeek began his labors, but the Young People's Liquidation society has already raised $500 toward the payment of the obligation and by systematic giving, the burden is constantly growing lighter.

The first Thursday evening in each month, the young people of the church meet in the parsonage for social and literary improvement. All young people who are interested in church work are invited to these meetings which have proved most helpful as well as entertaining to those who have attended.

It would be a mistake to attribute LaGrave's early advances and successes exclusively to its clergy. Then, as now, the congregation was blessed with talent. There were many members who had leadership ability. And over all, there was the blessing of God. One of LaGrave's earliest and outstanding lay members was John L. Benjamin, clothier, active in politics as a supervisor, and very involved in the church, serving as an officer in the consistory, choir director, and in many other capacities. Indeed, when in 1892 he suffered a "close shave" with death, not only the whole congregation, but the entire community, all agog, breathed a sign of relief and thanksgiving. With other fine lay leaders, such as B. DeGraaf, J. Gelock, C. Verberg, A. Oom, John Wierenga, M. Schram, it seems arbitrary to single out any one of them. Even so, a special citation regarding J.L. Benjamin is in order, inasmuch as he served as a pillar among pillars. His wife was almost his equal in involvement with the church. Her home was always open, and countless meetings took place in her parlor. The Sewing Circle and others gave occasional parties for her in appreciation for all her work.

A CLOSE SHAVE.

Supervisor John Benjamin
Narrowly Escapes a Horrible Fate.

Supervisor John Benjamin narrowly escaped being crushed to death by the elevator in the new county building shortly after 8 o'clock last night. Having occasion to use the elevator he opened the door and found that it had been left about half way between the first and second floors. In order to lower it Mr. Benjamin reached the lever rope with his arm, and in doing so he was obliged to lean well into the elevator shaft. He pulled the rope down and the elevator started up. Seeing that it was going in the wrong direction he reversed the lever and did so so suddenly that the elevator descended with great rapidity. The upper part of the cage caught him on the back of the head and carried him to the floor. As he struck he had presence of mind enough to jerk his head out of danger or he must have surely been instantly killed by having his skull crushed between the cage and floor. As it was Mr. Benjamin escaped with but slight injury to the scalp, which was cut by the blow. He was able to walk to Dr. L.E. Best's office, where his injury was dressed. It was a close shave and an experience that the supervisor does not care to repeat.

Supervisor John Benjamin had so far recovered from his injuries sustained in the elevator at the court house Saturday night, as to be able to attend to his duties at the dedication yesterday, but his head is pretty sore yet, and he shudders as he remembers how narrow was his escape from death.

A NEW SOCIETY.

Organized by the Young People of the
Lagrave Street Reformed Church.

The young people of the Lagrave Street Reformed Church completed the organization last Wednesday night of a Young People's Literary Society. The following officers were elected:

President — John L. Benjamin
Vice President — Gelmer Kuiper
Secretary — Miss Lizzie Quartel
Treasurer — Miss Jennie Quartel

These, with C.A. Benjamin, G.J. Haan and John D. Brummeler, will form the executive committee. The following standing committees were appointed:

Social Committee —
    Miss Lena Van Heulen
    Miss Anna Johnson
    Isaac Van Bree
    Cornelius Meerse
Entertainment Committee —
    Miss Anna Quartel
    Miss Jennie Semeyn
    Miss Connie Van Dam
    G.J. Haan
    B.H. Hoer

The meetings, which are to occur once a month, will be devoted to a literary programme, furnished by the entertainment committee, to consist of reading, speaking and music; and a large part of each evening will be given to the introduction and entertainment of strangers and guests.

The meetings will be held in the lecture room of the church, on Lagrave Street.

The society numbers thirty-one members now, which number will be increased, no doubt, to fifty or sixty before the season is over.

Under Rev. VanderBeek's direction, the congregation enlarged in membership and in activities during the first years of his tenure. A young people's organization, already in existence, was reorganized and enlarged. Adding to such endeavors as catechism and sunday school classes, and the Central Ladies Aid, a South End Ladies Aid was begun. A Young Misses Sewing Circle, later to be called the Young Ladies Missionary Society, saw the light of day. Quite a number of young people made profession of their faith. A mission Sunday school was undertaken in the Seymour School House, and in March of 1893, a church paper named *Church Chronicle* was begun. A monthly, it was destined for the short life of only twelve issues because of the panic of 1893.

Today, people think of the 1890s nostalgically. Indeed, it has been romanticized beyond recognition. The truth is that the decade seemed destined to corroborate all of Klaas Troon's dire predic-

The Church Chronicle *provided church news and information, an article or sermonette for adults, a children's column, and ads. See the Addendum for the inside pages of this same August, 1893 issue.*

tions, which had now been enlarged and extended to encompass the country as well as the church. It was the worst of times — financially and ideologically. Because there was no more frontier, some thought there was no more future. The census of 1890 revealed the fact that for the first time in our country's history, there were more people residing in the cities than in rural America. This brought out the doomsayers who were proven right when the depression of 1893 descended.

This panic had to do with Europe, railroads, inflation, and a host of varied factors. There were 15,000 business failures. Banks went bankrupt. Railroads too. Suddenly, out of sixty-five million people, there were four million jobless. Jacob Coxey led an army of 500 unemployed (Coxey's Army) from Ohio to Washington D.C., where they

were arrested for walking on the grass. Jack London hopped boxcars from California to join Coxey and wrote a book about it (*The Road*). Tremendous strikes — one of the biggest being the Pullman Strike in Chicago — were brutally crushed. Tremendous anger and anxiety spread everywhere. The monied people feared anarchy. With no income, President Cleveland, an able man, had to get J.P. Morgan to bail out the country. The political climate began building early for the election of 1896 in which William Jennings Bryan, Democrat and populist, got more votes than any other previous candidate in American history. However, he still lost to the Republican, William McKinley, in a watershed election. All the Troons fell on hard times. At age sixty-four, Klaas lost his job and never really worked again.

It was under these conditions that Rev. Vander-Beek and his band sought to advance the work and calling of the LaGrave Church. The denomination was not dormant. Between 1890 and 1907 there were two attempts at church union, neither very strong; one was with the big Northern Presbyterian Church and the other with the smaller United Presbyterian Church. Beets and Bosma were putting out their catechism books on doctrine. L.J. Hulst was writing on infra- and supralapsarianism. Professor J. Robbert was busy with his overview of Reformed Theology. Yet, denominationally, too, the economic climate was registering. *The Banner*, for example, founded by Rev. DeBaun, and now a denominational paper, went from appearing twice weekly to appearing only once a week.

At LaGrave there were harbingers of worse days to come. The Sunday School Mission at Wealthy and Lake Avenue never materialized, and the Mission Sabbath School on Grandville Avenue, after some ups and downs, merged with a church in the neighborhood. Some members of the consistory moved away, and a few others resigned. The budget was not being met. Every week the church fell farther behind. Rev. VanderBeek, heavyhearted, nevertheless applied himself with vigor and preached encouragingly to his flock.

It was thought that pledge cards might help both income and planning for the future, but this effort failed. A plea to the synod for aid brought no results. Pictures of the church and parsonage were placed on sale in various business establishments in the city to augment the income, but this, too, proved to be a vain effort. Meanwhile, because of widespread unemployment and a diminished membership, contributions to the church dipped to about four cents per week per person. Even so, it was thought that the congregation would yet weather the crisis, provided some drastic measures were taken. Accordingly, at a congregational meeting held October 18, 1897, the pastor's salary was reduced. With this, and a surge in the collecting of pew rent, it was felt that the congregation would manage. But, there was no rent coming in for ninety-three assigned seats. Efforts to collect from those who were in arrears bore little fruit.

Rev. VanderBeek, for his part, also sought to augment the income of the church. Early in 1897, he published a series of sermons under the title: "The Spiritual Thermometer."

His introduction can move hearts even today. He wrote:

Having been requested by a number of friends to have the discourses contained in this volume printed, I have responded to their wish in the hope of being able to contribute aid to the church of which I am pastor, which is now in financial need.

The people are an earnest and self-denying congregation and have struggled heroically to be self-sustaining during the four years of financial depression; but a number of their best supporters have met with reverses in business and are unequal to the responsibilities they at one time gladly assumed.

During the five years of my pastorate they have never solicited any outside aid; but are a congregation of workers who have willingly responded to the needs of their church. They have no knowledge of this step in their behalf, but they stand in need of encouragement from such as have Zion's cause at heart.

This is not an intent to beg, but if God's Holy Spirit should move the hearts of some to contribute aid to a willing people at this time, the writer will feel that his effort has been put forth in a worthy cause.

Yours fraternally,

Rev. S. I. VanderBeek
Pastor of LaGrave Street
Christian Reformed Church
Grand Rapids, Michigan

His booklet, *The Spiritual Thermometer,* consisted of three sermons whose titles and texts were:

"The Thermometer"
Exodus 35:29 "The children of Israel brought a willing offering unto the Lord, every man and woman whose heart made them willing to bring all manner of works, which the Lord had commanded to be made by the hand of Moses."

"The Atmosphere"
John 15:7 "As the Father hath loved me, so have I loved you; continue ye in my love."

"The Temperature"
Exodus 40:33-34 "So Moses finished the work. Then the cloud covered the tent of the congregation, and the glory of the Lord filled the tabernacle."

All three sermons were Biblical and practical. Thus did Rev. S. I. VanderBeek make his gallant effort to save his church by peddling three sermons at a dime apiece, for the price of the booklet was thirty cents. But there were few who bought. Dimes were scarce.

THE

Spiritual . . .

Thermometer.

A Series of Sermoms Delivered by Rev. S. I. Vanderbeek, Pastor
of the Lagrave Street Christian Reformed Church,
Grand Rapids, Mich.

PUBLISHED BY REQUEST.

PRICE, - - 30 CENTS.

RAMSEY, N. J.:
JOHN Y. DATER, BOOK AND JOB PRINTER,
1897

In August of 1898, Rev. VanderBeek, placing the well-being of his church ahead of himself, handed in his resignation. It relieved his congregation of the obligation of his support. On October 9, he preached his farewell sermon on II Corinthians 13:11: "Finally, brethren, farewell, be perfected, be comforted, be of the same mind; live in peace; and the God of love and peace shall be with you."

Rev. VanderBeek was a likeable man. His difficulties and subsequent resignation were due to circumstances beyond his control. There is no doubt that the trauma of his resignation affected the remainder of his days. After his resignation in 1898, he served no church until he went to Leonia, New Jersey in 1906. This was the same church his predecessor at LaGrave had served. From 1911 to 1919 he again served no church. It was in 1919 that he became emeritus. He died in 1924.

On October 11, 1898, two days after the farewell of its pastor, LaGrave assessed its situation and its hope for the future. The indebtedness had risen to $15,000. A motion was not only made, but carried, to suggest to the mortgage holder that the property be turned over to him, provided he waived the back interest and would allow the use of the church for two years with the parsonage offered for his immediate possession.

The next pastor of LaGrave, Dr. Henry Beets, would remember this period of LaGrave's history. As a historian, he would refer to it as, "A dark period of trial."

Chapter 7

THE SOUND OF MUSIC

Not yet in its teens, the LaGrave Church, along with the nineteenth century, seemed to be dying. After a difficult birth only a dozen years before, it teetered on the edge of extinction. It was surviving spiritually and ecclesiastically, but not economically. Years later, some would call it "the rich church." But in 1898, there was none poorer. The son of a Presbyterian minister, Grover Cleveland, President of the United States, had seen a terrible money panic engulfing the land. The result was a ruinous decade which threatened to sweep LaGrave aside.

In twelve short years, the first English-speaking Christian Reformed Church (but named the Fourth Holland Christian Reformed Church) had been distinctive — not just because of its language. It had been unusual in other ways as well. In the May 20, 1904, issue of *The Banner*, it was reported that "Classis Illinois desires that synod disapprove the church choir in our sacred worship." But LaGrave had incorporated a choir into its order of service from its very beginning. This made the sister churches unhappy. Indeed, LaGrave's pastor, Rev. J.Y. DeBaun, had been reprimanded for having included an anthem by the choir in the cornerstone laying ceremony rather than a Psalm sung by the people. This is not to say that the denomination was against music. In fact, "Singing Schools" (Choral Societies) flourished almost everywhere. But choirs were not permitted in the official worship services in the Christian Reformed churches until well into the twentieth century.

The Westminster Shorter Catechism begins by asking: "What is the chief end of man?" It answers, in part, as follows: "To glorify God . . ." Never does the church do so more directly than in song. This is the activity of the angels, and their sound of music is the sound of heaven. That it is also the sound of the church on earth was well understood by the members of the Christian Reformed Church around the turn of the century. Psalm singing was their heritage. The Lord was great and greatly to be praised! When God placed a church on earth, He gave it something to sing about. And so a church without music wasn't a church, as a Christian without a song wasn't a Christian. Klaas and Anna Troon had a reed organ in their parlor. It was their prize possession. As Klaas played, they both sang. The Christian sings, "O for a thousand tongues to sing my Great Redeemer's praise," so Klaas used the one he had.

Together the Troons could sing even on their darkest days — like Paul and Silas in Prison. Together with their fellow members in the Christian Reformed Church, they created a sound of music such as the world could not shut up, nor the devil silence.

In the Christian Reformed Church, that sound of music was the singing of Psalms, in distinction from hymns. Only outside of the official worship hour did they "Sing a New Song unto Jehovah." Within the Sunday order of worship, they sang only the old songs — the Psalms. It was a tradition they shared with some others. The Puritans in New England, Psalm singers all, didn't do as well. Generally, they sang less than a dozen of them, but sang them poorly. No two people sang alike. Their congregational singing sounded like 500 different tunes roaring out at the same time, often one or two notes apart. An eighteenth century New England minister wrote, "I, myself, have twice in one note paused to take breath." The Christian Reformed Hollanders, a century later, would do better. Most knew from memory the versified versions of all 150 Psalms. Uniting their voices, they could raise the roof, even though, sometimes, the whole notes they sang exceeded their breathing spans too.

Therefore, it seemed even more alien when La-Grave, adopting English as its language, sang in "foreign" sounds and accents and rhythms. Indeed, there were few who found the hymns familiar. Those who did were automatically placed in the choir to aid the congregation in singing. Generally, these were the younger people who, in every generation, adapt more easily. Thus the older members looked to the young to lead them in this part of the worship hour.

In its initial years, LaGrave was indeed fortunate to have three individuals who were largely responsible for the establishment of a sound musical tradition. They were the first pastor, Rev. J.Y. DeBaun, Mr. John L. Benjamin, and Mrs. Anna M. Maris. Rev. DeBaun had brought from New Jersey a few copies of a book called *The Family Psalmist*. It was a compilation by him of a small number of Psalms and hymns. As these were limited in number and needed by the choir, there was not much congregational singing at first. This situation was remedied by the printing of the words on sturdy cards which were supplied to the worshippers and were to be left in the seats.

J.L. Benjamin served as song leader and choir director. The first choir rehearsal took place in one of the homes of the congregation with about twenty people present — a number soon reduced to half. Even so, despite their fear of arousing the antagonism of the more conservative church members, they desired and prepared anthems for singing in the worship hour. They were supported in their effort by the kindly advice of their "dear old pastor." Meanwhile, Anna Maris served faithfully at the console of a hand-pumped organ.

In less than a year, the congregation supplied itself with a sufficient number of United Presbyterian Psalters, a book the Christian Reformed Church Synod would approve some twenty years later, in 1914. The small choir labored faithfully, in unbroken service, for about three years, leading the congregation through their musical paces. In 1891 it disbanded and was replaced by a quartet comprised of the Misses Anna Johnson and Anna Quartel and the Messrs. I. VanBree and E.H. Boer, who had served briefly as choir leader in its initial sessions. Anna Maris was still at the organ. G.J. Haan and J.L. Benjamin joined the quartet which was enlarged to a chorus and continued to the end of 1892.

This seemed to be a good move in terms of musical development, for these people represented the most talented and best voices in the congregation. They still led the membership in Sunday services, but they also went beyond this task to introduce a music of both spiritual and aesthetic worth.

Alas, the tradition that a church choir can sometimes be a source of tension is a universal one. Musical tastes differ — often more sharply than mildly. The departure of the first pastor and his calming presence may also have been a factor. Whatever the reasons, the choir dissolved, leaving J.L. Benjamin to lead the congregation for a time as precentor. It was but a few months before agitation for a new choir began. In April, 1893, Mr. Benjamin organized a choir which would be in continuous existence for the next twenty years. The man was indefatigable, evidenced not only in his church activities on the Lord's Day, but also in his business and political involvements. It was La-Grave Church, however, to which he gave first priority. His contribution to the social life of the congregation, which was considerable, too, inevitably involved more sounds of music.

Anna M. Maris was, perhaps, the only organist available when the LaGrave Church was organized. She was of great assistance and willingly served more than six years. Mr. A.J. Englewood

4th Holland Christian Reformed Church.

PLEASE LEAVE IN SEAT.

Psalm 84.

LORD GOD of hosts, how lovely
   The place where thou dost dwell!
Thy tabernacles holy
   In pleasantness excel.

2 My soul is longing, fainting,
   Jehovah's courts to see;
My heart and flesh are crying,
   O living God, for thee.

3 Behold, the sparrow findeth
   A house in which to rest,
The swallow hath discovered
   Where she may build her nest;

4 And where, securely sheltered,
   Her young she forth may bring;
So, Lord of hosts, thy altars
   I seek, my God, my King.

5 Blest who thy house inhabit,
   They ever give thee praise;
Blest all whom thou dost strengthen,
   Who love the sacred ways.

Ps. 122.

WITH JOY I hear my friends exclaim,
   ' Come let us in God's temple meet,'
Within thy gates, Jerusalem,
   Shall ever stand our willing feet.

2 A city built compact and fair,
   Jerus'lem stands, the sacred place,
To which the gathering tribes repair,
   Tribes of Jehovah's chosen race.

3 'Tis there by his command they meet,
   To render thanks and pay their
      vows;
And there is judgment's royal seat,
   There are the thrones of David's
      house.

4 Pray that Jerus'lem's peace endure,
   For all that love thee God will bless;
Peace dwell within thy walls secure,
   And joy within thy palaces.

Ps. 125.

HE that in God confideth,
   Like Zion Mount shall be,
Which ever more abideth
   Unmoved eternally.

2 As mountains, which defend her,
   Jerusalem surround,
His saints secure to render,
   God compasseth around.

3 The sinner's rod shall never
   On just men's lot abide,
Lest upright men should ever
   To sin be turned aside.

4 Thy goodness, Lord, our Savior,
   To all the good impart;
And ever show thy favor
   To men of upright heart.

Ps. 126.

WHEN Zion's bondage God turned
      back,
   As men that dreamed were we.
Then filled with laughter was our
      mouth,
   Our tongue with melody:

2 The heathen people said, The Lord
   Great things for them hath wrought,
The Lord hath done great things
      for us,
   Whence joy to us is brought.

3 As streams of water in the south,
   Our bondage, Lord, recall,
Who sow in tears, a reaping time
   Of joy enjoy they shall.

4 That man who, bearing precious seed;
   In going forth doth mourn,
He, doubtless, bringing back his
      sheaves,
   Rejoicing shall return.

Ps. 132.

FOR God of Zion hath made choice;
   There he desires to dwell.
This is my rest, here I will stay;
   For I do like it well.

11 Her food I'll greatly bless; her poor
   With bread will satisfy.
Her priests I'll clothe with health;
      Her saints
   Shall shout forth joyfully.

Sturdy pew cards provided the congregation with words to the Psalms that were sung in church

became the church organist in May, 1893. It was largely through his efforts that the church procured its first small portable pipe organ. There was tremendous enthusiasm among young and old alike to gather money for this project.

During this period, the LaGrave congregation became noted for its congregational singing. This was largely due to the great effort of Mr. Benjamin to involve young people with music.

Thus began a tradition still evident in the church. In the addendum in this volume, there is a listing of LaGrave organists and choir directors, all of whom contributed to an ongoing tradition of musical excellence that has become characteristic of LaGrave Church. An examination of its musical activities in the 1890s reveals La Grave's heritage. Consider these notices which appeared in the local press of that era.

40

WILL RENDER "DANIEL"

The Lagrave Street Choral Society of the Lagrave Street Christian Reformed church, under the direction of John L. Benjamin, is putting in its final rehearsals on cantata "Daniel," which will be given at the church Friday evening, February 15, with B.H. Boer in the title role and Mrs. A. Thomas, Miss Minnie Sherphorn, Messrs. G.J. Haan, Peter Quartel and J.D. Brummeler will take the remainder of the solos. This beautiful cantata has never been sung in this city, and as this society has been working on it all winter, something good may be expected. It will be given for the benefit of the above mentioned church, and as no admission fee will be charged, a beautiful libretto will be sold containing all the words of the cantata, and a collection will be taken up for the poor of the church.

CHRISTMAS EXERCISES.

The "Prince of Peace," a Christmas cantata, was well rendered by the choir of the Lagrave Street Christian Reformed Church under the direction of J.L. Benjamin. A finely rendered violin obligato by W.A. Weeks was worthy of much praise. Those who took leading parts were Miss Cora Hazenburg, Miss Anna Sluyter, Miss Minnie Scherphorn, J.L. Benjamin, Peter Quartel and James Benjamin. The accompaniment was played by A.J. Englewood.

ANNUAL TREAT.

Given by the Lagrave Street Reformed Sunday School Last Evening.

The eighth annual entertainment of the Lagrave Street Reformed Sunday School was held last evening. The large auditorium seating over seven hundred people was filled to standing room. The entertainment consisted of carols and speeches by young children which delighted the audience and elicited much applause. Choir, class and school singing formed the musical part of the program. On the pulpit was placed a large pyramid of oranges, while vari-colored boxes of candy were piled up in columns on either side. The performance closed with the singing of the Doxology.

PLEASANT ENTERTAINMENT

Mr. and Mrs. John Benjamin of No. 119 Lagrave Street entertained the young people of the Lagrave Street Christian Reformed Church at their home Wednesday evening. About a hundred accepted the invitation and after spending an hour or so in social intercourse, listened to the following program:

"Minstrels' Carnival" . . . . . .Excelsoir Banjo Club
Piano Duet . . . ."Neck and Neck" B.H. Boer and Miss Anna Johnson.
Guitar and Mandolin Quartet — Misses Marrin, Rasch, Saltsgiver and Beuter,
Recitation . ."The Pauper's Death Bed" Gelmer Kuiper.
Drum Solo . . . . .Edward Knapp
Baritone Solo . . . ."Fearless" B.H. Boer
"Limited Mall" . .Excelsior Banjo Club
Autoharp Solo . . . . .Frank Marrin
Soprano Solo (selected) . . . .Miss Anna Geyon
"Manhattan Beach March" . .Excelsior Banjo Club
"Good Night, Gentle Folks" . . . . Mixed Quartet
Misses Anna Johnson
Cornelia Benjamin
Messrs. Peter Quartel, B.H. Boer

The entire program was well rendered, the work of the Excelsior Banjo Club as usual being exceptionally fine, they being required to respond to frequent encores.

EASTER CANTATA

The LaGrave Street Christian Reformed Church choir is putting in its final rehearsals for the Easter cantata which will be given at the church, Tuesday evening, April 9. The work is composed by H.W. Porter, and entitled "The Resurrection" telling the story of the cross in solos, quartets, choruses, etc. The regular choir of twenty-four voices has been increased to about forty which with the organ, piano, and a string quartet will give a highly entertaining and edifying evening. The admission will be free, but a collection will be taken to defray the expenses of the concert.

The tradition continued into the new century. In December, 1904, the LaGrave choir of fifty voices presented the cantata, "Light of Life." *The Banner* reported that the music was "of high character, containing a part of Handel's *Messiah* and selections by Shelly, Geibel, and others." The next reference to *The Messiah* in *The Banner* appeared December 12, 1907, and read, in part, as follows:

> The chorus of the LaGrave Church numbering over forty voices, intends to give the cantata, *The Prince of Peace*, by J. Spencer Camp, on the evening of December 19th. The famous "Hallelujah Chorus," from Handel's *Messiah* will be sung as a special number by request.

In his book, *Fifty Years of Music at Calvin College* (p. 22), Professor Seymour Swets, one of J.L. Benjamin's successors as a LaGrave choir director, wondered "whether this was the first time that the "Hallelujah Chorus" was sung at LaGrave or in any of our churches." Today, the singing of that chorus takes place as a tradition at LaGrave each Easter and each fourth Sunday in Advent. *The Banner* of March 3, 1910, announced that:

> On Friday, March 11, a chorus of 48 voices expects to sing the oratorio *St. Paul, The Apostle*, by Trowbridge, at the LaGrave Church. There is a quartet of good soloists who, together with the chorus, will give some of the stirring scenes from the great apostle's life.

In 1907, the big year of the Semi-Centennial of the Christian Reformed denomination, LaGrave's choir director, J.L. Benjamin, directed a massed choir of 400 voices singing "O Praise the Lord, Our Jubilee We're Hailing" in the Dutch language. The following evening, the whole program was repeated in English. In addition to the music, both evenings saw five speakers giving five main addresses. Rev. H. VanderWerp wrote the cantata. The celebrations took place in the Auditorium Building on South Ionia Avenue.

It may be true that the musical selections and renditions of LaGrave's earliest choirs and choruses were not up to today's standards. It would be unfair to compare them with today's quality. But in zeal, enthusiasm, and commitment they set high standards.

Klaas Troon, rock-ribbed conservative, rejoiced in music. Cantatas, however, did not touch him as deeply as the Dutch Psalms. He worried about English hymns eventually finding entrance into Sunday services, particularly those of questionable theology. Despite the growing unpopularity of his position, he continued to warn against the dangers of Americanization. Years later, Professor Seymour Swets would articulate some of the things that made Klaas uneasy. In his book *Fifty Years of Music at Calvin College* (p. 28), Professor Swets wrote:

> It was all so very simple in the old days. But somewhere complications crept in and church music began to suffer. The Americanization process had a good deal to do with it, the taking over of the best, but more often the worst, of our middle-class American culture. By the early 1900s most of our church people sang hymns, though not in church.[c] A copy or two of *Gospel Hymns, No. 1 to 6* was found on almost every reed organ or piano, and the favorite pastime for young people as well as for many of the older ones was to "gather round" and sing hymns. With the advent of radio and evangelistic campaigns, new hymns with swinging rhythms became popular. Such hymns as "Since Jesus Came into My Heart" and "Love Lifted Me" were sung with gusto. Billy Sunday, Homer Rodeheaver, Bob Jones, Gypsy Smith, and many others introduced new hymn books with each new campaign. With much of radio still taboo, our people became easy victims of the evangelistic radio stations that beamed forth "messages" and frothy gospel songs all day long. No doubt many people were benefitted spiritually by these hymns, but the daily exposure to them created and developed a taste for this style of evangelistic song. No wonder that our Psalm tunes sounded drab in comparison. No wonder that there was a clamor for these peppy hymns in Sunday school and young people's meetings.
>
> With the passing of the older generation of organists who loved the Dutch Psalms there arose a new generation, often high school girls, who could play a little piano but who did not know Worp and Van Krieken and knew nothing about church music. These young people had no one to turn to for guidance and so skimmed off some of the froth they heard on the radio. Soon hundreds of these hymns and choruses were instantly available in the form of "sing-spiration" books.

Some of those hymns would eventually find their way into the pews of quite a few Christian Reformed churches, to be sung — if not in the service proper — in a hymn sing before the service. For its first century of existence, LaGrave has exercised great care in this matter, scrutinizing all of its hymns carefully for doctrinal soundness and musical excellence. That this is so, is due largely to those good beginnings when, then, as now, the sound of music was heard in praise of God.

The LaGrave mixed choir, Christmas, 1904.

Chapter 8

ENTER MR. JENKS

George Bancroft, historian, in a letter to his wife, wrote: "Each page of history may begin and end with 'Great is God and marvelous are His doings among the children of men.'"

LaGrave's darkest page of history was October 11, 1898. The congregation had decided to turn its property over to the mortgage holder. Its debt was astronomical! There was nothing left to do. Yet, this darkest of days, too, issued forth into the praise of God; for as Bancroft wrote to his wife, " 'By His providence, whereby He upholds all things and governs them according to His wise and gracious plan,'* the Lord sent help." He sent it from a most unexpected quarter.

Help had been sought from the synod. But none was forthcoming — neither from other Christian Reformed churches nor classis. They, too, were struggling as a result of the economic climate. It may have been that some individuals were secretly gloating over LaGrave's distress, having opposed its birth from the very beginning. Alas, such is the nature of the "old nature" in the Christian. It is dying, yet not dead. Even so, it must be observed — to the credit of Klaas Troon — that he did not rejoice in LaGrave's disaster. It is true that

he had fought its coming into existence. Indeed, no one had opposed it more. But the distress of others was never a source of comfort to him. And so it was Klaas, who had fought hard on the floor of classis to abort LaGrave's birth, who now reprimanded those few who interpreted LaGrave's plight in terms of divine retribution.

God sent help in the form of Mr. Samuel B. Jenks. Mr. Jenks was the man who held the mortgage. The members who had voted to turn the property back to him were in a more severe state of depression than the economy. A developing series of reversals had left them dazed, discouraged, and wondering. After so much struggle and prayer, and after a seeming hand of benediction over them for a decade of spiritual increase, there had come in quick succession mounting bills, a reduction of the pastor's salary, a reduction in membership, the pastor's proffered help through resignation, a sad farewell between shepherd and flock, and a congregational decision to return the property to Mr. Jenks. Was God not on their side? Had he been deaf to all their prayers?

*Lord's Day 10, Heidleberg Catechism

ASSIGNMENT OF_____ MORTGAGE *146 - 413*   LIBER 203.

From *George G. Briggs*

To *Samuel B. Jenks*

Received for Record *November 4th* A. D. 18*93* at *10 1/3* o'clock *A.* M.

John T Gould Register.

Know all Men by these Presents, That I, *George G. Briggs of the City of Grand Rapids, County of Kent and State of Michigan,*_____

of the first part, for and in consideration of the sum of *Ten Thousand Sixty and 25/100 Dollars ($10,060.25/100)*_____

_____ lawful money of the United States of America, to me_____ in hand paid by *Samuel B. Jenks of the City of Grand Rapids, County and State aforesaid,*_____

of the second part, at or before the ensealing or delivery of these presents, the receipt whereof is hereby acknowledged, have granted, bargained, sold, assigned, transferred, and set over, and BY THESE PRESENTS do grant, bargain, sell, assign, transfer, and set over unto the said party of the second part a_____ certain INDENTURE__OF MORTGAGE_____, made bearing date the *Fifteenth* day of *March*_____ one thousand eight hundred and *Eighty nine*_____,

by the Fourth Holland Christian Reformed Church of Grand Rapids, Kent County, Michigan, to William H. Van Leeuwen, and recorded in the Register's office of the County of Kent, State of Michigan, in Liber 146 of Mortgages, at pages 413, 414 and 415, and which said mortgage was by the William H. Van Leeuwen assigned to George G. Briggs, on the 23rd. day of July A.D. 1889. and which said Assignment was duly

recorded in the Register's Office of the County of *Kent, State of Michigan,*_____ in Liber *142*_____ of Mortgages, at Page *422*_____ with all and_____ singular the premises therein mentioned and described, together with the *Bond*_____ or obligation therein also mentioned, and the moneys now due_____, and the interest that may hereafter grow due thereon: TO HAVE AND TO HOLD the same unto the *said*_____ party of the second part *his heirs*_____ and a signs, FOREVER, subject only to the proviso in the said Indenture of Mortgage mentioned. And I_____ do hereby authorize and appoint the said party of the second part, *my*_____ true and lawful Attorney, irrevocable in *my*_____ name or otherwise, but at *his*_____ proper costs and charges, to have, use, and take all lawful ways and means for the recovery of the sum or sums of money now due and owing, or hereafter to become due and owing, upon the said *Bond and*_____ _____ Mortgage, and in case of payment to give acquittance or other sufficient discharge, as fully as_____ might or could do if these presents were not made; and I_____ do hereby, for *myself*_____ *my*_____ heirs, executors, and administrators, covenant, promise, and agree to and with the said party of the second part, that there is *at the date hereof, due*_____ upon the said *Bond and*_____ Mortgage, the sum of *Ten Thousand Sixty and 25/100 Dollars ($10,060.25/100)*_____

and that *I*_____ *have*_____ good, right, and lawful authority to grant, bargain, and sell the same in manner aforesaid_____

Sealed and Delivered the Seventeenth day of April 1891

In Presence of

Chas. Chandler
M. Elizabeth Race

George G. Briggs (SEAL)

State of *Michigan*
County of *Kent* } ss.

On this *Seventeenth* day of *April A. D.* One Thousand Eight Hundred and *Ninety one*, before me, *a Notary Public in and for said*_____ County, personally appeared *George G. Briggs, to me known to be* the *person* described in and who executed the *within* instrument and acknowledged the same to be *his* free act and deed_____

Charles Chandler,
Notary Public, Kent Co. Mich.

Mr. Samuel B. Jenks held the mortgage on the Fourth Holland Christian Reformed Church

The first pastor, Rev. J.Y. DeBaun, had made a tremendous contribution to the birth and life of the church. Many people after him would do the same. It would be unwise to attempt to list them for, undoubtedly, so many would be missed. But if such a compilation of names were attempted, it would have to include one who wasn't a member at all, yet who lives today in LaGrave's annals as one of its great benfactors.

MR. JENKS!

Who was he? Was he Protestant, Roman Catholic, or neither? Was he Congregationalist or Lutheran? Was he a believer, an agnostic, or an atheist? It is strange that LaGrave's records tell us almost nothing about him. All that we do know is that he was a capitalist. An investor. He built and owned the Herkimer Hotel on Division Avenue, naming it after the county in New York where he was born. To this day it carries his name carved in stone. Jenks! Before the disaster of 1893, it had been good business to loan money to churches. After the crash, Mr. Jenks, no doubt, was also affected. But whether his reversals were major or minor, he was in the business of making money. Therefore, it was altogether likely that he would have taken back the property of LaGrave, in view of an enormous debt of $15,000 which, humanly speaking could never be paid by a discouraged membership, rapidly diminishing in members.

It was a surprise, therefore, when Mr. Jenks graciously refused the return of the property; that he was willing to wait; and that, in fact, he encouraged a defeated, disheartened congregation to look forward, to find an energetic pastor with vision, and to move ahead with hope into the new century soon to arrive.

It could have been otherwise!

Dutch Christian Reformed people were resented by some Grand Rapids citizens, then as now, either for their nationality, their faith, or both. Mr. Jenks might have been one of them. Like the sneering black-caped villain in old-fashioned plays, evicting the poor widow out into the cold for being behind in the rent, Mr. Jenks, too, might not only have been short on patience, but sinister. It would not have been the first time. Instead, he acted in the spirit of Christ, although he might not have professed Him as his personal Saviour.

It is preferable to think that he did. But what if he didn't? Either way, as future historian Henry Beets would write, "God moved his heart."

The Lord works in mysterious ways His wonders to perform. King Cyrus, of Old Testament fame, a stranger to the Jewish faith, nevertheless, gave orders for the rebuilding of the temple in Jerusalem. One who was unfamiliar with Jehovah restored the vessels of His house. In so doing, Cyrus was God's unwitting instrument. He was, as Mr. Jenks, God's rescuing presence. It was Emerson, no Calvinist, who said, "Our helm is given up to a better guidance than our own." The struggling LaGravites of 1893 felt depleted, but God was long beforehand with their souls. Without knowing, perhaps, Mr. Jenks, as Cyrus, achieved God's plan. Isaiah called Cyrus "The Lord's Shepherd." So, for one brief meeting, Mr. Jenks was LaGrave's shepherd, even though he had never set foot in the Christian Reformed Theological School and had never been ordained into the Christian Reformed or any other ministry.

Local Capitalist Claimed by Death

SAMUEL BUSHNELL JENKS.

After a residence in Grand Rapids of 45 years, Mr. Jenks died suddenly at his home, 109 Washington street, early yesterday morning aged 77 years.

He came to this city in the early 70's and engaged in lumbering. At the time of his death he had extensive timber holdings in Michigan and in the south and west.

He was prominently identified with many of the local furniture companies. He was the owner of the Herkimer hotel.

God did not create a church in 1887 without assuming responsibility for it. If it seemed to the membership that the clay was breaking in the potter's hands, they were forgetting that the chiefest blessings often come by way of calamities which, in God's leading, are never more than a mask. When Winston Churchill stood before the United States Congress, he said that he was aware of an appointed plan. Perhaps Cyrus was not. Perhaps Mr. Jenks was not. Perhaps Mr. Jenks was a Christian, but Arminian in his theology. But both Mr. Jenks and the LaGrave Church had been predestined to meet. As Cyrus was a foreordained intrument of the Lord of history, so Mr. Jenks was God's chosen agent for the continuance of LaGrave's history. We are not told whether Cyrus was good or bad. The Bible does not label him. History's verdict does — as good and bad — yet more good than bad. Whatever his character, and whatever the character of Mr. Jenks, a sovereign God uses a variety of human tools to achieve His purposes.

Years later, in the history of the Christian Reformed Church, there would be a devastating debate regarding the common grace of God. LaGrave Church, along with the denomination, and the whole cause of Christ, would be hurt by it. It is hoped that Mr. Jenks was the object of God's special grace. But if not, then God's common grace — allowing him to be such a man of means and giving him the ability to be gracious to a struggling congregation was grace indeed! How marvelously God works all things together for the good of those who love Him!

Thus, in the history of LaGrave, there came about this strange, yet wonderful interlude. Like a bit player on a stage, like a meteor in the sky, Mr. Jenks entered, and Mr. Jenks exited. God can work His wonders in the twinkling of an eye. And whomever He selects as His instrument may be entirely unconscious of the end he serves.

Chapter 9

A CENTURY OF GOLD

The depression of the 1890s was not only gone, but forgotten, when the nation entered into what some called "The Century of Gold." Senator Chauncey DePew, of New York, said on the Senate floor, "There is not a man here who does not feel 400 percent bigger in 1900 than he did in 1896." His colleague, Mark Hanna, crowed, "Furnaces are glowing, spindles are singing their song, happiness comes to all with prosperity." The Reverend Newell Dwight Hillis of Brooklyn, gave it his best ministerial insight: "Laws are becoming more just, rulers humane, music is becoming sweeter, and books wiser." Despite a welter of problems — child labor, teeming slums, wide-spread political corruption, and ruthless corporations — the faith of America sang the inevitability of its progress. Henry James wrote: "The will to grow was everwhere written large, and to grow at no matter what or whose expense." In a cartoon entitled "Reading The Will — The Inheritance of the Twentieth Century," the Nineteenth Century — an old man — held up a document which read, "I hereby devise and bequeath to my sole heir — the Twentieth Century — The Chinese Imbroglio, The South African War, The Philippine Question, The Sultan of Turkey, A Few South American Scraps, and several

useful inventions." But the Twentieth Century, a feckless youth in sporty attire, whistled nonchalantly as he scarcely paid attention. Meanwhile, President William McKinley, addressing Congress, said: "At the outgoing of the old and the incoming of the new century, you begin the last session of the 56th Congress with evidences on every hand of individual and national prosperity."

So it seemed. Americans were blissfully unaware that they had ushered in the bloodiest of centuries. Darwin and liberal theologians had made their contribution to the national notion that everywhere, and in every way, the world was getting better and better.

In 1900, America was made up of forty-five states and 76 million people, whose average wage was 22¢ an hour. Eleven million of the people, however, were farmers whose numbers would decrease annually as cities and factories beckoned. But if wages and income were low — so were the prices.

Few people — eighteen out of a thousand — had phones, and none had radios or refrigerators. Keeping up with the Joneses had not yet become a factor. It was a simple time in which the government, recovered from the ills of the 1890s, showed a surplus and a balanced budget, more or

Meat and Poultry Prices

Spring Chicken	7¢lb.	Roosters	15¢ea.	Turkey	10¢lb.	Veal	10¢lb.
Beef	10¢lb.	Hens	7¢lb.	Duck	6¢lb.	Breakfast Bacon	12½¢lb.
Sausage	12½¢lb.	Pork	10¢lb.	Duck, Dressed	10¢lb.	Goose	5¢lb.

Grocery Prices

PRODUCE AND DAIRY PRODUCTS

Red Apples	30¢pk.	Dried Apricots	10¢lb.
Seed Potatoes	35¢bu.	Dried Prunes	5¢lb.
Onion Sets	3 qt.25¢	Eggs	12¢doz.
Oranges	20¢doz.	Butter	18¢lb.
Lemons	15¢doz.	Swiss Cheese	25¢lb.

HOUSEWARES

Scrub Brush	15¢	Starch	10¢
Lye	5¢	Toilet Soap	3 for 15¢
Garden Seed	2 for 5¢	Candles	1 Box 15¢

CANNED GOODS

Golden Cream Corn	10¢	Boston Baked Beans	10¢
String Beans	10¢	Oysters	20¢
Tomatoes	20¢	Jams	10¢
Early June Peas	10¢	Green Turtle Meat	$2.75
Sliced Peaches	25¢	Sardines in Oil	5¢

STAPLES

Tea	40¢	Sugar	100 lbs. $5.80
Coffee	15¢lb.	Salt	100 lbs. 20¢
Cocoa	25¢	Salad Dressing	25¢
Macaroni	10¢	Baking Powder	10¢
Hominy Grits	10¢	Gelatine	15¢

Department Store Prices

LADIES' WEAR

Tailor-made Suit	$10.00	Waist	$3.00
Skirt	$4.00	Corset	40¢
Chemise	50¢	Shawl	50¢
Bracelet	35¢	Silk Petticoat	$5.00
Shoes	$1.50	Bead Purse	50¢

MEN'S WEAR

Fancy Suit	$9.00	Coat and Vest	$7.00
Trousers	$1.25	Linen Collar	25¢
Shirts	50¢	Hat	$2.00
Woolen hose	15¢	Underwear	50¢
Suspenders	25¢	Work Shoes	$1.25

HOUSE FURNISHINGS

Blanket	35¢	Wallpaper	roll 5¢
Carpet	12¢ yd.	42-Piece Dinner Set	$2.95
Hammock	$3.50	Sheet, Double Bed	58¢

DRESS GOODS

Gingham	12½¢yd.	Sewing Machines	$12.00
Madras Cloth	10¢yd.	Embroidery	8¢
Taffeta	85¢yd.	Silk	50¢yd.
Calico	6¢yd.	Sewing Pattern	10¢
Pins	box 5¢	Damask	40¢yd.

less, which would continue until President Dwight Eisenhower did it for the last time in 1960. For almost two generations there had been no major wars, but diphtheria, typhoid, malaria, and pneumonia claimed victims in high numbers.

The population was augmented annually — alarmingly so, some felt — by immigrants; a half-million in 1900, and by 1905, a million a year. Ellis Island processed thousands daily. Thomas Watson, native-born politician, wailed: "The scum of creation has been dumped on us! The most dangerous and corrupting hordes of the old world have invaded us! The vice and crime which they have planted in our midst are sick and terrifying." Others saw it all as part of a nation's progress and growing strength — a nation which, it was predicted, would bring about 150-mile-an-hour trains, home ice-making machines, and much more, before the new century ran its course.

The first decade of the Century of Gold saw such people as Robert E. Peary, who placed his footprints on the North Pole; William Randolph Hearst, of newspaper fame; and William Jennings Bryan, Democrat and populist orator who, fighting the gold standard in favor of a silver-based currency, cried: "You shall not crucify mankind on a cross of gold." J. Pierpont Morgan was the financier, and Booker T. Washington, former slave, founded Tuskegee Institute in Alabama as the first Negro college. But above all these stalwarts stood the real man of the decade, Theodore Roosevelt, President of the United States from 1901-1909, the man with the Square Deal. William Allen White wrote: "I have never known another person so vital nor another man so dear." "Teddy" Roosevelt was the father of "Alice," the very image of the "Gibson Girl," of whom her father said, "I can do one of two things. I can be president of the United States, or I can control Alice. I cannot possibly do both."

Cigarette companies printed baseball cards with pictures of such giants as Ty Cobb. Honus Wagner refused to be included because he didn't want to encourage children to smoke. The bookish ones read all about Frank Merriwell and delighted in Booth Tarkington's *Penrod.* (" 'Penrod, what excuse have you to offer before I report your case to the principal?' The word 'principal' struck him in the vitals. Grand Inquisitor, Grand Khan, Sultan, Emperor, Tsar, Caesar Augustus — these are comparable.")

The new century saw eight thousand horseless carriages in the country, but people were looking

The "Gibson Girl" was created by the American artist Charles Dana Gibson. She was portrayed as attractive, athletic, poised, and intelligent.

for another name. Motorcycle, petrocar, viamote, and mocle were all tried. Gradually, "automobile" became the label for the rich man's toy. Meanwhile, Orville and Wilbur Wright got something else off the ground, when, in Kitty Hawk, North Carolina, they flew a contraption 852 feet in fifty-nine seconds, while Americans sang, "It's a Grand Old Flag" (originally "rag") and "In the Good Old Summertime," which sold a million copies.

The Christian Reformed denomination, at forty-three years of age, moved into this Century of Gold. The LaGrave congregation, barely surviving the old century, was just entering its teens. The year of our Lord, 1900, would not, however, usher in a new Paradise — neither for the country, nor the world. But it would bring with it a golden decade for the denomination. Writing in *The Banner* of September 13, 1935, the Rev. W. Groen stated:

The golden era of our denominational history was undoubtedly the period between 1900 and 1915. Whoever can recall these days must at times wish that the Golden Age would return.

12 Pages In Two Parts

Virginian-Pilot.

VOL. XIX. NO. 68.   NORFOLK, VA., FRIDAY DECEMBER 18, 1903. TWELVE PAGES.   THREE CENTS PER COPY.

FLYING MACHINE SOARS 3 MILES IN TEETH OF HIGH WIND OVER SAND HILLS AND WAVES AT KITTY HAWK ON CAROLINA COAST

THEODORE ROOSEVELT

COMMANDER PEARY'S PRELIMINARY ACCOUNT OF HIS SUCCESSFUL VOYAGE TO THE NORTH POLE

He Sends to The Times by Wireless a Summary, to be Followed by His Full Report—Record of His Swift Progress to the Utmost North.

FROM CAPE COLUMBIA UP IN 37 DAYS, BACK IN 16 DAYS

Prof. Ross G. Marvin, of Cornell, Drowned on April 10, Forty-five Miles North of Cape Columbia, While Leading the Supporting Party.

BATTLE HARBOR, Labrador, Via Wireless Cape Ray, N. F., Sept. 8. As it may be impossible to get my full story through in time for to-morrow's TIMES, partly as a prelude which may stimulate interest and partly to forestall possible leaks, I am sending you a brief summary of my voyage to the North Pole, which is to be printed exactly as written.

SUMMARY OF NORTH POLAR EXPEDITION OF THE PEARY ARCTIC CLUB.

The steamer Roosevelt left New York on July 6, 1908; left Sydney on July 17; arrived at Cape York, Greenland, August 1; left Etah, Greenland, August 8; arrived Cape Sheridan, at Grantland, September 1; wintered at Cape Sheridan.

The sledge expedition left the Roosevelt February 15, 1909, and started for the North. Arrived at Cape Columbia March 1; passed British record March 2; delayed by open water March 2 and 3; held up by open water March 4 to 11; crossed the 84th parallel March 11; encountered open lead March 15; crossed 85th parallel March 18; crossed 86th parallel March 23d; encountered open lead March 23d; passed Norwegian record March 23d; passed Italian record March 24th; encountered open lead March 26th; crossed 87th parallel March 27th; passed American record March 28; encountered open lead March 28; held up by open water March 29; crossed 88th parallel April 2; crossed 89th parallel April 4; North Pole April 6.

All returning left North Pole April 7, reached Cape Columbia April 23, arriving on board Roosevelt April 27.

The Roosevelt left Cape Sheridan July 18, passed Cape Sabine August 8; left Cape York August 26; arrived at Indian Harbor with all members of expedition returning in good health except Prof. Ross G. Marvin, unfortunately drowned April 10, when forty-five miles north of Cape Columbia, returning from 86° North Latitude in command of the supporting party.
ROBERT E. PEARY.

MAP SHOWING PEARY'S ROUTE TO THE POLE.

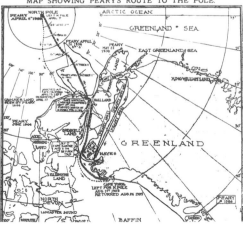

NO BALLOON ATTACHED TO AID IT

Three Years of Hard, Secret Work by Two Ohio Brothers Crowned With Success

ACCOMPLISHED WHAT LANGLEY FAILED AT

With Man as Passenger Huge Machine Flew Like Bird Under Perfect Control

BOX KITE PRINCIPLE WITH TWO PROPELLERS

51

It was indeed a period of growth, as the statistics of the *Yearbooks* of that era reveal.

1900	1915
7 Classes	13 Classes
10,614 families	16,407 families
17,584 communicants	34,608 communicants
53,794 souls	86,779 souls
144 churches	223 churches
98 ministers	154 ministers

A continuous stream of immigrants from the Netherlands, deplored by politician Thomas Watson, contributed significantly to the increase of these statistics. But if these "Hollanders" came to America, the great melting pot, they refused to melt. Instead, together with those already here and in the denomination, they remained a separate people. Rev. W. Groen, whose article in the 1935 *Banner* has already been cited, continued his commentary as follows:

Our denomination was self-contained in that Golden Age. The dominant language in our churches was a foreign language. The ideas and purposes of our people were very much akin to those of the land from which they had come. Only occasionally did currents of thought that influenced American life touch our denomination. Excepting in very few places where our people formed a rather large part of the population, our denomination was not noticed. Our numbers were so few and our isolation so complete that we were entirely self-contained. Our denomination was a very small drop of oil floating on the great sea of American life. Moreover, there was a loyalty to and pride of our denomination that was striking. Every member felt that he was Christian Reformed. The happenings within the denomination and the discussions in *De Wachter* were the dominant issues within the home and the friendly circle. In many cases a secular newspaper was taboo, and there was no knowledge of world happenings beside what *De Wachter* and other papers of a semi-religious nature would state. Hence the denomination was the little world in which our people lived.

The outlook of our people upon religion was chiefly a doctrinal one. Concerning ethical questions there was little difference of opinion. What was worldly and what was not was well known. The manner of keeping the Lord's Day was well nigh uniform in all our families. Whatever discussions and controversies existed were concerning abstract doctrinal matters.

There were two doctrinal tendencies in the denomination — one with a pietistic, separatist

emphasis harkening back to 1834, and an opposing view flavored by the teachings and writings of Abraham Kuyper, theologian, author, teacher, and statesman in the Netherlands. The issues between these two camps were often sharply drawn, with each side seeking to persuade the other, rather than expel. The questions they debated not only outweighed but completely obliterated all community, national, or world concerns. Whether one was an infralapsarian or a supralapsarian was far more important than whether one was a Republican or a Democrat.

The LaGrave Church was also a part of this picture. Its preoccupations paralleled those of the denomination. As has already been suggested, its desire for English in the worship services was not so much motivated by a wish to be progressive or evangelistically outreaching, as by the desire to keep the young people from drifting off into "those American churches" and the American world. Despite the fact that its first two ministers were "American" — a unique distinction — LaGrave, too, thanks to Mr. Jenks, contemplated moving into the twentieth century with high walls in splendid isolation from the world. That this did not happen was due, in large part, to its third pastor whom the Lord sent to LaGrave in 1899. Henry Beets was from "the old country." Henry Beets was "from Iowa." These two biographical facts hardly indicated a man of broad vision who, as one almost before his time, would open windows to the world for both LaGrave and the denomination. In so doing, he brought the Fourth Holland Christian Reformed Church (soon to be known as LaGrave) — if not a century — surely a decade-and-a-half of gold.

REVEREND AND MRS. HENRY BEETS 1899–1915

LaGrave overcomes struggles with renewed vision; a revitalized church expands its mission program

Chapter 10

SOLI DEO GLORIA

It was 1898. The LaGrave congregation possessed a beautiful church of Romanesque architecture and natural brick. Ivy climbed its walls, adding a touch of graciousness. The sanctuary seated five hundred people. The pulpit was its focal point. Behind it, the west wall supported a mahogany wooded arch above which a circular stained glass window dominated. This circular window was later replaced by the Rose Window, which was made of colorful stained glass depicting Christ in prayer in the Garden of Gethsemane. The choir loft and organ, adding to an atmosphere of reverence, were located immediately to the right of the pulpit; a pulpit which, in the parlance of that day, was vacant.

But not for long! Twice, LaGrave had successfully looked eastward to New Jersey for ministers. This time, under the leading of God, it turned its eyes westward to Sioux Center, Iowa. Mr. Jenks had advised the congregation to struggle forward and to seek an energetic leader. LaGrave could not have found anyone filled with more energy, stamina, and dedication than "Dominee" Beets.

Henry Beets was born January 5, 1869, in Alkmaar — of Dutch cheese market fame — the environs in which he spent the first seventeen years of his life. His mother died when he was

A view of the sanctuary of the new LaGrave Christian Reformed Church, 1898.

twelve days old. Raised by his father and stepmother, neither of whom were Christians, he became a farmhand at a very early age. His education was extremely limited. Even so, there were harbingers of what was to come. For example, he kept a diary. He was eternally inquisitive. He was restless. He dreamt of the New World. Thus, not yet eighteen, he booked passage and, travelling "steerage," crossed the Atlantic. Was it coincidence that this great future American passed the

53

Statue of Liberty ("Give me your tired, your poor, your huddled masses yearning to breathe free. Send (these, the homeless, tempest-tossed to me. I lift my lamp beside the golden door!") and landed on American soil on America's birthday? The year was 1886. With the Fourth of July celebrations in full swing, it was hard for young Henry to make rhyme or reason of Christians making such a "heathen racket" in appreciation for the boon of liberty.

With the clothes he wore, a revolver and ammunition (LaGrave's only gun-tot'n' preacher), a railway ticket, and seven silver dollars, he headed for an uncle in Prairie View, Kansas. Soon he was on his own. He worked hard. He found employment where he could. He didn't always make ends meet. In June, 1888, he was almost killed by lightning — a traumatic experience LaGrave's ninth pastor would also undergo years later. The Lord used it to move young Henry's heart closer to His own. Henry decided to go into the ministry and began his studies at the Theological School of the Christian Reformed Church in North America, Grand Rapids, Michigan, in 1888 and completed his studies in 1894.

During his first summer vacation, Henry sold books in Western Michigan, including Grand Haven, where he met a lovely young lady, Clara Poel, who was destined to be his wife. After six years of hard study, selling books, writing for newspapers, teaching grade school, and doing missionary work in South Dakota, he accepted a call to Sioux Center, Iowa. Two months later, at age twenty-six, he married Clara, age twenty-two. Their honeymoon was a train trip to Iowa where they stayed four years.

Ministers' calls are serious business — not only for those who extend them, but also for those who receive them. Even through much prayer, the Lord's will is not always unerringly ascertained. Sometimes calls are accepted or declined for wrong reasons. Sometimes the whole process is viewed with cynicism. A preacher's daughter, so the story goes, may have been making an educated guess when she told her friend that her father would, no doubt, accept his call because, although he was in the study praying, her mother was in the bedroom packing. Most ministers and their wives, however, earnestly seek God's will and follow the leading of the Holy Spirit as best they can. So it was with Rev. and Mrs. Henry Beets when, in the providence of God, he received the call to become the third pastor of the LaGrave Church.

Today we speak of first class and tourist travel — both are pretty nice ways of getting around. In the days of Dutch pilgrimage to the USA, travel was first class, second class, third class, and then steerage. Steerage was deep in the bowel of the ship with no ventilation, no comforts, no fancy plumbing, no entertainment, no parties, no beauty operators. A do-it-yourself type of travel, accompanied by lots of mice, rats, and vermin, and a pretty skimpy menu well suited to those trying to trim waistlines before Metrecal™ was discovered ... This maiden voyage of Henry Beets was quite a contrast to one he made in 1934 when he returned to the Netherlands as a guest, first class, of the Holland American Steamship Lines, to be knighted by Her Majesty, Queen Wilhelmina.

W. C. Beets, *LaGrave News*
"LaGraviana #8"
April, 1963, VOL. IX

Henry Beets was nineteen, living in Luctor, Kansas, and working as a clerk in the Poppen and VanDiest store. From his diary:

Lightning struck our store while I was standing behind the show case. I shall never forget this moment. A body of fire resembling a blue ball, fell directly in front of me, tumbled with celerity, and disappeared. The thought of Eternity, of perpetual misery without salvation, struck my mind. I felt I would be lost without Jesus as Redeemer for my countless sins. That night I wept, prayed, and thanked God for saving my life and not calling me before His tribunal. I had never before seriously thought about God. Since this, the peace of God has wrought a change in my heart and I believe that Jesus Christ is my Savior.

Henry Beets attended Theological School in both the old and the new schools. The old original school was located at 43 Williams Street, S.W., a block west of Division Avenue. The Christian elementary school pupils went directly to the Theological School for their preparatory years. The new Theological School, dedicated in 1892, was located on the corner of Franklin and Madison, and included Calvin College. It later became Christian High School.

Reverend Henry Beets

Henry Beets's impressions of Grand Rapids, as recorded in his diary:

I am not yet used to the rustle and bustle of a great city like Grand Rapids, much less to the dark walls and sombre rooms of our Theological Seminary. Grand Rapids is a large and prosperous city. New houses, mostly of lumber, are arising everywhere in the suburbs. Downtown, all is activity and business. Planing mills are buzzing, engines smoking, and shops of all kinds are producing articles of every description. The city is situated on the banks of the Grand River, a broad but shallow stream. The chief industry is the manufacture of furniture. A larger amount of the inhabitants are foreigners by birth. I am told 20,000 of them are Dutch (Hollanders). When promenading the streets, one would imagine to be in Holland. Everywhere I see old country folks with black silk caps, queer and short broadcloth jackets, ditto breeches, and the indispensible wooden shoes which clatter on the sidewalks like horses' feet on the pavement. A short and smoky Gouda pipe between the lips usually completes the costume. There are also saloons in Grand Rapids. This liqour traffic is a stain on a progressive city like this and ought to be blotted out of existence . . . The suburbs of this city are being beautified by numerous trees planted by every wayside and around almost every dwelling.

W. C. Beets, *LaGrave News*
"LaGraviana #18"
June, 1974, VOL. X

His own words, written afterwards, best describe his feelings upon weighing LaGrave's invitation:

Somehow I had a strong desire to enter the English work but dared not accept, feeling insufficient for the task of ministering to a congregation of its standing and culture. Some tried to dissuade me from going to a church that was practically bankrupt. But the Lord made it so clear to me that I had to undertake the work, that never, even for one minute, have I doubted that the Master wanted me here.

And so, Providence sent this man with a Dutch accent to salvage His church at LaGrave. On June 4, 1899, Rev. Henry Beets preached his inaugural sermon on Psalm 51:12b,13: "Uphold me with Thy free spirit, then will I teach transgressors Thy way and sinners shall be converted unto Thee."

Henry and Clara Beets moved into the parsonage with two children and almost no furniture. It was a fine house, but it really required a tenant with a larger salary. Rev. Beets "enjoyed" a salary of $600, a third of which was required for coal for the furnace. The neighborhood was lovely. George G. Steketee, the former mayor of Grand Rapids, was a neighbor. He lived on the corner of LaGrave and Oakes. On the other corner, the Herpolsheimer family was ensconced. The presidents of two large breweries lived on the same block. All came to the parsonage to pay their respects.

Mr. Kelly, one of the brewers, even brought "a fifth" as a gift, a present Henry Beets — enemy of all drink — graciously accepted and put away for medicinal purposes. The Pecks, of Peck's Drug Stores, lived on Jefferson. The Pennel Apartments on Oakes and the Iowa Apartments on Jefferson were prestigious places.

Gradually, the parsonage was better equipped and became the social center of the church. It was also the site for many congregational and denominational affairs. Only a five-minute walk from Union Station, the Beets's residence, cheaper than the Pantlind,* became a hotel. Guests were frequent, making the mistress of the manse the whole hospitality committee of the church. She also became the mother of a third son, William Clarence, born on a Sunday morning, June 2, 1901, just in time for church.

Undertaking what some called a hopeless task, and what was surely a difficult one, Rev. Beets found his work signally blessed of the Lord. A new spirit pervaded the congregation. The members willingly followed their new leader whose enthusiasm was contagious. The church, which a short time before seemed close to extinction, became firmly established once again. The membership grew from 102 families, 156 communicants, and 455 souls, to 150 families, 262 communicants, and 648 souls. The debt, which in 1898 seemed insurmountable, was completely paid by 1912, the year of the Quarter-Centennial. The Central Ladies Aid, organized in 1899 in the home of Mrs. Quartel, and other auxiliaries, grew strong. The young people responded especially well to the new pastor. It was a remarkable sight to see so many catechumens, with willing hands, digging out a basement beneath a portion of the church for the creation of a catechism room. It was probably more fun digging it than reciting their lessons in it. Clearly, a period of progress and prosperity had begun!

Long known for its musical activities, the congregation continued to enjoy its choir. The *Grand Rapids Herald* of June 21, 1900, carried the following news item:

> There was no meeting of the synod last night. The delegates attended the mid-week meeting of the LaGrave Church. Instead of the regular service, the La-Grave Church choir sang a sacred cantata entitled *Saul of Tarsus*. The soloists were Marie VanderWerf, Anna Sluyter, Cora Hazenberg, Abe Hazenberg, and Peter Quartel.

* A large hotel in Grand Rapids.

THE PARSONAGE.

The parsonage had a large porch about thirty-five feet long, a vestibule, and a great hall with an imposing stairway to the upstairs opening. From the hall, via sliding oak doors, was a formal sitting room with a fireplace, a great big parlor with a marble fireplace, a bedroom . . . and a dining room with a plate rail and wallpaper made from burlap. This room had a small stove which burned wood. There was also a great big kitchen heated with a large wood-burning stove which heated the area, the water, and the food.

Grand Rapids was really a furniture city. In those days, Mr. Wierenga . . . sold us wood cuttings from the factories. He dumped them into the great big cellar with its dirt floor. The basement had a fruit cellar, a potato bin, and one furnace that ate coal and gave off vast quantities of ashes which had to be hauled away. You people of the Natural Gas Age just don't realize what you have missed.

The downstairs lavatory had the water reservoir toward the ceiling, and by pulling a chain, the water came down by gravitation — usually, at least . . . Our baths always were taken on Saturday night in the kitchen in an old-style round laundry tub. The hot water was lifted out of the reservoir in the woodburning stove.

W. C. Beets, *LaGrave News*
"LaGraviana #23"
March, 1965, VOL. XI

The pen of Henry Beets, it seems, never stopped. He wrote a lengthy article for the *Grand Rapids Press* on the Christian Reformed denomination. It appeared in 1900. Together with Menno J. Bosma, he co-authored *A Sacred History For Juniors* (1901), *A Sacred History For Seniors* (1902), and an enlargement of *The Borstius Primer* (1903).

On September 5, 1901, President William McKinley journeyed to Buffalo, New York, to deliver a major address on the lowering of tariffs by reciprocal agreements. The following day, at a public reception held in the Temple of Music at the Pan American Exposition Building, hundreds

ATTEMPT MADE UPON LIFE OF THE PRESIDENT

Dastardly Attack Made During Reception Yesterday.

Anarchist Was Overpowered and Lodged in Jail—Boasted of His Deed and Said "I Am An Anarchist; I Have Done My Duty"— Country Overwhelmed With Grief at Attack on Life of ...

EX-ATTORNEY GENERAL GRIGGS HAD WARNED McKINLEY

NEW YORK, Sept. 6.—Former Attorney General Griggs, in discussing at Paterson N. J., the shooting of President McKinley, said: "I warned him against this very thing. Time and time again I asked him for his country's if not for his ow...

... to have a body guard when he went ...t at me. He

WAS LEON CZOLGOSZ

ANARCHIST WHO SHOT M'KINLEY MAKES CONFESSION.

stood in line to shake the president's hand. One of them, an anarchist named Leon Czolgosz, shot the president through the stomach with a revolver hidden in a bandage around his right hand. The finest doctors in the land did their best to save McKinley's life, but he died on September 14. He was mourned throughout the civilized world. Services were held in England, France, and other countries. LaGrave Church also held a service. The *Grand Rapids Herald* of September 20, carried a report concerning it.

> One of the most powerful and certainly the most dramatic sermons preached in connection with the memorial services for President McKinley held in local churches yesterday was that of the Rev. Henry Beets in the LaGrave Avenue Chr. Ref. Church. The text came from II Samuel 2:23, choosing the following words: "As many as came to the place where Asahel fell down and died, stood still." The congregation joined the choir in singing "Lead Kindly Light Amid Th' Encircling Gloom" and the hymn "God Moves in a Mysterious Way." The service closed with the singing of "America" and "The Doxology." The church was tastefully decorated in black and white bunting, the American flag, and a draped picture of the late president.

In a burst of patriotism, Henry Beets, with his perpetual motion pen, dashed off a two-hundred page book on the life of President McKinley and had it off the press twenty-eight days after the president died. He wrote it in Dutch because he wished to communicate his thoughts to as great a part of the Christian Reformed constituency as possible. It was well received and sold for seventy-five cents. He also wrote a biography on the life of President Abraham Lincoln. Both McKinley and Lincoln had risen from humble beginnings. It would not have been possible in the old country with its caste system. Henry Beets thrilled to America where such things could happen and issued a bold call for a faster pace of Americanization among the Christian Reformed Hollanders. Indeed, he turned composer and wrote "Song of the Holland Americans."

In 1901, the congregation reduced its debt by $1,350, and raised the salary of its pastor to $900, with a bonus of $50. The *Press* printed, as news, that LaGrave's receipts had totalled $3,907.02, and its expenses $3,803.53. There was no connection between the bonus and the pastor's visit to the Netherlands the following year, 1902, sixteen years after he came to America. He travelled second class this time, not steerage, with Rev. Jacob Noordewier, as both had been delegated to attend the synodical meetings of De Gereformeerde Kerken in the Netherlands. The LaGrave congregation gave its pastor a ten-week leave of absence for this denominational assignment. (Its ninth pastor would be given three weeks off for the same assignment in 1974, not because the congregation was less liberal, but travel more swift). Upon his return, Rev. Beets assumed his added duties as stated clerk of the denomination — a new and permanent position created by the synod. Thus, in addition to all his labors, the pastor now had also to prepare the agenda and write the *Acts* of the succeeding synods. He would function in this capacity for the next forty years.

LaGrave's pastor was also functioning, most capably, as the editor of *The Banner,* writing a steady stream of editorials on such subjects as "The Half Way Covenant," "Church Union," "Hypocrisy in the Pulpit," "John Calvin," "The Methodist Church Lowering the Bars," "Free Masonry," "Ball Room Dancing," "Demon Rum," "Indian Missions," and many more. Meanwhile, Beets continued to tend to his pastoral and preaching assignments to the satisfaction of the congregation. An examination of the annual statement of 1904 tells us much about the state of the church.

Song of the Holland-Americans
Wien Neerlandsch Bloed

English Text by HENRY BEETS

Moderately Slow / Matig langzaam

Melodie: J. M. WILMS

1 Come ye who boast of Dutch de-scent, Sons of New Nether-land, And ye who reached our friendly shores With west-ern pil-grim band! U-nite with us in fes-tive song, Song which the heart e-lates And sing the praises of our land Our own U-nit-ed States Our own U-nit-ed States.

Wien Neerlandsch bloed in de a-ders vloeit, Van vreem de smet-ten vrij; Wiens hart voor Land en Ko-ning gloeit, Ver-heff' den zang als wij Hij stell' met ons, ver-eend van zin, Met on-be-klem-de borst Het God-ge-val-lig' feest-lied in Voor Va-der-land en Vorst, Voor Va-der-land en Vorst.

Copyright MCMVI by Rev. Henry Beets

We love the land across the sea
We glory in its past.
We pray for its prosperity,
May it forever last!
But tho we love old Holland still,
We love Columbia more,
The land our sons and brethren fill
From east to western shore.

We praise the beauty of our land
Displayed by rocks and rills.
Its fertile plains, its mighty streams,
Its mountains, lakes and hills;
We praise its glory-laden past,
Which made our country free,
Its institutions, grand and strong,
Its opportunity.

O God of nations, bless our land,
Its every place and state
From where the dark Atlantic rolls
Unto the Golden Gate;
O bless our rulers and our flag,
Uphold our liberty,
Make us a blessing to the world,
A praise, Lord, unto Thee.

One special boon, our fathers' God,
We crave from Thy right hand:
Make us a blessing more and more,
To our beloved land;
Infuse the best of all our past,
The noblest of our traits,
Into the life, into the deed
Of our United States!

Bescherm, o God! bewaak den grond,
Waarop onz' adem gaat;
De plek, waar onze wieg op stond,
Waar eens ons graf op staat.
Wij smeeken van Uw' Vaderhand,
Met diep geroerde borst,
Behoud voor 't lieve Vaderland,
Voor Vaderland en Vorst.

Bescherm hem, God! bewaak zijn' troon,
Op duurzaam recht gebouwd;
Blink altoos in ons oog zijn' kroon
Nog meer door deugd dan goud!
Steun Gij den scepter dien hij torst,
Bestier hem in zijn hand;
Beziel, o God! bewaar den Vorst,
De Vorst en 't Vaderland.

Van hier, van hier, wat wenschen smeedt
Voor een van beide alleen;
Voor ons gevoel, in lief en leed,
Zijn Land en Koning éen.
Verhoor, o God! zijn' aanroep niet
Wie ooit hen scheiden dorst,
Maar hoor het éen, het eigen lied,
Voor Vaderland en Vorst.

Dring' luid van uit ons feestgedruisch
Die beê Uw' Hemel in:
Bewaar den Vorst, bewaar zijn huis
En ons, zijn huisgezin;
Doe nog ons laatst ons jongst gezang
Dien eigen wensch gestand:
Bewaar, o God! den Koning lang
En 't lieve Vaderland.

59

LaGrave Street
Christian Reformed Church

ANNUAL STATEMENT,

MAY 1, 1904

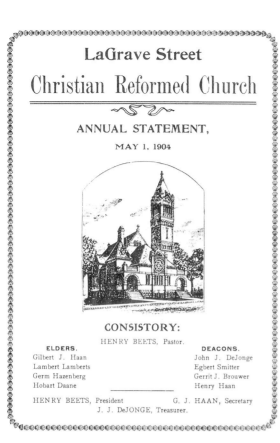

CONSISTORY:

HENRY BEETS, Pastor.

ELDERS.	DEACONS.
Gilbert J. Haan	John J. DeJonge
Lambert Lamberts	Egbert Smitter
Germ Hazenberg	Gerrit J. Brouwer
Hobart Daane	Henry Haan

HENRY BEETS, President   G. J. HAAN, Secretary

J. J. DeJONGE, Treasurer.

LaGRAVE STREET CHRISTIAN REFORMED CHURCH.

Financial Statement.

RECEIPTS.

	1903-04	1902-03	Increase	Decrease
Balance on hand	$ 93 01	12 96	80 05	
Weekly Offerings	1803 76	1782 90	20 86	
Collections	1572 27	1401 25	171 02	
Sewing Circles:				
Central	100 00	150 00		50 00
South End	100 00	100 00		
Young Ladies'	100 00	100 00		
Sabbath School	175 00	200 00		25 00
Class of 8 girls	5 66		5 66	
Young People—Balance collected on Motor	56 31		56 31	
Flood Sufferers	40 80		40 80	
Missions	274 82	106 05	168 77	
	$4321 63	3853 16	468 47	
Total Receipts	$4228 62			

DISBURSEMENTS.

	1903-04	1902-03	Increase	Decrease
Pastor's Salary and Supplies	$ 938 00	980 00		42 00
Janitor's Salary	150 00	150 00		
Music	96 12	74 90	21 22	
Light	72 72	86 20		13 48
Fuel	114 45	100 40	14 05	
Water	18 00	18 00		
Interest	360 00	364 25		4 25
Insurance	90 00		90 00	
Printing and Stationery	16 62	12 75	3 87	

Repairs	214 93	126 02	88 91	
Motor for Organ	79 24		79 24	
Tax on Mortgage	123 33	231 47		108 14
Sundries	83 63	67 76	15 87	
Theological School	120 00		120 00	
Emeriti Fund	24 00	44 00		20 00
E. B. P. Fund	10 00		10 00	
Holland Home	24 78	22 00	2 78	
Charity	110 00	92 35	17 65	
Home Mission	140 20	48 50	91 70	
Foreign Mission	103 20	56 55	46 65	
Jewish Mission	3 00	14 00		11 00
U. P. Mission, Rev. Kruidenier	16 13		16 13	
Dr. Krull's Mission	26 72		26 72	
Flood Sufferers	40 80		40 80	
Finland Famine		71 00		71 00
Church Debt	$1300 00	1200 00	100 00	
	$4275 87	3760 15	515 72	

SUMMARY.

Balance on hand May 1st, 1903	$ 93 01	
Received for Current Expenses	4228 62	
Total Receipts		$4321 63
Paid for Current Expenses	$2357 04	
Paid for various Church Funds and Benevolences	618 83	
Paid for Church Debt	1300 00	
		$4275 87
Balance on hand		$45 76

In addition to the above our Young People have raised the magnificent sum of $626.37, and placed in our church a beautiful organ at a cost of $587.61 and presented the church with $56.31 for a motor.

CHURCH MEMBERSHIP.

Communicants		226	
Received by Letter		10	
Received by Confession		18	
		254	
Removed by Death	3		
Transferred 13 and erased 10	23		
	26	26	
		228	228
Members by Baptism		349	
Received by Letter and Births		24	
		373	
Transferred	17		
By Confession	18		
By Death	4		
	39	39	
		334	334
Total Number Enrolled		562	
Total Number Families		127	

There were seven deaths that year. Ten people were erased, mostly for disciplinary action because of membership in secret societies. The budget required about sixty-five cents a week per family. The statement indicated that the young people, far from tired because of digging a basement for a catechism room, had contributed a sizeable sum for an organ with a motor, thus eliminating the position of organ pumper. There seems to have been a famine, too, in Finland, to which the members contributed.

WE SHALL HAVE MUSIC

In the month of January, 1904, our young people formed different clubs of ten, whose members pledged themselves to pay at least 5¢ per week toward collecting money for a pipe organ. They also persuaded others to pledge. What a friendly rivalry there was between "tens," and what rejoicing when already in the fall of the same year the organ was installed — and completely paid for.

LaGrave's growth in the early 1900s could not be pictured as a line rising steadily on a graph. Even then, there was the move to the suburbs. At first, this did not encourage membership transfers to outlying churches where services were in Dutch. Transportation was mostly on foot, and when more English-speaking congregations began to appear, shifts in congregational allegiance occurred. There were some who walked to La-Grave from as far away as the corner of Burton and Eastern. But, all things being equal, more chose the neighboring churches. Broadway (now Westview), Burton Heights (a daughter church), Sherman Street, Bethel — all came into being with the blessing of LaGrave. They did, however, take away from the membership. When Burton Heights was formed in 1905, close to fifteen percent of LaGrave's membership transferred to this new church. As always, LaGrave not only recovered after a temporary loss in membership but moved ahead again.

Not until 1918 did synod decide that the use of the common or individual cup in communion was a local matter. Each congregation could decide for itself. But long before that date, the issue was a major one — also at LaGrave. There were those who took opposing positions on this question for theological reasons. The real catalyst causing the debate, however, was not theological but hygienic in nature. Tuberculosis, called consumption, was a dreaded killer in the early years of the twentieth century. For this reason, an increasing number of church members favored the individual cup. La-Grave and its pastor took what measures they could. Thus there appeared in the *Press* of January 6, 1913, the following item:

> CHURCH IS AIRED:
> WILL BE A REGULAR FEATURE!
> While the hymn preceding the sermon at LaGrave was being sung last night, the ushers opened all windows and doors (this was January — ed.) This was arranged by the pastor and the Anti-Tuberculosis Society. This will be a feature at every service in the future.

Newspaper coverage of the churches, as seen by the above notice, was excellent in those days. There were many papers, and competition among them was keen. The larger ones had church reporters. All the downtown churches, with the exception of Central Reformed — for some unknown reason — had a representative of the *Press* present in their morning services. Monday's papers, therefore, contained digests of many messages. The reporters seldom failed to attend LaGrave's services. Generally, the music was excellent and Henry Beets was always interesting. In May of 1905, the *Press* quoted from a sermon by Rev. Beets as follows:

> Grand Rapids should repent! The wickedness of the city has aroused the wrath of God; our saloons run full blast on the Sabbath day; our billboards are covered with indecent prints; Sunday ball games are tolerated; street cars carry thousands of pleasure seekers to Reeds Lake on Sunday to misspend the Holy Day of God. Vendors are allowed on our streets; stores are kept open needlessly; liberalism invades our pulpits; and worldliness our churches.

The sermon closed as follows:

> It seems as though God is crying out to Grand Rapids: "Bring forth better fruit, or I will show mine anger!"

There was a spirited response to this report on the part of many readers. One was entitled "Pinhead Preaching." Another said, "If Henry Beets is correct in ascribing the smallpox epidemic to the wrath of God, I would like to know why the scourge fell on so many upright Holland families rather than the saloon keepers and law breakers."

With so much to do, it is a wonder that Pastor Beets and his wife had time for relaxation outside of their church activities. There is evidence, however, that life, busy as it was, was not all work. On November 19, 1906, Rev. and Mrs. Beets went to the Pantlind and dined on "blue points (oysters), hearts of celery, cream of tomatoe aux croutons, tranche of halibut sauce remoulade, olives and radishes, filet mignon de boeuf aux champignons (mushrooms), green peas, larded spring chicken au cresson, pommes risolles (potatoes), salad de saison, neapolitan la cream, fancy assorted cakes, cheese, coffee."

So much energy needed fuel!

In 1907, Klaas Troon died. Although he expired in the new century, his heart had never left the old one. His closing years had brought an added burden — the death of his oldest son, Dirk, who years before, had left the Christian Reformed Church because of its "Dutchiness," and from whom Klaas had largely remained estranged. His wife would survive him by ten years. His daughter, who had married, remained with him at First Church. In the last year of Klaas's life, his youngest son Pieter, with his wife and two children, Trina and John, transferred to LaGrave. But Klaas did not know this, for in his closing year he was no longer "aware."

It was just as well that it was thus, for Klaas considered Henry Beets, along with some others, a mixed blessing. In this he was not alone. Klaas Troon was the salt of the earth. But he was also a rock. Rock salt. He could not be moved. He considered "Americanizers," such as Beets, the bane of the church. He predicted that before the new century was out, the Christian Reformed denomination would go liberal.

In 1909, twenty ministers and fifty lay members met in the LaGrave Church and founded the Christian Psychopathic Hospital, now known as Pine Rest Christian Hospital. Dr. G. Stuart, a LaGrave member, became its first medical director.

Life in the parsonage seemed no less busy than New York's Grand Central Station — with growing boys, daily visitors, many meetings, and a pastor whose work load was ever expanding. But there was also time for fun and play. The Beets's family set a good example for the congregation and the neighbors in Sabbath observance. The boys were not allowed to play in the street on Sunday. But with as much energy as their father — who could expend his on the Sabbath duties — the Beets's boys, with no sermon to preach, were sometimes

difficult to contain. Fortunately, they could work off some excess energy Sunday afternoons playing in a yard surrounded by a high fence. But on one of those Sunday afternoons, Clarence hit a ball through one of the stained glass windows. It was there for all to see when the worshippers gathered for the evening service.

> *My mother cured spring fever with a heavy dose of sulphur and molasses. For worms, she spread gun powder on Dutch rye bread which we ate for breakfast. This produced an annual spring house cleaning, which apparently worked. If all families were as healthy as ours, the doctors would be on the relief rolls. The sulphur, molasses, and gun powder treatment ended abruptly one day when mother, by mistake, threw the gun powder and the sulphur in the kitchen stove. The house committee was headed by . . . Mr. C. Borrendamme (father of Mrs. Bertha Franken — ed.) In his opinion, a little sickness would have been cheaper than the repairs on the parsonage, then located at 107 LaGrave.*
>
> W. C. Beets, *LaGrave News*
> "LaGraviana #10"
> June, 1963, VOL. IX

Rev. Henry Beets, in addition to all his other duties and activities, became more and more involved with mission work. His legacy of interest in this area of the Lord's work is still one of LaGrave's characteristics. Mission collection boxes were installed at all of the sanctuary exits and were designated for "Jewish," "Home," and "Heathen" mission work. A booklet of 1911, promoting mission interest at LaGrave, mentioned a Miss Rosback, missionary at the Rehoboth Mission School for Indian Children and the urgency of helping an Indian child who was a pupil at the school.

Community affairs involved Rev. Beets too. He was a familiar figure at City Hall. He served on the Library Commission. Indeed, he appeared on the national scene as well, as an old newspaper clipping reveals:

THE REV. HENRY BEETS OFFERED OPENING PRAYER

The Rev. Henry Beets, pastor of the LaGrave Street Christian Reformed church, had the honor when in Washington to be invited to offer prayer at the opening of the session of the House Monday. The prayer as given in the Congressional Record was as follows:

Gracious God, who art in heaven, we bless Thy holy name for the rest and privileges of the Sabbath of yesterday. We bless Thee for all of Thy gifts unto us as individuals, as families, and as a nation. Forgive us graciously that we do not sufficiently appreciate Thy blessings toward us.

Forgive us all of our sins of omission and of commission.

And, as we are assembled here at this moment, we ask of Thee that Thou vouchsafe to us Thy blessing in every way.

Let Thy Favor be extended unto this House of Representatives, unto every one of its members, and especially unto the speaker. Let Thy blessing also be showered upon our senate and our acting vice president, and let our Congress be blessed with Thy gifts of light and wisdom and righteousness, that all of its deliberations and resolutions may be a blessing to our commonwealth.

We ask Thee in a special manner to remember the respected and honored head of our nation, our President, Theodore Roosevelt. Wilt Thou bless him, O God, in body, in mind, and in spirit, that he may be a blessing to our land, and, if possible, to all mankind? We ask of Thee to remember in Thy favor his cabinet, and our army and our navy, and everything pertaining to the executive branch of our government.

Let Thy favor rest upon our Supreme Court and upon our lower courts, that our laws may be administered in keeping with Thy divine principles of justice and of love.

Remember all of our states and territories and those that are in authority, as well as all people under them. Wilt Thou cause our prosperity to continue? Let peace and righteousness prevail.

And wilt Thou even use us as an instrument, O God, if possible, that Thy Kingdom may come by means of our national activities?

Wilt Thou hear us and accept of us and be gracious unto us and all of our interests? We ask it of Thee, Father of Mercies, for the sake of Jesus, Thy Son, and through the Holy Spirit. Amen.

Able as he was, the pastor could not possibly have accomplished what he did without the prayers and cooperation of the congregation and the able and even outstanding assistance of the consistory. Standing (left to right): Jas. Benjamins, J. Michmershuizen, D. TerMolen, C. Borrendamme. Seated: G. J. Rooks, J. VanDuinen, G. J. Haan, the Pastor, C. J. Brouwer, G. Hazenberg, H. Daane.

The young people, too, continued their involvement with their church. Their season's activities were always well-planned and advertised. The vitality of the Young People's Society is evident in a sample of their programs.

In 1912, LaGrave Church, twenty-five years of age, celebrated its Quarter-Centennial. Henry Beets preached an appropriate message based on Psalm 48:9: "We have thought on Thy loving-kindness, O God, in the midst of Thy temple." Titling his message, "Thinking on God's Loving-Kindness," he exhorted the congregation, by way of a historical sketch, to consider that kindness:

    I. In the Slow Launching of Our Movement
    II. In Our Hard Initial Struggle
    III. In a Dark Period of Trial
    IV. In Our Present Conditions.

A souvenir booklet using the title of Rev. Beets's sermon and containing appropriate pictures, was issued for the occasion. It was an unforgettable evening for those who attended. Ten days before, at the consistory meeting, the treasurer had displayed the mortgage and the last note with notice: "Paid in full."

Baptized Members

...of the...

Lagrave Street
Christian Reformed Church

Grand Rapids, Mich.

THE CONSISTORY of our church, desirous of wiping out the entire indebtedness now resting upon our church property, before we celebrate our Quarter-Centennial, February, 1912, hereby appeals to you for a liberal subscription for that purpose.

The congregational meeting, held December 4, 1911, unanimously expressed itself in favor of the proposal. The suggestion was adopted that each head of our families and every adult baptized member pay AT LEAST ONE PER CENT of his or her annual income.

Brethren and Sisters, NOW is the time to show that we appreciate our church. Let us, as one of mind and heart, all put our shoulders to the wheel.

WE CAN PAY OFF THAT $1700 IF WE WILL. May the Lord prosper our purpose, to His glory. Exodus 25:21-23.

Please, place your signature before the amount printed below and mail this paper direct to our Treasurer, in the enclosed, self-addressed envelope. It is understood that the money will have to be paid only when enough is pledged to cover the entire indebtedness. If need be you can pay in two installments, viz., January 1 and February 1, 1912.

ON OR BEFORE FEBRUARY 1, 1912, I promise to pay to the Treasurer of the Fourth (Lagrave St.) Christian Reformed Church, of Grand Rapids, Mich., the amount which I have set opposite my signature.

$ 5.00			35.00
10.00			40.00
15.00			50.00
20.00			75.00
25.00			100.00
30.00			$

PAYS ALL THE DEBT

Lagrave Street Christian Reformed Church Is Free Now.

DUE TO THE PASTOR

Rev. Henry Beets Gets Results In Thirteen Years.

Organization Doubles Membership and Minister Finds Time to Devote to Writing.

Rev. Henry Beets, pastor of Lagrave Street Christian Reformed church, which this week celebrated its quarter centennial, is in the thirteenth year of his ministry with this organization, having come here in June, 1899. During this time the church has increased from 156 to nearly 300 communicants with 650 souls in its parish. The last of the debt on the $20,000 building and parsonage was discharged this month.

This earnest plea for funds to liquidate the church debt met with great success as noted in the headline which appeared in the Grand Rapids Press, February 24, 1912.

In 1914, the Christian Reformed denomination took over *The Banner* and continued its editor, Rev. Henry Beets, for twenty-five years. Prior to this, *The Banner* was privately printed, governed by a board of directors, and had its office in the home of the editor.

The young people, with their undiminished enthusiasm, enabled the church to buy a fine new Austin organ, which was properly dedicated.

In 1915, Henry Beets, after the longest pastorate in the annals of the fifty-eight-year-old history of the Christian Reformed Church, left LaGrave to become the pastor of the Burton Heights Church. The congregation was sad to see him leave. He had placed such a stamp upon the church and, in the eyes of most, had become so identified with it as to preclude his leaving. But he wasn't leaving — really. He was staying in the family — merely moving in with a daughter, Burton Heights. In five years he would return to join the members of LaGrave in the pews. As denominational director of missions and editor of *The Banner* and stated clerk, the Lord had given him so much to do that he had to lay his pastoral and preaching work aside. For the rest of his life, he was a familiar and faithful figure at LaGrave's worship services and activities.

By the end of Rev. Beets's tenure, LaGrave's reputation, in the eyes of a large segment of the denomination, had been established. The general assessment of LaGrave paralleled Klaas Troon's opinion that it was a "liberal" church even though it proclaimed the infallible Word, upheld the three forms of unity, preached the Heidelberg Catechism, observed all denominational obligations and standards, and submitted annually to the church visitation by classis.

With the perspective of time, it is possible to analyze this erroneous and unfair assessment. It was based, in part, on LaGrave's role as the first English-speaking Christian Reformed Church in the world. The fact that it had a choir as part of its worship services was also a contributing factor. What must also not be overlooked was its choice of clergymen. Its first two pastors had come from an American background. Its third pastor, Henry Beets — although born in Holland — was, if possible, more American in character and personality than his predecessors with whom he contributed to the "flavor" of LaGrave. Had early assessments labelled the congregation "progressive," they would have been more accurate — and fair. But "progressive" translated into "liberal" in that day — perhaps in this day as well.

Henry Beets was on the move. As a result, he sometimes outran his contemporaries. He was wise enough, however, as wise leaders instinctively are, to slow his steps on occasion, in consideration for those who followed. Even so, he pioneered on the mission front, the college front, an English periodical front, a patriotic front, an Americanization front, and, therefore, was followed — sometimes at some distance — by a wary constituency.

He was cosmopolitan where others were provincial, ecumenical where others were exclusive, thinking only in terms of "our people" versus "outsiders." His love of America had something to do with his conversion in a country where the burden of his heart rolled away. For this reason, he could never fully disapprove of the flamboyant Billy Sunday, as so many of his esteemed brethren in the denomination. After all, Billy gave the country the shaking it needed; and so, when push came to shove, Beets endorsed the ex-ballplayer evangelist. For when all was said and done, Billy Sunday was a blessing for a land Beets loved and for whose president he frequently prayed, that the man in the White House might not yield to the

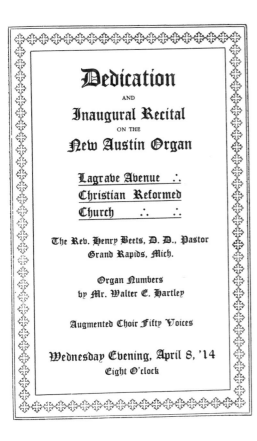

Dedication

AND

Inaugural Recital

ON THE

New Austin Organ

Lagrave Avenue ∴

Christian Reformed

Church ∴ ∴

The Rev. Henry Beets, D. D., Pastor
Grand Rapids, Mich.

Organ Numbers
by Mr. Walter E. Hartley

Augmented Choir Fifty Voices

Wednesday Evening, April 8, '14
Eight O'clock

Description of Organ

THIS Instrument was built by the Austin Organ Company of Hartford, Conn., builders enjoying the best of reputation for high-grade work. One of the main features of the Austin Organ is the Universal Air Chest System, which is used by them exclusively. It provides some important and unique advantages, among them being a perfect distribution of pressure to all pipes, as each one has its own valve opening directly into the air chest, the pressure of which cannot possibly vary.

This chest may be compared to a small room which can readily be entered by means of air-tight doors, so that persons can actually be within the air pressure itself even while the organ is in operation, and thus all the mechanism is readily accessible from the pressure side of the instrument, and at the same time it greatly simplifies the action of the organ.

The specifications of the instrument follow and it will be seen from them that for an organ of this size there is an unusual and excellent variety of beautiful tone qualities which can best be judged by hearing them.

It will also be noticed that the pipes of the various stops are extended an extra octave, 73 pipes being furnished, while 61 is the usual compass. These extensions make the octave couplers effective throughout the entire compass of the key-board. Instead of the regular stop knobs placed at the side of the Console the organ is controlled by stop keys placed just above the keys, in addition to twelve adjustable combination pistons affecting the stops and couplers of each manual and pedal organ.

SPECIFICATIONS

GREAT ORGAN. Three Stops—*Compass CC to C4-61 notes*

Open Diapason	8ft. 73 pipes metal	Dulciana	8 ft. 73 pipes metal
Clarabella	8 " 73 " wood		

SWELL ORGAN. Six Stops—*Compass CC to C4 - 61 notes*

Violin Diapason	8 ft. 73 pipes, metal	Oboe	8 ft. 73 pipes, reed
Rohr Flute	8 " 73 " wood	Viol D' Orchestra	8 " 73 " tin
Salicional	8 " 73 " tin	Tremulant	
Harmonic Flute	4 " 73 " metal		

PEDAL ORGAN. Two Stops—*Compass CCC to G - 32 notes*

Bourdon 16 ft. 32 pipes, wood
Lieblich Gedack, (Placed in Swell Box) 16 ft. 32 notes, wood

COUPLERS. Twelve

To Great. Great Sub.	To Swell. Swell Sub.
Great Unison off.	Swell Unison off.
Great Octave.	Swell Octave.
Swell Sub.	To Pedal. Great to Pedal Union.
Swell Unison.	Swell to Pedal Union.
Swell Octave.	Swell to Pedal Octave.

ADJUSTABLE PISTON COMBINATIONS. Twelve

Six double acting pistons, moving stop-keys to control Great and Pedal stops and couplers.

Six double acting pistons, moving stop-keys to control Swell and Pedal stops and couplers.

Three pedals adjustable for controlling all stops and couplers.
Balanced Crescendo and Diminuendo pedal, adjustable, not moving registers.
Balanced Swell Pedal.
Great to Pedal reversible.
Sforzando Pedal.

Program

Hallelujah Chorus (Messiah)	*Handel*
CHORUS	

Prayer	
REV. BEETS	

Traumerei	*Schumann*
MR. HARTLEY	

Psalm 100 (page 314)	
CONGREGATION	

*Suite Gothique   *Boellmann*
  I. Chorale
    II. Minuet
      III. Prayer
        IV. Toccata

Pastorale	*Flagler*

Prelude and Fugue in B Flat	*Bach*
Widor Ed., Vol. II., No. VIII.	

Largo (New World Symphony)	*Dvorak*
MR. HARTLEY	

Psalm 150 (page 466)	
CONGREGATION	

Address	
REV. BEETS	

Offering

Allegro Cantabile (Symphony V.)	*Widor*
MR. HARTLEY	

Praise the Lord	*Randegger*
CHORUS	

Humoresque	*Dvorak*
Berceuse	*Delbruck*
Gavotte (Mignon)	*Thomas*
Meditation	*Sturges*
*Largo (Xerxes)	*Handel*
March (Occasional Oratorio)	
MR. HARTLEY	

Remarks and Prayer	*Rev. Beets*

Doxology

Benediction

*By Request

temptations of his office, nor grow insensitive to the profanity to which he was exposed, nor yield to pressure to join the lodge, nor attend the theater, nor travel needlessly on the Lord's Day.

Henry Beets made frequent Fourth of July speeches. In them he worried about the power of excessive money over legislators and votes. He prayed for farmers and was partial to labor — a leaning he had acquired in his Kansas days where he had heard the great Samuel Gompers. In his patriotic addresses, Beets warned against Mormonism, the hierarchical power of Rome, secret societies, the Ku Klux Klan, American expansionism as in the Philippines, and, above all, strong drink. Along with Ate Dykstra, a local businessman and politician (and grandfather of LaGrave's ninth mistress of the manse), he thundered against the saloons. Worldliness, too, roused him to eloquent warnings. There were many things he was against. Even so, he was a positivist. There were more things he was "for." There was country. And there was God. But not in that order. And there was the church — along with God.

Perhaps Henry Beets can best be summed up as an American Calvinist — the first in the Christian Reformed Church. The teachings of Abraham Kuyper, in the Netherlands, enjoyed his complete embrace. Kuyperian Calvinism, with its world and life view, with its emphasis of God's sovereignty — in and over all spheres of life — had his enthusiastic endorsement. In his zeal for it, he even imputed this comprehensive conception of the infallible Word of God to the founders of LaGrave who, in truth, were more separatist than Kuyperian. It was an emphasis that many would carry forward into the days ahead. Armed with it, Henry Beets was a vessel of the grace of God for LaGrave, and for the denomination and community as well. It is fitting, therefore, to close this chapter with that most Calvinistic of expressions which Henry Beets so often used as his closing word in speeches, sermons, articles, and even conversations:

Soli Deo Gloria!

Chapter 11

ALL THE MEMBERS — MINISTERS

So far, this chronicle of LaGrave seems largely made up of the history of its clergy. This requires some explanation. There is, for these annals a dearth of material with which to reconstruct LaGrave's distant past. Most churches kept poor records years ago, and LaGrave was no exception. Few had the foresight to appoint historians or archives committees. Minutes, when kept, were stored in homes — and lost. Then, too, in some churches, the "dominee" had such a strong and charismatic personality that he was placed on a pedestal, the result being that his congregation stood in his shadow. The stories of churches and their ministers were often intertwined, with the former colored by the latter.

There is a deeper reason why the history of any church cannot really be told. It is one which has nothing to do with lost records. A church is people. To recount the history of a church, therefore, requires the telling of each member's story. We do not always think of the church as people. We think of it rather as an institution to which people belong. We think of the history of a church in terms of how it has been organized, disorganized, and reorganized. We trace its life in the minutes of its ruling body. But the Church of Jesus Christ, and any local expression of it, is an organism such as is described in I Corinthians chapter 12.

In such a body, there is no Biblical distinction between clergy and laity. In Reformed theology, the army of the church, as in "Onward Christian Soldiers," is not made up of privates (members) and generals (clergy). As today's LaGrave bulletins manifest, "All the members are ministers." There is no top and bottom. In the institutional church, there is a difference between the Pope and an acolyte. In the organizational church, there is a distinction between a Bishop and his auxiliary — a hierarchy that simplifies the history. But who can chronicle the church as an organism? It is impossible. God is its sole historian.

Therefore, it is important, at this juncture, to recognize all the members of LaGrave, both past and present. The first three pastors of the church accomplished nothing alone. "The eye cannot say unto the hand, I have no need of thee, nor again the head to the feet, I have no need of you," (I Corinthians 12:21). The focus, thus far, has centered, in large part, on the pulpit. But this does not imply that the pew is secondary. In the life of a church, a minister's role is a determinative one. Yet, in the eyes of God, the widow's mite might do as much. The faithful prayers of the most self-effacing member in all LaGrave's history may have blessed the church more than the combined efforts of many who were more prominent.

In the writing of congregational histories, it is good to be aware of at least three tendencies. The first is the temptation to cite only the leading members. Certainly, LaGrave has had no lack of them. Yet, mentioning their names runs a risk, for by whose measure does one measure? What is considered prominent on earth may be considered obscure in heaven — and vice versa. The second tendency is to select from among those prominent only such as have made significant contributions of time, talent, and/or money to the life of the congregation. Generally excluded from local church chronicles are those whose efforts were more Kingdom directed in distinction from congregation oriented, even though they, too, were engaged in precisely such pursuits as were urged upon them by a Reformed pulpit — namely, reaching out, as Christians should, into their own respective spheres of endeavor. Surely this, too, is part of the story of any church whose members take seriously the Bible-centered commissions which all receive!

If illustrations are to be used, wisdom dictates that they be set forth cautiously and that they be selected from among those who left LaGrave for the church above, rather than from among the living. Doing so, we could surely cite, from among many equally worthy, such lay members as Professor Jacob VandenBosch, Professor A. Rooks, Dr. W. Harry Jellema, Mr. William B. Eerdmans, Sr., and the esteemed Garret Heyns as among the gifted who gave of themselves as consistory members and who served in other capacities in the work of the church. Less involved, perhaps, were such members as Professor Henry VanAndel and Dr. Henry Zylstra, whose efforts were almost totally directed outward from their church to the field of Christian education; and Professor B. K. Kuiper, who taught at Calvin College as did VanAndel and Zylstra. B. K. Kuiper also taught in our seminary, served for a time as editor of *De Wachter,* as editor of *The Christian Journal,* as editor-in-chief of a Christian Publishing House, and as an author.

These names are taken, somewhat at random, from among those of the Lord's gifted children who, for parts of their earthly sojourn, were members of LaGrave. It is done to emphasize that their stories, too, are part of the history of their local church, even though they served more exclusively in the area of Kingdom endeavors.

The third tendency in recounting the saga of a church, particularly if its beginnings were in another era, is to ignore — almost totally — the contributions of the women. For one thing, the ministers' wives, if mentioned at all, receive little more than deferential nods. The fact is that the Lord knows — and most people do not — what contributions and sacrifices they make and how much of them goes into the makeup and history of the churches of which they and their husbands are members. As for the women in general, congregations simply could not survive without them. The fact that this history can be written at all is due, to an astonishing degree, to the work and prayers of the women of LaGrave.

To bring all the foregoing threads together in an effort to pay tribute to the lay men and women of the LaGrave Church, we select one from among them all as their representative. In thanking the Lord for him, we give thanks to the King of the Church for each and every member of the body of Christ in that local expression of it — the LaGrave Church — for the past one hundred years! The one selected lived long ago. Even so, there was something about him that would make him fit into this century as well as the last. He was Mr. John Gelock.

John Gelock

John Gelock was not the only Hollander to adjust his name. Some, upon coming to America, made radical changes — Bruinooge to Browneye or Browning or just plain Brown. Others made minor adjustments in spelling — Vanden Berge to Vanden Berg, De Jongh to De Young, Smit to Smith, Yongste simply to Young. Jan Gelok, tired of correcting those who insisted on misspelling his name, finally yielded and began to write it the American way — John Gelock. It was characteristic of him. He gave in easily on minor points, but on the major ones he was the Rock of Gibraltar.

John was born in the Netherlands (Oud-Vassemeer) — the very same place from which Theodore Roosevelt traced his roots. John's parents were poor, and of Reformed persuasion. In his fifteenth year, John experienced a spiritual struggle which resulted in his profession of faith. His firmness and resolution where principle was concerned were soon evident. There was a law in the Netherlands, a holdover from the Napoleonic times, that assemblies in excess of nineteen people were disallowed. For transgression of this law, on principle, John was repeatedly fined until his debt to the government amounted to 1200 guilders. The penalty was finally cancelled.

John, as was the custom of the day, followed in his father's trade and became a wagonmaker. He married, became a widower, and married again. He came to America with his family in 1850. Arriving in Grand Rapids — after a brief sojourn in Rochester, New York — he resumed his trade, setting up a shop on the corner of Market and Louis Streets. The Lord prospered him remarkably. Indeed, he might have become a wealthy man. But he preferred to give his time — as much of it as possible — to church and Kingdom work.

At the advice of friends, he joined the Second Reformed Church of Grand Rapids. His devotion and qualities for spiritual leadership soon became evident, and he was chosen to serve first as a deacon, then as an elder. Unhappiness with certain policies and tendencies, a doctrinal laxity, and reports concerning the Reformed Churches in the East precipitated his resignation from the Second Reformed Church in 1856. This took place a year before the Christian Reformed denomination — of which he was one of the founding fathers — was born.

He recorded his motives. His decision to affiliate with the Reformed Church had been hasty and ill-informed. He was disturbed by Arminian tendencies. Catechism preaching, catechetical instruction, and church discipline were not uniformly practiced. Masons were admitted to membership. Disturbing rumors and investigations of further denominational aberrations were quashed. In view of these consideration, John Gelock felt himself free to accept the option he had been given to "bid the Reformed Church a fraternal adieu." He did not do so as a petty fault-finder, but as a man of conviction. Having developed keen theological antennae in the Netherlands, he applied his sound discernment to the establishment of a new denomination. A year later, his name was on the charter of the First Christian Reformed Church in Grand Rapids.

John Gelock took an active part in the life of the new denomination. In 1872, together with J. DeJonge and B. DeGraaf, he represented his denomination at the synod of the Christian Reformed Church in the Netherlands. There, he and his fellow travellers were hardly welcome as representatives of the new denomination. The cold reception was due to the fact that one of the Dutch leaders was a brother-in-law of Dr. A. Van Raalte, founder of the Reformed Church in America, the denomination which Gelock and his associates had left. John Gelock sought to assure the esteemed brethren that he and his colleagues had not been motivated by pettiness. Even so, they gained no recognition for their new denomination. They were, however, commended for their evident loyalty to the Reformed faith.

At home, John Gelock also capably defended the existence of his denomination, not just orally, but in articles he wrote in *De Wachter.* Throughout these affairs, principial in nature, he was unyielding. On other matters, more peripheral in nature, he continued to show his adaptability, as in the matter of the singing of hymns — against which sterner defenders of the faith raised their voices. Thus he continued — a pillar elder in the First Christian Reformed Church of Grand Rapids (Bates Street).

If it was his firmness in principial matters that precipitated his departure from the Second Reformed Church, it was his pliability in all other matters that brought about his exit from the First Christian Reformed Church. Long convinced that Americanization was not only inevitable but desirable, he refused to represent his consistory at classis because it had determined to prevent the birth of what was to become his church's unwanted daughter — LaGrave. He could not find it within himself to support his beloved pastor, Rev. J. H. Vos in his vehement opposition to an English-speaking church. On this language question Gelock stood squarely opposed to his fellow elder, Klaas Troon, when that battle was won — or lost — depending on who was recounting it. La-Grave Church was organized as the Fourth Holland Christian Reformed Church; and John Gelock joined it. Indeed, the same year it was founded (1887), John Gelock was elected one of its elders. He served in this capacity until the Lord called him home in 1889. Jacob VandenBosch, a LaGrave member, gave belated recognition to this outstanding layman in the pages of *The Reformed Journal,* (April, 1958, p. 17.) In the final paragraph he wrote:

> We rise from the contemplation of the life of John Gelock, feeling that we have been in the presence, as it were, of a worthy character who nobly served the church of Christ. Balanced in judgment; moderate in expression; ready to yield in the interests of peace, but unyielding when a fundamental truth, as he saw it, was at stake; loved because of his open nature and friendliness; trusted because of his integrity, John Gelock was a leader of whose memory the church need not be ashamed. Though very likely not agreeing with his views on some minor issues, we must be fair and judge him in the light of his time. He loved the church and its work because he loved Christ. Thinking of him we are reminded of the sacred injunction, "Remember them who have the rule over you; who have spoken unto you the Word of God; who faith follow, considering the end of their conversation."

He is presented in this history, once again — this time as representative of all LaGrave's members through the years — as we salute each and all.

It is interesting to observe that, although John Gelock served as elder for only the first two years of the first English-speaking church's existence, nevertheless, through the years, LaGrave has manifested the same characteristics that were his — firm in principle, yet pliable in all other matters. These are traits which insure both the solidity and the contemporaneity of any church. It should be a fervent desire and prayer on the part of the LaGrave members to maintain these characteristics throughout the next century, if the Lord tarries, and until He comes again.

REVEREND AND MRS. WILLIAM STUART 1915–1925

LaGrave continues to reach out to the world as its pastor nurtures
concern for Christian education

Chapter 12

WHITHER ARE WE DRIFTING?

"Whither Are We Drifting?" This has been the theme of countless sermons in countless decades. But when the Reverend James K. Thompson, in Muskogee, Oklahoma, preached on it in June of 1914, it had never seemed more pertinent. The country was no more adrift than it had ever been. Even so, for those who were attuned, there were harbingers of things to come. Hectic changes were looming on the horizon, but only as a cloud the size of a man's hand. The end of the decade, however, would see the close of what some called "The Age of Innocence."

There were cultural developments. Grover Cleveland had said earlier, "The relative positions to be assumed by men and women in the working out of our civilization were arranged long ago by a higher intelligence than ours." Yet, by 1920, the new woman had emerged who by 1980 would have "come a long way, baby." On June 4, 1919, Congress passed the 19th amendment to the constitution, stating that no citizen could be denied the right to vote "on account of sex." However, it would still take awhile before women would be admitted to congregational meetings in Christian Reformed churches.

Writers like Booth Tarkington and Zane Grey continued to entertain. But others like H. G. Wells, Walter Lippman, and Theodore Dreiser, and poets like Carl Sandberg, Robert Frost, and Vachel Lindsay put a new tang in the air. But it was polluted by the "Tin Lizzie," America's fond designation for the Model T. Henry Ford, its creator, said, "The way to make automobiles is to make one automobile like another automobile, to make them all alike, to make them come through the factory just alike." He didn't care what color they were painted "as long as they are all black." Along with Thomas Edison and the Wright brothers, he propelled the nation forward.

Meanwhile, the Christian Reformed Church had its own propellants, notably B. K. Kuiper, who would later join LaGrave, and Henry Beets, who had left LaGrave to serve its daughter, Burton Heights. Both continued their positive leadership towards Americanization. LaGrave Church, as well, would move along under the leadership of its fourth pastor, Rev. William Stuart, who came in 1915 and remained for a fruitful ministry of ten years.

William Stuart was born in Assen, the Netherlands, in 1875. His father, Albert Stuart, was a native of the Netherlands but of Scottish descent. Albert, a jeweler by trade, was of Reformed persuasion, and a strong supporter of Christian education. His son, William, after leaving LaGrave, would devote his life to Christian education by teaching Bible at the Grand Rapids Christian High School.

Young William came to the United States, to Colorado, at the age of sixteen. Shortly thereafter, he moved to Orange City, Iowa, where he attended the Northwestern Classical Academy. From there, he went to Calvin College, and then to Princeton Theological Seminary, where he remained for three years. He won a Hebrew scholarship which allowed him to study abroad at Leipzig University.

After his ordination to the ministry, he became a home missionary. He travelled extensively on horseback in pursuance of his pastoral tasks. The Christian Reformed Church of Manhattan, Montana, was one of the results of his missionary endeavors. Thereafter, he became pastor of the Sully, Iowa church (1905) and the Church of Third Roseland, Chicago, Illinois (1908). It was while laboring there that he received and accepted the call to LaGrave. He came with his wife, Helena Knook Stuart, and daughters, Gezina, Frances, and Lenore. His brother, Dr. Gerrit Stuart, also a member of LaGrave, was a psychiatrist — the third to practice in Grand Rapids and the first on the staff of the Christian Psychopathic Hospital (now Pine Rest Christian Hospital). Later, after the death of his wife, William would marry a widow, Gertrude Boer (nee Brouwer), mother of Gordon and Lois (DeLoof).

The story of William Stuart at LaGrave is one that is filled with human interest. He was an engaging speaker in the pulpit. There were those who would walk miles to hear him. His style was simple and direct. He never wrote out his sermons, but chose rather to speak from a small outline on two halves of a small sheet of paper on which names and places were underlined in red ink. It was the teaching element in his preaching that distinguished his sermons and made them characteristically his own. As one parishioner said, "He sharpens my wits." His tremendous knowledge of the Bible, his lucid exposition, coupled with his straightforward manner, made him outstanding.

He was as intriguing out of the pulpit as he was in it. He had the capacity of friendship. Mr. Hubert Daane, an elder, and partner in the Daane and Witters store, was a close friend. The members of the church sometimes referred to them as "David

Reverend William Stuart

and Jonathan." Professor Jacob VandenBosch, also an elder, was very close to William Stuart as well. Rev. W. P. VanWyk, pastor of the Eastern Avenue Christian Reformed Church, and William Stuart were also inseparable. (Rev. VanWyk took time from his pastoral duties to travel to Detroit to baptize LaGrave's ninth pastor.) Together with his friend VanWyk, Rev. Stuart wrote a compendium. He wrote other books as well.

Rev. Stuart was also a family man. Ministers' families are often neglected and take second place to hosts of ministerial occupations and preoccupations. Without slighting his calling, Rev.

The Stuart family had made some root beer. Rev. Stuart saved a few bottles for a better fizz, as he felt that the children drank it too quickly. One night there was the sound of gunfire. Five shots. The family hurriedly dressed and went outside. Rev. Stuart was sure that someone in the neighborhood had gone berserk. After a bit they all went back to bed. The crisis was over. Then the Reverend saw a trickle of something coming from the closet door. This became known as the night of the great root beer blow up.

Reminiscenses by
Frances Stuart Monsma

Stuart generally managed not only to be home for tea time, but to serve the beverage — accompanied with one cookie for everybody. It became a ritual and a memory to be treasured by his daughters. Like Peter Marshall, Rev. Stuart was a great game player, cherishing Rook above all, which he played with his wife, his brother Gerrit, and sister-in-law Sebrina — with the shades drawn, lest he become a stumbling block to the flock. He also found time, on occasion, to play a game or two with others, such as the custodian Mr. Barney Diepstra. A more distinguished looking custodian was Mr. Lakke, whose wife peeled potatoes too thick, and who, himself, peeled the English language outrageously.

> The custodian, Mr. Lakke, had invented his own version of Yankee Dutch. When members came to church functions carrying packages and looking for places to deposit them, he invariably said, "Putsa here." He was gallant and helpful with older ladies who had difficulty rising, assisting them while saying, "Uppie, Uppie."

The family enjoyed their dinner hour. Always the educator, Rev. Stuart wanted his children to be well informed. Therefore, few subjects were taboo for discussion during the meal. Some of the remembered topics would fit into our modern world as, for example, a conversation on homosexuality. Had one of the family members written a book on "Life in the LaGrave Parsonage with Rev. William Stuart," it would have sold well. Also, it would have given insights and ideas as to how to make a house a home, complete with what is today referred to as "quality time for the children."

But the house and neighborhood had some disadvantages. Mrs. Stuart (Helena) wished for another neighborhood in which to raise her daughters. When Rev. Stuart conveyed this thought to the consistory, the elders and deacons said, "Find the place you like."

Before Rev. Stuart arrived, Rev. Beets had already been approached regarding the building of a new parsonage. One of the LaGrave parishioners had built a house at 616 College S.E. which Dr. Beets very much admired. When he moved to Burton Heights, his new consistory agreed with his assessment of the house on College; they used its floor plan for the building of a new parsonage on 2050 Francis S.E. It was the residence at 616 College S.E. that was purchased by LaGrave as its new parsonage, and the Stuarts became its happy occupants.

LaGrave's new parsonage was purchased for $12,000 and the old one was converted into a much needed church house. The building was given some minor alterations to enhance its usefulness for church meetings, societies, and activities. It was used until 1939 when it was replaced by LaGrave's present parish house.

Meanwhile, the sanctuary, too, received some improvements and changes. The members had now been joined by their pastor in what was a generalized move to the suburbs. Yet, even though some members affiliated with closer neighborhood churches, the membership statistics for LaGrave increased to where, in 1925 — the year Rev. Stuart left to become Bible teacher at the Christian High School — there were 207 families. LaGrave was now firmly established as a downtown church. The statistics a few years before (1919) revealed the fact that LaGrave increased Rev. Stuart's salary by $500, making him, at $2,500, the highest paid minister in the denomination.

It was during Rev. Stuart's tenure that one of the congregation's most important dates, October 10, 1920, occurred. China was to become a new mission field for the Christian Reformed Church. Rev. J. C. DeKorne, Dr. Lee S. Huizenga,

The parsonage at 616 College S.E.

and Rev. Harry Dykstra were to be the pioneers. LaGrave had the rare privilege of being the calling and supporting church of Dr. Huizenga. Rev. Stuart read the liturgical form and Dr. Huizenga responded with sincerity, saying: "I do with all my heart." Henry Beets, former pastor and denominational director of missions, was present to deliver the sermon. He spoke on the text: "Lift up your eyes and look on the fields, for they are white already to harvest."

Lee S. Huizenga had worked his way through Calvin College. Intense, and thoroughly dedicated, he worked too hard. In the late months of 1905, he suffered from complete nervous and physical exhaustion. As a change of pace, he worked for the mission board as industrial manager of Indian Missions.

In New Mexico, Lee gained more than his health. Matilda VanDyken, from Grand Haven, Michigan, had gone to the great Southwest as a missionary. In God's providence, Lee and Matilda met and married.

Lee S. Huizenga married Matilda VanDyken, September 22, 1909

Dr. Huizenga became the pastor of the Englewood Christian Reformed Church in New Jersey. Taking this pastorate provided him with the wherewithal to enroll in New York's Homeopathic Medical College to study medicine. His salary came to $66.66 per month. The barest household necessities required thirty dollars. Another thirty dollars were needed for commuting to New York and for school expenses. Six dollars and sixty-six cents went to the Lord. Thus the Huizengas gave their whole lives, plus their tithe. Dr. Huizenga, quite literally, gave his life, July 14, 1945, when he died in a Japanese prison camp — almost twenty-five years after his commissioning at La-Grave. Lee S. Huizenga was both an ordained clergyman and a medical doctor. He did pioneering work among the lepers. His picture hangs in the parish house. The saga of his life and letters is found in the LaGrave Centennial Library, compiled by Mr. Loren Dykstra. Rev. L. J. Lamberts, Sr., father of Dr. Austin Lamberts, LaGrave member, wrote a fascinating biography of Dr. Lee S. Huizenga, entitled *Life Story of Lee S. Huizenga.*

If a full choir was not available, quartets or small groups would provide music for LaGrave's services. This quartet participated prior to 1915. From left to right: Cornelius Scherphorn, Anna Oosting, John Jeltes (pianist), Margaret Sluyter, P. Henry Sluyter.

During the Stuart years, mission interest and support was not limited to Dr. Lee S. Huizenga. LaGrave gave liberally to such causes as Jewish Missions, Indian Missions, General Home Missions, and the South American Fund. In 1919, it contributed to the support of an Indian boy.

Musically, LaGrave continued as the only Christian Reformed Church with a choir as part of its worship services. A male chorus furnished the Sunday anthems from 1915-1920 when it was temporarily replaced by a quartet. Its members were Mrs. Martin Daane, soprano; Mrs. G. J. Stuart, alto; Mr. H. Oosterhuis, tenor; and Mr. C. Werkema, bass. Miss Anne VanDomelen, indomitable lifelong LaGrave worker, later to marry Marinus Scherphorn, sang a solo entitled, "Christ Is All," at Dr. Lee S. Huizenga's inaugural service. In 1922, Harry Dice, LaGrave's fourth choir director, organized a mixed choir — as they called it, which has continued in unbroken service to this present day. It was Rev. Stuart's idea and was accomplished at his insistence.

There were three developments outside LaGrave, each of which made its impact on the life of the congregation during the pastorate of Rev. Stuart. The first pertained to the denomination and its enforcement of doctrinal orthodoxy. Rev. H. Bultema of the First Christian Reformed Church of Muskegon, Michigan, wrote a book entitled *Maranatha* in which he not only expressed certain millenial views, but views on the unity of the church in all dispensations, and on the Kingship of Christ. On the latter subjects, he was adjudged as being in error. His persistence in his position led to his departure from the denomination.

Another crisis developed centering on Dr. R. Janssen who was professor of Old Testament at Calvin Seminary. He was charged with making statements that came close to "modernism" and with having a view of scripture and its origins which was more humanistic than faith oriented. This whole controversy culminated in his departure from the seminary and from the church.

The "common grace" issue involving the pastor of Eastern Avenue Christian Reformed Church, Dr. H. Hoeksema, also surfaced in this time frame. He and Rev. H. Danhof, of Kalamazoo, Michigan, held views which, in the opinions of many, were out of harmony with the Bible and the confessions of the church. It was another controversy and issued, as did the others, in a departure of the principals from the denominational ranks. All three episodes affected all the churches and their members — LaGrave not excepted. Estrangements developed, even within family circles, as members held to opposing views and chose opposite sides. It was a harsh denominational environment in which Rev. Stuart gave steady leadership as the shepherd of the LaGrave flock.

A second development, outside LaGrave, yet profoundly affecting its life, was national and international in scope. The First World War descended. The year Rev. Stuart came to LaGrave, the Lusitania was sunk by German might. When America entered the war, the Christian Reformed people supported their country, even though, initially, they had been polarized. Henry Beets, and others, didn't like the British, as they still harbored feelings aroused by the Boer War in South Africa. The American churches viewed Christian Reformed and Reformed people of Holland origin with suspicion. They did not always distinguish between Dutch and Deutsch. The pastor of the Fountain Street Baptist Church (it has since dropped the word "Baptist"), thoroughly liberal in his theology, preached a sermon in which he linked Christian Reformed orthodoxy, Calvin's bloody theology, and Christian Schools with un-Americanism. Even progressives like Professor

STATE OF WAR IS DECLARED

The Grand Rapids Herald

THIRTY-THIRD YEAR.   GRAND RAPIDS, MICH., TUESDAY MORNING, APRIL 3, 1917.   PRICE THREE CENTS.

U.S. CITIZENS LOST AS AZTEC IS TORPEDOED

WILSON URGES CONGRESS TO ACCEPT GAUGE OF BATTLE AT ONCE AND END GREAT WAR

DEMS ORGANIZE HOUSE; CLARK IS AGAIN SPEAKER

ELLIS MORE THAN 1600 VOTES BEHIND OPPONENT, FULLER

BRING GERMANY TO TERMS IN NAME OF

WILSON'S WAR MESSAGE

DON'T FORGET!

YESTERDAY'S VICTORS.

City Commissioners.
At Large—Philo C. Fuller.
First Ward—William Oltman,
Julius Tisch.
Second Ward—William J. Clark,
Christian Gallmeyer.
Third Ward—William E. Tallmadge, Daniel Kelly.
Supervisors.
First Ward—Louis Kregel, Charles Serfling.
Third Ward—William Haan.
Board of Education.
Henry E. Crow, C. M. Alden, Mrs.
George P. Wanty.
Short Term—John W. Scott.
Library Commissioner.
Gustavo Wolf.
Judge Circuit Court.
Willis B. Perkins, John. B. McDonald, William B. Brown.
Park Bonds.
Lost overwhelmingly.
State Election.
Republican state ticket carried Grand Rapids, Kent county and the state of Michigan by normal Republican majorities.
Constitutional Amendments.
Probably all have carried in Grand Rapids with the possible exception of that one increasing the levies of state officials.

FORMER MAYOR BADLY BEATEN IN CHARTER RACE

CITIZENS LEAGUE CANDIDATES ARE ALL SUCCESSFUL IN TUESDAY'S ELECTION.

CITY HALL EMPTIED; NEW FACES APPEAR

Not One of Men Elected Has Served City in Governmental Capacity—Oltman and Tisch Win in First Ward.

George E. Ellis defeated for the first time a year ago after having been five terms mayor of Grand Rapids.

The World.

"Circulation Books Open to All"

NEW YORK, SATURDAY, MAY 8, 1915.

TWO TORPEDOES SINK LUSITANIA; MANY AMERICANS AMONG 1,200 LOST; PRESIDENT, STUNNED, IN SECLUSION.

Liner Attacked Supposedly by German Submarine Off the Irish Coast, and Goes Down in Fifteen Minutes—Luncheon Being Served at the Time—Survivors Picked Up From Lifeboats. — Queenstown. Forty Miles Distant—Regarding 1,254 — Cunard Line Says "First Officer — Ship Left New York Last Saturday — Prominent New Yorkers, Who Di—

LUSITANIA, HER CAPTAIN, AND PLACE WHERE SHE WAS HIT

S.S. LUSITANIA

Captain W. T. TURNER.

WASHINGTON, SILENT, AWAITS ADVICES ON AMERICANS' FATE

CUNARD OFFICES CLOSE AS LIST OF THE DEAD GROWS

Ford
THE UNIVERSAL CAR

Yes—you buy something more than a marvelous automobile when you buy the Ford. No matter where you are—nearby you'll find a Ford service station. There's something better than a guarantee back of the Ford—and we'll sell seventy-five thousand of them this year.

All Fords are Model T's—all alike except the bodies. The two passenger runabout costs $500—the five passenger touring car $690—the delivery car $700—the town car $900—f. o. b. Detroit, completely equipped. Get latest catalogue from Ford Motor Co.

SUFFRAGE WINS FIGHT OF 40

SENATE ADOPTS AMENDMENT BY MARGIN OF TWO

FORD GUNS FIRE PRO-GERMANISM CHARGE IN SUIT

AUTO, KING TURNS BATTERIES

IF PEACE TREATY IS MENACE TO AMERICA SENATE SHOULD NOT RATIFY IT, TAFT HOLDS

PITTSBURGH, June 24.—"Germany will sign the peace treaty," said former President William Howard Taft, who is here today to make two addresses at mass meetings furthering the League to Enforce Peace.

"There is a lull in the peace proceedings just now," the former president continued. "All are waiting for the action of Germany so the treaty can be brought home and laid before the senate foreign relations committee.

Jacob VandenBosch, a LaGrave elder, was accused of being pro-German and, therefore, opposed to his own country. Another Christian Reformed leader of some stature had the colors of the German flag painted on his porch with graffiti, telling him to be an American and to buy war bonds — of which he had already bought three. Christian Reformed Churches were "flagged," a procedure which involved breaking into the church to drape the pulpit with the stars and stripes. In Iowa, no meetings in a foreign tongue were permitted unless full translations were furnished in advance. The Christian Reformed Church of Peoria, Iowa, whose pastor was Rev. J. J. Weersing, was burned to the ground by the townspeople. Meanwhile, the war was raging.

LaGrave Church, being an English-speaking pioneer church, suffered fewer barbs than those Christian Reformed churches which were still holding to the mother tongue. There is no doubt that a frenzied patriotism, fanned by Germany and unfair to the Holland Americans, hastened the process of Americanization in some quarters. LaGrave, in this period of time, maintained its congregational life, supported its country, and prayed for peace.

A third happening that left its imprint on all, LaGrave included, was the flu epidemic that killed eighteen million people worldwide. Mrs. Klaas Troon, who had survived her husband for a decade, succumbed to it as well. She had reached her eighties and had seen much change in the world and in her own denomination. Throughout the last ten years of her life, she had held to the views and prejudices of her late husband, Klaas, partly by conviction and partly in loyalty to him. She was glad that her husband did not live to see their son Pieter and his family transfer to the very church whose organization her husband had fought. Pieter's son, John, was now in his teens, a member of the LaGrave Young People's Society. His grandmother worried about the reports that LaGrave was a liberal church. There were those who agreed with her.

After the war, there was a generalized feeling among the faithful that the world was moving to its end. With the Christian British conquest of Palestine, the persecution of American Christians in Turkey, a resurgence of religious cults, the spread of flickers (movies) and flappers (short-skirted hussies), apocalyptic premillenarianism was a dominant note in American conservative Protestantism that predicted the imminence

Missionaries debarking at Shanghai from the steamship China, *November 23, 1920. Top: Dr. and Mrs. Lee S. Huizenga and children; Middle: Reverend and Mrs. Harry Dykstra; Bottom: Reverend and Mrs. J.C. DeKorne and children.*

of the end. Rev. Stuart again steered a careful course amidst all these currents and cross currents.

Thus the Stuart years were far from uneventful, both for the pastor and the members. In 1918, the Christian Reformed denomination joined the Federal Council of Churches and withdrew in 1924. Its entrance coincided with the war hysteria — which explained it. Its exit coincided with the denomination's efforts to maintain doctrinal purity — which, again, explained it. Actions, as well as texts, are often accounted for by their contexts. At any rate, it was an action and reaction that did not go unnoticed in LaGrave Church, which had some ecumenical leanings. In 1924, the first radio broadcast in Grand Rapids occurred — another harbinger of the future. Was it a possible tool in the work of spreading the Gospel? It would be some years yet before the Back To God Hour would be born and more years before LaGrave's ninth pastor would serve for a time as its president.

Rev. William Stuart's evident penchant for teaching made his call to another kind of work inevitable. He had a special gift, and so, from 1925 until his death in 1941, he taught Bible and kindred subjects in the Grand Rapids Christian High School. He died of a stroke in Sparrow Hospital in Lansing, Michigan, where he had gone to visit a daughter. The Lord called His faithful servant home. Rev. Stuart's funeral service took place in the church he loved — LaGrave. The attendance proved his popularity. It had been his wish that such an event be devoid of ostentation. Rev. Herman Bel, sixth pastor of LaGrave, read the scripture. Professor Seymour Swets, fifth director of LaGrave's choir, sang a solo. Dr. Edward Masselink, seventh pastor of LaGrave, preached the sermon on II Corinthians 5:20: "We are ambassadors for Christ." Rev. Henry Beets, third pastor of LaGrave, wrote a touching "In Memoriam" in the pages of *The Banner.*

Austin Farrer, warden of Keble College, Oxford, and one of England's most famous theologians, once observed that a familiar prayer in commemoration of benefactors declares that God is to be praised as well in the dead as in the living. He maintained that to honor the excellence of His handiwork in those who have died is to honor Him. Thus, in cherishing the memory of LaGrave's fourth minister, we cherish the Maker of him, and of us all, and exalt God's holy name.

During the Stuart years at LaGrave, there were those in the denomination who had veered off in various directions — via the Bultemas, Janssens, and Hoeksemas. Some others, who had come to LaGrave mistaking its progressiveness for liberalism, would soon move on again. Others, overcompensating for developments they viewed with alarm, went further to the right, seeking shelter in ultraconservatism.

Far away, a new religion was born — communism — hailed by many, even in America. Some women saw the 19th amendment as an end, but more beheld it as only a beginning. An ever increasing prosperity nurtured materialism and worldliness. A new president, Calvin Coolidge, monosyllabic, muttered that the business of America was business. All this, and more, closed an age of innocence. The Rev. James K. Thompson, of Muskogee, Oklahoma, was a prophet. The ten years that followed his sermon would, indeed, see drift. It would result in what would later be referred to as "The Roaring Twenties."

In the middle of it all, a plain spoken, direct, gifted, no-nonsense preacher at LaGrave Church, his hand firmly at the helm, steered a steady course.

REVEREND AND MRS. R. B. KUIPER 1925–1929

*A gifted preacher and writer is a "herald for truth" as "worldly
amusements" and "new doctrines" threaten*

Chapter 13

HERALDS FOR TRUTH

Pieter Troon turned sixty-five the year Rev. Stuart began teaching at Grand Rapids Christian High School. LaGrave would miss its pastor. Pieter had served as an elder in the LaGrave consistory under Stuart, along with such fellow elders and stalwarts as Dewey Blocksma, Henry Stehouwer, A.J. Rooks, Matthew Houtman, and J.G. VandenBosch. His son, John, had made profession of his faith during Stuart's tenure. John was now at the University of Chicago Medical School. Pieter was proud of him. Soon now his son would be known as Dr. Troon.

Pieter thought his son took after his grandfather. Klaas had always been a lover of animals. Pieter remembered the day his father had successfully operated on one of their chickens. It had straw stuck in its crop. He had also amputated a rabbit's crushed paw, and the rabbit had lived. But Pieter worried about John being in Chicago with its 400 gangster murders a year. Some called it the "Kingdom of Al Capone."

His father, Klaas, had always viewed the future with apprehension. He said that the church was growing indifferent in his day and would grow increasingly lukewarm. The world, even as the Bible said, would grow even worse. As a young man, Pieter had taken issue with his father on

some of these matters. He had joined LaGrave in his fortieth year, after his father was no longer "aware." Even so, there had been his mother, whose silence on the subject had made him feel a little disloyal. However, he was soon assured, because although LaGrave was progressive, it was, nevertheless, doctrinally sound. He had been blessed by the ministries of both Henry Beets and William Stuart. It had been a good church for the nurture of his daughter, Gertrude, who had married and was living in Kalamazoo, and for his son, John. But now, with John — a young man in Chicago — Pieter thought again of his own father, Klaas, whose dire predictions considering the state of Chicago — to say nothing of the country — seemed surprisingly sound, if not downright brilliant.

A spirit of frivolity reigned in the nation. Women were getting their hair bobbed, wearing knee-high dresses, and smoking cigarettes. Pieter lit a cigar and continued his "strain" of thought. Everybody in Chicago, if not in Grand Rapids, seemed to be dancing the Charleston. Hip flasks, bath tub gin, and speak-easies abounded under prohibition, in a kind of unrestrained hedonism. The movies were sweeping the land. It was predicted that soon there would be "talkies" — movies with sound. Moral standards were definitely lowering. Even his son had taken a course in "Freud." Young people laughed at being reprimanded, especially in many colleges where racoon-coated students seemed to be doing nothing but partying. They ignored the warnings of the moralizers by singing: "In the meantime, in-between-time, ain't we got fun?" Hollywood fanned such flames. Clara Bow* gave an entirely new meaning to the harmless pronoun "it."

Was his son doing any social dancing? A female revivalist in Portland, Oregon, had said, "Social dancing is the first and easiest step to hell." Pieter had read it in the paper. Billy Sunday sounded similar warnings. Of course, you couldn't always trust those popular evangelists. There was Aimee Semple McPherson in California. Some of the most religious were the biggest racketeers.

The country also seemed to be getting more and more sports crazy. Babe Ruth, the home run king, Gertrude Ederle, who swam the English Channel, Red Grange of football fame, Dempsey and Tunney, prize fighters — these were the modern gods. Altogether, the country seemed

*Hollywood actress made world famous for her role in the film *It*.

more occupied with pleasure (crossword puzzles, gum chewing, marathon dancing, and Miss America contests) than anything else, except the dollar bill.

Pieter had done pretty well in that department himself. He was well able to pay John's expenses in medical school. Having a lucrative paint business was only a part of his prosperity. He was doing very well in the stock market also. The same people who said insurance was wrong, felt that buying and selling stocks was wrong. Pieter disagreed. It wasn't gambling. Without a stock market, businesses could never grow. He couldn't believe what he was worth — on paper. His father, Klaas, would have been astounded! Everywhere there seemed to be a fiscal euphoria. Radios were selling like hotcakes. Cars, too. Installment buying, with "easy little payments," was the rule. The Sears Roebuck Catalog was the bible. Relatives in the old country could not believe the paradise Pieter inhabited. Of course, Bruce Barton had gone too far. Everybody was reading his best seller, *The Man Nobody Knows*. In it, Barton put forth the thesis that the title character (Jesus) was the world's greatest salesman.

Such was Pieter's world in 1925; a world in which Clarence Darrow and William Jennings Bryan debated in the famous Scopes or "monkey trial;" in which ninety percent of America's wealth rested in the hands of thirteen percent of its citizens; in which blacks lived in economic slavery; and in which the Ku Klux Klan grew to five million strong. It was true that there were myriads untouched by the spirit of the age. They still read their Bibles and went to church. But these things were less on Pieter's mind than the worldliness that was growing and the madness it fed. He hoped that his son would come home unscathed from the world. And he prayed that whoever succeeded Rev. Stuart would be a solid man.

His hope and prayer were both realized. It would be several years before his son, John, would return. But Rev. Stuart's successor appeared promptly. He was the Reverend R.B. Kuiper.

"R.B.," as he was known, was born January 31, 1886, in the Netherlands, where his father, the Rev. Klaas Kuiper, served as pastor in several Reformed churches. R.B. was the sixth child of eight. There was Barend (B.K. whom we have already met in these pages), Rolena, Lubberdena (active for many years in the American Federation of Reformed Young Women's Societies), Anton, Jan (father-in-law of the late Rev. Peter Eldersveld), Rienk Bouke (R.B.), Hendrik (an educator in the Christian schools of the Midwest, and one of the founders of the National Union of Christian Schools), and Herman (a respected minister in the Christian Reformed Church, and a professor in Calvin Seminary).

Coming to this country in 1891 with his parents, R.B. lived first in Grand Haven, Michigan, and later in Chicago, Illinois. He obtained his A.B. degree from the University of Chicago. He furthered his education at the University of Indiana, Calvin Theological Seminary, and Princeton Seminary. In 1912, he was ordained as minister of the Christian Reformed Church at Overisel, Michigan. In the year that he graduated from Calvin Seminary, he married Marie Jansen, who was the supervising principal of the West Side Christian School of Grand Rapids, Michigan. Three children were born to them: Marietta Rolena, who married Rev. Edward Heerema; a son, Klaudius; and Kathryn Junia, who died at the age of two. R.B. served the West Leonard Christian Reformed Church of Grand Rapids, Michigan, from 1914-1917, at which time he became pastor of the

Reverend R. B. Kuiper

Sherman Street Christian Reformed Church of that city. In 1923, he left the Christian Reformed Church to become pastor of the Second Reformed Church of Kalamazoo, Michigan. It was there, in 1925, that he received and accepted the call from LaGrave to serve as its pastor.

Pieter Troon and his fellow members were not disappointed with their new minister. It was apparent that R.B. was a pulpiteer of unusual stature. The Christian Reformed denomination was blessed with a considerable number of men who were talented in the pulpit. The initials R.B. stood for "rijk begaafd" (richly talented), according to the editor of *De Wachter*. Others, admirers all, said that R.B. stood for "roaring bull." He had some mannerisms which he excused by saying that if all people were entitled to one idiosyncrasy, preachers were entitled to two. His piercing eyes held his audiences, as did his crisp speech. He avoided clichés and had the rare ability to dramatize what he had to say. He expounded and elucidated great truths in such a way as to make them simple and clear and exciting — even for the twelve-year-olds in his congregation. His pulpit magnetism drew some of his former parishioners in the city to affiliate with LaGrave. Thus,

when R.B. Kuiper had been LaGrave's pastor for only a short time, A.J. Rooks was able to write these words about him in LaGrave's fortieth anniversary booklet:

During the year and one-half that our present pastor, the Rev. R.B. Kuiper is with us, much prosperity may already be observed. The membership has enlarged to 235 families; our contribution to the salary of our missionary pastor (Dr. Lee S. Huizenga) has been increased to $2,500; the debt incurred with the recent improvements of the church auditorium has been practically wiped out. That the pastor is prized can easily be observed from the attendance at church services.

The fortieth anniversary of LaGrave was celebrated February 24, 1927, at 6:30 P.M., at the Fountain Street Baptist Church parish house — complete with "perfection salad."

The quartet, which took a part in the evening's proceedings, included a former director of the LaGrave choir, Harry Dice, and his successor, Seymour Swets, who would function as the choir's director for the next thirty-seven years.

Professor Swets had come from South Holland, Illinois. The move to Grand Rapids, Michigan, was motivated, in large part, by considerations for Christian education. Seymour attended Grand Rapids Christian High School and graduated from Calvin College in 1923. He attended the University of Michigan and obtained a master's degree

in history. At this point, he was persuaded to return to Calvin College where he taught all kinds of courses, including physics. He had wed Wilma Hilarides. It would prove to be a happy marriage, as was evidenced in the dedication of his book, *Fifty Years of Music at Calvin College,* which appeared in 1973 and in which he wrote: "To my wife Wilma, who supported me through all these years with sweet encouragement and patient endurance; whose talent for homemaking built for us a happy home and enabled us to share a life that was filled with music."

In 1923, the Board of Trustees of Calvin College appointed Seymour Swets to the Chair of Music and Public Speaking, even though he was, at that time, in pursuit of his master's degree in history. His forthcoming appointment was contingent on his obtaining this degree. This hardly made sense; yet, in the providence of God, it did, for Seymour Swets had always held music as his first love. But Calvin College offered no courses in this field. As a member of its glee clubs, he had travelled to many Christian Reformed churches in various areas of the country and taken the pulse of the denomination — musically and otherwise. A concerned grandmother in Sioux County, Iowa, had asked him in Dutch, "How is it at Calvin College? Is there any religion left, or is it all English?" That he could handle such remarks diplomatically was part of his credentials. In view of all the experience he had had with three years of vocal lessons, six years of glee club concerts, four years of quartet experience — including two summers of barnstorming the West with an average of four concerts a week for eight weeks, including readings and solos — in addition to three years of "precentoring" in chapel services, Seymour Swets accepted the appointment. Until his retirement, he filled his place on Calvin's faculty with competence and honor. He became known as "Mr. Christian Reformed Music." Indeed, no one in his time influenced the course of music in the denomination more.

It was this man who would serve as the director of the LaGrave choir until 1962. Thus, in the second half of the 1920s, the LaGrave Church had both a preacher and a music director who were outstanding in their respective fields of work.

In 1926, in his second year at LaGrave as the pastor, Rev. R.B. Kuiper's book, *As to Being Reformed*, appeared. Having just served as the minister of a Reformed church in Kalamazoo and having returned to the Christian Reformed Church, he compared the two denominations. He found motes and beams in the Reformed denomination but also lamented with equal feeling certain conditions in the Christian Reformed church. He wrote guardedly regarding the union of these two churches, expressing the view that it could not happen unless agreement was obtained on certain doctrinal matters — the Masonic Lodge, catechism preaching, and Christian schools. The book found a ready sale and much response.

If the LaGrave congregation didn't know it yet, they knew it now — their pastor spoke fearlessly and stood for the fundamentals without compromise. Even so, there were those who continued to characterize LaGrave as the liberal church. Forty years later, the editor of *The Banner,* Rev. John VanderPloeg, wrote in the May 20, 1966 issue: "For most of us, few books stand out long in our memories, but the mark left upon me by reading R.B.'s *As to Being Reformed*, many years ago, has not yet been forgotten."

One evening, shortly after coming to LaGrave, R.B. and his wife entertained a small group at the parsonage, including LaGrave's former pastor, Rev. William Stuart and his wife. Rev. Stuart had been a colleague of R.B.'s father in Chicago. Talk centered on the congregation Rev. Stuart had led for ten years and which R.B. was just beginning to serve. According to Rev. Edward Heerema's book on R.B., Rev. Stuart ended the conversation with his characteristic forthrightness and brevity: "I'm sure you can handle it."

Professor Seymour Swets

In the pulpit, R.B. poured himself into his favorite subject, "The Grace of God," but not without warning the congregation against the perils of ungodliness. One member of the church complained to him, saying that she was tired of hearing about hell. Nevertheless, as always, R.B. did what he thought was his duty. The eternal destiny of the souls that were in his care filled his preaching with urgency and eloquence. He could be blunt. "Modernism is perfectly despicable!" "Modernism is damnable!" His sermons, however, were not just warnings and predominately negative; they were positive and Christ-centered — an emphasis he equated with Calvinism which he thought was "the most nearly perfect interpretation of Christianity." Pieter Troon wrote to his son, John, in Chicago, "How often, in church, I wish for your presence so that you, too, could hear the marvelous sermons of our minister."

Jean Boelkins Clelland remembers R.B. Kuiper as a preacher who could get carried away. Once he preached all through the Sunday School hour. No one minded.

Another member, William B. Eerdmans, publisher, having similar thoughts, determined to make some of the sermons available to the general public. R.B. had launched himself into a short series of messages on the subject of worldliness. It was a matter of growing concern. Indeed, the synod of the denomination felt that it could not be ignored. Agitation on this matter increased throughout the decade. There were floods of sermons, articles, appeals, and books all dealing with the sins of the age. Pietists, Fundamentalists, and the "holiness" churches were particularly verbal, if not always articulate. Billy Sunday was clearly convinced that the country was "going to hell in a handbasket" — whatever that meant. It was clear that a thoroughly Biblical answer to the whole matter was needed. R.B. undertook to provide the answer, believing that preaching should always be relevant to the needs of God's people. The series of sermons that ensued were stenographically recorded and published in a book entitled *Not of the World,* which appeared in 1929 and was dedicated to the members of the LaGrave congregation.

The title of the book was taken from Christ's intercessory prayer, recorded in John 17:16. The first message in the series, based on I Corinthians 5:9,10 and entitled "Mingling with the World (A Good Mixer)," was divided into the following points:

A. The Christian Can Mingle with the World
B. The Christian May Mingle with the World
C. The Christ Must Mingle with the World
D. This Mingling Has Its Proper Limitations

The sermon, "Enjoying the World (A Healthy Human)," based on I Corinthians 7:31, was divided into two points:

A. To Use This World Is Perfectly Proper
B. To Use It to the Full Is Perfectly Foolish.

Another message entitled, "Overcoming the World (A Victorious Soldier)," based on I John 5:4, was also divided into two points:

A. What It Means to Overcome the World
B. What It Is That Overcomes the World

Other messages in the series were as follows:

"Differing From the World (A True Aristocrat)" Romans 12:2
"Hated by the World (A Happy Martyr)" John 16:33
"Travelling Through the World (A Yearning Pilgrim)" Hebrews 11:13
"Owning the World (A Multimillionaire)" I Corinthians 3:22,23
"Evangelizing the World (An Ardent Missionary)" Mark 16:15

As always, the complex was simplified, the mystery made plain. The Bible did not enjoin separatism. In R.B.'s words, to do that "we would have to jump off the globe. Try it, and see how far you get!" To participate in the world and to be involved, as we must, presents hazards. Yet, "In attempting to avoid every possible danger, we would be driven to the absurd position of the mother who forbade her children to go near the water until they had learned to swim."

R.B.'s illustrations always hit the mark. When the series was published, Pieter Troon bought several copies, sending one to his daughter in Kalamazoo and one to his son in Chicago.

The denomination availed itself of the talents of LaGrave's pastor. He was placed on several committees. One, mandated to introduce more hymns into Christian Reformed worship services, resulted in the new Psalter Hymnal of 1934. R.B. served on this committee, together with his choir director, Seymour Swets. The synod of 1926 placed him on a committee to study worldly amusements. The adoption of its report, in 1928, was to become a celebrated matter in the annals of Christian Reformed history. The report began

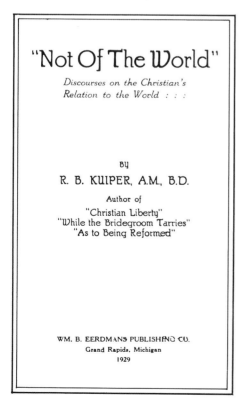

"Not Of The World"

Discourses on the Christian's Relation to the World : : :

BY

R. B. KUIPER, A.M., B.D.

Author of
"Christian Liberty"
"While the Bridegroom Tarries"
"As to Being Reformed"

WM. B. EERDMANS PUBLISHING CO.
Grand Rapids, Michigan
1929

by asserting Christian liberty, yet went on to mention such restrictions as the committee felt were
in harmony with subordinating the physical to the
spiritual and the temporal to the eternal. Christian liberty was further limited to the point at
which offense to others began. The result of all
this proscribed movie attendance, card playing,
and dancing. These three "don'ts" would play an
important role in the history of the denomination,
and for several decades were identified by some
as the essence of what it meant to be Christian
Reformed.

According to the book containing his biography, written by his son-in-law Edward Heerema,
R.B. regretted the fact that the report on worldly
amusements was interpreted as singling out certain sins. R.B. felt this discredited the report.
Such an interpretation gave the false impression
that a mere avoidance of movies, card playing,
and dancing left one innocent of worldliness.

However that may have been, there was another
drama unfolding at this time involving R.B.'s
brother, B.K. As earlier noted, the latter had
served the church brilliantly. But B.K. was as ec-
centric as he was brilliant and thereby destined to
be in and out of hot water in the years ahead. It all
came to a climax at about the time his brother,
R.B., as reporter for the committee on worldly
amusements, surfaced with a document at the
synod of 1928 which was adopted and which,
among other things, inveighed against worldly
amusements such as the movies. Alas, brother
B.K., who had been teaching at the seminary, had

been seen coming out of such an establishment
by a layman. B.K.'s explanation that he had entered the movie house merely to adjust his new
dental plates did not satisfy the concerned layman. The Oakdale Park consistory asked classis
to overture synod not to reappoint B.K. Kuiper as
a teacher in the seminary. Despite a three-hour
defense on his own behalf — before the highest
ecclesiastical body of the church — in which he
was more concerned about influencing the thinking of synod on amusements than securing his
own reappointment, B.K. was terminated. The
vote was approximately ten to seventy.

Henry Beets, church historian, and highly esteemed as even-handed, wrote:

> The majority of minister delegates, nearly all of
> whom were pupils of the amiable and able pro-
> fessor, would have voted to give him another
> chance. But some of his unguarded utterances
> during the second part of his defense and, later
> on, his rather sudden about-face were factors of
> his own making which turned the vote of many
> against him. And for this he has only himself
> to blame.

Henry Beets added, "We feel sorry for the
brother." Henry Zwaanstra wrote: "From a
broader historical perspective, it seems that B.K.
not only acted, but was acted upon." But no one
wrote about the irony of history wherein two
brothers played a large role in the synod — R.B.
who brought a report on worldly amusements
that was adopted and B.K. who was terminated as
a professor in the seminary on that same issue.
R.B. would go on from LaGrave to serve as president of Calvin College (1930-1933), chairman of
the faculty of Westminster Seminary and head of
its department of practical theology (1933-1952),
and president of Calvin Seminary (1952-1956).
B.K., on the other hand, was finished. John J.
Timmerman, in his book, *Promises to Keep*,
(pp. 37-38), would write about B.K. years later
as follows:

> The remainder of this talented man's life was
> mournful . . . With all his talents, he ended as a
> withered branch. While I was studying at North-
> western University, I often . . . came home from
> there around midnight. I saw him frequently
> between eleven and twelve walking the almost
> deserted streets, or just standing on a corner
> chewing on a dead cigar. It must have been
> 3 A.M. in his soul . . .

B.K. was a faithful member of LaGrave Church
until his death in 1961 when the Lord took him to
the Church Triumphant. In those years, he was a

faithful and stimulating member of its Men's Society — The Brotherhood. Deafness in his later years did not stop him from attending its meetings.

The termination of his brother's services saddened R.B. He loved B.K. and was to him all that a brother should be.

The Board of Trustees of Calvin College and Seminary had not far to look when they were casting about for a new president of the college. R.B. accepted the appointment, thus terminating his services as pastor at LaGrave. Pieter Troon was not the only one who was disappointed. Indeed, when he learned of R.B.'s acceptance of the call to Calvin College, it was as if the roof had caved in on him.

The same year that R.B. accepted the call that took him away from LaGrave, the roof did cave in for millions more. Charles Lindbergh, in 1927, had made the world smaller with his flight to France, but the 1929 crash of the stock market made it a broken world. "While Jerusalem had only one wailing wall, on Wall Street every wall was wet with tears." So said one of its inhabitants. The president of Union Cigar plummeted, along with his stocks. He jumped, or fell, from the ledge of a New York hotel. Others, not able to face financial disaster, stopped the world and got off — suicides all. One woman asked, "How could I lose $100,000? I never had $100,000." So it was with Pieter Troon. He had invested heavily. He had stocks. But the numbers were all on paper. It was fortunate that his son had almost finished his medical training. From now on, he and many of his fellow members at LaGrave would have to pull in their belts. Would LaGrave suffer and almost disappear with this depression as it almost had during the Grover Cleveland disaster? How quickly things changed! One year LaGrave and its members flourished — with the denomination's most popular pastor. The next year they lost him — he was gone.

And so was the economy!

Years later, as professor of homiletics at Westminster Seminary, R.B. would speak on the importance of the context of a text in determining its meaning. It was the context of the 1920s that explained much of R.B.'s emphasis and ministry during his LaGrave years. A very practical preacher, he addressed himself to the world in which he and his parishioners lived. With prosperity running rampant, with modernism's voice increasing in the pulpits of the land, and with worldliness creeping into the pews, his sermons were not made up of soft guesses and inferences and tentative conclusions. Instead of being shaped by the day, he sought to bring about a new dawn. Thus he preached, and would in later years urge his students to preach similarly, "The Word, the Whole Word, and Nothing but the Word."

The March 1931 issue of *Christianity Today* printed his sermon "What Is Truth?"* based on John 18:38 ("Pilate said to him, what is truth?"). In 1987, there are still many who remember hearing him preach it. Sermons seldom live that long, yet even today his message on "Truth" comes alive off the page. It was first preached in the LaGrave Church. The man who preached the Word, the whole Word, and nothing but the Word, preached the Truth, the whole Truth, and nothing but the Truth. For the Word and Truth are one.

In II Timothy 4:2 we read: "Preach the word." R.B. often made reference to it. The Greek word for "preach" literally means "herald."

That's what he did!

That's what he was!

*See Addendum

REVEREND AND MRS. HERMAN BEL 1932–1939

With "two Bels and eight chimes" in the parsonage, LaGrave endures
the threadbare thirties encouraged by a lively music program

Chapter 14

THE THREADBARE THIRTIES

The full effect of the depression was not felt immediately. By 1939, when the worst of it was over, forty million people had learned to live with poverty. It was a decade in which many businessmen slipped from being home owners to room renters and even to wandering in the streets. Top grade salesmen were reduced to selling apples on street corners. Countless thousands slept under Hoover blankets (newspapers for warmth) on park benches and sported Hoover flags (empty pants pockets turned inside out). Herbert Hoover himself, able engineer but hapless president, learned on his last day in office, March 3, 1933, that the country's banking system had collapsed. Will Rogers, court jester for the whole country, said, "We are the first nation in history to go to the poor house in an automobile." Alas, with unemployment soaring to 25 to 30 percent of the work force, there were fewer and fewer cars.

The decade did not lack for pied pipers: Father Charles E. Coughlin in Royal Oak, Michigan, and Huey Long in Louisiana. John L. Lewis's leonine head loomed everywhere. As the Czar of Labor ("labor, like Israel, has many sorrows"), he looked and sounded awesome. His critics claimed his head was only his neck "haired over." None rose higher in the decade, however, than Franklin Delano Roosevelt, president of the United States.

Franklin D. Roosevelt brought America the "New Deal," and through the lean years, fed the nation with alphabet soup. N.R.A. (National Recovery Administration), C.C.C. (Civilian Conservation Corps), P.W.A. (Public Works Administration), W.P.A. (Work Progress Administration), and more. There were those who took to hissing the president. Others put their faith in him; but he couldn't prevent such natural disasters as tornadoes and the dust storms, nor could he banish the evil deeds of men. Lindbergh's baby was kidnapped, and John Dillinger earned his title of "Public Enemy Number One." But Roosevelt did put a firm hand on the helm of the ship of state.

Meanwhile, citizens sought solace where they could. Prohibition ended. Orphan Annie, Tarzan, and Dick Tracy became preoccupations, via the funnies. Kate Smith, Fibber McGee and Molly, Major Bowes, and many more caught America's ear. George Bernard Shaw, returning home to England from a visit to the new world, said there were three things he would remember: the Rocky Mountains, the Statue of Liberty, and Amos and Andy. But Hollywood took America's eyes, as well

LaGrave's ninth pastor, in his teens in the thirties, was "peddling" cabbages in the streets of Detroit instead of writing them for The Banner. *A nickel a piece! One customer turned his nickel over in his hand several times before giving it up. "You don't see many of these nowadays," he said.*

as her ears, despite the Christian Reformed Church synodical stance of 1928. Opulence on the silver screen helped Americans to forget their pinched existences as they lived the stars' lives vicariously and fantasized in downtown Palaces and neighborhood Bijous.

Before the 1939 World's Fair in New York would top the decade and Hitler topple Europe, there would be those who would wonder whether Germany's dictator, Hitler, or Mussolini in Italy, or Stalin in Russia was the anti-Christ, or if Roosevelt's N.R.A. symbol (the blue eagle) was the mark of the beast. For, in American towns and cities, fundamentalism, tabernacleism (tent revivals), and a growing retinue of itinerant evangelists were seeing all sorts of current events predicted in Bible prophesy and as signs of the times and warnings of the imminence of Judgment Day. The people of the British Isles, identified by some as the lost ten tribes, were restoring Palestine! The secrets of the Pyramids were predicting a world conflagration!

The Christian Reformed Church, as much as possible, sought isolation from much of what the thirties brought. Having worked through the Bultema, Janssen, Hoeksema, and worldliness challenges, it settled down to a repetitious recital of its distinctive features — complete with warnings against their erosion. With immigration from the Netherlands disappearing and the language question mostly settled, it sought to consolidate its gains and build its walls. Between a great depression at the beginning of the decade and a great war at its end, the Christian Reformed Church developed an "us and them," an "insiders and outsiders" mentality — almost to the point of paranoia. It sought escape from being contaminated by both fundamentalism and modernism. Its *Banner* repeatedly sounded the alarm, awakening all to vigilance. At mid-decade, *The Calvin Forum,* a monthly, was born — once more sounding Abraham Kuyper's progressive note, which was dear to the hearts of both Henry Beets and

B.K. Kuiper. Even so, the denomination sought preservation in a more cautious "mind of safety." Dr. W. Harry Jellema, professor of philosophy at Calvin College, the faculty's most luminous mind, asked too many questions with his Socratic method and gave too few answers, according to some. He departed for the University of Indiana.

LaGrave Church, despite its stalwart and altogether reliable former pastors and its own commitment to the Gospel of Jesus Christ, continued to be suspect in the eyes of many. Some of its members were too much involved with the community! It preferred its ministers in robes rather than the standard Prince Albert coats and striped trousers! It nurtured its choir! Etc., etc. A member of the Franklin Street Christian Reformed Church visited LaGrave and felt "humbled" because he had harbored erroneous and unfair attitudes towards what turned out to be a solid, rather than a liberal, congregation. But its pulpit was vacant. Rev. R.B. Kuiper had left, and his replacement was slow in coming. The congregation extended calls, but they were not accepted.

There were other churches that had sustained long vacancies. Relatively speaking, Christian Reformed churches, rooted in their theology rather than their pastors, sustained empty parsonages much better than some congregations of other denominations. This spoke well of their stability. Often, elders would read sermons to congregations who remained faithful in their attendance. Even so, vacancies were to be endured but terminated as soon as possible. Orchestras could do better without conductors than congregations without pastors. Thus, LaGrave prayed earnestly, but the Lord sent no undershepherd to His flock. It was, therefore, a time of testing. LaGrave had been signally blessed through the presence of its first five ministers. No two of them had been alike. Their ministries at LaGrave had complemented each other in a remarkable way.

During its vacancy period, which would last from 1929 to 1932, the church sustained its membership roll. A few families left, but others came. Among the latter was Dr. John Troon, who returned to Grand Rapids to begin his practice as a general practitioner.

The medical scene in 1930 was a challenging one. The most common operations were thyroidectomies and mastoidectomies. Many died of meningitis. Annual polio epidemics were a scourge. Victims of scarlet fever were removed to the "pest house" on Fuller Avenue. There were no

PASTORLESS!

We used to have a pastor,
  In short, was called R.B.
He came to us from Kalamazoo,
  To preach for you and me.

He always had a message,
  When he'd the truth unfold.
His style was just that simple,
  To profit young and old.

No doubt this is the reason,
  That he was loved by all,
But now you see what happened
  Just then he gets a call.

From regions unexpected,
  Once and again they came;
That threw us in the balance,
  Westminster won the game.

This placed an added burden,
  Upon his neighbor Bill;
We mean the Rev. Stuart,
  Whose place he'd come to fill.

Though many years our pastor,
  And now our youth he feeds;
He stayed within our circle,
  To help us in our needs.

His best years he has given,
  Completely of his time;
To us, who hold him in esteem,
  True love will ever climb.

And now he is our counselor,
  To serve us with advice;
We do enjoy his sermons, too,
  They're wisdom to the wise.

While thus we are assisted,
  From other sources too;
The fact that we are pastorless,
  Has proven to be true.

And think of our consistory,
  Elders and deacons, twelve;
Men that must sacrifice their time,
  And into problems delve.

We know they are most capable,
  And love to do the right;
And satisfying all us folks,
  Requires all their might.

They have had several trios formed,
  Of preachers far and near;
One duo also and quartet,
  Good judgment was made clear.

O, how our hearts go out to them,
  As down the list they go;
The yearbook as a guide they take
  To form a slate, you know.

A — hasn't been there long enough,
  B — is but rarely known;
Of C — it is quite often said,
  He's too much on the throne.

D — seems a little prejudiced,
  No church should have a choir;
Although where he is serving now,
  He's surely full of fire.

And E — who has a sickly wife,
  His station wouldn't leave;
The change of climate won't permit
  It might cost her her life.

So now you see how difficult,
  A task it seems to be;
First of all to make a slate.
  And then to pick out three.

And don't forget that officers,
  Are men like you and me;
Each has his likes and dislikes, too,
  Which otherwise can't be.

But while these methods are employed,
  Our prayers they must afford;
Intelligent then cast our vote,
  And leave it to the Lord.

We know He rules the hearts of men
  And ever guides His church;
He tests our faith, but after all
  Won't leave us in the lurch.

So let us then together stand,
  United as one man
With faith in God expressed in prayer,
  And do the best we can.

Gerrit Spoelstra

antibiotics. Poverty had placed many on the welfare lists; they were not apt to call on the doctor when he was needed. Some of the widows in the LaGrave Church knitted booties for Dr. Troon's wife who was expecting. It was something they could do for their doctor who made house calls and didn't charge if they couldn't pay. The result was enough booties for a centipede. Many mothers gave birth at home. They were encouraged to do so if they were on welfare. The state paid Dr. Troon fifteen dollars for every home delivery. There were no abortions — except illegal ones which resulted in many deaths. There was little treatment for tuberculosis, the social diseases, and other ills. Many in the church, and more in the denomination, had stayed alive in the past — or so they thought — by taking Dr. Pieter's "Zokoro," a medicine for which ads appeared with religious regularity in the church papers, and which enhanced another kind of regularity. "Zokoro" was good for upset stomach, indigestion, coated tongue, flatulence, loss of appetitie, headache, nervousness, restlessness, and loss of sleep when these troubles were due to constipation. Dr. Pieter's formula contained senna, fennel, mandrake root, peppermint, spearmint, mountain mint, horsemint, sarsaparilla, sassafras, hyssop, blessed thistle, dittany, ground ivy, johnswort, lemon balm, sage, spikenard, and yarrow. The fact that it contained fourteen percent alcohol gave a warm feeling in the stomach. Eighteen fluid ounces cost $1.90. Dr. Troon did not prescribe it. On those occasions when he was called out of the consistory meeting (he became a deacon soon after his return) because of a phone call from someone in distress, he could sometimes be overheard prescribing a little whiskey.

At the University of Chicago, John Troon had studied under the remarkable Professor Maud Slye whose discovery of cancer by inheritance had been reported in *Time* magazine. Professor Slye had autopsied over 100,000 mice — the subjects of her experiments. On the basis of her findings, she discovered that susceptibility to cancer was inheritable, but that it could be bred out of a family by a judicious marriage. Susceptibility alone, however, was not enough to insure a person's developing a cancer. There had to be an external factor as well, for example, a bruise. Dr. Troon had been impressed, albeit not convinced, by her findings.

The LaGrave congregation was privileged to hear various preachers and professors. Being located in Grand Rapids, Michigan, there was no dearth of pulpit supply possibilities. However, it was not the same as having a permanent shepherd. The LaGrave congregation continued to issue calls. It sent an invitiation to a minister in the East. His name was Herman Bel. Twice before, LaGrave had obtained a minister from that part of the country. But Rev. Bel declined. It was another disappointment. The Lord, however, furnished a wonderful, although temporary, solution. Seminarian Bastian Kruithof had taught a year at Christian High School in Grand Rapids. Rev. Stuart thought highly of him. Others, too, traced promises of greatness in him. Mr. Kruithof had entered Calvin Seminary with a view to entering the ministry. He was a remarkable student-preacher. The LaGrave consistory delegated Elder A.J. (Dean) Rooks to engage him for preaching and catechism teaching. It proved to be a mutually rewarding arrangement. Bastian Kruithof needed financial comfort, and LaGrave needed spiritual comfort. The arrangement continued for about six months. The student-preacher appeared in the pulpit once each Sunday, alternating between morning and evening services. During the week, he taught LaGrave's catechism classes at Neland Avenue Christian Reformed Church — a more convenient location for the smaller children. He taught a class on Sundays as well and led the lesson study at the Sunday School teachers' meetings on Fridays, under the direction of LaGrave's Sunday School superintendent, Mr. Dewey Blocksma.

The elders furnished Mr. Kruithof with a pulpit robe which, alas, was several sizes too large for his small frame. He obliged, but observed that he would rather preach in Saul's armor than in Saul's

Reverend Bastian Kruithof

tent. Between morning services and catechism, he would enjoy coffee and cake with Mr. Lakke, the custodian, ("putsa here, uppie, uppie") in the church house. Mr. Lakke, an ardent Kuyperian — partly due to the fact that he had personally met the great Abraham Kuyper in the old country — invariably engaged the coffee-drinking, cake-eating, budding theologian in heavy discussions on Calvinism.

The pulpit experience, a great education for Mr. Kruithof, was no less profitable for the congregation. In his preaching, the young student occasionally made references to bits and pieces of great poetry or literature whenever it served his point. It was something different and especially enlarged the horizons of some of his younger hearers. Once, when his watch stopped, Mr. Kruithof went overtime — a happening good naturedly remembered when, upon his departure, the congregation presented him with a gold watch. He could have stayed. The members wanted to call him. It would have been a wonderful marriage of shepherd and flock. But Mr. Kruithof wished to broaden his education. After graduation from Calvin Seminary, he headed in the direction of the University of Michigan. He went on to become an author, and, for years, a member of the faculty of Hope College, Holland, Michigan, where he taught Bible and related subjects.

During his stay at LaGrave, it was Bastian Kruithof's goal to preach a no-peppermint ser-

At the expiration of the time during which the LaGrave Avenue Christian Reformed Congregation of Grand Rapids Michigan has had the pleasure and the honor of having had our Brother **Bastiaan Kruithof** labor in its midst as Preacher and as Teacher the Consistory of LaGrave Avenue Church wishes to express its hearty appreciation and gratitude to Mr. Kruithof for the excellent work he has done.

The Lord has bestowed extraordinary gifts upon our Brother, and in the performance of his duties he has displayed conscientious devotion and great zeal and talent.

It is the hope and prayer of LaGrave Ave Consistory that under the guidance of the Holy Spirit these gifts may come to ever greater development.

Mr. Kruithof may rest assured that the Consistory is loath to part with his services, and that in the hearts of its members he will always have a warm place.

Hoping that Gods richest blessings may attend the person and the labors of our Brother, the Consistory commends him to the blessings and the mercies of our Covenant God, and to the Christian Reformed Churches

Done in the Consistory this 18th day of January 1932.

Albert J. Rooks, Vice Presus
John H. Spaland, Secretary

mon. He set for himself quite a task in a congregation which, in that day, always took in its theology along with a mint or two. No one knows if he succeeded, but everyone knew that he preached exceedingly well. LaGrave sent him on his way, not only with a gold watch, but with a resolution written on parchment in beautiful handwriting.

When it had become clear that Mr. Kruithof would continue with his studies, the consistory was led by the Holy Spirit to reconsider the name of Herman Bel who had declined its earlier invitation. The congregation, agreeing with the consistory, extended a second call to him. Rev. Bel, in Paterson, New Jersey, found the decision exceedingly difficult to make. He wrote two letters, one accepting LaGrave's call, and the other declining. An elder of the Paterson church was called to the parsonage. After prayer, the elder chose the envelope that was an acceptance to LaGrave Church. Thus, LaGrave's sixth pastor came by lot.

93

Bethel Christian Reformed Church

Organized December 27, 1921

193-197 Haledon Avenue

Paterson, N. J.

Jan.2,1932

Rev. Herman Bel, Minister
193 N. 9th Street
Phone: Armory 4-2155-M.

The LaGrave Ave Chr.Ref.Church,
Grand Rapids,Mich.

Dear Brethren and Sisters in the Lord:

The time has come to decide what to do with your call.I need not inform you that it has been on my mind ever since I received it.The last week it has burdened me beyond expression.It seemed impossible for me to come to a decision.My own people begged me to stay,if possible,and many of your congregation pleaded with me to accept,if at all possible.

I have compared the needs of the two congregations over and over again but found it impossible to reach a decision by this means.

Emotionally I have been swayed back and forth.My people are dear to me; you can not blame me for that,and I certainly hate to think of leaving them after a period of only three years.

When I considered the question of personal fitness I invariably came to the conclusion that I fit in best where I am now.

I can conscientiously say that I have earnestly prayed that the Lord to give me light.I have asked him to take the burden of the call away from me if it should be His will that I stay in Bethel,or to detach me from my present charge,if He wants me to go.

And now the time for a decision has come.I am not detached from my present charge and I am not loose from LaGrave.Only one thing is left for me to do and that is write two letters,the one containing an acceptance and the other a declination.This I am doing.The matter is now finally and absolutely in God's hand.Whatever He decides that will I do.If this letter be sent to you,then you have herewith the answer:''I'll come over and help you.''

May God's blessing rest on His own choice,and may He comfort the loyal people whose loss is your gain.

Yours in Christ,

Herman Bel

94

Rev. Herman Bel was born in 1886 in Uithuizen, the Netherlands. At the age of five, he lost his mother in death. He soon learned to care for his younger brother while his father worked. At the age of twelve, be became a farmhand. It was a hard life. In his seventeenth year, he came to the United States to live with an uncle and aunt in Grand Rapids, Michigan. Before his arrival, he suffered a serious injury while attempting to board a train in Chicago. The accident changed his life. Impressed with God's care over him, he felt led of the Lord to enter the ministry. He began his studies in 1907.

Upon completion of his course, he married Tena Dykstra, with whom he would share a loving and fruitful relationship for many years. His first church was in Rochester, New York. Four years later, he moved to Detroit, Michigan, where he met LaGrave's ninth pastor who, occasionally, at the age of one year, interrupted his sermons. Herman Bel's tenure in Detroit coincided with a time in which the Motor City was suffering from the Purple Gang Wars. Many of the mobsters drove Buicks. So did Rev. Bel. Did he move to Muskegon after three years because his Buick was mistakenly targeted? Some say the story is apocryphal. After two years in Muskegon, he accepted a call to the Fourth Christian Reformed Church of Chicago. While there, he pursued graduate work at Lewis Institute and McCormick Theological Seminary. In 1928, the Lord led him to the Bethel Church in Paterson, New Jersey. Four years later, he accepted LaGrave's second invitation. He was installed on February 14, 1932.

Reverend Herman Bel

niality, common sense, practicality, and sense of humor energized one and all. With a house full of children, the whole family was hailed as "two Bels and eight little chimes" at a reception for the new minister.

His catechism classes became an institution. Some of them continued at the Neland Avenue Church. The Saturday classes, however, were conducted at LaGrave in the basement room under the church, dug out years before by the catechumens of Rev. Henry Beets. The unique feature of Rev. Bel's Saturday classes was the transportation. He owned a big, seven-passenger Buick, acquired to accommodate his rather sizeable family. Always practical, he converted it on Saturdays into the church's first bus. Every hour, Saturday mornings, he taught a different class, the members of which were chauffered to church in the ministerial Buick by son, Al; then son, Tennyson; and later, son, John. All the children were picked up at their homes and brought to church, where others were loaded in to be returned to their respective places. None of the children wanted to miss catechism because they had so much fun riding the shuttle. However, when they came to class, they were expected to know their lesson.

There was never a dull moment at the parsonage. The children constantly brought strings of friends home with them. This was particularly true on Sundays when Mrs. Bel and her daughters

> *Officiants in the installation of LaGrave's sixth pastor were Rev. Henry Beets and Rev. William Stuart, LaGrave's third and fourth pastors, and Dr. George Goris who would become LaGrave's eighth pastor. Rev. Bel's inaugual sermon was entitled, "The Whole Council of God."*

It was apparent to the members of the LaGrave congregation why the Lord had directed them to Herman Bel a second time. Obviously, he was the right man, in the right place, at the right time. The depression had settled in. The change in climate it brought — to both church and community — depressed morale as well as the economy. In such a setting, Herman Bel's disposition, conge-

> On January 18, 1935, Mrs. Hazenburg and Mrs. Dooge brought a new black robe to the manse. It was a gift from the South End Ladies Circle. Rev. Bel felt very self-conscious in his new robe. He was the first among his fellow Christian Reformed clergymen to wear such a garment, for the distinctive pulpit attire in those days was the Prince Albert coat and the grey striped trousers. The congregations's reaction to the robe, mixed at first, soon changed to unanimous approval. Later, another robe was supplied — for visiting ministers.

> LaGrave's ninth pastor once played pool with Rev. Bel just before an evening service. He was the guest of Al and Tenny. Rev. Bel couldn't finish the game because "it was time for church."

> LaGrave was still being criticized for having a choir. Rev. Bel not only defended it, but aggressively promulgated the concept of choirs in more Christian Reformed churches. Once, at a meeting of Inter-Now (a monthly gathering of Christian Reformed clergymen and their wives), he said, "As a preacher in the pulpit, I would rather be without my right arm than do without the choir."

Alyce Lantinga

would make mountains of sandwiches. Everyone was welcome for coffee or to share a meal. The third floor had a pool table and a ping-pong table. It was a great gathering place.

Adrian Kett and his wife, members of LaGrave Church, were resident caretakers of Calvin College dormitory. They had no family of their own. Nevertheless, they had three floors of young men to supervise and feed. It was no small task. Holidays were particularly difficult and lonely for those students who were too far from home to spend such important days with their families. To make things at the dorm more homelike, Rev. and Mrs. Bel and all eight children would eat the Thanksgiving meal with (Pa and Ma) Kett and "the boys."

In 1937, LaGrave celebrated its fiftieth birthday. To mark the occasion, B. K. Kuiper, long since dismissed as a teacher at the seminary, wrote a word of appreciation of the pastor:

The church now numbers 254 families, 596 communicants, and a total membership of 917. The services on Sunday draw large congregations which listen attentively to the earnest preaching of our pastor.

A program to mark the occasion took place on February 24, 1937, with Mr. Dewey Blocksma as toastmaster. Once again, it took place at the Fountain Street Baptist Church.

Among other things, the program offered a piano solo by Mrs. G. (Alyce) Lantinga. The year before the fiftieth birthday party, "Alyce" had become LaGrave's organist. She would continue in that capacity for a remarkable forty-two years, retiring in 1978.

Alyce (nee VanderMey) was born in New Era, Michigan. She inherited perfect pitch from her mother and displayed musical talent at an early age. At age fourteen, she attended the Sherwood Music School in Chicago with her sixteen-year-old sister, Marie.

At age nineteen, she undertook organ studies with Harold Tower, organist for many years at St. Mark's Episcopal Church of Grand Rapids. She was soon playing the organ at the Wyoming Park Christian Reformed Church, and then at the Sherman Street Christian Reformed Church, followed by six years as assistant organist at St. Mark's. She also served at East Congregational, Bethany Reformed, Central Reformed, and Westminster Presbyterian churches — all in Grand Rapids.

In 1933, Alyce VanderMey married Garret Lantinga, a businessman. In 1936, she was approached by LaGrave to serve as organist at an annual salary of $150 for all services, including weddings and funerals. She accepted the offer and took over the duties of her immediate predecessors, Ethel Leestma and Alyde VandenBerge, presiding at the console of LaGrave's two-manual Austin organ.

The church house, where the custodian lived, was connected to the sanctuary by a dungeon-like passageway. Choir members moved from the front room of the church house where rehearsals took place, through the passageway to the back of the organ, then through a walkway between organ pipes, and into the choir loft. The choir seating was in front of and to either side of the organ console.

The placement of the choir and organ in the sanctuary did not lend itself to the choir being directed by its leader. It was for this reason that Alyce gave the choir its cues with motions of her head.

Coupled with teaching — at one point up to sixty-six students — and playing at church, there was the matter of raising five children. Sometimes, dressing them was finished during the five-mile ride downtown. Even-paced, she was imperturbable, a quality that served her well amidst all that was required of her. Jane Dorr and Helen Bolt, assistant organists, ably substituted during her absences. Later, her daughter, Evelyn, would also serve as her assistant.

LaGrave Church was indeed fortunate to obtain the services of so able and faithful an organist as Alyce Lantinga proved to be. Other churches soon recognized her talent. Along with LaGrave's choir director, Seymour Swets, Alyce Lantinga did much to raise musical standards in the denomination. Besides playing in Grand Rapids, she played organ dedications in churches in Jenison, Grandville, Grand Haven, Kalamazoo, Zeeland, Cadillac — all in Michigan. The editor of *The Banner* recognized her denominational contribution, together with others, when he placed her

picture on the cover of the denominational paper's October 2, 1953 issue with the following commentary:

> The purpose of our cover picture is not to give prominence to one of our organists above all others. We want our readers to regard the person whose likeness appears in this conspicuous place merely as a representative — an outstanding one to be sure — of a large group of men and women who not only love music, and have learned to play the greatest of all musical instruments, but have dedicated their skill to the service of God through the edification of the church in public worship.

The fiftieth anniversary of the LaGrave Church, for which Alyce Lantinga played a piano solo, had been preceded the Sunday before by services of thanksgiving. Both morning and evening saw the sanctuary filled to capacity. At the beginning of both services, the choir proceeded down the aisle singing "Onward, Christian soldiers." The pastor, Rev. H. Bel, was the liturgist. In the evening, he was assisted by a former pastor, Rev. W. Stuart. In the morning, the Rev. David D. Bonnema, pastor of LaGrave's mother church (Bates Street), preached on the words found in Romans 15:13. In the evening, Dr. Edward Masselink, pastor of LaGrave's daughter church (Burton Heights), spoke on John 6:5–11.

One Sunday morning, Alyce entered the choir room with a teddy bear under her arm. Herb, her son, had decided it would be nice to have it at church. Nonchalantly, Alyce placed it on the piano as the pre-service rehearsal began.

Rev. Herman Bel continued his excellent leadership. He was not only well accepted in the congregation but in the denomination and community as well. Having an outgoing nature, he made contacts with ministers of other denominations very easily. There were those in the denomination who did not approve. He was highly criticized for being the first Christian Reformed minister to join the Downtown Ministerial Conference.

> *Rev. Bel believed in being fair. Five church members owned grocery stores: J. Kos, A. Botting, R. Brinks, P. Mellema, and H. Daane. Every month, groceries were bought at a different store.*

Pastor Bel had felt a growing need for a parish house to replace the old parsonage. The latter served as a meeting place and provided living quarters for the custodian. The congregation shared this feeling. Thus, during Rev. Bel's tenure, the parish house was built. Pledges were made. Loans were obtained from members and through ads in *The Banner* at four percent interest. The letter to the congregation which sought loans over the signature of Alfred H. VanKeulen, chairman of the parish house project, described the interest rate as "commensurate with present day conditions and considerably more than is now available in savings accounts." It was 1939 and the depression was largely spent. Even so, it took a while before the indebtedness incurred was liquidated.

The building project was not without mishap. The builder, in excavating four feet below the foundation level of the church, had taken a chance and lost. A section of the north wall collapsed. The *Grand Rapids Press* carried a picture of the tragedy. The organ was visible from the outside. Huge braces were applied to shore up the remainder of the wall where huge cracks appeared. Damages were estimated to be from eight to ten thousand dollars. Services of worship were held at Westminster Presbyterian Church the following Sunday evenings. The morning service on the first Sunday after the collapse and all services on succeeding Sundays were held at Calvin College. The pastor, Rev. Bel, missed all the excitement. He was vacationing.

—Grand Rapids Press Photographer

Church Organ Loses Housing

Most of the north wall of Lagrave Avenue Christian Reformed church will have to be replaced because a section at the rear, as shown in the picture, collapsed Monday afternoon while excavating work was proceeding for the new parish house. The organ was visible from the outside through the section of the wall that collapsed and several large cracks developed before the wall was braced to guard against further collapse. Damage to the edifice will amount to thousands of dollars, the city building inspector's office said.

It was in 1937 that Rev. William D. VanderWerp retired from his last charge in Spring Lake, Michigan. Upon moving to Grand Rapids, he and his family joined LaGrave Church where he began to serve as Rev. Bel's assistant. Before the parish house was completed, Pastor Bel received and accepted a call to serve the Berwyn Christian Reformed Church in Chicago, Illinois, and to teach Bible at the Chicago Christian High School. It was the latter task, fully as much as the former, that appealed to his young heart. The fact that he had to drive the school bus everyday was no deterrant to his activist nature. Rev. Bel had never been afraid of work, including the kind that made his hands dirty. His face in perennial smile was missed. He returned for the dedication of the parish house — a dream of the congregation before Rev. Bel came which was shelved by the depression but activated and then realized largely because of his inspiration and drive.

The *Grand Rapids Press* of February 17, 1940, announced that over one thousand people had attended the dedication ceremony of LaGrave's new $50,000 parish house. Three former pastors, an assistant pastor, and a pastor-elect had participated in the event. Highlights of the program were addresses by Rev. Bel, who had just left the church, and Dr. E. Masselink, who would be coming to serve as LaGrave's seventh pastor in March. Brief addresses were also given by Rev. Henry Beets and Rev. William Stuart, former pastors. The keys to the building were presented to Rev. VanderWerp, vice president of the consistory, who spoke on behalf of the congregation. Dr. E. S. Sevensma, chairman, and committee members Erwin L. Haan, Garret Heyns, Bert Vandenberg, and A. VanSledright had made all the arrangements.

RECYCLING THE 1930s' WAY

To earn money for such things as Children's Retreat and the fund for the new parish house, the South End Circle prepared noontime chicken dinners in the church basement for businessmen. On one occasion, there was such a large attendance that the women ran out of dishes. Someone suggested carrying the dirty dishes in dish pans to the parsonage and washing them quickly with the hot water from the bathtub. Tress Pastoor and Ruth Vanden-Berg chuckled as they reminisced about "doing dishes in the bathtub" and what fun the ladies had working on those projects.

FINANCIAL REPORT OF GENERAL TREASURER
Fiscal Year Ended December 1, 1937

Balance on Hand, December 1, 1936 .... $ 943.74

Receipts

Pledges	$7,587.16	
Open Collections	3,256.55	
Special Collections	348.95	11,192.66
		$12,136.40

Disbursements

Pastor's Salary	$3,300.00	
Janitor's Salary	1,200.00	
Choir Director's Salary	273.00	
Organist's Salary	312.00	
New Auto for Pastor	817.90	
50th Anniversary Expense	382.90	
Supplies	180.63	
Utilities	394.64	
Charity	1,460.46	
Printing and Stationery	384.57	
Fuel	427.94	
Repairs	360.40	
Red Cross Flood Relief	102.52	
American Federation Y. M. S.	25.00	
G. R. Minister's Association	5.00	
Insurance	282.15	
Kent County Poor Farm	16.08	
Advertising	30.00	
Pulpit Supply	120.00	
Calvin College and Seminary	762.00	
Classical Expense	68.58	
Emeritus Fund	406.40	
Radio Services	38.10	
Student Fund	101.60	
Synodical Expense	101.60	
New Parish House Expense	36.77	
Holland Home—Thanksgiving Collection	111.82	11,702.06
Balance on hand, December 1, 1937		$ 434.34

* * *

Building Fund

Balance on Hand, December 1, 1936 .... none

Receipts

Gifts	$ 836.06	
Bank Interest	5.02	$ 841.08
		$ 841.08
Disbursements		none
Balance on Hand, December 1, 1937		$ 841.08

LEO B. DICE, *General Treasurer.*

[7]

REPORT OF MISSION FUNDS
Fiscal Year Ending November 30, 1937

Receipts

Pledges —		
1st Quarter	$1,022.20	
2nd Quarter	1,032.95	
3rd Quarter	917.60	
4th Quarter	1,253.06	$ 4,225.81
Catechism		94.30
Ladies Missionary Society		100.00
Sunday School		150.00
Central Ladies Aid—for Red Cross		25.00
Special Collection—Pentecost		96.59
Special Collection—Other		366.98
Balance on Hand, December 1, 1936		43.32
		$ 5,102.00

Disbursements

Dr. Lee S. Huizenga	$2,400.00	
Indian and China Mission	739.00	
City of G. R. Missions	204.00	
Jewish Missions	165.50	
Church Extension	254.80	
Church Subsidy	418.00	
South American Missions	28.60	
Hoboken Seaman's Home	28.60	
Church Aid	102.00	
Emergency Fund	75.00	
Bethesda Sanatorium	56.25	
Denver Poor	37.50	
Gideons	18.75	
Faith, Prayer, and Tract League	18.75	
American Bible Society	18.75	
Christian High School	87.50	
Christian Education	352.50	
Mission Festival	10.00	
Hebrew Christian Alliance of America	10.00	
Second Christian Ref. Church of Denver	50.00	
Board of Missions—Map of Indian Field	1.50	
Red Cross	25.00	$ 5,102.00
Balance on Hand		none

BASTIAN BLOK, *Treasurer.*

[8]

Even in hard times, LaGrave was faithful in its giving.

The parish house became an instant beehive. The first people to be married in it were Helen Pylman and Henry Boss. The second wedding held in the lounge was a double one. Rev. Bel returned from Chicago to perform the ceremony for two of his daughters, Helen and Stella, on June 20, 1940.

There were criticisms. It was an extravagance that the first Christian Reformed church to erect a parish house should build the facility with room to feed three hundred people and a kitchen complete with restaurant equipment — including steam cookers and coffee urns! The money might better have been used for missions! Years later, however, other Christian Reformed churches would build even finer parish house facilities.

After Chicago, Herman Bel would serve one more church — the Christian Reformed Church in Dorr, Michigan. While there, he suffered a heart attack and was forced to retire in 1957. His years of service were fruitful; his term of service at LaGrave signally blessed. He had served during the depression years. Yet, as he and the congregation discovered together, hardships often bring such spiritual rewards as prosperity can seldom furnish. It was a time when the LaGrave people, individually and together, had to call upon their spiritual resources. Doing this, they discovered God's grace anew. Thus, a time of want became a time of plenty. Mutual care and concern came to a greater expression. Members became more aware of each other and of each other's needs. In retrospect, Pieter Troon said of the depression, "I wouldn't want to go through it again, but I wouldn't have missed it either." And so, with Rev. Bel in the pulpit, the threadbare thirties were rich indeed.

DR. AND MRS. EDWARD J. MASSELINK 1940–1944

Characterized by Mrs. Masselink as "tough years," LaGrave mourns three war dead; a new parish house facilitates Christian hospitality

Chapter 15

WAR AND (PEACE)

In 1939, Germany invaded Poland. France and Great Britain declared war. Italy overran Albania. Russia attacked Finland. But in America, "Gone with the Wind" (GWTW) and "The Wizard of Oz" were movies which, although out of bounds for Christian Reformed people, received more attention than the gathering worldwide storm. Indeed, young Americans on campuses were so busy swallowing goldfish and putting nickels in jukeboxes to hear Wee Bonnie Baker ("Oh, Johnny, Oh") that they couldn't be bothered with what was going on a whole ocean away. Neither could the guns of war be heard at 107 LaGrave. However, Rev. Bel did pray for peace abroad and so did the congregation.

In 1940, the world moved closer to the brink. There were those whose greatest concern was President Roosevelt's appointment of Myron Taylor as his personal ambassador to the Pope, and Fulton Sheen, Roman Catholic priest, who was gathering a following on radio. There were those of Dutch descent who, remembering the Spanish Inquisition and the persecution of their forebearers, were still sensitive to such things. However, what awakened the Dutch, and others, to the approaching brink, was the German conquest of the Netherlands. It brought Hitler a lot closer than

an ocean away. *Time* reported:

> Crucial in the first hours of the huge Blitzkrieg in Holland was the parachutists' battle for Rotterdam. The Dutch rallied fiercely, but in a few days it was all over. Resolute Queen Wilhelmina fled to London.

Pastor Martin Niemoller, German hero of World War I and an ex-submarine commander — but now in a concentration camp on half rations, double labor, rock breaking, road building, and ditch digging — had said, "Not you, Herr Hitler, but God is my Führer." Would LaGrave's freedom of worship be threatened too? President Roosevelt, running for a third term, reassured the country: "I have said it before, but I shall say it again and again and again — your boys are not going to be sent into any foreign war." It was less reassuring, however, when, after defeating Wendell Wilkie in the election, he asked congress for 1.8 billion dollars to finance the greatest peacetime military buildup in U.S. history.

It was in this world context that the Lord sent one of his soldiers, Rev. Herman Bel, LaGrave's pastor, to Chicago Illinois; and enlisted another to take Rev. Bel's place at LaGrave. In 1915, daughter Burton Heights had called mother LaGrave's pastor, Rev. H. Beets. Now, a quarter of a century

later, mother LaGrave called daughter Burton Heights's pastor, Dr. Edward Masselink. He arrived in March 1940. Turnabout was fair play.

Edward Masselink was born in 1901 in Meservey, Iowa, near Mason City. His father, Gerrit H., had come to America from Graafschap, Bentheim, Germany, in 1881. His mother, Etta, (nee Poets) followed a year later. Father and mother married and lived in Reeman, Michigan, where Mr. Masselink served as the first elder of the new church in that town. Soon they moved to take up farming in Meservey, Iowa. There was a Christian Reformed Church there which disbanded a year after Edward was born. That there is no casual connection between these two events is certain, in view of how the future would reveal Edward as a builder, not a disbander of churches. In 1902, the family moved to Edgerton, Minnesota. Edward was one of nine children — seven boys and two girls. Of the boys, four (Edward, William, John, and George) would become ministers.

The proverbial one-room country schoolhouse started Edward on a long educational journey that would take him to Baxter Christian School, Grand Rapids, Michigan (1914); Calvin College (1915); Grundy College, Grundy Center, Iowa (1916); the University of Chicago, Illinois (1919); Princeton Theological Seminary, New Jersey (1922); and Southern Baptist Seminary, Louisville, Kentucky (1926) where he earned a Ph.D. degree. In 1927, he became pastor of the Trinity Reformed Church, and in 1929, he entered the Christian Reformed ministry at the Burton

In 1885, a terrible storm hit Reeman, Michigan. Fire from lightning destroyed the Masselink log cabin and barn. It killed one of their oxen. The other, badly burned, had to be destroyed. Rev. Henry Walkotten, father of Dr. Henry Walkotten (future chairman of the LaGrave building project), visited Dr. Masselink's parents. He saw their poverty and strongly recommended a move to Iowa and a new beginning. In the spring of 1892, Gerrit and Etta Masselink took Rev. Walkotten's advice and moved to Merservey.

Heights Church; both churches were in Grand Rapids, Michigan. He was a bachelor pastor, immensely popular, whose lot in life many matchmakers — both in and out of his church — sought to improve.

But it was not until 1939 that he would wed. The woman of his choice was Clazina Baker, daughter of Rev. Henry Baker. After a year of marriage, Dr. Masselink accepted the call to LaGrave. The Masselinks moved into the parsonage. It was an easy transfer because, as noted earlier, the houses were nearly identical. The Masselinks could almost hear the happy shouts of "the two Bels and the eight chimes" echoing from the walls. The cordial hospitality of the previous occupants soon became real. A little old lady appeared on the doorstep with the announcement

Call Letter

The Rev. _L. Masselink_
2050 Francis Avenue,
Grand Rapids Mich.

Grace, Mercy and Peace from God our Father and Jesus Christ our Lord.

The Consistory of the _Christian_ Reformed Church at _La Grave Avenue_ herewith has the honor and the pleasure to inform you, that from a previously made nomination of _three_ you, Rev. _L. Masselink_ have been chosen by _majority_ vote at a legal congregational meeting held on the _22d_ day of _January_ 19_40_ to be their Minister of the Word and of the Sacraments.

On behalf of said congregation we therefore extend to you the call, and come to you with the urgent request: "Come over and help us."

The labors that we expect of you—should it please God to send you to us—are: Preaching twice on the Lord's Day, attending to catechetical instruction, to family visiting and calling on the sick, and furthermore of all things that pertain to the work of a faithful and diligent servant of the Lord, all these agreeably to the Word of God, as interpreted by our Forms of Unity and the Church Order of Dordrecht, as amended by the rules of our Church.

Convinced that the laborer is worthy of his hire, and to encourage you in the discharge of your duties, and to free you from all worldly cares and avocations while you are dispensing spiritual blessings to us, we, the Elders and Deacons of the _La Grave Avenue_ _Christian_ Reformed Church do promise and oblige ourselves to pay you the sum of _Three thousand_ dollars, in _monthly_ payments, yearly, and every year as long as you continue the Minister of this Church, together with free use of parsonage, the free use of a telephone _____

Moreover, we promise free transportation of yourself, your family and your belongings (under provisions as stipulated in Articles 5, 10 and 11 of our Church Order.)

Now, dear Reverend Brother, may the King of His Church so impress this call upon your heart and give you light, that you may arrive at a decision that is pleasing to Him and if possible for us mutually gratifying.

Done in Consistory, this _twenty second_ day of _January_ 19_40_ and subscribed with our names.

The Consistory of the _Christian_ Reformed Church of _La Grave Avenue_

Deacons:	Elders:
Arthur Van Sledright	W. J. Vanderwerf
John K. Huizinga	Henderik V. Laане
Erwin L. Haan	John Yonkman
Bert Vandenberg	Dr. J. Bruinsma
Albert Nieboer	G. J. Rooks
Bastian t Blok	C. J. Van Porpumelen
Jay DeBoer	Lаммe Lерра
Arthur Franken	John Kos

R. L. Veenstra →Counselor.

WM. B. EERDMANS PUBLISHING CO., GRAND RAPIDS, MICH.

Dr. Edward J. Masselink

that she always had her Sunday dinners with the Bels — an arrangement that had been very satisfactory for her.

The *Grand Rapids Press* announced the installation service of Dr. Edward Masselink on March 31, 1940, as being a unique event, inasmuch as it would involve four brothers. Rev. W. D. VanderWerp, LaGrave's assistant pastor, would be the liturgist. Rev. William Masselink of the Alpine Avenue Christian Reformed Church, would preach the sermon. Rev. John Masselink of Kalamazoo, Michigan, would charge the pastor. Rev. George Masselink of the Presbyterian Church of Stockbridge, Michigan, would read scripture. LaGrave's third pastor, Rev. Henry Beets, was slated to charge the congregation, and Rev. William Stuart, LaGrave's fourth pastor, would pronounce the benediction. The *Press* further informed its readers that the new minister would preach his inaugural sermon in the evening. The previous Wednesday, the congregation had honored the pastor and his wife at a reception. The welcome party for the new minister coincided with the opening of the new parish house.

Rev. Bel had worked long and hard to replace the old former parsonage with a more adequate and badly needed facility. The congregation had wisely built when the depression prices were still in effect. Even so, it was a considerable financial undertaking. Conditioned by the depression, and still remembering the Mr. Jenks's affair, the members were especially sensitive to debt. Ladies

groups worried about paying for the furnishings. The debt sparked an excitement and enthusiasm that one sees only in new churches. With a singleness of purpose, all set about to cancel it out. The congregation drew together. The congregation pulled together.

Church basements were the usual place for meetings in those days. A parish house was something else! Thus, LaGrave was flooded with requests for weddings, receptions, luncheons, and celebrations of all kinds. The women of the congregation worked hard to service a variety of functions and affairs. The Central Ladies Aid peeled carloads of potatoes. The other women's auxiliaries were organized for serving assignments. There was no paid caterer. Tireless, and a wizard with food, Mrs. Wesley Karsies deserved plaudits. So did Mrs. Fred Bosma, Mrs. Martin Kalsbeek, Mrs. Martin VerMerris, and many more. Besides making themselves available for other organizations, the LaGrave women sponsored their own bazaars, and other activities, in order to generate funds for debt reduction.

An altogether different result of the appearance of the parish house was the increase in societies and society activities. The Senior Fellowship, spear-headed by Mr. William B. Eerdmans, with its meetings in the church lounge, became a well attended activity. Mr. Eerdmans also served as a program committee of one, bringing in excellent speakers. Alternating with this Tuesday evening activity was the Mr. and Mrs. Club. With competence and congeniality, Florence Hekman served as its first president.

The new pastor and his wife came to LaGrave with high anticipation and resolve to work as a team. Together, they plunged into a heavy schedule of calling in order to get to know each and all.

The plan for the pastor and his wife to call on all the members as soon as possible was interrupted by the birth of their first child, Ellen, July 10, 1940. This was the first birth in the LaGrave parsonage since that of Dr. W. Clarence Beets in 1901. Nineteen months later, Ellen was joined by a baby sister, Carolyn, born Feb. 25, 1942.

from "The Masselinks Came to LaGrave"
by Clazina Masselink

Long before jogging was fashionable, the pastor and his wife, depending on who had the car, were seen establishing track records between the parsonage at 616 College and the church at 107 LaGrave. Ladies Auxiliaries and catechism classes kept them moving. Rev. VanderWerp, the assistant pastor, and Dr. Masselink and his wife, taught catechism on Wednesday afternoons and evenings. There were classes on Monday evenings and Sunday mornings also. Rev. VanderWerp also made calls on shut-ins. While making his calls, he would leave his wife at the parsonage, for she was senile and could not be left alone.

The downtown churches took turns broadcasting their services over a local station. LaGrave joined in, taking its turn, and was once again criticized for suspicious ecumenicalism. It was, however, in the style of Henry Beets who had pioneered in this regard and set an example. The women of LaGrave belonged to the Inter-Denominational Missionary Union and participated in the World Day of Prayer. Protests against this sort of activity appeared, on occasion, in the pages of *The Banner.*

There were some questions regarding LaGrave that had some basis. In the earlier years, the percentage of its children attending Christian Schools, although high, was not as high as in other Christian Reformed churches. It would rise perceptibly as time went on. Community involvement was higher. The appearance of LaGrave names in newspapers in connection with community social events, was sometimes misinterpreted. Some felt that LaGrave had less regard for the *Church Order* and for liturgical forms which were denominationally constructed and recommended. There were reassurances, however, for those who wondered. When the Inter-Denominational Missionary Union became the World Council of Church Women, LaGrave withdrew. Meanwhile, Dr. Masselink's reputation was considerable, as he was held in high esteem and considered both sound and well informed. It was for this reason that the denomination made demands on his time; but finding himself in an exceedingly busy pastorate, he had little time to spare. Nevertheless, Dr. Masselink was willing to extend and expend himself — and did.

The consistory, on the other hand, was not as considerate as it would become in later years. The rule for vacation time after only a full year of serv-

H. Daane and G. J. Rooks were designated as honorary elders, for want of better liturgical nomenclature. Whereas other elders served three-year terms, honorary elders were kept in consistory in order that the church might profit from their wisdom and advice. In later years, Mr. George VanWesep would function in that same capacity.

ice was strictly observed. In 1941, the Home Mission Board requested the use of LaGrave's pastor for an experiment in evangelism called "Preaching Missions." Dr. George Goris and Dr. Masselink had been chosen to conduct a series of services in Whitinsville, Massachusetts, and Midland Park, New Jersey. The consistory consented, providing Dr. Masselink considered it his vacation. The same policy prevailed with respect to the newly purchased Camp Roger. Dr. Masselink had been a member of the board which purchased the site and brought the camp into being. He was granted a brief time as counselor, but, again, as part of his vacation. Thus did LaGrave's pastor spend his vacation "capturing the flag" and becoming the confidant of boys.

Work at LaGrave seemed to proliferate. The parish house had enlarged the work and increased the scope. The war added much more to the pastor's tasks. Young men leaving for service had to be visited. By 1944, over ninety of LaGrave's sons were in the Armed Forces.* Dr. John Troon was one of them. His father, Pieter, had died just before he left for overseas duty. Dr. Masselink wanted to stay in touch with all of them. But how?

He found the answer in a dusty forgotten corner of the church basement. It was Providence! There he stumbled on an antiquated mimeograph machine. No one could remember how it got there, or whose it was. The pastor took it home. After cleaning, repairing, and oiling the machine, Dr. Masselink made space for it in a corner of his study. A monthly letter was mimeographed and mailed, personalized with brief comments written in long hand by the pastor. Soon, return letters began to come, requiring a reference file for ready access before the next month's mailing. It was a huge task, but a necessary one. It all happened in the days before LaGrave had a church office, a secretary, and an expense account. Dr. and Mrs. Masselink bought a lot of stamps. Mean-

*See Addendum

ABOUT THE SERVICEMEN

Most of the draftees were to report to Union Station on Ionia Avenue. If it was at all possible, I accompanied my husband to see them off. Those goodbye scenes at the station will stay with me — crowded — noisy — clusters of families, red-eyed, the departing servicemen with infants on their arms, small groups with heads bowed in prayer, sweethearts' parting embraces, a young girl running along the tracks as the train was leaving to have a last glimpse of the one she loved.

Some received orders to report directly to Detroit. I remember visits to the parsonage of worried husbands with requests for special pastoral care. There was concern for material welfare as well. I believe a serviceman's pay was $65 a month.

Several families had more than one star in their window.

One by one we had seen our young men leave us — our prime young men — and our doctors. One of these young men was Warren Pylman, a member of the choir. It was his turn to leave. Ed asked him to sing one last song for us. He sang, *"His Eye Is On The Sparrow." It was a very emotional time.*

How straight and tall and handsome they all looked when they came home on leave, often just before going overseas. I remember when John Dekker returned long enough to marry his sweetheart, Viola Reminga. When the minister asked, "Do you take this woman to be your lawful wedded wife?" he replied crisply, "I do, sir."

One of the real concerns for our young servicemen was that they would be tempted to marry girls who did not share their faith. I can think of two specific cases where the young women were converted by following a plan of daily reading the same scripture portion as their future spouse, obeying the urging of their pastor.

A wartime ministry had unusual challenges. The gas rationing, the tensions, the separated families, the sugar shortages. When one wanted to entertain, all of it required perhaps a little more ingenuity than in peacetime.

from: "Memoirs"
by Clazina Masselink

---

while, the servicemen were remembered each Sunday in prayer. Then, too, the Ladies Missionary Society held a service of prayer each month for the boys in uniform. Mrs. Anne Scherphorn was one of its presidents during this period of time. All the mothers and wives attended faithfully.

Today the bulletins of the church are a major weekly undertaking. The routine was a little different in the days of Dr. Masselink. The members called in their announcements to the parsonage. Seymour Swets called in the anthems. On Thursday mornings, Dr. Masselink "wrote it up" and Mr. G. J. Rooks took it to the Etheridge printing shop.

Not only did LaGrave have many members in the armed services, but there were others who had moved to Detroit and environs to find war work. The Ypsilanti Chapel sprang up. LaGrave's ninth pastor, serving in Dearborn, Michigan, in his first charge, preached frequently for this group, thus meeting some who were members of LaGrave. To do so, he had to use up some of his valuable rationing stamps. LaGrave's members, and the rest of the country as well, were not accustomed to wartime sacrifice. WPB Directive No. 1 to OPA, January 1942, instituting rationing, came as a shock! Suddenly, U.S. citizens were stuck with a mess of little books and stamps that limited the food and gas they could buy. The instructions were incomprehensible.

RATIONING STAMPS INSTRUCTIONS

All RED and BLUE stamps in War Ration Book 4 are WORTH 10 POINTS EACH. RED and BLUE TOKENS are WORTH 1 POINT EACH. RED and BLUE TOKENS are used to make CHANGE for RED and BLUE stamps only when purchase is made. IMPORTANT. POINT VALUES of BROWN and GREEN STAMPS are NOT changed.

No. 388754 EH

4

UNITED STATES OF AMERICA
OFFICE OF PRICE ADMINISTRATION

WAR RATION BOOK FOUR

Issued to *Bertha H. Dykstra*

(Print first, middle, and last names)

Complete address *1818 Kalamazoo Ave. S.E.*

Grand Rapids, Michigan.

READ BEFORE SIGNING

In accepting this book, I recognize that it remains the property of the United States Government. I will use it only in the manner and for the purposes authorized by the Office of Price Administration.

Void if Altered

(Signature)

It is a criminal offense to violate rationing regulations.

OPA Form R-145

16—35670-1

Gasoline rationing was especially unpopular. "A" cards limited drivers to a mere three gallons a week. Ministers received "C" cards, entitling them to the maximum. Some LaGrave members, living a distance away and having only "A" cards, began limiting their church attendance at LaGrave, choosing to go to neighborhood churches. Many found it impossible to come twice on Sunday.

Housewives paid grocers in stamps, as well as cash. Because a pound of butter cost sixteen points, and margarine only four, many switched. With steak at twelve points a pound, many turned to hamburger at seven points. Baby food (4½ oz. jar) was a merciful one point. However, compared to what was going on far away — rationing, brownouts (cutting down on the electricity), watching for enemy planes that never came — making do with a scarcity of hairpins and glass eyes was trivia. The fact was that in crucial 1943, the U.S. living standard was one-sixth higher than it was in 1939. Business generally prospered. LaGrave members were successfully whittling down the debt on the parish house. Dr. John Troon, home on leave, found life essentially unchanged. His son and daughter, Jack and Karen, were growing. Jack had just entered Christian High; Karen was enrolled at Oakdale Christian School. His wife was doing her war bit at Butterworth Hospital, along with other doctors' wives. Together with the whole nation, she listened to Edward R. Murrow's mesmerizing voice from overseas, "This is London," and read the papers reporting the actions of draft boards and rationing stamp scandals. She also read *The*

Banner and its reports on the activities of the chaplains and camp pastors. The Christian Reformed church, it seemed, was concerned for its young men, scattered worldwide.

Setting out with a healthy balance of $300 for the year 1941, the consistory launched the congregation into the new year with prayer and a proposed budget.

PROPOSED GENERAL BUDGET FOR 1942

Pastor's Salary	$ 3,200.00
Assistant Pastor's Salary	600.00
Custodian's Salary	1,320.00
Choir Director	364.00
Organist	364.00
Pulpit Supply	125.00
Charity	2,000.00
Printing and Stationery	500.00
Utilities	1,500.00
Insurance	300.00
Maintenance and Repairs	500.00
Supplies	200.00
Parking Lot	72.00
Calvin College and Seminary	892.50
Ministers' Pension and Relief	408.00
Classical Expenses	51.00
Synodical Expenses	25.50
Synodical Radio	63.75
Bethesda Sanatorium	50.00
Christian Schools	500.00
Christian High School	500.00
Contingent Fund	500.00
Total	$14,035.75

PROPOSED MISSION BUDGET FOR 1942

Dr. Huizenga's Salary	$2,400.00
Indian Missions	943.50
China Missions	239.70
Sudan Missions	81.60
Church Help	191.25
Church Extension	382.50
Fund for Needy Churches	573.75
Jewish Missions	145.35
City Missions	255.00
South American Mission	63.75
Hoboken Seamen's Home	25.00
Gideons	25.00
Faith, Prayer & Tract League	25.00
American Bible Society	25.00
League of Evangelical Students	10.00
Ann Arbor	76.50
Contingent Fund	100.00
Total	$5,562.90

Society life was flourishing. The new parish house was wonderful. Activities centered around:

Central Ladies Aid: Mrs. W. Stuart, President
South End Ladies Aid: Mrs. E. Gaikema,
                                            President
Esther Circle: Mrs. E. Haan, President
Ladies Missionary Society: Mrs. J.F. Stuit,
                                            President
Brotherhood: Professor A.J. Rooks,
                                            President
Business Girls Club: Mrs. R. VanderWilt,
                                            President
Senior Fellowship Club: Mr. W.B. Eerdmans,
                                            President
Mr. and Mrs. Club: Mr. R. Brander, President
Boys Club: H. VerMerris, R. Brander,
                        A.C. Kinkema — Sponsors
Young Mens Society: E. VerMerris, President
Girls Club: Mrs. P. Gezon, Sponsor

In their round of visits, Dr. and Mrs. Masselink met Mrs. Maris, a distinguished lady in her late seventies. She reminded them that she had been LaGrave's first organist. In all the years, however, she had not joined the church by a profession of her faith. She lived on Division Avenue above the Bear Wheel Alignment establishment, across the street and south of the old Post Office building. Grace Posthuma, LaGrave member, was her housekeeper and companion. A widow, Mrs. Maris never had children. On the stairway approaching her living quarters was a landing on which were placed a desk, chair, and filing cabinet. This was her "office." There were posted office hours for her tenants around town to pay their rent. She had been the first woman in town to obtain an automobile driver's license. Tooling

Anna M. Maris, on the occasion of her 80th birthday, February 28, 1940

down the avenue, she had been one of the town's Gibson Girls.

On a visit one day, Dr. Masselink mentioned the need of improving LaGrave's organ. It had given years of service and needed attention. Mrs. Maris responded by saying that the matter had been on her mind as well. In fact, she had entertained thoughts of contributing the sum of $12,000 for the purchase of a new instrument to be given in memory of her husband.

The Maris organ, as it came to be called, was installed. Its cost exceeded the original figure by quite a bit. The instrument was as large as could possibly be accommodated by the space available. The large pipes had to be stashed underneath the platform. It was a three-manual Aeolian-Skinner instrument. When it was dismantled years later (1959) and stored, it was discovered that one sixteen-foot base pipe under the flooring had never been connected. The two-manual Austin Organ, which it replaced, was sold to Calvin College where it is still in use.

At the dedication service of the organ, Mrs. Maris, though advanced in years, played the doxology. She insisted that Alyce Lantinga be seated beside her to help set the stops. Dr. C. Harold Einecke, organist at Park Congregational Church, came to give an organ recital on the Maris Memorial Organ.

Dr. Masselink took Mrs. Maris to hear several organs in town. Dr. C. Harold Einecke, organist at Park Congregational Church, was especially helpful. Mrs. Maris wanted an organ like "that one." He said to her, "Mrs. Maris, did you know that there is a stop on the organ named for you? — Unda Maris."

———————

One evening, at a meeting of the Senior Fellowship, Dr. Masselink asked Mrs. Maris if she would consent to play. "Only if you will sing a solo," was the reply. Dr. Masselink sang the solo as best he could. Those present listened as best they could. It was all for the cause.

from: "The Masselinks Came to LaGrave"
by Clazina Masselink

TO DEDICATE NEW ORGAN AT CHURCH WEDNESDAY NIGHT

Dedicatory services for the new Maris Memorial organ of the LaGrave Avenue Christian Reformed Church will be held Wednesday evening in the church auditorium. The organ is the gift of Mrs. A. M. Maris, first organist of the LaGrave Avenue church, in memory of her husband.

Mrs. Alyce Lantinga, organist of the church, will play the dedicatory service by request of the congregation. The church choir under direction of Prof. Seymour Swets will sing. The dedicatory address will be given by Rev. E.J. Masselink, pastor.

The organ is the last to be made or installed in the United States for the duration. G. Donald Harrison, president of the Aeolian Skinner Company of Boston, will be present at the dedication service with Walter Hardy, architect who installed the organ.

WEDNESDAY EVENING, MARCH THIRTY-FIRST
NINETEEN HUNDRED AND FORTY-THREE

The DEDICATION

▼

CALL TO WORSHIP

THE SCRIPTURE

THE PRESENTATION OF THE ORGAN

RECEPTION OF THE KEYS and RESPONSE by John Spalink, Chairman of the Building Committee

THE DOXOLOGY
(Sung by the congregation with Mrs. Maris at the console of the organ. The congregation will kindly rise).

DEDICATORY MESSAGE AND PRAYER....Rev. Edward J. Masselink

CONGREGATIONAL HYMN—"Beautiful Savior"—No. 373

THE CHOIR—"Behold Now, Praise the Lord!".............................*Titcomb*

▼

MARIS MEMORIAL ORGAN

This organ is a gift of Mrs. A. M. Maris to the LaGrave Avenue Christian Reformed Church in memory of her husband, Mr. Anthony Maris, who worshipped with her for many years in this church. Mrs. Maris was the first organist of the LaGrave Avenue Church when it was organized in 1887. At that time the church was meeting in the Powers building, and afterward in Luce's Hall, with Rev. J. Y. De Baun as minister. Since that time Mrs. Maris has been associated with this church, and both she and her husband were always deeply interested in its music. The gift of this organ as a memorial is a fitting perpetuation of that mutual interest, and is a fitting climax of many years of service in this church.

All too soon, from LaGrave's standpoint, Dr. Masselink received a call to serve as the pastor of the First Christian Reformed Church in Cicero, Illinois. The congregation wanted him to remain. Many spoke to him. Mr. William B. Eerdmans, a leader in the congregation, made an earnest plea as the congregation's spokesman. This made Dr. Masselink's decision all the more difficult, inasmuch as he felt led to accept the invitation to the Cicero church. It was during this time, while giving prayerful consideration to his call, that he went to visit Mrs. Maris again. He wished to speak to her about her status as an adherent, but not a confessing member of the church. He felt that she should take her stand for the Lord. The Holy Spirit had gone before him, as was evident by her reply. She said she had been having the same thought. She said, "If I don't come now, I never will."

Although it was wintertime, Mrs. Maris came to the consistory, desiring to make profession of faith. She did just that. She was over eighty years of age. Her public profession, before the congregation, took place after Dr. and Mrs. Masselink and children had left.

In 1950, having served in Cicero, Illinois, for six years, Dr. Masselink became the pastor of the Twelfth Street Christian Reformed Church of Grand Rapids. In 1955, he went to serve the Central Avenue Christian Reformed Church in Holland, Michigan. In 1962, he became the pastor of the Thirty-Sixth Street Christian Reformed Church in Wyoming, Michigan. During all these charges, he took a leadership role in the denomination as well. His scholarship was widely recognized, as was his gift — both as a speaker and writer.

LaGrave did not forget the Masselinks. When its eighth pastor — Dr. George Goris — left, Dr. Masselink's name was again placed in nomination; the Lord's plans, however, were otherwise. Nor did the Masselinks forget LaGrave, for they rejoined the LaGrave congregation when Dr. Masselink became an emeritus minister in 1966, retiring to write, study, preach, and serve as editor of *The Cynosure*. At this time, Dr. Masselink also became an associate pastor of LaGrave.

The years 1940—1944 were taxing and heavy for LaGrave and the whole country. For those years, the Lord provided the congregation with a man who, besides all his other talents, had the gift and the energy to stay in touch — amazingly — on a personal basis with all the sheep in the flock.

Many of these sheep were scattered because of the war. But wherever they were, at home or abroad, they heard from their pastor —

About the Gospel of Peace.

In September of 1944, on the 26th of that month, one of LaGrave's servicemen died. He was the son of James (LaGrave's chief usher) and Jean Dice. Dr. Masselink returned from Cicero, Illinois, to conduct the funeral. It was a sad day for the whole family of LaGrave. One of its many servicemen had fallen and would not return. Dr. Masselink addressed words of comfort to the family and prayed, as he had so often from LaGrave's pulpit, for peace.

Donald E. Dice was a Lieutenant in the United States Army, first member of LaGrave Church to give his life in the service of his country. He died in active duty near Warrenton, Georgia, while stationed at Shaw Field, Sumter, South Carolina, on September 26, 1944. ("Mail Call," November, 1944)

IN MEMORIAM
DONALD E. DICE
BORN DEC. 22, 1923
DIED SEPT. 26, 1944

Chapter 16

A FRIENDLY CHURCH

"When people visit a church and do not return, it is not necessarily because the doctrine is wrong, or the preaching poor, but because of the indifference shown the stranger."

"I have learned that the number one complaint about our churches is not our facilities, our programs, our sermons, but rather the coldness — the unfriendliness."

Both of the above quotations were uttered in England; the first by a rector and the second by a bishop. They are presented to show that the problem focused upon is not regional. When Paul told the Romans to practice hospitality and when he reminded Timothy to entertain strangers for, thereby, some have entertained angels unawares, the Lord, through His servant, was addressing the church everywhere, and of all ages. The King of the Church, when on this earth, put out His hand to all. He knew the loneliness that pervaded everywhere — not only in the wilderness, but in the cities where the population was concentrated.

From the very beginning, LaGrave, following Christ's example, tried to maintain an open door and an outstretched hand. In so doing, there have been some difficulties. In the earlier years, the Dutch people were clannish, as were all ethnic

groups made up of immigrants. Additionally, it was not the nature of the Hollander to be outgoing. When the Christian Reformed Church was born, these aforementioned dynamics were compounded. It was said by some that the members of the new denomination considered themselves purer Christians than those of the Reformed Church. They were viewed by others as "holier than thou." Stories were told about St. Peter tiptoeing as he whispered to a new arrival, a Methodist, "Don't disturb these Christian Reformed people," he shushed, "they think they're the only ones up here." Others told stories about how those Christian Reformed people, with their insistence on the Dutch language for worship services, truly believed that God was a Hollander. They were afraid of converting an "American" for — what in the world would they do with him?!

Obviously, many of these remarks and stories were unfair; they caricatured unkindly. Even so, the observations of the rector and bishop, descriptive of churches far away, applied in Grand Rapids as well.

As has already been observed, LaGrave and "English" came into being in the Christian Reformed denomination first of all not because of some great missionary impulse to reach out to others so much as an effort to keep the young people within the fold. They wanted as few as possible to follow Klaas and Anna Troon's son, Dirk, who left for Methodist pastures. However, once LaGrave was established, its outreach possibilities came more and more into focus. In this enlargement of its vision, it was greatly helped and encouraged by its first two pastors who, long since, had been acclimated to the American scene. Henry Beets, its third pastor, was especially instrumental in putting the Christian Reformed denomination on the map, so far as the non-Christian Reformed world was concerned. Out of concern for the young people, there was an effort to "bring them in," and once in, not to "freeze them out." When Pieter Troon transferred to LaGrave in 1900, it was the friendliness of the congregation and its pastor that drew him. Through the many years of his membership, until his death, Professor Jacob VandenBosch was Mr. Hospitality to one and all — never forgetting a name. Visitors seldom escaped without a hearty welcome from Dewey Blocksma. These typified a spirit that came to be identified with the Christian Reformed downtown church. Few services were without visitors. Not all were personally greeted. No church can claim a perfect record. But most left having been welcomed.

Dewey Blocksma

Professor Jacob VandenBosch

Efforts to invite others into the fellowship of the church took various forms. In the thirties and after, neighbors were called on in a mission outreach. Men were invited to a Sunday morning Bible class. Meanwhile, there was inreach as well as outreach. New ideas were encouraged in order to insure an open door and a friendly face.

Dr. Gerrit Stuart, psychiatrist, and brother of LaGrave's fourth pastor, had long been concerned with the needs of the alcoholic. He wondered, in particular, concerning the propriety of serving wine at communion services. There were those who had "a weakness." It was at his suggestion that the consistory substituted grape juice for wine, but not without considerable debate on the part of the elders and much criticism from other churches. There were those who felt that the substitution contained an implied criticism of the Lord himself who had obviously used the ferment of the grape in the institution of the sacrament. The change in policy — now the practice — was characteristic of LaGrave's concern for the individual.

That same concern surfaced in other ways. Most Christian Reformed churches were made up of communicant and baptized members. LaGrave recognized a third category, called "adherents." For many years, Mrs. Maris, whose gift to the church is recounted in the previous chapter, was of that status. There were others. There were some who, because of lodge membership, could not be members of the church. A denominational ruling forbade it. LaGrave was fully supportive of that stance. Nevertheless, there were many who charged LaGrave with "harboring Masons." The fact was that the church sought to be friendly towards those who, for their own reasons, attended LaGrave services regularly but preferred not to relinquish their membership in a secret society. Such persons, though not admitted to membership, nevertheless, experienced the LaGrave hand of fellowship and were listed as "adherents."

A similar spirit was evidenced towards those who were not persuaded on the matter of Christian education and, therefore, sent their children to the public school. LaGrave's pastors were all strong supporters of Christian education. Indeed, three of them left the LaGrave pulpit in order to enter this field. The article of the *Church Order* which stated that all consistories should support the cause of Christian education was fully honored by the LaGrave Church, both in sermons and with offerings. But what of such individual members whose convictions, before God, led them in another direction? In some Christian Reformed churches, such people were objects of discipline. In almost all, indeed, if not in all Christian Reformed churches, such individuals were not considered eligible to serve as elders or deacons. LaGrave refused to go to that extreme. Again, it made room for differences. While strongly upholding Christian education, it did not bar from service such individuals who manifested a different emphasis as long as they accepted the church's commitment to the Christian school. Such tolerance was again misinterpreted by some as liberalism. It wasn't. The tolerance, however, had wonderful by-products.

The congregational meetings were always cordial, in a day when some of them were harsh experiences in other places. The good spirit prevailing at congregational meetings was also manifested between pastors and flock. When LaGrave's ninth pastor received its call, and when he sought advice from its previous four ministers, each in his own way supported what LaGrave's eighth pastor said: "You'll never serve a better church." For this reason, so many members, who through the years had left LaGrave, returned and rejoined when it was possible — including former pastors and their families.

In England, where some are still aware of a pecking order, the janitor of the church, known as the "verger," enjoys great respectability. In the Netherlands travellers have explored churches escorted by well dressed gentlemen in high hats. Seemingly of exalted rank, they turned out to be the "kosters" (custodians). In the earlier years, LaGrave gave equal consideration to such persons, affording personal housing quarters for Mr. Lakke in the church house and incorporating roomy living quarters for the janitor and his wife on the upper level of the new parish house. Its first occupants, Sy and Mary VanderPloeg, set high standards in the care of a church building. Mr. B.

WHAT DO YOU DO
SUNDAYS
Between 12 and 1 P.M.

IT'S ONLY AN HOUR

The Men's Bible Class of the
Lagrave Ave. Christian Reformed Church
(109 Lagrave Avenue)

Meets in its Special Room
EVERY SUNDAY NOON
for Fellowship and Bible Study

You are Cordially Invited to Attend

This card was not only distributed in church, but also in various locations around the downtown area

Mr. James Dice, chief usher for 37 years

Diepstra, Mr. E. Brouwer, and others, preceded the VanderPloegs as custodians. Mr. and Mrs. Howard VerMerris, and others, succeeded them. The VanderPloegs, it was felt by a few, were overly clean — an opinion which they and the majority viewed as a compliment. But, although they placed cleanliness next to godliness, they did not place cleanliness before godliness, as some, making sinners who have mud on their souls unwelcome because they have mud on their soles. The VanderPloegs, et. al., were instructed to personify, as much as possible, the friendly character of the church to both members and visitors.

With an increasing impersonalization of society as a whole, the maintenance of LaGrave's friendly spirit towards those within and without was a concern. Increasing urbanization of life caused many to view their neighbors through the wrong end of their binoculars. The modern pace of life scarcely left time for giving others individual concern. The size of the church allowed too many to get lost in the crowd. In such a setting, it was easy to mandate committees with hospitality responsibilities which, in smaller churches, would simply be assumed as the task of each and all. Then, too, LaGrave's services had a relative formality about them, and some members — as in any large church — were less outgoing than others. Thus, very early in its history, LaGrave organized a corp of ushers in a day when only the "American"

churches had them. It was, again, something that was viewed with suspicion by some. Out of necessity, by the mid thirties, many churches had followed suit, for crowds everywhere were large and facilities not always adequate. Mr. James Dice served as chief usher for *thirty-seven* years. A grateful congregation gave him recognition for his dedication and faithfulness at a special reception. During his tenure, a service without him hardly seemed a LaGrave service. Church greeters were also appointed to receive guests and strangers and to make them feel welcome. Visitors signing the registry received cards, and worshippers took time to greet one another in the pews — such practices as these are still observed. Solomon wrote: "He that winneth souls is wise." A church, therefore, as well as the individual Christian, must be winsome.

Paul, writing to the Ephesians, observed that Christ who loved the church and gave Himself for it sought "to present it unto Himself a glorious church, not having spot or wrinkle, or any such thing — that it should be holy and without blemish." As with every church, LaGrave is not without its spots and wrinkles. In an attempt to be what it ought to be, LaGrave, among other things, has endeavored to practice hospitality; for in a century of grace it may often, unknowingly, have entertained angels.

DR. AND MRS. GEORGE GORIS 1945–1952

A war ends and a new pastor arrives in 1945 signalling years of peace, growth, and revitalized mission

Chapter 17

A WATERSHED YEAR

Karen Troon was about fifteen when Dr. and Mrs. Masselink left for Illinois. Her father, John, was still in the service. So was her brother, Jack. He had joined the Marines. Her mother was active in the South End Ladies Aid and still spent time at Butterworth Hospital, as did so many other doctors' wives. Adolescents were now being referred to as "teenagers." Girls like Karen, and others her age, were discovering a new profession called "baby-sitting."

With so many away in the service of their country, the younger boys were now the biggest men in town. With the depression over, they, as Karen, had some money in their pockets. They spent some of it where the whole gang got together for milk shakes while listening to the jukebox — "This Is the Army, Mr. Jones." "Der Fuehrer's Face," by Spike Jones, made them all laugh. Karen still liked "In the Mood," but her mother's favorite was "When the Lights Go on Again All Over the World."

Even with fathers and brothers in the service, the war seemed far away. There was an overwhelming urge for all girls to dress alike, and Karen was no exception. "Jitterbugging" was out, her mother said, and her daughter was an obedient girl. But Friday night slumber parties were

okay. While spending the night at Karen's, some of her friends read her new magazine, *Seventeen,* shrewdly published by some enterprising people who had discovered a new market. One evening they all looked at an article about a new singer in New York, Frank Sinatra, who made the girls swoon. It all seemed more exciting than catechism, for which Karen was generally prepared. Her homework for Christian High School was regularly completed also. She usually studied in the den. On the piano stood a picture of her father, John, and grandfather, Pieter. On another wall, there were large oval pictures of her great-grandparents, Klaas and Anna Troon. They looked very stern.

Such was the state of affairs in the Troon clan when Dr. and Mrs. George Goris came to LaGrave. George Goris was born in Lafayette, Indiana, on February 22, 1895. His father, Cornelius, as his father before him, was a dedicated Christian and worker in the church. A covenant God led young George in his father's footsteps. He made his profession of faith at the early age of fourteen years. Two pastors, H. M. VanderPloeg and D. H. Kromminga (who would later teach history at Calvin Seminary), together with his parents, were influential in George Goris's decision to seek his life's

Dr. George Goris

work in the Christian ministry.

George Goris graduated from Calvin College and Seminary in 1918. He married Jennie Brink of Kalamazoo, Michigan, with whom he shared forty-five years of a blessed union in the Lord. In 1919, he graduated from Princeton Seminary in New Jersey with a Th.M. degree, studying under the great Reformed theologians, Warfield, Vos, and Hodge. He majored in systematic theology. That same year, he began his ministry as pastor of the Eastmanville Christian Reformed Church, Michigan. His inaugural sermon, based on Galatians 4:14, was entitled "Glorying in the Cross." It was something he did all his days. He practiced what he preached. In 1927, he accepted the call to the Christian Reformed Church of Englewood, New Jersey. While there, he studied at Union Theological Seminary and Columbia University, from which he obtained his doctor of philosophy degree.

In 1930, Dr. Goris became pastor of the Fuller Avenue Christian Reformed Church, Grand Rapids, Michigan, where his eventual successor and ninth pastor of LaGrave was serving as accompanist for the Fuller Avenue male chorus, an organization that was receiving attention by giving concerts in surrounding towns. In 1941, Dr. Goris assumed pastoral duties at the Sherman Street Christian Reformed Church of Grand Rapids — a congregation whose birth LaGrave

had encouraged in 1907. A number of their charter members had come from LaGrave. In 1944, when Dr. E. Masselink strongly felt the call to Cicero, Illinois, he approached Dr. Goris regarding LaGrave, feeling that his qualifications and personality uniquely fitted the church's needs. Dr. Goris replied that such a call, if it came, would receive earnest and prayerful consideration.

That call to LaGrave materialized. It came in the Providence of God, quite apart from Dr. Masselink's intuition. Thus, in January of 1945, LaGrave received its eighth pastor. At the service of installation, Karen Troon was impressed with the new minister's dignified and striking appearance.

Dr. Henry Beets charged the new minister in his own characteristic way. He said:

Always speak a good word for the Lord Jesus Christ . . . And tell us a great deal about the Holy Spirit . . . And tell us about the Father. In His electing love. We are Calvinists. We love to hear the very word "Election." It was precious to the fathers and founders of LaGrave Avenue . . . And don't forget to tell us much of the Covenant of Grace and its promises. Especially when we think of the boys across. We need its consoling promises. And the next charge I lay upon you as an older preacher is, be much engaged in prayer. I happen to know an old preacher who was blessed wonderfully in his ministry. He happened to be a relative of mine. So I asked him one day, "To what do you ascribe the great blessedness on your labors?" He told me, "It is not that I am such an eloquent preacher. But, I attribute the blessing of God on my ministry to much private prayer. I will tell you, as my relative, what I do. Monday morning I am half an hour or so on my knees and I pray for every family living east of my parsonage; Tuesday morning for the families to the west; Wednesday for those north of my home; and Thursday morning for those to the south. It seems God's blessing rests upon my intercession." Brother Goris, use part of your time for prayer for us, in the various parts of the city . . . And I charge you further, do much personal work . . . As a rule the Lord does not convert people en masse, although He has done so occasionally. We have had such in the history of Eastern Avenue. But as a rule, handpicked fruit is the most lasting fruit. Especially among the young . . . And finally, keep us a real mission-minded church. LaGrave Avenue at present is the only congregation in our denomination supporting a missionary entirely on its own hook: Dr. Lee S. Huizenga. But he is a semi-captive. He is getting older. We need new recruits . . .

Alas, the same year Henry Beets spoke of Dr. Lee S. Huizenga, the great missionary to China died — a prisoner. He had worked in Jukao, Japan. But war clouds broke in 1937–1938. With Japan launching its offensive, it became necessary for him to leave the hospital where plans were already afoot for expansion and go to Shanghai.

The busy years in Shanghai were perhaps the happiest time in Dr. Huizenga's life because of the great opportunities they presented for practicing his skills as a doctor and preaching his sermons as a minister in a time of severe need. The work continued until the year of Pearl Harbor (1941) when his freedoms were restricted. Early in 1943, Dr. and Mrs. Lee S. Huizenga and their entire family, Dr. Ann, Eunice, Faith, Philip, Myrtle and her husband Rev. Oscar Wells and their daughter Shannon, had been interned in a concentration camp in Shanghai. In the fall of 1943, Dr. Ann Huizenga and the Wells family were released. They returned to the United States on the ship Gripsholm. Dr. Huizenga died on July 14, 1945, in a hospital just outside the Chapei Civil Assembly Center concentration camp in Shanghai, China. His daughter, Myrtle Wells, wrote:

> . . . one day the Lord took father by the hand and led him over Jordan. I don't know how or where, but I can see the Master place a crown of glory on father's head and smilingly say, "Well done, thou good and faithful servant."

The congregation mourned his passing.

REMEMBRANCES OF SHANGHAI

. . . Countless numbers had become victims of tuberculosis. A mat shed and a few cots were the humble beginnings of a 250 bed, well-equipped hospital. Jewish refugees sought advice and help, and they were not turned away. A mission and clinic were opened for their relief. The medical care of the patients at the Door of Hope was another responsibility put upon father's shoulders. Sick calls were a part of each day and many a night. Father's pen was never idle. Sermons were always in the making and often in demand. Articles were written and letters never forgotten. He was loved by all and was everyone's friend.

Myrtle Wells (daughter of Dr. Lee S. Huizenga)
from *The Banner,* November 2, 1945

DR. LEE S. HUIZENGA

"We recall his graduation from Calvin Seminary. He and one of his own classsmates, the Rev. L. J. Lamberts, spoke at the commencement exercises. His oration was a stirring plea for missions in South America. However, the Lord led his steps to China.

He and Dr. J. C. DeKorne were the first missionaries of our denomination to that great nation. They had the responsibility of selecting the location of our new mission field, subject to the approval of synod.

Being a physician, as well as a minister, Rev. Lee Huizenga took special training in the treatment of leprosy and conducted a clinic for these unfortunates. He wrote various articles concerning the treatment of this ancient and modern disease.

We remember the anxiety of his devoted wife that he might become a leper. But the Lord protected him from the contagion in a wonderful way. He entertained the ideal that his work might expand into a leprosarium of larger proportions, serving the unfortunates in the leper colony.

In Missions, he and his talented family lived and moved and had their being, serving the Lord with marvelous devotion. Many religious tracts and articles that he had written kept the cause of missions before us.

To have had him as our missionary is a great privilege for our congregation. The Lord called him to his eternal reward out of a Japanese prison camp.

We hope Mrs. Huizenga and children may soon all be in our midst to attend the memorial service for this noted missionary of the Lord."

Martin J. Wyngaarden

It is interesting to note that Shannon Wells, granddaughter of Dr. and Mrs. Lee S. Huizenga, was a member of the team on the space shuttle Discovery which was launched on June 16, 1985.

Roger Niewold made the final supreme sacrifice for his country on January 11, 1945, in Belgium. He died at his post of duty, while in action as a medical aide with the Third Army.

Roger was nineteen years old and had graduated from Central High School at the close of the first term in January 1944, entering the army in April and being sent overseas in October.

We share the sorrow of the bereaved family and commend them to the God of grace for comfort in their great loss.

> IN MEMORIAM
> ROGER J. NIEWOLD
> BORN JULY 26, 1926
> DIED JAN. 11, 1945

John Spalink Jr., was born in Muskegon, Michigan, January 17, 1922. He attended Ottawa Hills High School. He was active in sports and served as captain of the football team in his senior year, 1940, when he graduated. He entered service in February 1943. After three months of training at Camp Roberts, Calif., he went overseas. He was killed in action at Lupas, Luzon, Feb. 4, 1945, and was given a Christian burial with military honors in the cemetery at Santa Barbara, Luzon, Philippine Islands.

(Mail Call, May 1945, p. 3)

> IN MEMORIAM
> JOHN SPALINK JR.
> BORN JANUARY 17, 1922
> DIED FEBRUARY 4, 1945

LaGrave had not had a church paper since the appearance of *The Chronicle.* It was short-lived in the 1890s because of the depression of that decade. Now the church had a monthly again. Its name was *Mail Call.* It was born in order that the church could stay in touch with its servicemen. The editor-in-chief was Dr. M. J. Wyngaarden who was succeeded by Dr. Goris. A large staff assisted. *Mail Call* consisted of twenty-eight book size pages. The bulk of it was devoted to news concerning the servicemen. An editorial, a message from the pastor, and news from home completed its pages.

The March issue of 1945 contained news concerning LaGrave's second war casualty.

How many more would the war claim before it was over? Roger died one year after graduating from high school and less than three months after going overseas. Thirty days later, John Spalink Jr., would also make the supreme sacrifice.

Roger J. Niewold

John J. Spalink, Jr.

Along with those LaGrave sons who lost their lives in World War II, many others were exposed to great dangers, yet spared. News concerning them and their hazardous involvements appeared in LaGrave's *Mail Call* and also in the Grand Rapids's newspapers. One of them, Howard Dekker, completed thirty-five missions in the Eighth AAF over Europe, ten of them as a navigator.

MEDAL, PROMOTION ARRIVE TOGETHER

The past month has been a busy one for Lt. Howard R. Dekker, 23, whose wife, Louise, resides at 902 Dickinson St., SE.

Since the middle of May he has bagged one Nazi plane, won the air medal as a bombardier, completed training as a navigator and received his promotion to first lieutenant in the air corps, according to news pieced together from letters to his wife and news dispatches from his headquarters in the European theater of operations.

He shot down the enemy plane while on his 13th mission, and had completed 16 missions before the invasion started. He was slated for a week or two in a rest camp, but when the big push began all such leaves were cancelled.

The air medal was awarded to him for his first five missions, and his promotion came in mid-May. Since he arrived overseas in March he has been flying as bombardier on a Fortress with the Eighth A.A.F. while training as a navigator.

Lt. Dekker, a former student at Christian and Ottawa Hills high schools, entered the service in February, 1943, and received his bombardier's wings and commission at Roswell, N. M., in September.

He is the son of Mrs. Gertrude Dekker, 820 Alexander St., SE., and before his induction was engaged in book binding here.

Dr. Goris had hardly begun his ministry at LaGrave when, already, he had conducted two memorial services for sons of the congregation who had made the supreme sacrifice, bringing the total to three. Mercifully, there were no more. On May 8, 1945, VE (Victory in Europe) Day was celebrated. Franklin Delano Roosevelt had died one month before. Thus, the president did not experience the hour of triumph. Most Christian Reformed churches celebrated with an evening service. LaGrave held a well attended thanksgiving service at 3 P.M. in the afternoon. Karen Troon

Germans Announce:

SURRENDER!

Vol. CV No. 35,943   Copyright 1911   FRIDAY, APRIL 13, 1945   THREE CENTS In New York City

President Roosevelt Is Dead;
Truman Sworn In as Successor

Our Navy Radios:

JAPS QUIT

Tokyo Signals Its Ships

was there. She and her mother held hands. The *Grand Rapids Press,* on VE Day, featured a picture of a soldier's mother and his fiancee holding a telegram reporting their soldier's death in the Pacific area. It was a poignant reminder and emblematic of the fact that the war was only half finished. Thus, Grand Rapids greeted VE Day with more prayers then cheers. President Harry Truman officially proclaimed victory in Europe. Whistles blew. Church bells rang. And George Goris addressed his hearers on the words of II Samuel 7:18:

> Then David the king went in, and sat before Jehovah; and he said, "Who am I, O Lord Jehovah, and what is my house, that Thou hast brought me thus far?"

His sermon title and divisions, were:

> "Evaluating Our Great Blessings
>   As We Sit Before Jehovah"
>
> I. As we sit in wonder
> II. As we sit in humility

He told his hearers, grateful for war's end in Europe, that:

> It is only when we sit before Jehovah that we see things in their proper perspective.

He spoke of sitting in wonder.

> In wonder we saw the hand of God in history when, at Dunkirk, a mist hung over the channel at the crucial time and the Lord allowed 225,000 men to escape to England. The wonderful hand of God in history is no less clear from the fact that, at Pearl Harbor, God blinded the eyes of the Japanese, so that they did not see how destructive the blow had been, and how nearly our whole fleet in the Pacific had been wiped out.

He spoke of sitting in humility.

> David said, "Who am I?" It was an expression of deep unworthiness . . . Who are my people, my fellow Americans, that this great victory should come to us? We are deeply conscious of the profanity, the Sabbath desecration, filth and immorality present in our cities. We know we are spending far more for liquor, cigarettes, and cosmetics, than for education, religion, and missions. Though we acknowledge humbly the bravery of our men in uniform and the sacrifices of our servicemen and women, as well as the genius of our military leaders, we still exclaim with the Psalmist, "Who are we that Thou shouldest bring us thus far?"

It was an unforgettable service; the joy tempered with humility. LaGrave's pastor was a deeply spiritual man. The members sensed in him a Godly leader.

Easter Sunday also came in May of 1945. At 10 A.M., the sanctuary was already filled for the 10:30 service. Ushers wore pink carnations. A large basket of white lilies and white snapdragons decorated the chancel area. The choir processed down the aisle, singing "Christ the Lord Is Risen Today." The anthems, "He Arose," "Easter Hallelujah" (soloist: Ted Vanderveen), and "Resurrection Song" were fittingly rendered with Alyce Lantinga at the organ. Dr. Goris preached on the theme, "Seeking the Living Among the Dead," a message based on Luke 24:5, wherein he identified our Lord as among the living, and because of Him, also Donald E. Dice, Roger Niewold, and John Spalink Jr. — LaGrave's three fallen men in battle — they, too, were not dead.

The Easter service was described for the men overseas in *Mail Call*. In an attempt to convey a touch of home, an article was included entitled "The Hats," in which some twenty-seven appearing in the Easter service were described. Among them:

Mrs. G. Goris
  Black straw, black veil, with pussy willows scattered in it.

Mrs. H. DeBoer
  Small green hat and veil with a white flower.

Mrs. J. Hartger
  Black hat and veil with white flowers on top.

Mrs. A. Botting
  Dark brown tailored hat trimmed with a white ribbon.

Mrs. Leo Yonkers
  Large brown hat.

Mrs. Leo Dice
  A black sailor with a pink dotted veil.

Mrs. D. Etheridge
  If there was a hat, it was covered with pink and blue flowers.

Mrs. Bert Vandenberg
  A large navy blue.

Mrs. J. Dekker
  Black with a pretty pink rose on it.

Mrs. Wesley DeYoung
  A cute black hat with purple and pink flowers over her right ear.

> Dr. Goris's favorite text was from Isaiah 6: "In the year that King Uzziah died, I saw also the Lord sitting upon a throne, high and lifted up, and his train filled the temple."
>
> He had a keen sense of the holiness of God. The services he conducted were infused with the spirit of Isaiah 6.

LaGrave's men in service appreciated mail from home. Almost all responded when they were able; some with brief notes and some with pictures. Others wrote at great length and, indeed, with Christian eloquence. Henry Zylstra's description of a Sunday in the Philippines appeared in the June, 1945, *Mail Call* and touched the hearts of all:

If Jesus had come to this Island, He would have spoken in terms of ponies and carabacs, of the rice and cane, of fish ponds and palay, of bancas and paraos. The children would have been here for Him to speak to, and the many burdened and heavily laden, and the poor, oh, so many. The lepers, too, though now they are no longer shouting "Unclean," for they have been sent to the Leprosaria. Even the toll-gates are here, actually barring the roads, except now when trucks and tanks must have right-of-way, with who knows what Matthew, catering to priest and provincial governor, sitting at the receipt of custom. These are here, and there are temples in which devout women, chastened by sorrow, are praying earnestly for respite from the grief of war. And although there are no money changers in them, they are just outside the gate fighting their cocks for a gamble and exchanging seventy centavos in coin for a hundred in paper — and hoarding the silver to promote the business.

These He would have dispersed, and He would have spoken straight out, as among us only the righteous or the humble can, pointing His finger first at the priest in his glistening Packard, and then at the widow's child who wants the leavings from the soldier's plate. He would have spoken, I think, had He been on this Island then, not of the wheat and the chaff, but of the palay and the rice, and how by much beating this comes out polished from that, and fit for the Father's use. He would have been at the barrio well where the Artesian water springs, and the women are washing clothes, telling them of the other cleansing that goes beyond the raiment.

The enemy says the Filipinos are Orientals. Yes, but not Buddhists, Shintoists, or Moslems. They are Christians. Listen to the names, to the Christian culture, the heavenly music of the sound of them: Josephine, Eulogio, Visitacion, Coledonio, Natividad, Angela, and Gloria. There is that in these names and shows that His lines are gone out through all the earth. This leaven has quickened the whole loaf of the world.

My work has kept me from attending services today. But I thought of a prayer, written by a saint long ago: "Lord, we pray not for tranquility, nor that our tribulations may cease; we pray for Thy Spirit and Thy Love, that Thou grant us strength and grace to overcome adversity; through Jesus Christ, Amen."

Dr. Goris read these words to Karen Troon's catechism class. Karen was especially touched. She had been thinking about making profession of faith. She made it.

On August 6, 1945, the atom bomb was dropped on Hiroshima. It altered the world. It would affect all future history. Its implications were not immediately realized. President Harry Truman had made the mind-choking decision and, thereby, hastened VJ (Victory over Japan) Day, proclaimed for September 2. LaGrave's VJ service was held earlier, on the same evening that marked the news of Japan's surrender. The congregation sang:

Hallelujah! Hallelujah!
In His temple God be praised.
In the high and heavenly places
Be the sounding anthem raised.

The choir continued the exalted theme. It sang Handel's "Hallelujah Chorus." The service contained a strong missionary note. There was prayer that the clinic the late Dr. Lee S. Huizenga had hoped for would arise with the dawning of a new day in the Far East.

There were still more events that occurred in 1945 that would have great bearing on the future of LaGrave and the world. One of them was the rise of television as a means of entertainment. The Christian Reformed Church was still standing by its decisions of 1928. Card playing, dancing, and movies continued out of bounds. But the boys who were returning to their homes would not return to their former isolation. Having seen the larger world, they found it impossible to return to the restraints of their smaller one. Nor could those who had remained at home forever keep the world from coming into their living rooms and lives. They were discouraged from buying television sets. *The Banner* took a dim view of them. But a few were already buying — with Christian Reformed antennae (installed out of sight — in attics). The day would come when some dire predictions would be realized. But in the post war euphoria, not many were listening.

In October of 1945, LaGrave observed the semi-centennial of Rev. Henry Beets. Fifty years before, he had been ordained. The Lord had given him much to do; and Rev. Beets had sought to serve Him with all his might. The consistory requested him to observe his semi-centennial by preaching a sermon to the congregation. Rev. Beets preached on Psalm 71:17: "O God, Thou hast taught me from my youth, and hitherto I have declared Thy wondrous works." A reception and celebration was attended by LaGrave's members and many, many visitors.

And so, a most significant year came to a close. A watershed year. Dr. John Troon came home. His son, Jack, was still in Europe. They had met in Noordwyk Aan Zee, in the Netherlands, shortly after VE Day. It was the place where John's grandfather and Jack's great-grandfather, Klaas, had been born. They had seen a record of his birth in an old book in the town hall. Jack would come home the following year. By that time, Dr. John Troon, his wife, and daughter Karen would have moved to Ann Arbor, Michigan, where Dr. Troon would do cancer research for the university.

Dr. George Goris had come to LaGrave. Prior to his arrival, the memorial service for Donald E. Dice had taken place. Two more servicemen, Roger Niewold and John Spalink, Jr., had also offered their lives. Dr. Lee S. Huizenga had died. The war in Europe had ended, and the war in the East as well. LaGrave, together with the whole wide world, entered the atomic age. The walls of Christian Reformed isolation were crumbling. Servicemen were beginning to come home, looking the same, and yet different. Some expected a return to former ways. But everything had changed, and nothing would be the same again —

Except Jesus Christ, the same yesterday, today, and forever.

Chapter 18

"GO YE INTO ALL THE WORLD..."

It had been surprisingly easy for Dr. John Troon and his son, Jack, to readjust to civilian life. The small army of psychologists and counselors who stood ready to help returning servicemen through the crisis of reentry into civilian ranks received fewer calls than had been anticipated. Wacs and Waves (G.I. Janes), starved for feminine frills, retooled with ruffles and home permanents ("Which twin has the Toni?"). But housing was a problem.

Many ex-G.I.s enjoyed membership in the 52–20 Club, named for the unemployment pay of $20 for 52 weeks granted to discharged servicemen. By August, 1946, six million had drawn an average of two months' benefits. General Omar Bradley, Veterans' Administrator, began worrying that the boys would never go back to work. But they did. In fact, getting a job was less of a problem than many had anticipated.

Television was attacking radio (Milton Berle — Texaco Star Theater), but radio was still holding its own. (Fred Allen said Arthur Godfrey had a barefoot voice.) Meanwhile, something new — the singing commercial — was attacking both ("Chiquita Banana," "Pepsi-Cola Hits the Spot").

There was a baby boom, with thirty million of them born from 1942–1950. It brought "Howdy Doody Time" into millions of homes via television. It also prompted the "scandalous" Kinsey Report on "Sexual Behavior in the Human Male." Some were much more interested in pyramid clubs whereby, theoretically, everybody could make a bundle. John Troon, having moved with his family to Ann Arbor where he was driving a Kaiser-Fraser product, was much more interested in the promise of penicillin, a newly discovered drug.

Politically, it was a time wherein Senator Arthur Vandenberg of Grand Rapids, Michigan, dominated American foreign policy. His fellow citizen, Gerald Ford, left for congress where John F. Kennedy had preceded him by two years. Another congressman, Richard Nixon, was stalking Alger Hiss and communism. Truman defeated Dewey and "also rans" Thurmond and Wallace. Senator Bilbo wanted all blacks deported to Liberia. Warren Austin became the country's first delegate to the United Nations. The *Grand Rapids Press,* located a few blocks from LaGrave Church, reported all these happenings, and more. But it paid no attention to a young man dressed in a "zoot suit" (wide lapels; broad, baggy trousers narrowed at the ankles — all accompanied by a watch chain dangling to the knees) who placed an

ad for a planned local revival. Few came. Yet, before the decade would end, Billy Graham would draw 300 thousand into a Los Angeles tent where he would claim six thousand conversions.

This was the world in which Dr. Goris conducted his ministry at LaGrave and in which his life exemplified his teaching. He had long before demonstrated his feeling for people. In many Christian Reformed churches, family visitation generally included the questions: "Do you go to the theater?", "Do you play cards?", "Do you dance?" Dr. Goris's questions were always different. He would ask: "Can you look back on this year and see that you have grown spiritually?"

Dr. Goris had a background in psychology which was put to good use in both superintendent Reynolds Brander's Sunday school teachers' meetings and in sermons. He often mentioned the need for pastoral counseling, a somewhat revolutionary idea when he first promulgated it in the 1930s in Christian Reformed circles.

Thus, he championed the individual. If someone in the choir had never been offered a solo part, he encouraged the director to consider it, even if the voice in question was not the most talented. He emphasized psychology along with theology. Dr. Goris was a dignified man with a hearty laugh — and a huge heart. A man who, when offered a raise in the threadbare thirties, refused it, saying: "I wish to suffer with my people."

The denomination recognized his talents. Earlier in this narrative, it was reported that he was sent on preaching missions with his predecessor at LaGrave, Dr. E. Masselink. He stayed in touch with Dr. John Troon in Ann Arbor, who was now attending the campus chapel. Dr. Goris had formed it while pastor of the Fuller Avenue Christian Reformed Church. Indeed, he had served briefly as the first campus chaplain. LaGrave's ninth pastor, succeeding Dr. Goris, would later serve for a time as president of its governing body. One of LaGrave's future assistant pastors, Donald Postema, would assume and continue that work. While at Sherman Street Christian Reformed Church, Grand Rapids, Michigan, Dr. Goris took another leave of absence to serve as pastor to the servicemen in Washington D.C. While there, he organized the Christian Reformed Church of that city.

It was Dr. Goris's concern for neighborhood children that initiated a neighborhood evangelism program under the direction of Grace Wiers. She was a daughter of Mr. and Mrs. John Pleune,

members of LaGrave. Dr. Goris insisted that Mrs. Wiers attend the Reformed Bible Institute, now Reformed Bible College, for instruction in doctrine. With the help of the South End Ladies Aid, the Esther Circle, and the Business Girls Club, a class for neighborhood children and mothers was begun. Up to fifty children attended, while a dozen mothers came for coffee and Bible study. Mrs. Wiers visited the homes of these children and their mothers, encouraging them in family life and home care, but always as an evangelist, for that was uppermost in her mind. Not everyone in the congregation supported this neighborhood venture. Indeed, some were opposed to this effort, feeling a rescue mission a more appropriate setting. However, there was solid support from others. Mr. William B. Eerdmans contributed in a financial way. Wurzburg's Department Store always rented the Wm. B. Eerdmans Publishing Company's parking lot for the annual Santa Claus Parade. Mrs. Wiers received this money; both Mr. and Mrs. Eerdmans were solid supporters. Gordon Boer, Evangeline DePew, Grace Rooks, Johanna Scholten, and Marie VanBeek were always reliable helpers. This work was carried on for five years.

In 1952, LaGrave sent Mrs. Grace Wiers to work in the Wayland, Michigan, area. Rev. Henry Guikema, son-in-law of Mrs. Henry DeBoer (granddaughter of LaGrave's first pastor), was surveying the area ascertaining its mission potential. The Moline Christian Reformed Church, located

Mrs. Grace Wiers (MacNaughton), neighborhood evangelist for LaGrave Avenue Christian Reformed Church

in an area adjacent to Wayland, assisted in this work which resulted in the formation of the Wayland Christian Reformed Church, organized in 1957. In the absence of Mrs. Wiers, LaGrave's neighborhood work would continue, taking various forms.

The November 22, 1947, issue of the *Grand Rapids Press* included a picture of Rev. W. D. VanderWerp in recognition of his Golden Jubilee of ordination as a minister. Rev. VanderWerp had retired in 1937. He served his last church in New Era, Michigan. Upon moving to Grand Rapids, he was engaged to serve as assistant pastor at LaGrave, a position he filled under the Revs. H. Bel, E. Masselink, and G. Goris. The newspaper article said:

> In the same church in which he preached his first sermon 53 years ago as a seminarian, Rev. William D. VanderWerp Sunday will preach a sermon commemorating the fiftieth anniversary of his ordination as a minister in the Christian Reformed Church.
>
> Mr. VanderWerp, who has served the LaGrave Church as assistant pastor since 1937 and who was a member of the church in college and seminary days will be honored by the congregation at the 10:30 morning service there with Dr. George Goris, pastor, presiding and with his three children present: Rev. Donald W. VanderWerp, Plymouth Congregational Church, Barnevelt, Wisconsin; Rev. Marvin J. VanderWerp, Warren Park Christian Reformed Church, Chicago, Illinois; and Mrs. Richard VanderWilt of Grand Rapids, Michigan. Mrs. VanderWerp, the former Nellie Sarah Schram, to whom he was married July 1, 1897, died December 31, 1946 . . . The topic of his anniversary sermon will be "Remember the Works of the Lord."

Reverend W.D. VanderWerp

Church life at LaGrave prospered with Dr. Goris in the pulpit. Those who could not find seating in the sanctuary were accommodated in the parish house lounge. Small open windows allowed a limited view to a few who were seated there. But all could hear, aided by an "intercom." The voice of the preacher was a box on a wall which housed the speaker system.

With the blessing of the consistory, Dr. and Mrs. Goris left the parsonage on College, S.E., and moved into their own home on Somerset, N.E., built by LaGrave member Albert Bel, son of Rev. H. Bel. This happened in a day when few, if any, Christian Reformed parish ministers lived in their own houses.

The Goris home on Somerset, N.E.

On October 29, 1947, the Lord took to Himself Rev. Henry Beets who, by this time, had become something of an elder statesman in the denomination. His passing was mourned by the congregation, the community, and the whole denomination. An era had passed. His name would live on. Indeed, it was not long after his death that the LaGrave Henry Beets Mission Society came into being.

In later years, Dr. W. Clarence Beets, son of Rev. Beets, described the birth of the society bearing his father's name and wrote:

> The Henry Beets Mission Society is probably misnamed! It should really be the George Goris Mission Society. This organization was entirely the brainchild of the late Dr. George Goris who, very fortunately, was our pastor during the tremendously challenging period in Oriental history during the late 1940s. He recognized that frequently the "King's" business requires haste, and he had the audacity to formulate the highly unconventional method (for our church circles, at least) of sending in commando forces when and where needed, without recourse to burdensome red tape.

The LaGrave Henry Beets Mission Society arose out of developments in other parts of the world. Great Britain was losing its empire and, seeing the handwriting on the wall, gave Lord Louis Mountbatten complete authority in aiding and abetting the birth of India as an independent nation. However, a United India — the dream of Mahatma Gandhi — was not to be. Its principal groups of people, Hindus and Moslems, like oil and water, could not fuse. On August 15, 1947, they determined on separation — the Hindus going South, and the Moslems North. The result was upheaval and two countries — India and Pakistan. In the resultant migration, long columns of people moved past each other in opposite directions. India lost many of its leaders and professionals.

While this was taking place, Dr. John Vroon and his wife Theresa, members of LaGrave Church, were serving in the midst of this upheaval as missionaries for the United Presbyterian Church. Our denomination had not been able to place them. Because of widespread disease and the threat to public health in a most chaotic time, there was great need for hospitals in many areas, including Lahore, one of the major cities in West Pakistan. It was too large a project for any one church. Thus, Anglican, Methodist, Presbyterian Churches, the Salvation Army, and, ultimately, the LaGrave Christian Reformed Church joined together in founding the United Christian Hospital of LaHore, Pakistan. It was a non-denominational effort, and the Vroons lost no time in

> *John and Theresa Vroon were supported, in large part, by the Littlefield Presbyterian Church of Dearborn, Michigan. Convinced of the call to the mission field, they did not interpret their Mission Board's inability to support them as a door closed by Providence. La-Grave's ninth pastor, serving the Dearborn Christian Reformed Church, scheduled a collection for the Vroons, which was given to the Littlefield Presbyterian Church.*

seeking help. Specifically, they sought to enlist Dr. Ralph Blocksma and his wife Ruth, LaGrave members. This led to the formation of the Henry Beets Mission Society, an organization bypassing boards and other protocol for the direct support of the Blocksmas and their appearance on the scene, sooner rather than later.

Sunday, December 12, 1948, was communion Sunday. It was an ideal time for an offering for the new mission society. Permission was granted by the consistory. Publicity, some appropriate messages by Dr. Goris plus a live appearance by Ralph and Ruth Blocksma, whose presence inspired confidence, preceded the date of the offering. The estimated need was $8,500. The response exceeded the goal as $9,080.09 was received.

Soon the Blocksmas met the Vroons in Pakistan. Ralph was immediately pressed into service

Dr. and Mrs. John Vroon and children Anton, Judith, Ronald, and Marchiene

in the hospital, and Ruth became a teacher to the children of the missionaries. Their salary the first year was $2,040, plus $800 as allowances for the children, plus another $150 for language study. There was also a vacation allowance of $350, hardly an optional item because of the heat and the frequent bouts of sickness the family experienced from amoebic dysentery to malaria. Through all the experiences, they were buoyed and upheld by the prayers of the LaGrave congregation and supported through its Henry Beets Mission Society. Dr. Blocksma, in appreciation, wrote:

> . . . You don't know what a reputation the Henry Beets Mission Society and the LaGrave Church are developing in this part of the world. And in New York too (the seat of several large missionary boards). You have set a new mark in seizing the initiative in a new missionary venture and wholeheartedly getting behind it with money and personnel. Things like this just don't happen in this world. It is a situation without parallel.

Soon after the Blocksmas' arrival in Lahore, at Dr. Blocksma's request, the Henry Beets Mission Society sent Eunice Huizenga, daughter of Lee Huizenga, as a well-qualified laboratory technician. She trained the natives to carry on the laboratory work. Then Betty Herrema was sent to establish a school of nursing. Later, Frieda Ens (sister of Ruth Blocksma) became manager of the hospital. When she finished her term of duty, the Henry Beets Mission Society sent a LaGrave member, Marian Postema, to take her place. Still later, Miss Feenstra was appointed and financed to take over the laboratory. Thus did LaGrave, with Dr. Goris as its pastor, undertake mission projects — one in the neighborhood and another far away. Once before, LaGrave had undertaken the sole support of a missionary abroad — Dr. Lee S. Huizenga in China. Now, again, it did the same with Dr. Blocksma in Pakistan.

When one of the members of the Henry Beets Mission Society learned of the heat in Pakistan and that the anesthetic ether evaporated before it reached the patient's nostrils, he bought from Arthur Boot (a LaGrave member) a large air conditioner for the operative suite. I suppose it is still there. That was sent December 19, 1950.

Dr. W. Clarence Beets

Dr. and Mrs. Ralph Blocksma and children Dewey, Julia, and Mary

SURGEON'S SOLILOQUY

O Lord, mysterious are your ways, too wonderful to comprehend.
By what morphic miracle did your fingers mold my flesh
  in the Stygian darkness of my mother's womb?
Whence the cosmic Intelligence that set in rhythm the atoms of my DNA
  to match the whirling of celestial spheres?
Did not your Presence give initial thrust to that first heartbeat at that
  instant when the tree of vessels with its vital liquid burden was prepared?
What heavenly impulse led my microscopic brain to push out filaments of fragile
  nerve to join in perfect pattern of construction, so in embryonic night
  my eyes could perfectly be prepared for day?

Surely you ordained creation of that rich amniotic lake beneath my mother's heart,
  proclaimed it would not always be my home, timed that first breath miracle
  of air to find alveoli receptive to the revolutionary atmospheric change.
There in the endometrial flux with the primordial union of two cells
  did you bring forth a man-child ready for the father-mother love
  and his Creator's world of majesty and confusion.

O Lord how marvelous are your works, how impenetrable the ultimate mysteries
  of your universe, yet how massive the strivings of science
  to wrestle from You your secrets.
White-coated gnomes in forests of glass work with arrogant sophistry
  to solve vexing enigmas of created life - pursuing
  threads of investigation unravelling endlessly . . . . . .
It is enough for me, O Lord, to know
  that in love You created me deep in the pelvis of the mother you had chosen,
  that You knew my name from eternity before I found life in mitosis,
  that Your fingers shaped not only my nose and face and limbs, but
  my mind, my abilities, my destiny.

Your greatness is too marvelous for me to comprehend, your love like the cosmos
  in volume, your creative power beyond all comprehension . . .
You have saturated my mind with your grandeur, and I will praise you with
  all my being forever and forever.

Ralph Blocksma
September 17, 1984

In the latter half of the forties, Grand Rapids's first television station began operations. The city was cited as the first in the nation to fluoridate its public water system. Dr. Goris voted for Rev. Albert C. Keith to serve as president of the Grand Rapids Ministerial Association, the first black, locally or nationally, to serve in this interracial capacity. And Grand Rapids earned the tribute of "All-America City," the first award of its kind in the nation. Grand Rapids was a good place to live. LaGrave's members were doing their part to make it so.

All was not peace, however. Politically, a reform movement dedicated to clean government, with many Christian Reformed people making up its rank and file, fought the Frank McKay machine. Denominationally, too, there were tensions. A generational change was taking place in college and seminary, bringing ideological stress. There was the "seminary situation." There were new professors, some of whom were thought to deviate from old paths. More often, tensions were psychological rather than theological. Many of the debates, including those in the pages of *The Banner,* received the attention and concern of the general laity. But, if other churches and their memberships involved themselves more with these denominational issues, LaGrave and its pastor involved themselves less. The church at 107 LaGrave S.E., Grand Rapids, Michigan, seemed a step removed. And, yet, its denominational loyalty was not in doubt. The financial quotas were observed, and Dr. Goris continued to receive recognition, serving as an officer of synod and in other capacities such as vice president of the Calvin Board of Trustees and president of the publication committee of the denomination.

At the end of 1952, Dr. Goris received and accepted a call to the Hope Christian Reformed Church in Grandville, Michigan. The congregation bade him and Mrs. Goris a reluctant farewell. Their two sons, Donald and Howard, and their families, remained at LaGrave. In 1963, three years past the usual age of retirement, and after ten years of service in Grandville, the Lord translated George Goris, suddenly and unexpectedly, to the place prepared for him above. Rev. Emo VanHalsema wrote a fitting "In Memoriam" in the pages of *De Wachter.* Rev. William Masselink wrote a similar tribute and sketch of his life in *The Banner:*

> Dr. Goris was a lifelong leader in the Christian Reformed Church. He was thoroughly ground-ed in the faith, extensively educated to meet all the academic qualifications, well balanced in his approach to church problems, a gifted preacher, a highly cultured soul, and all this was related to a humble, pious, God-fearing character. The beauty of Jesus was truly seen in him. His ethical life was constantly revealed in his preaching and conversation as he was among us.

After his death, his wife, Jennie Goris, returned to LaGrave Church. The congregation continued to hold her in high esteem, as it had before their separation, and did so until her death on February 21, 1983.

LaGrave had now gone from 1887 to 1952, a total of sixty-five years. During that span of time, it had lived through two great economic depressions and two great world wars. The Lord had given eight pastors to the church, all different, and all dedicated. Through them, He had brought His Word to His people. In those sixty-five years, many members had come and gone, some by death, some by transfer to other churches in other cities, or the same city. Some, too, had left; for, like Demas, they loved this present world.

LaGrave, in the early years, kept records imperfectly and, sometimes, indifferently. Furthermore, not all the records were preserved. Only the Lord makes and keeps perfect books. Therefore, only the Lord can give the complete statistics for the first two-thirds of LaGrave's first one hundred years — births, deaths, professions of faith, marriages, transfers, erasures, resignations, reaffirmations, etc. Much of the seed fell on good ground. But some of it fell on stoney soil. A narrative of the LaGrave story is not complete without the expression of a hope that those who were unresponsive to LaGrave's ministry accepted Christ before their deaths. Or, if still living, have responded or will respond to the Master's call.

The last third of LaGrave's first century of existence would bring greater perils than those before. For the time ahead would be one of unparalleled prosperity, astonishing progress, and frighteningly destructive potentialities.

Chapter 19

ABIDE WITH ME

On the local scene, Henry Schultze, President of Calvin College, said that it was "five minutes to twelve." That was the title of a speech he made in which he urged support for a building program to expand the facilities of Calvin College. There were those who reacted by asking: "Why build at all if it is this late on the clock of human history?"

On the international scene, others, with the atomic bomb in mind, said even more dramatically that it was "three minutes to midnight." Those who were persuaded dug bomb shelters in their backyards. Enterprising companies sold underground cubicles for $1,995, complete with storage space for canned goods. Russia had the A-bomb, and Harry Truman, President of the United States, said: "We have no time left." But bomb shelters found little use beyond being storage spaces for garden tools and old snow tires.

Truman's suspicion of an aggressive communism was vindicated on June 25, 1950, when a massive invasion force from communist North Korea rolled into South Korea. American G.I.s were ordered to the battlefield again. The United States was at war for the second time in five years. Once more, LaGrave's young men were called upon, although this time in lesser numbers.

J. Robert Oppenheimer, the frail and soft-spoken genius who had headed the A-bomb project at Los Alamos, sadly said: "In some crude sense, which no vulgarity, no humor, no overstatement can quite extinguish, the physicists have known sin and this is a knowledge they cannot lose."

This gnawing sense of guilt did not stop Edward Teller, a beetle-browed, brilliant, Hungarian-born physicist, from pursuing the hydrogen bomb. His work in a laboratory in Livermore, California, proved successful. On November 1, 1952, while scientists peered through special smoked glasses on ships and planes fifty miles away, the largest explosion ever created by man obliterated an entire island. Eniwetok, an atoll in the Marshall Islands in the Pacific, with its palm trees and coconuts, simply disappeared from the face of the earth beneath an enormous mushroom cloud.

In its shadow, life went on. In Grand Rapids, Michigan, as elsewhere, people found solace in shutting out the grim realities of a new age. Barbecue pits in back yards were more fun — and cheaper than bomb shelters. "Gunsmoke" on television, Eisenhower in the White House, and Edmund Hillary on top of Mt. Everest helped to blot out such unthinkable realities as Russia's H-bomb

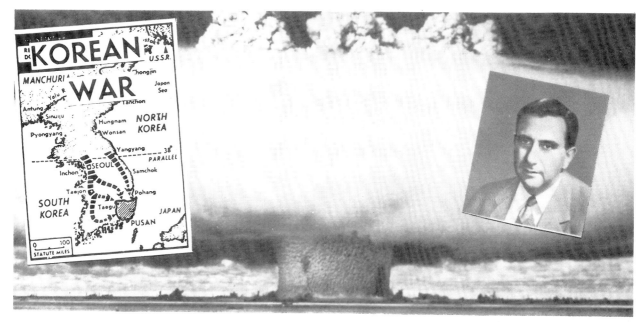

On the edge of disaster . . .

In 1969, LaGrave's ninth pastor and his wife, Rev. Jacob and Anne Eppinga, on sabbatical in Cambridge, England, lived upstairs, in Mullion House, on the edge of town. The son of Edward Teller (father of the hydrogen bomb) and his wife lived downstairs. The Tellers and the Eppingas became friends. One subject was never discussed — the H-bomb.

explosion in Siberia in 1953 and America's second test at Bikini Atoll nine months later. The world had gone mad, but there were few sermons about such mind-boggling developments as science had brought about. Rev. Leonard Trap, whose widow and son would join LaGrave after his death, wrote in *The Banner* that he could now understand II Peter 3:10 better, where the apostle wrote about the "elements melting with fervent heat." But if he and others like him were sobered, the lighter mood of the country seemed more appealing, especially to the young, including the youth of the church. "They are too well adjusted," wrote Cecil DeBoer of Calvin College in the *Calvin Forum* of August 1953, "and too apathetic to care . . . Never since the Reformation has a younger generation had less to fall back upon . . . But . . . considering the kind of world they are about to inherit, perhaps, one should pray for them rather than complain."

Thus, a decade which lifted the curtain upon a possible imminent apocalyptic holocaust, be-

came the decade of Marilyn Monroe, flying saucers, and Elvis Presley who took America from pop to rock (Awophopaloobop alapbamboom! Tutti-frutti! All-rootie! tutti-frutti! All-rootie!). Davy Crockett became America's pied piper on television. The older set followed quiz shows and funnyman Milton Berle so totally that Edward R. Murrow — himself the decade's top TV commentator — labelled the boob tube the true opiate of the people. Fred Allen, a radio humorist, sounded more like an Old Testament Amos when he said, "Television is a triumph of equipment over people, and the minds that control it are so small that you could put them in the navel of a flea and still have enough room beside them for a network vice-president's heart."

There were other opiates. Norman Vincent Peale poured syrup from his pulpit. "Dear Abby" fielded the funniest questions and gave the wittiest answers. Students practiced togetherness — twenty-two in a phone booth, forty in a Volkswagon — and challenged each other with hula hoops. True, Americans shivered at the movies viewing Nevil Shute's "On the Beach," a film depicting the end of life on earth as the aftermath of nuclear war. But the result was more graveyard humor than revival:

And we will all go together when we go,
Every Hottentot and every Eskimo;
When the air becomes uranious,
We will all go simultaneous,
Yes, we will all go together when we go.

. . . society seemed to be losing itself in fads and causes

It would be wrong, however, to imply that all were eating and drinking and making merry on the edge of disaster. In Grand Rapids, there were some who seized the theological challenge of the fifties by producing a new publication, *The Reformed Journal.* Others, one month later, equally motivated and equally responsive to the hour — but with a greater mind for safety — gave birth to another paper, *The Torch and Trumpet,* now *The Outlook.* In Montgomery, Alabama, a young black minister, Martin Luther King, emerging as the leader of a movement that would contribute to the altering of America, encouraged a bus boycott by his people. All did not accept the divinity of an Elvis Presley who drew broadsides of wrath from scores of columnists and commentators. The Reverend William J. Shannon of *The Catholic Sun,* said, "Catholics are angry. What right does he have to behave like a sex maniac in public before millions of impressionable kids?" Jack Gould of *The New York Times* wrote, "When Presley executes his bumps and grinds, it must be remembered by the Columbia Broadcasting System that even the 12-year-old's curiosity may be overstimulated."

A Century of Grace, the history of the LaGrave Church, cannot be understood without viewing the background against which it was received. With the beginning of the second half of the twentieth century, the church moved into a different world, wholly other than the one from which it had emerged. The effects were not immediately apparent. LaGrave would move on from its eighth to its ninth pastor. It would enter into a new flurry of activity. But, its members and their children would be profoundly affected in their living and in their thinking by events around them. In some ways, they would be more influenced by the world, than influencing it. Jackie Gleason, television entertainer whose situation comedy, "The Honeymooners," presented acceptable humor in the fifties, and who was more of a thinker than many realized, said of Elvis Presley, "He can't last. I tell you flatly — he can't last." In this, he proved to be completely inaccurate, as the emerging culture would demonstrate.

And so, after the fifties, LaGravites lived in a different world from those in the first half of the century. So much had happened since 1887. So much more would come about beginning with the fifth decade of the twentieth century. LaGrave's founders might possibly have related to their church and denomination in the 1940s, but they would have been unable to find themselves after the revolution of the sixties, whose roots had sprouted in the fifties. Had it been possible for Klaas and Anna Troon of the nineteenth century to visit with their great-grandchildren, Jack and Karen Troon, in the second half of the twentieth century, the gap would have been much more than generational, even though all were Christians. Only the gospel thread would relate them. And so, the church of divine origin, including La-Grave, would prevail against the considerable onslaughts of the fifties and succeeding decades. In church, the members of LaGrave sang:

Change and decay in all around I see;
O Thou who changest not, abide with me.

He did!

Some seized the theological challenges of the '50s and responded through the printed word

LAGRAVE AVENUE CHRISTIAN REFORMED CHURCH
SANCTUARY WINDOWS

CHANCEL WINDOW

The Great Commission chancel window, with its five lancets, depicts Christ's commission to His disciples: "Go ye, therefore, and teach all nations, baptizing them in the name of the Father and the Son and the Holy Ghost." (Matthew 28:19)

CENTER THREE LANCETS:

Christ commissioning His disciples, superimposed upon an open Bible; Reformers and missionaries spread out left and right to uplifted hands of peoples of the world.

TOP OF LANCETS:

A. A dove and escalloped shell, representing the descending of the Holy Spirit at Christ's baptism; St. Stephen, the first Christian martyr
B. An angel with trumpet, attesting to Christ's ascension
C. The ascended Christ with the dove of the Holy Spirit
D. An angel with cymbals, attesting to Christ's ascension
E. Grapes, wheat, and the Holy Chalice as symbols of Holy Communion; St. Paul on the road to Damascus, called to preach the Gospel

REREDOS AND COMMUNION TABLE
(in front of the Great Commission Window)

The reredos (a decorated screen behind the altar in a church) displays a beautiful wood carving of the Lord's Last Supper. It is the work of Joseph F. Wolters.

The decorative carvings on the reredos and around the communion table are leaves and fruit of the vine, symbolizing the wine.

AISLE WINDOWS
The windows on the east and west sides of the sanctuary are divided into 12 bays, each with 3 lancets — with the exception of bay number 7. The bays depict scenes in the life of Jesus, from his birth to his ascension into heaven.

BAY NUMBER ONE: (on the west wall)
   the birth of Jesus

   A. wise men; sheep
   B. shepherds; lamb
   C. angel; Mary and babe; Mary, Joseph, Jesus, and Simeon in the temple

BAY NUMBER TWO:
   Boy Jesus in the Temple at Jerusalem confounding the learned doctors with his questions

   A. rabbis; flight to Egypt
   B. Boy Jesus in temple; rabbis
   C. Mary and Joseph; rabbis

BAY NUMBER THREE:
John the Baptist baptizing Jesus in the River Jordan and Jesus' temptation in the wilderness

    A. Jesus' baptism; bystanders
    B. Dove (Holy Spirit); John the Baptist; bystanders
    C. Jesus tempted in the wilderness; temple (pinnacle)

BAY NUMBER FOUR:
the calling of the disciples, with the large central scene showing Jesus beckoning to the fishermen Peter and Andrew

    A. Jesus and Matthew (follow me)
    B. miraculous catch
    C. Jesus and Nathaniel

BAY NUMBER FIVE:
Jesus' first miracle, that of turning water into wine at the wedding feast of Cana

    A. wedding in Cana; servant pouring wine
    B. miracle of water changed to wine
    C. John the Baptist in prison (with shell overhead symbolizing John as baptizer of Jesus); lame man being lowered through the roof to be healed

BAY NUMBER SIX:
the Sermon on the Mount

    A. Jesus stilling waves
    B. listeners to Sermon on the Mount; light under bushel (Matthew 5:15)
    C. listeners to Sermon on the Mount; the birds have a nest (Matthew 8:20)

BAY NUMBER SEVEN:
the feeding of the five thousand

    A. ruler asking Jesus to raise sick daughter (Matthew 9:18); Jesus feeding the five thousand

    B. Andrew bringing boy with loaves and fishes to feed the five thousand

BAY NUMBER EIGHT:
Jesus' Transfiguration where He appears in company with Moses and Elias

    A. Jesus preaching foreboding events, Luke 9:22f, Mark 8:31f, Matthew 16:21f

    B. God's voice, Moses, and Elijah

    C. Transfigured Christ; Jesus and rich young man

BAY NUMBER NINE:

Palm Sunday — Jesus' triumphal entry into Jerusalem

  A. Jesus driving the money changers from the Temple

  B. Jesus entering Jerusalem on donkey

  C. people waving palms; widow and her mite

BAY NUMBER TEN:

the Last Supper with all the disciples seated at the table

  A. betrayal by a kiss from Judas

  B. Lord's Supper (note that at the table Judas is not haloed)

  C. feet washing

BAY NUMBER ELEVEN:
the Passion and Crucifixion of Jesus

    A. Jesus beaten by soldiers
    B. Crucifixion
    C. Jesus before Pilate

BAY NUMBER TWELVE:
Jesus' Resurrection from the tomb, bearing the banner of victory

    A. Jesus supping with disciples; blinded soldier
    B. the Resurrection of Jesus Christ
    C. angel and women at the empty tomb; Jesus and doubting Thomas

BALCONY ROSE WINDOW

This Rose Window was removed from the chancel of the original sanctuary and now graces the balcony of the new. In richly colored stained glass, it depicts Christ our Lord praying in the Garden of Gethsemane.

THE DEWEY BATTJES MEMORIAL CHAPEL WINDOWS

ROSE WINDOW

(over outside entrance to chapel)

shows Christ with arms outstretched, bidding people to "Come unto Me . . ."

CLERESTORY WINDOWS

Symbols of Christ's twelve apostles based on the character
and activities of these men as revealed in the Scriptures

1. ST. PETER: Crossed keys recall Peter's confession and our Lord's statement regarding the Office of the Keyes, which He committed to the church on earth. (Matthew 16:13-19)

2. ST. JAMES: The staff, wallet, and hat signify his pilgrimages. The scriptural reference upon the scroll, indicates Christ's Incarnation. (John 1:14)

3. ST. JOHN: The eagle is one of the four beasts mentioned in the fourth chapter of Revelation, which are thought to refer to evangelists. John's Gospel from first to last soars on eagles' sings to the very throne of Heaven.

4. ST. ANDREW: Crossed fish recall his original occupation and his call to become a fisher of men.

5. ST. BARTHOLOMEW: When Philip sought out Bartholomew to tell him about Christ, he found him under a fig tree, hence the fruit and leaves of the fig. The folded hands before an open book refer to the fact that Bartholomew seems to have been a withdrawn man who spent much time in meditation.

6. ST. PHILIP: A basket, two loaves of bread, and a Tau Cross, recalling his remark when our Lord fed the multitude. (John 6:7)

7. ST. THOMAS: Thomas reaches out to feel the wounds in Christ's outstretched palms, whereupon he made his great confession, "My Lord and my God!" (John 20:28)

8. ST. MATTHEW: The winged man is the symbol of Matthew, because that evangelist begins his Gospel by tracing the human descent of our Lord. This is one of the four beasts derived from Revelation mentioned in relation to John.

9. ST. JAMES the Less: James the Less is characterized by the lily-of-the-valley, that fragrant but modest flower which is a symbol of humility.

10. ST. THADDAEUS: This apostle sailed far on missionary journeys with Simon, hence his symbol is a sailing vessel.

11. ST. SIMON: Simon was a zealot and thus his symbol is the symbol of Christian zeal, a cross flamant (a cross with flame-like edges).

12. ST. MATTHIAS: This apostle, who was chosen by lot to take the palce of Judas, has for his symbol the paper bearing his name, which decided his fate, and the Easter lily referring to the fact that he witnessed the Resurrection.

FOUR THREE-LANCET BAY WINDOWS (on west wall)

BAY NUMBER ONE:

Christ's intimate ministry

A. Christ with woman at the well; Christ with Nicodemus

B. Christ blessing the children; (Hannah taking child Samuel to Eli the priest)

C. Christ calling Zaccheus from a tree; Christ at Mary and Martha's house

BAY NUMBER TWO:

Christ as preacher — His parables

A. Parable of the prodigal son; "The Good Shepherd gives His life for His sheep"

B. Christ advises, "Consider the lilies . . . how they grow . . . ;" The house on the rock

C. Parable of the Good Samaritan; parable of the sower

BAY NUMBER THREE:

Various types of prayers

A. Moses' intercessory prayer for the Israelites who had worshipped the golden calf; Daniel continued his habit of praying — even in the lions' den

B. Christ teaching the Lord's Prayer; Christ's prayer for mercy and grace, in the Garden of Gethsemane

C. Cornelius, the centurion, praying and being guided to seek out Peter; David's prayer of confession, derived from Psalm 51

BAY NUMBER FOUR:

Christ, the Great Physician

A. Woman with issue of blood, touching hem of Christ's garment; one leper out of ten returns to thank Christ for his healing

B. Christ healing blind Bartimeus; Christ casting out a devil from a child brought to Him immediately after His transfiguration

C. Christ speaking to the centurion whose faith was so great (Matthew 8:8-10)

THE FRESCOES

In the narthex of LaGrave are the four awe-inspiring frescoes painted by Reynold Weidenaar, who was a member of LaGrave. In the Addendum is a complete explanation of the fresco artform.

FRESCO NUMBER ONE

This small fresco depicts Christ framed by church pillars. It had been discarded by the artist because of inferior plaster material but was rescued by Rev. Eppinga and is now preserved under glass.

FRESCO NUMBER TWO

    The Great Commission fresco depicts mankind struggling in despair and evil, seeking the meaning of life and man's purpose on earth and his destiny through a variety of religions. In the center is Jesus Christ, the only hope of all the world. Small portraits of contemporary religious leaders and missionaries are spotted around the Cross.

FRESCO NUMBER THREE
Depicts pre-Reformation Christian leaders: Paul at Philippi, Constantine at Milvia, Augustine at Hippo, Boniface at Friesland, Wycliffe at Lutterworth, and Savonarola at Florence.

FRESCO NUMBER FOUR
Depicts Reformation leaders: Hus at Constance, Luther at Wittenberg, Calvin at Geneva, William at Leyden, Farel at Geneva, and Knox at Edinburg.

THE DEKKER MEMORIAL
(located in the Tower Room)

This contemporary art piece, designed in part by Douglas Pettinga, was given as a memorial for David Dekker who died in the Vietnam War. It depicts the dove of peace breaking through the wall man has built between himself and God.

AN ACCOMPANYING PLAQUE READS AS FOLLOWS:

Dedicated to the men who have given their lives in the service of their country.

In the tender compassion of our God, the morning sun from heaven will rise upon us, to shine on those who live in darkness, under the cloud of death, and to guide our feet into the way of peace.
Luke 1:78, 79

A second plaque lists LaGrave's war dead.

REVEREND AND MRS. JACOB D. EPPINGA 1954–1987

A century of grace finds LaGrave seeking to confirm God's work in the city and the world

Chapter 20

LENGTHENING THE CORDS

I
t was 1952. Dr. George Goris had gone to serve the Hope Christian Reformed Church of Grandville, Michigan. LaGrave's ninth pastor, Jacob Dirk Eppinga, would not arrive until January of 1954. In the interim, Rev. J. Herbert Brink, a Presbyterian minister from Cleveland, Ohio, provided part-time pastoral services. He had returned to Calvin Seminary in order to enter the Christian Reformed ministry. Shortly after the new pastor's arrival, Rev. Brink received an invitation to become the minister of a Christian Reformed Church in Holland, Michigan. His friends at LaGrave bade him Godspeed.

Rev. Eppinga was born in Detroit, Michigan, in 1917. He attended Calvin College and Westminster Seminary in Philadelphia, where one of his professors was Rev. R.B. Kuiper, who had been LaGrave's fifth pastor. After taking a graduate year at Calvin Seminary, he became pastor of the Dearborn, Michigan, Christian Reformed Church in 1945. Seven years later, he moved to the Highland Hills Christian Reformed Church of Grand Rapids, Michigan, where he served for two years. While studying at Westminster, he married Anne Batts of Detroit, Michigan. Jacob and Anne, together with their four children, Richard, Jay, Susan, and Deanna came to LaGrave in the first month of 1954.

The installation service of January 17, 1954, involved LaGrave's three most recent pastors. Dr. Edward Masselink, using Psalm 84 as his choice of scripture, preached a sermon entitled, "A Heavenly Promise for an Earthly Ministry." Dr. George Goris presided over the installation, reading from the appropriate formulary. Dr. Martin Wyngaarden, who had just retired as vice president of the consistory, charged the new pastor. Rev. H. Bel followed by charging the congregation. In the evening, Pastor Eppinga based his inaugural message on the words of Psalm 124, "Our Help Is in the Name of the Lord."

Pastor Eppinga had purchased a new pair of shoes for the occasion of his installation. They were brown. In the company of Masselink's, Goris's, Bel's, and Wyngaarden's black shoes and their black robes, and his own black robe, his brown shoes — in plain sight of all — pained him in more ways than one. Alas, he had so hoped to make a good initial impression!

In the week following, there was a consistory party at the Peninsular Club and a congregational reception held on the lower level of the parish

New Pastor At LaGrave

Rev. J. D. Eppinga to Be Installed Sunday

REV. J. D. EPPINGA.

Rev. Jacob D. Eppinga, former pastor of Highland Hills Christian Reformed church, will be installed as pastor of LaGrave Avenue Christian Reformed church Sunday at the 10.30 a. m. service.

Dr. Martin J. Wyngaarden, vice president of the church's consistory, and three of its former pastors will participate in the ceremony. The former pastors are Dr. George Goris, now pastor of Hope Christian Reformed church of Grandville; Dr. Edward J. Masselink, pastor of Twelfth Street Christian Reformed church, and Rev. Herman Bel of Dorr. Dr. Goris is in charge of arrangements and Dr. Masselink will preach the sermon.

Mr. Eppinga will preach his first sermon in his new pulpit at the 7 p. m. service Sunday. LaGrave Avenue church will be his third pastorate. A graduate of Calvin college and Westminster Theological seminary, he completed a year of postgraduate work at Calvin seminary in 1944 and served a church at Dearborn until 1951, when he came to the newly-organized Highland Hills church.

He is secretary of the Evangelical Ministerial Union and second vice president of Calvin College Alumni association. The Eppingas will move Feb. 1 into LaGrave church's new parsonage at 2443 Oakwood av., SE.

house. Dr. Garret Heyns served as chairman. The program introduced the various organizations to the new pastor and unfolded as follows:

Women's Organizations . Mrs. R. VanderWilt
Sunday School . . . . Reynolds Brander
Henry Beets Mission Society . . . W. C. Beets
Young People . . . . Roger Boerema
The Brotherhood . . . . . . Wm. B. Eerdmans
Mr. and Mrs. Club . . . . Gordon Buter
Music . . . . Choir
Closing Remarks . . . . J. D. Eppinga

LaGrave's ninth pastor undertook his responsibilities with a measure of trepidation. Some felt he was too young and lacking in ecclesiastical stature. He received letters — some signed and some anonymous — alerting him to the liberalism of LaGrave and giving him warning. Others wrote expressing disappointment, for they feared he had accepted LaGrave's call for reasons of prestige and money.

There were two items that were of more concern to him than the negative reactions he had received — LaGrave had no parsonage and the membership rolls had been lost. LaGrave had

gone out of the parsonage business when Dr. Goris had purchased his own house. It was now necessary to find another. Meanwhile, the church had to pay rent to the Highland Hills Church for providing the Eppingas with housing. It was an awkward arrangement which was soon remedied with the purchase of a residence in East Grand Rapids, at 2443 Oakwood S.E.

The parsonage at 2443 Oakwood, S.E.

136

The project of recovering a membership roll took longer than the project of finding a parsonage and pointed up the need for a church office and secretary. Mrs. Greta VanYsseldyke was engaged, and office equipment was purchased and installed in a room adjacent to the custodian's quarters on the upper level of the parish house. As soon as the church office was functioning, a church monthly called *LaGrave News* saw the light of day. In the latter part of 1957, Mrs. Greta VanYsseldyke, due to ill health, resigned as church secretary. Mrs. Ruth Snoek replaced her in January 1958. She was a providential "find," and remains with the church to this present writing and continues to be a blessing to all.

Volume I, No. 1, of the *LaGrave News* appeared in October in 1954. Its predecessors (*The Chronicle*, 1890s, *Mail Call*, 1940s) were short-lived. The *LaGrave News* hoped for a longer life and a larger purpose. The closing paragraph of the first-page introduction read:

> Perhaps it will be possible to keep you posted on such items as: consistory matters (what do these men do in their meetings anyway!), our sick and shut-ins (we have quite a few), our monthly calendar of activities (to help you plan

Ruth Pell had worked at the Children's Bible Hour prior to her marriage to John Snoek and until shortly before the birth of their first child. John and Ruth's weekend honeymoon was spent chaperoning the children to Chicago, Illinois, where the CBH telecast was to originate from the sanctuary of the Lorimer Memorial Baptist Church. All the children had to be camera-ready by 10 A.M. broadcast time — a duty Ruth accomplished with the help of some of the older children — and John.

When Ruth came to LaGrave, her children, David and Paulette, were in the 2nd and 3rd grades respectively. LaGrave was a good employer. During the summer months when her children needed her, Ruth was allowed to remain home except for one day a week when she prepared the bulletin. LaGrave felt that it should not employ a mother full-time, and so this arrangement was made. She carried out her office duties from her home the rest of the week.

ahead), our servicemen (we are trying to keep in touch with them every month), and other items of a more miscellaneous character. We pray that this effort will be good for our church.

The same first issue of the *LaGrave News* carried the notice that Mr. John Maliepaard, seminarian, would take up duties as a part-time assistant to the pastor. In this manner, LaGrave sought to expand its youth work and the work of community evangelization. He would be succeeded by other seminarians in the decade of the fifties: Clarence Nyenhuis, who would later enter a ministry in Missions; and Donald Postema, whom the Lord would eventually choose to serve as our campus chaplain at the chapel in Ann Arbor, Michigan. In the 1950s, the campus chapel was directed by a committee whose chairman was Dr. George Goris; later Rev. Eppinga succeeded Dr. Goris in this capacity.

On the evening of September 21, 1954, the formation of the LaGrave Christian Education Society was approved at the suggestion of the consistory. This society sought to broaden the base of support for Christian education by extending the responsibility to everyone in the congregation and assuring the schools of full tuition payment for each student. This arrangement freed the members from being subjected to repeated school drives for financial emergencies and deficiencies. It further helped school boards

Ruth Snoek became secretary of LaGrave in 1958.

LA GRAVE

NEWS

OCTOBER 1954, Vol. I, #1

PUBLISHED BY THE LA GRAVE AVENUE CHRISTIAN REFORMED CHURCH
107 LA GRAVE AVE., S. E., GRAND RAPIDS, MICHIGAN

OCTOBER SCHEDULE

3rd	Sunday Services
	Sunday School
	Young Men's Forward Club
4th	Catechism Classes
5th	Catechism classes
	Esther Circle
	Proposed Christian Education Society Meeting
6th	Central Circle
	Choir Practice
7th	Ladies Missionary Society
10th	Sunday Services
	Sunday School
	Catechism
11th	Consistory Meeting
	Catechism
	Friendship Club
12th	Sr. Fellowship Club
13th	South End Circle
	Choir Practice
17th	Sunday Services
	Sunday School
	Catechism
18th	Catechism
19th	Esther Circle
	Mr. and Mrs. Club, Barbecue at Townsend Park
20th	Central Circle
	Choir Practice
	South End Circle, a Coffee at home of Mrs. Wm. Pastoor
24th	Sunday Services
	Sunday School
	Catechism
25th	Consistory Meeting
	Catechism
	Friendship Club
26th	Fellowship Club
27th	South End Circle
	Choir Practice
29th	Stanley Brush Demonstration at the home of Mrs. M. Roskam sponsored by South End Circle.

SOMETHING NEW

GREETINGS FROM LAGRAVE! Beginning with this news letter we hope to visit you through the mail box every month. Our Sunday bulletin is far too small to carry all the items which we would like to bring to the attention of the congregation. Nor is it proper that the paper you carry to your pew contain "just everything". The pulpit, too, is not the place to send forth anything in the way of announcements except the most urgent and important. We hope, therefore, that the "LaGrave News" will fill a real need and find a real welcome.

Perhaps it will be possible to keep you posted on such items as: Consistory matters, (What do these men do in their meetings, anyway!) our sick and shut-ins (we have quite a few), our monthly calendar of activities (to help you plan ahead), our servicemen, (we are trying to keep in touch with them every month), and other items of a more miscellaneous character. We pray that this effort will be for the good of our Church.

AN INVITATION

Any organization wishing to avail itself of these pages for announcements, news items, or matters of general interest, is invited to do so.

Please send copy to the Church Office by the 20th of every month.

to concentrate on education rather than finances. So called "Booster Clubs" in the East had proven successful and were cited as models. Thus, the LaGrave Christian Education Society came into existence — another first for LaGrave in the Grand Rapids area.

Mr. Gordon Buter served as its first president. Other moving figures were Dr. Orren Bolt, Jack Peterson, and William B. Eerdmans. It did not take long for the society to win widespread praise from Christian school leaders in the area. Other churches soon followed LaGrave's example.

Christian Education Society
of the
LaGrave Avenue Christian Reformed Church

BULLETIN
SEPT. 1955

La Grave Avenue Christian Reformed Church
167 LA GRAVE AVENUE, SOUTHEAST
GRAND RAPIDS 3, MICHIGAN

Dear Congregation:

[letter text]

Jacob D. Eppinga

Be a Booster for Christian Education!

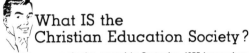

What IS the Christian Education Society?

It is an organization created in September, 1955 by members of the LaGrave Ave. Christian Reformed Church.

What is Its Purpose?

To create an interest (financial and otherwise) among the members of the church in Christian education.

How Do I Become a Member?

If you are a member of LaGrave and wish to participate in the work of the society hand in your name to the Secretary. Application forms can be found in a box next to bulletin board in the parish house.

I Do Not Have Children in School. How Can I Participate in Society Activities?

For you, too, participation is easy.

1. Come to the periodic meetings of the society.

2. Make monthly contributions to the society through the envelopes you have received for this purpose.

What Does the Society Do With the Money it Receives?

1. Money received from parents for the cost of educating their children is sent to the schools as designated by the parents.

2. Special gifts are distributed to the Christian schools that our children attend in proportion to the number of LaGrave children in each of these schools.

What are the Practical Benefits of This Society?

1. It spreads the interest in and support of Christian education to ALL members of the church, not just to those with children in school.

2. If our societies and others like it, can raise enough money to cover the total cost of educating our children in the Christian schools it will not be necessary to have periodic campaigns for Christian education.

3. It provides a means to relieve school boards of some of the financial problems and permits them to spend more time on the educational problems.

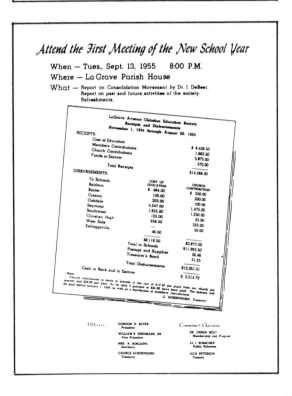

Attend the First Meeting of the New School Year

When — Tues., Sept. 13, 1955   8:00 P.M.
Where — La Grave Parish House
What — Report on Consolidation Movement by Dr. J. DeBeer. Report on past and future activities of the society. Refreshments.

LaGrave Avenue Christian Education Society
Receipts and Disbursements
November 1, 1954 through August 20, 1955

RECEIPTS:
Cost of Education
  Members Contributions $ 8,458.50
  Church Contributions   1,662.50
  Funds in Escrow   3,875.00
                                     570.00
      Total Receipts $14,566.00

DISBURSEMENTS:
To Schools   COST OF   CHURCH
                  EDUCATION   CONTRIBUTION
  Baldwin $ 484.00 $ 250.00
  Creston   100.00   200.00
  Oakdale   203.00   100.00
  Seymour   4,247.00
  Southeast   1,855.00   1,475.00
  Christian High   125.00   1,250.00
  West Side   958.50   25.00
  Kelloggville   525.00
                     46.00   50.00
                  ————   ————
                  $8,118.50 $3,875.00
  Total to Schools $11,993.50
  Postage and Supplies   26.46
  Treasurer's Bond   31.25
      Total Disbursements $12,051.21

  Cash in Bank and in Escrow $ 2,514.79

G. SCHERPHORN, Treasurer

Officers:
GORDON H. BUTER President
WILLIAM B. EERDMANS, SR. Vice President
MRS. R. BOELKINS Secretary
GEORGE SCHERPHORN Treasurer

Committee Chairmen:
DR. ORREN BOLT Membership and Program
AL J. BOSSCHER Public Relations
JACK PETERSON Finance

The fall of 1954 was eventful for other reasons:

Dr. Ralph Blocksma, back from Pakistan, was serving as the president of the Henry Beets Mission Society which had been formed for his support.

An announcement was made by the consistory, a harbinger of something that would materialize later and prove to be a great blessing in the life of the congregation:

DEACONESSES!

Should we have them? There are those who are convinced that there is need in this respect. Surely the idea is scriptural. At one of the meetings of the consistory sometime ago, it was the united opinion that we could move in this direction. Whether by appointment or election, the office would fill a real need in a church such as ours. What is your opinion?

from *LaGrave News*, Nov., 1954.

A neighborhood evangelism effort was initiated, involving seventy-five members of the church who volunteered to ring door bells on Sunday afternoons, distributing Bibles, tracts, and extending personal invitations to attend LaGrave's services.

The pastor published his first book, *The Soul of the City.*

A PASTOR SPEAKS TO.....

J. D. EPPINGA

In 1953, just prior to his arrival at LaGrave, Pastor Eppinga had a brush with lightning. He was on the golf course and had just hit a golf ball. He followed through (as all good golfers do) with his club aloft and suddenly became a human lightning rod. He was knocked to the ground. Such experiences, as others have also testified, are not without their spiritual dimensions.

In 1961, cruising all night in a police car, he assisted in apprehending a man who had robbed a store on the corner of Jefferson and Wealthy.

In 1982, Pastor Eppinga was himself robbed, at gun point, in the LaGrave Church parking lot. Ministers do not always lead sheltered lives.

By February of 1955, LaGrave was supporting another missionary, Miss Betty Feenstra, in Pakistan. She was soon joined by Miss Marian Postema. At home, an anonymous donor had provided the congregation with two tape recording machines for the recording and distribution of Sunday's sermons to the shut-ins. The first sermon recorded, entitled "God, the Sparrow, and You" included not only the voice of the pastor, but also the voice of the taxi dispatcher across the street. His messages, radioed to drivers here and there in the city, were occasionally mysteriously picked up by LaGrave's P. A. system. Visitors were often startled by what seemed to be a voice from heaven interrupting the sermon and telling them to proceed to certain areas of the city.

A NEW BOOK

The announcement regarding the pastor's book was followed by a favorable review in the Grand Rapids Press. *"Rev. J. D. Eppinga, pastor of LaGrave Avenue Christian Reformed Church, is the author of a new book,* The Soul of the City, *published by W. B. Eerdmans Publishing Company. It is his first published work. The idea came to Mr. Eppinga while he was pastor of a church in Dearborn, Michigan. It consists of ten chapters on 'Talks to the City' . . . " Mrs. Roy (Esther) Bielema undertook the selling of this book and the proceeds went to the support of the Pine Rest Children's Retreat.*

It was also in February of 1955 that the first series of weekly Lenten luncheons was scheduled. Dr. Richard Boelkins, the originator of the idea, conceived of it as a missionary outreach effort in which the businessmen of the congregation could invite their unchurched friends to a luncheon where they would afterwards hear a Gospel message. The effort proved to be so successful that another series was immediately scheduled for the following year. These Lenten luncheons were discontinued after eighteen years because of a diminishing attendance, due partially to a number of imitations in various parts of the city and the multiplication of small Bible study breakfast groups. The four speakers for the first Lenten Luncheon Series were:

Mr. Sydney Youngsma,
    Development Secretary, Calvin College
Rev. Harold Leestma, Pastor,
    Garfield Reformed Church
Rev. Harold Dekker,
    Professor of Missions, Calvin Seminary
Dr. Peter Eldersveld,
    Radio Minister, Back to God Hour

February of 1955 brought still more developments. At the annual congregational meeting in December, 1954, the pastor had been authorized to appoint a special study committee to investigate the needs of the church regarding the expansion and improvement of the church building. The committee was to report within ninety days. Five years before, a recommendation to build a new structure had been defeated. The sanctuary, with its dark wood, was possessed of a particularly worshipful atmosphere, but deterioration had set in. The carpet runners in the aisles were not only threadbare, but had holes in them. A builder had worried about the soundness of the north wall.

The committee, appointed in December of 1954, reporting before its deadline, wrote that while it was important for the congregation to know what the committee was doing, it was equally important for the committee to know what the congregation was thinking. Accordingly, a questionnaire was circulated asking opinions on the following five points with respect to LaGrave's facility:

WHAT SHALL WE DO?

1. Do nothing! Leave things as they are.
2. Create and husband a building fund.
3. Remodel our present facilities with the thought of temporarily solving our lack of seating capacity.
4. Build a new church on our present site.
5. Abandon our present site with the thought of building entirely new facilities elsewhere.

Thus, the initial steps were taken which, although unknown at the time, would lead to the erection of a new sanctuary on the present site.

There was another question on which the congregation was polled — much smaller, yet, surprisingly, just as difficult. Morning services began at 10:30 A.M. There were those who favored 11 A.M. Others were supporters of the 10 A.M. idea. Older members favored an earlier hour. Parents with children leaned in the direction of a later time. The whole matter sparked a surprising amount of debate, mostly motivated by considerations of habit, inclination, and convenience. Amazingly, when the vote revealed a preponderant feeling for 10 A.M., all debate disappeared. But, whereas most members arrived in plenty of time for the 10:30 service, the majority now came just in the nick of time for the 10 A.M. hour.

COFFEE TIME

Another tempest in a teapot concerned coffee after church — a beverage Hollanders could scarcely do without. A few were going to Holly's Restaurant, one block from church. To counter this growing tendency, coffee was served in the lower level of the parish house. A collection plate was positioned next to the coffee urn to defray expenses. Some asked, "What is the difference if we pay at Holly's or here?" This resulted in the disappearance of the collection plate and the slight enlargement of a line item in the budget. Heretofore, the ship of LaGrave had floated on a sea of coffee. Now it sailed on an ocean of it.

In June of 1955, the synod of the denomination named LaGrave Church as its convener. Delegates gathered from everywhere for the service of worship. The LaGrave choir, under the direction of Professor Seymour Swets with Alyce Lantinga at the organ, contributed significantly to an evening of inspiration. It was a great event in the life of the congregation and would be repeated two more times in the new sanctuary — in 1978 and in 1987.

LaGrave services didn't often receive international attention, but its prayer service for the synod of 1955 was reported and described at some length in the October, 1955, issue of *Centraal Weekblad,* a church paper in the Netherlands. The reporter, Rev. P. G. Kunst, described the service as follows. The late Dr. Henry Zylstra, a member of LaGrave, provided the English translation in the October, 1955, issue of the *LaGrave News:*

The synod of 1955 was ushered in by means of a dignified prayer service in the LaGrave Avenue Church, the church of one of the older congregations in Grand Rapids. It is a distinguished-looking church, its interior decorated in the darker color tones, and having stained glass windows and a beautiful organ. Of the pipes and framework of this organ nothing can be seen. At LaGrave, as in so many churches, the business end of the organ is concealed behind a protective shield, done in Gothic style.

The organist, Mrs. Lantinga, knows marvelously well how to handle the stops and keys. She plays Bach and Barowski with wonderful poise. Along about a quarter to eight, the minister, Rev. J. D. Eppinga, comes walking down the length of the church. When he is seated, and the organ plays softly on, one hears, intermingled with the notes of the organ, the voice of a man, which seems to be coming nearer as it sings. The sound of singing swells and swells. Now there are women's voices too. A moment later and it is evident just what is going on. Very gradually, as in a procession, a church choir of approximately thirty members marches down the broad aisle to the front. Organist and choir are in remarkable harmony with each other, and there sounds through this church most imposingly a severely restrained anthem. The congregation picks up the note of the choir and strongly joins in with: "The Church's One Foundation Is Jesus Christ Her Lord."

At several points in the service we listen to this choir as it presents a piece from Schackley, "Put on the Whole Armor of God," and a piece from Herbert, "Let Mount Zion Rejoice." I must confess that I have to get used to such a choir at church. When I see them sitting there in the loft alongside of the rostrum, all severely garbed in the long lavendar robes trimmed in silver gray, the loose sleeves also lined with the lovely silver silk . . . well, I say to myself, "That is something the old Dr. VanRaalte ought to have seen and heard." Still, the role of this choir was most certainly not a disturbing element in the service. As a matter of fact, it ministered to and it supported the congregation in its service of prayer.

The whole service gave the impression of having been carefully planned and executed. Everything was done in good order. This can be said also of the way in which the collection was announced and gathered. Six collectors presented themselves and lined up in front of the pulpit. In a short prayer consisting of two sentences God was asked to prepare the hearts of those present for a generous gift and to receive the offering for Jesus' sake.

The local pastor spoke on John 16 and selected as core of his sermon a part of verse 13: the guidance of the Holy Spirit. The sermon was remarkable in a number of ways, of which I appreciated most of all the brilliant structure and composition of the sentences. Here was an American speaking who articulated and enunciated his words carefully, and did not wrap them in all sorts of disturbing impurities of pronunciation. It was, in short, a beautiful evening, and it converged in the end upon a heartfelt prayer for the work of the synod.

In the fall of 1955, and in preparation for its annual congregational meeting, the LaGrave consistory recommended women suffrage at all church meetings. The women in the church were requested to be present as voting members at a special spring congregational meeting. The recommendation to make this a permanent arrangement passed unanimously. Few women were present. The following year, many more appeared. A few congregations made similar decisions. Synod was also moving in this direction — but slowly. Ironically, all Christian school society meetings, where women might have been expected to be present and voting, were strictly masculine.

The year 1955 also saw LaGrave's Henry Beets Mission Society undertake a new challenge. The South India Mission Field had been abandoned by the denomination, leaving its native minister, Rev. Arthur Ramiah, in a difficult strait. The reasons were controversial. The consistory expressed concern for this challenging field. Before the consistory could communicate its concern to the classis, the Henry Beets Mission Society once again by-passed an abundance of ecclesiastical red tape and announced that it would serve as a collecting agency for any and all contributions for the support of Rev. and Mrs. Ramiah until such time as the work could be taken over by another denomination or agency. LaGrave's daughter church, Burton Heights, responded because the formal membership papers of Rev. and Mrs. Ramiah rested with them. Thus, many members of the Burton Heights church and individuals from as far away as California sent contributions to the LaGrave Henry Beets Mission Society. These gifts, combined with those of the society, made it possible for the Ramiahs to continue their ministry in South India. In supporting this effort, the LaGrave Henry Beets Mission Society sustained a measure of criticism from those in the denomination who, for right or wrong reasons, were disenchanted with the Ramiahs. At the end of this period of time, the local Anglican Church of South India took over the field — including the ministry of the Ramiahs.

At the annual congregational meeting held in December, 1955, the consistory was authorized to organize a board of deaconesses. It was an idea conceived in 1954, whose time had come. The consistory asked each women's organization to appoint two of their members to serve in this capacity — a tradition which continues to this day. The following women were the first deaconesses:

Central Ladies Aid
  Mrs. Ralph VandenBerg
  Mrs. Martin VerMerris

Esther Circle
  Mrs. Wesley Karsies
  Mrs. John Stuit Sr.

Friendship Club
  Mrs. Harold VanVliet
  Mrs. Gerard Prins

Ladies Missionary Society
  Mrs. John R. Huizinga
  Mrs. William Stuart

South End Circle
  Mrs. Cornelius Troost
  Mrs. Marinus Scherphorn

The deaconesses, in a service of installation and dedication, were charged to call on the sick and shut-ins, to read scripture and offer prayer and comfort, and to work closely with the pastor. This organization continues faithfully to fulfill its task and has been a source of inestimable blessings to very many.

Television, in the 1950s, was moving ever onward and forward. Area churches were asked if they would be willing to have their worship services televised. LaGrave took its turn. On these Sundays, the televised service was at 10 A.M. and the service in the sanctuary at 11 A.M. Because the televised services were originally held in the studio and space was limited, tickets were made available on a first-come, first-serve basis. Ini-

On those occasions in which LaGrave's services were televised, studio engineers would hold up signs towards the end of the sermon: "Five More Minutes." Sixty seconds later, another saying: "Four Minutes." The pastor hoped that this would not give the members of the congregation any ideas.

Children under twelve were not permitted in television audiences. They were photogenic. They were also distracting. When objections to such discrimination rose to a considerable height, LaGrave declined to take its turn the next time it was invited to have part of its congregation worship "on the air" in the studio.

Most television stations in the fifties had a religious sign-on and sign-off. Periodically, LaGrave's ninth pastor would tape a number of prayers and brief meditations to be aired early in the morning and very late at night on WOOD TV. Surprisingly, there were many early risers and late retirers who saw him on television.

LaGrave's ninth pastor was also heard on radio. Substituting for Dr. Peter Eldersveld, he preached for a time on The Back to God Hour. The recording sessions were at Calvin College and the Radio Choir furnished the music.

tially, the whole arrangement was viewed as an opportunity for witness. After a time, the disruptive aspects caused the consistory to reconsider, despite many letters of appreciation from the general viewing area, including Holland and Muskegon — some containing contributions.

In the fall of 1956, it was decided to hold weekly Advent services on Wednesdays from noon to 1 P.M. for downtown office workers and Christmas shoppers. The month of December was a busy time for downtown merchants. LaGrave's meager parking facilities were always filled. The mission committee saw an opportunity. For several years, until its building program, Advent mid-week noon services brought significant numbers for prayer and devotions.

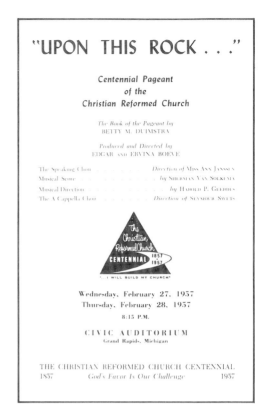

Centennial logo and program cover of the pageant "Upon This Rock." The production was written by Betty M. Duimstra and produced and directed by Edgar and Ervina Boeve to celebrate the 100th birthday of the Christian Reformed Denomination

In 1957, the Christian Reformed denomination celebrated one hundred years of existence. A pageant, "Upon this Rock," was presented at the Civic Auditorium in honor of this event. Many other activities marked the Centennial. Several sight-sound presentations were produced in connection with the denomination's century of existence, including one on the Heidelberg Catechism, written and produced by LaGrave's own Rev. Eppinga. The same year, LaGrave Church observed its 70th birthday. In Hungary, the freedom fighters lost out to Russia and communism. Quite a number of Hungarians were able to come to the United States as expatriates. Three of them were immediately sponsored by LaGrave: Dr. Theodore Thuri Nagy, an elderly gentleman who at one time had served as a lawyer and member of the Hungarian Department of the Interior; and Joseph Uhrin and Andros Liptai, two younger men — still in their teens — who found adjustment to Grand Rapids and American ways far easier than Dr. Nagy. LaGrave rented a house for them at 256 Prospect S. E. where Dr. Nagy proceeded to grow huge red peppers and other exotic foods in the garden. Eventually, Dr. Nagy was able to return to his native land. Frank Davidhazy, friend and fellow Hungarian from New York, together with the pastor, bade him farewell. Upon his arrival in Hun-

gary, Dr. Nagy sent a card to LaGrave. "Many hand kisses," it said. He died shortly thereafter. His was a sad story of the burdens carried by those who are displaced by war and man's inhumanity to man.

NEW ARRIVALS

Andros Liptai initially stayed at the home of the pastor. For his first good meal in his new country, Anne Eppinga made Hungarian goulash. It was the first time he had ever eaten it. He disliked it.

LaGrave also sponsored a Hungarian family. Mr. Julius Kubin, a photographer, and his wife Helen were expecting a new arrival in the family. There were three older children. The two oldest were enrolled in Seymour Christian School.

Not only the presence of the Hungarian refugees alerted LaGrave to the grim realities and potentialities of life, but the existence and threat of the H-bomb in the hands of communists was in the forefront of many minds. In fact, the LaGrave

Church parish house basement was designated as a fallout shelter by Civil Defense. An appropriate designation was attached to the front of the building indicating that 370 people could be accommodated in LaGrave's facilities. The pastor was given a badge and an I. D. card permitting him to move about freely in case of an emergency. Furthermore, he was obliged to go to Battle Creek to attend training sessions to gain understanding in handling emergency situations in the event of war and to become aware of the potency and the effects of the bomb. The pastor was required to return annually for refresher sessions. He did so for four years.

A more likely source of destruction, according to some, was not Russia, but nature. In 1956, a very destructive tornado had skirted the city. The consistory had adopted and announced a permanent policy for the cancellation of worship services during tornado alerts. This action, too, was in keeping with the wishes of Civil Defense.

Dr. John Vroon with the pastor of a mission church in Australia, Cuba, Reverend Eppinga, and John Huizinga

---

A SLEEPLESS NIGHT

Pastor Eppinga discarded the letter which sought assistance for the Christian witness in Cuba. It was a form letter, similar to countless other pleas coming almost weekly from everywhere. That night, Rev. Eppinga was unable to sleep; the Cuban letter repeatedly came to mind. The next morning he went to church early to rescue the letter from his wastebasket before the custodian could throw it in the incinerator. He gave it to Mr. Neil VanMalsen, chairman of the mission committee, whose subsequent inquiry led LaGrave and, eventually, the denomination to undertake this mission field.

In the spring of 1957, the pastor received a letter from Cuba. It was written by a native evangelist, Vicente Izquierdo, who sought moral and financial support. Bessie Izquierdo, his wife, had come to Cuba years before from a Christian Reformed church in New Jersey to do mission work there. The LaGrave consistory, upon recommendation from its mission committee, decided to send a team to investigate the field: Mr. John Huizinga, an elder and businessman; Dr. John Vroon, whose experience as a missionary was valuable; and Pastor Eppinga. In a moment of foresight, the team decided to invite Rev. Henry Evenhouse, Denominational Director of Foreign Missions, to accompany them.

CLOSE CALL

When LaGrave's team for investigating the Cuban mission field was lodged in Jauey Grande, Fidel Castro was in the hills plotting his revolution and creating disturbances. The local mayor, loyal to the Batista government, felt the security of the American visitors threatened. Upon his urging, a taxi was hired to drive eighty miles to the Havana Airport, along back roads, to secure a safe exit for the Americans. Close to the city, the taxi, with its Christian Reformed cargo, was stopped at gun point, but allowed to pass. The LaGrave delegation spent the following night, uncomfortably, in a small room in the airport and flew to Miami the following afternoon. It took less than an hour to land on freedom's soil — a whole world away from what was left behind.

These four returned with a favorable report and recommended that the consistory undertake the support of the small church and Christian school in Jauey Grande, and eight other missions in the Mantanzas Province of Central Cuba. This recommendation was adopted. After prayerful consideration of all the factors involved, the consistory unanimously further adopted the following communication to be sent to the Board of Foreign Missions of the Christian Reformed Church in North America. (Reported in the *LaGrave News*, Oct., 1955.)

Esteemed Brethren:

Sometime ago a committee from our church, together with your secretary, made an investigation of the mission work done by Reverend and Mrs. Vicente Izquierdo in Jauey Grande in the Mantanzas Province of Central Cuba.

This committee, to a man, was tremendously impressed with the marvelous work done and was inspired by the possibility of carrying out the great commission of our Lord in this island.

After prayerful consideration of the factors involved, the LaGrave Avenue consistory, at its meeting last Monday evening, September 16, 1957, unanimously adopted the following resolutions:

1. That the LaGrave Avenue Church consistory petition the Board of Foreign Missions to guide the project of LaGrave Avenue Church in sending aid to the Cuba Interior Gospel Mission, Inc., this aid to be contingent upon the expressed willingness of that mission to develop its work and its churches along Reformed lines and to consist initially of financial help to be followed by the sending of an ordained missionary to Cuba to serve that mission in the teaching of Reformed truth, the establishment of Reformed Church policy, and the wise extension of the work to areas accessible to the Gospel message.

2. It was further moved, supported and carried that LaGrave Avenue Church invite our foreign board to consider Cuba as a mission field of the Christian Reformed Church and to so request synod.

In view of the marvelous blessings which the Lord has granted to the work in Cuba, the urgent need for help, and the fact that no financial assistance is requested of the board in the resolution, we humbly ask that our petition be granted, that the board assist LaGrave Avenue Church with its experience and knowledge of mission development. For many, many years, LaGrave has been eagerly awaiting an opportunity to enter a new mission field and sincerely believes that the invitation from Cuba to "come over and help us" is in the way of Divine Providence.

We shall be deeply grateful to God for the privilege of spearheading this project which, we earnestly pray, will lead to the establishment of a prosperous native Christian Reformed Church in Cuba.

> Respectfully submitted,
> For the LaGrave Avenue
>   Christian Reformed Church,
> Signed: C. VanMalsen,
>   Vice President

"Lift up your eyes and look on the fields; for they are white already to harvest"
JOHN 4:35

Reverend and Mrs. Clarence Nyenhuis with son, Steven

146

For a period of time, LaGrave Church was the sole support of this mission field. Once again, the Henry Beets Mission Society, helping LaGrave's consistory and congregation in their mission efforts, justified its existence by providing the support and assistance — from Pakistan to South India to Cuba. Thereafter, the Cuban field was taken over by the denomination which sustained and supervised the work. LaGrave's assistant to the pastor, Clarence Nyenhuis, having successfully finished his work at Calvin Seminary, was ordained in 1958 and became our church's missionary to Cuba. When Castro triumphed, Rev. and Mrs. Nyenhuis moved to Miami where they undertook Cuban refugee work. One refugee family, Mr. and Mrs. Benito Infante and their three children, Jose, Illeana, and Anamaria, found a warm home in the hearts of the LaGrave congregation.

With great rejoicing, the Henry Beets Mission Society, the mission committee of the consistory, and the congregation, granted support to Dr. John and Theresa Vroon when they accepted the call to serve as Christian Reformed missionaries in Nigeria in June 1958.

The Henry Beets Mission Society was also active on the local scene, supporting neighborhood outreaches that were over and above the church budget. Occasionally, the society sponsored public meetings at which missionaries spoke. One such speaker was Dr. L. Nelson Bell, father-in-law of Rev. Billy Graham. He spoke in LaGrave Church to a large audience on the evening of February 5, 1958.

> As a summer project, LaGrave began sending some of its young people to work at mission stations out East and West. The Henry Beets Mission Society offered to support this venture. This activity anticipated the Summer Workers In Missions (SWIM) which was to become a denomination-wide activity.

The LaGrave congregation, without the involvement of the Henry Beets Mission Society, undertook a part in the support of Rev. Earl Dykema, missionary in Crown Point, New Mexico. The Izquierdos, Vroons, and Dykemas wrote faithfully and informatively concerning their work, and the congregation remembered them all in its prayers.

January 1, 1958, Boy Scout Troop 342 became a LaGrave sponsored organization. The denomination's Calvinist Cadet Corps was to become a strong and excellent organization in later years. But in 1957, it was weak and groping for an identity it could not find, particularly at LaGrave. After much deliberation and prayer, it was thought that joining with the Boy Scouts of America would give the sons of LaGrave an opportunity to witness not only in the Grand Valley Council but to such boys outside the congregation who might be attracted by the name. This was the rationale behind the beginning of the Boy Scout movement at LaGrave. Its first scoutmaster was Reynolds Brander. He was succeeded by Dale Korthuis, who gave years of dedicated service.

In the spring of 1958, the young adults of the church held meetings at a vesper hour before the evening service. The attendance at these meetings was generally between 20 and 40, but it soon peaked to *120–140,* a remarkable phenomenon. A light lunch was provided and followed by a variety of programs — all held in youth hall on the lower level of the parish house. After adjournment, most of the young people attended the evening service. This organization was called Young Adults.

Sabbath observance in the fifties was still more traditional than what, regrettably, it would become in the seventies and eighties. In the fifties, the young people were much more receptive to proffered church invitations and activities. Not far away, Calvin students on the old campus site endured long Sunday afternoons and the grim prospect of no supper. Thus, the timing was right for a great "singles" ministry. The Young Adults filled a real vacuum in the lives of these young people. Many who came found their future life partners.

WHEW!

After finishing Sunday dinner for their own families, sisters Sena Houtman and Betty Brown would go down to church and prepare supper for the Young Adults. Attendance at this meal was often more than one hundred! Sena's daughter, Marie, and Betty's son, Art, were leaders of the organization.

Karen Troon, a Calvin student from Ann Arbor and a former member of LaGrave, was happy to be back in her old church again where she attended Young Adults and the evening worship services. Her parents had joined the Ann Arbor Presbyterian Church. They continued their support of the Ann Arbor chapel but felt the need of a congregational home for themselves. Her brother, Jack, had moved to California.

After seven or eight years, a few other Christian Reformed churches organized similar young people's groups. Simultaneously, Calvin College moved farther out to the Knollcrest Campus, and the cultural revolution of the sixties began to take hold. The result was that attendance at Young Adults began to dwindle. For as long as it lasted, it proved a blessing to many.

And so, the busy decade of the fifties came to a close. The pastor, with enough to do within the church, continued to function as a member of several denominational committees. Locally, he served as chairman of the Hospital Chaplaincy Committee and the Evangelical Ministerial Union. He also served with the local cancer and TB societies and the YMCA.

The congregation had developed, organized, and refined the neighborhood convassing program. Palm Sunday afternoons saw seventy to eighty members fan out to assigned blocks for door-to-door calling. This, together with the other activities reported in this chapter, showed LaGrave's concern for, and involvement with the world around it — locally, nationally and internationally.

A new vision began to evolve at LaGrave in the 1950s — slowly at first but with ever increasing momentum and excitement. The congregation was moving towards the building of its new house of worship.

Through all this lengthening of the cords, ran the thread of the weekly Sunday services — the focal point — the Lord Jesus Christ, the King of the Church.

Chapter 21

"BUILD A HOUSE UNTO MY NAME..."

People go into buildings. But buildings also go into people. Each influences the other. Edgar Guest was right when he observed that "It takes a heap of livin' to make a house a home." But he said nothing about the transforming influence physical surroundings can have on people as well. The aging LaGrave sanctuary contributed to the spiritual experience of the worshippers who entered. This was true for the casual visitor as well as for those who were more sentimentally attached. But there were deficiencies. Organ and choir were inadequately housed. The pulpit, table, and baptismal font were forced into an awkward arrangement. The general layout made weddings difficult. Even so, the members loved their sanctuary with its dark wood and "churchy" feeling. Accordingly, occasional references to the physical inadequacies were ignored, filed for future consideration or, as was more often the case, viewed as expressions of disloyalty. During the tenure of Dr. George Goris, an attempt to assess the adequacy of LaGrave's facility was quickly dropped.

By the mid-fifties, sentiment for a building study had grown strong enough to warrant the attention of a congregational meeting. It was evident that to repair the building would require considerable effort and expense. Before the congregation set out on such a course, good stewardship required not only a cost estimate for full repair but also an overview of the alternatives.

Prayerful consideration was given to the possibility of moving to a new location. This produced many varied opinions. LaGrave Church was located in a dying neighborhood. The parishioners no longer lived in its vicinity. For these and other reasons, some members urged a search for a new site. Many were of a different persuasion. The downtown area would eventually improve. In addition, it was important to maintain a Reformed ministry in the core area of the city. LaGrave's providential location presented an opportunity to minister to the downtrodden of the inner city. Too many churches were already moving to the suburbs. "If some other downtown churches will never relocate, why should we?" The latter sentiment often included a reference to the permanency of St. Andrew's Cathedral, located a block south and west of LaGrave Church. There were times when the debate shed more *heat* than light. Mrs. William Stuart, widow of LaGrave's fourth pastor, took no position on the question. Rising above such considerations as population shifts and traffic patterns, she said at a congregational

The interior view of the original LaGrave Avenue Christian Reformed Church

meeting, "I have been listening to all the pros and cons of our devoted and earnest parishioners and my only comment is that we will never be a dying church — wherever we are — as long as God is in our midst."

At that same meeting, the congregation approved an appropriation of a sum not to exceed $4,000 for the purpose of obtaining tentative plans, sketches, and estimates with a view towards remodeling or rebuilding on the present site. At a subsequent congregational meeting (November 18, 1955), the study committee (J. Spalink, chairman, N. DeGraaf, J. Huizinga, B. Vandenberg, H. Walkotten) presented a proposal to rebuild at the same location. It lacked the necessary two-thirds majority by seven votes. Two months later, on January 27, 1956, by a nearly unanimous vote, the congregation made a historic decision and authorized the consistory to:

1. Proceed with the preparation of plans for a new church with a seating capacity of about 950. This church to be planned for the present site on LaGrave Avenue. (The congregation will be asked to give final authorization after plans have been presented.)

2. Purchase the property directly to the south of our present property on which an option is held.

3. Secure options on further property boarding on Cherry Street.

from *LaGrave News*, March, 1956

Because final authorization was to be given pending the presentation of plans, some began to have second thoughts. The first sketches of a new church revealed a quarter pie-shaped building with a free standing tower. There were strong negative congregational vibrations. A second set of sketches showing a church of neo-Gothic design caught everyone's imagination. At a congregational meeting where the second sketch was unveiled, there was total silence for almost ten seconds followed by enthusiastic applause.

One member who firmly opposed a new building project was Professor Jacob VandenBosch. He was a respected leader of long standing in the congregation whose love for LaGrave was passionate. He spoke with great eloquence in favor of repairing the old building. He became the spokesman for all who agreed with him — including a few who were counting the cost and were opposed because of financial considerations. When the congregation rejected his plea and voted for a new church, many wondered how Professor VandenBosch would react. Those who called on him seeking his financial support were not prepared for his response. Professor VandenBosch volunteered an extremely liberal pledge with the promise to increase it if necessary. He said the Lord had led the congregation in their decision. He would support one hundred percent what he had opposed.

Henry Walkotten, D.D.S., a member of the study committee, had become increasingly involved. He was the contact man with the architectural firm of Daverman and Company. Mr. Russ Pullen, who made the sketch that won the hearts of the LaGrave members and also drew the subsequent plans, related well to Dr. Walkotten. When the congregation approved Mr. Pullen's work, Dr. Walkotten was the unanimous choice of all to serve as the building chairman. A better selection could not have been made. He literally "ate, dreamt, and slept" his assignment. Henry Walkotten spent long hours in the public library familiarizing himself with church architecture, organ building, and related matters. He consulted far and wide with experts in the field of church construction and found their knowledge invaluable. The members of his committee who ably assisted him were:

Dr. Henry J. Walkotten

John Spalink	Deputy Chairman
Edward Hekman	Finance
Bert Vandenberg	Survey
Elias VanSweden . . .	Construction
Herbert VanderMey . .	Special Gifts
Richard Boelkins	Designs
Donald Battjes	Chapel Coordinator
Seymour Swets	Interior Appointments

These men all served as chairmen of their respective subcommittees. Mr. Casey Wondergem, not a member of LaGrave, was hired to oversee a pledge drive. With the exception of Mr. Wondergem, all the work was done by volunteers. There were too many to name. Representative of them all were Gordon Hartger and Thomas Kullgren, co-treasurers, who contributed countless

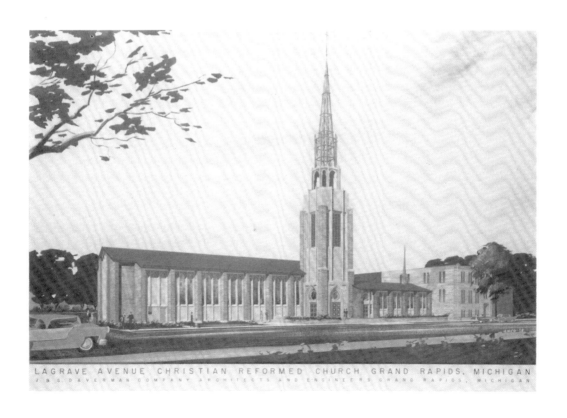

LAGRAVE AVENUE CHRISTIAN REFORMED CHURCH GRAND RAPIDS, MICHIGAN
J & S DAVERMAN COMPANY ARCHITECTS AND ENGINEERS GRAND RAPIDS, MICHIGAN

evenings to the financial matters of the building projects. The Building Fund Drive raised $252,000 in a period of three years. In 1960, the church would borrow $300,000 from the Old Kent Bank at 5½% interest. The theme of the entire project, "Build a House Unto My Name," was taken from I Kings 5:5.

In the spring of 1959, the congregation was informed that moving day was imminent. It would be a test of the cohesiveness of the congregation. It would also be a disconcerting experience requiring patience and understanding on the part of all. LaGrave was very fortunate in having accommodating neighbors. The Central Seventh Day Adventist Church, just west of the church, offered its facilities for Sunday mornings and Westminster Presbyterian Church, a block north, offered for Sunday evening services. All society and church school activities continued in the parish house. These arrangements were all made quietly and efficiently by George VanWesep, vice president of the consistory.

Demolition of the old hallowed sanctuary was scheduled for the first week in June 1959. The sanctuary was open every day for meditation and prayer for two weeks before the arrival of the wrecking ball. Mr. G. J. Rooks, honorary elder,

came every day to sit quietly in the pew where he had worshipped for so many years. Others, too, availed themselves of this opportunity. Many shed tears. The final service took place at 7 P. M., Sunday, May 31, 1959. Rev. Eppinga took his text from I Kings 5:5 which contained the theme of the building project. The sermon was entitled, "Build a House Unto My Name . . . " (See Addendum.) The choir sang "Give Thanks to God" by Worps-Old, and "Let Mount Zion Rejoice" by Herbert. The service ended with a solemn recessional of the choir followed by the congregation. When all had exited, Rev. Eppinga closed the doors. The bulletin for that day contained the following announcement:

> To observe the closing days in the present sanctuary, we were pleased to have with us the past few weeks three of our former pastors. Next Sunday we will meet in the morning at the Central Seventh Day Adventist Church directly behind the parish house. Services are scheduled for 9:30 and 11:00 A. M. In the evening, the service is scheduled for 7:00 P. M. and will be held in the Westminster Presbyterian Church across the street and one block north.

Early on Monday morning a surprising number of parishioners gathered across the street from

Demolition of the old sanctuary began Monday, June 1, 1959

TRANSITION

Nostalgia gripped us in God's house of prayer
The sad last time we met together there
In the dear sanctuary set apart
With special meaning in each separate heart;
The evening sunlight, gift of gentle May,
Lingered as if to hold this precious day,
Touching familiar faces in the choir,
Resting on pew and pulpit, slanting higher
To reach the picture of our Lord above,
Which had so often drawn our gaze of love.

Hush trembled, unplayed music, song unsung,
Echoing silence when a bell is rung,
With thankful joy mixed with some inward tears,
Our hearts re-captured moments down the years,
Not just one year for Him but seventy one.
May God have stamped them with his own "Well done"!
We may achieve the goals for which we pray,
Present to God still richer fruits one day,
Yet in our hearts fond memories will dwell
Of the vine-covered church we loved so well.

Josie Pangborn
LaGrave member

152

THE TOWER

The old church tower was stately,
 The old church tower was tall,
Its age-wise head uplifted,
 Its grace embraced us all:
Above the city's clamor,
 Above the city's grime,
It stood erect observing
 The changing ways of time.

It spoke a special language
 To wind and sun and rain,
And for those precious secrets
 Some listened but in vain:
The sensitive could hear them,
 Perhaps you heard them too,
The hopes and aspirations
 The winds relayed to you.

The old church tower has fallen,
 The old church tower is gone,
Yet in the winds it whispers
 "Press on, old friends, press on!
If what you have accomplished
 Thrives as it has begun,
There will rise spiritual, lasting,
 A tower to bless each one."

 Josie Pangborn

the church. Mr. E. VanSweden and Mr. A. Bel arranged for demolition work to begin that morning. Jay DeBoer, Albert Bosscher, Roy Bielema, and others were supervising the removal of the sanctuary furnishings which had been sold. Fortunately, Reynolds Weidenaar, artist and member of the congregation, had made his etching of the LaGrave tower just before it was demolished. By noon, most of those parishioners who had come to pay their last respects had melted away. Saying farewell to the old sanctuary had been a greater emotional wrench than had been anticipated. Rev. Eppinga led those assembled on the sidewalk in singing:

> I love Thy Church, O God!
> Her walls before Thee stand,
> Dear as the apple of Thine eye,
> And graven on Thy hand.

Because the Central Seventh Day Adventist Church sanctuary was so small, LaGrave had to conduct two morning services — 9:30 and 11:00 A. M. Some parishioners chose the 9:30 service. More came at 11:00 A. M. Church school was conducted during the second service. Many preferred the evening service where "all could be together."

The morning arrangement seemed to split the congregation into two parts. Many friends, meeting each other coming and going to and from the services, were glad this schedule was only temporary. The division in the communion of the saints was serious. Church attendance, good in the morning, better in the evening, was contrary to the usual pattern. It was evident, however, that the congregation was cohesive and that it would survive the temporary inconveniences.

As the building project progressed, Dr. Walkotten announced a list of items suitable to give as memorials or special gifts for the new facility. A surprising number of members came forward to avail themselves of this opportunity. (See Addendum.) The congregation was grateful for the generosity of these individuals. At the same time, it was announced that as soon as the new roof was over their heads they would move in, even though the interior work would not be completed.

True Dutch thrift influenced many decisions. The Willett Studios of Philadelphia, Pennsylvania would design and install the Great Commission window, but the lancet windows on the east and west walls would be of frosted glass until they could be replaced with more appropriate leaded windows at a cost of one thousand dollars a piece. Individuals and families would be given the opportunity to donate one or more as memorials.

The thirty-five lancet windows, eighteen on one side and seventeen on the other, would depict the life of Christ from His birth through His resurrection. Traditional leaded glass would be combined with a more modern idiom in the execution of the art work of these windows.

The Great Commission window in the chancel area, donated in memory of Dr. Henry Beets, was done in a new art form, of which there were only two other examples in the entire country. It was executed in a new and exciting technique consisting of brilliantly colored potmetal dalles — about an inch thick — cut and chipped to a desired size, then set in specially prepared concrete and reinforced with steel bars bent to fit the design. This beautiful five-lancet window, besides illustrating Christ's ascension, would vividly depict the divine command given to Jesus' disciples, "Go ye therefore, and teach all nations, baptizing them in the Name of the Father and the Son and of the Holy Ghost." (Matthew 28:19.) Below is a simple sketch giving the artist's general idea. For a more detailed description, see the color section.

> *A gracious Roman Catholic friend who had a sense of humor was approached for a donation for the LaGrave building project. He said that as a good Roman Catholic he could contribute nothing to the raising of Protestant walls, but he would be glad to make a contribution to the cost of tearing the old building down.*

> *The Willett Studios' original design of the Great Commission window contained a recognizable likeness of Albert Schweitzer, the doctor in Africa whose motto, "Reverence For Life," together with his other accomplishments, had made him world famous. Inasmuch as the building committee wished no specific individuals to be included outside of Bible figures, Mr. Willett was asked to alter the figure of the modern missionary in a pith helmet so that he would not be identified with Dr. Schweitzer, whose theology was far removed from that of John Calvin.*

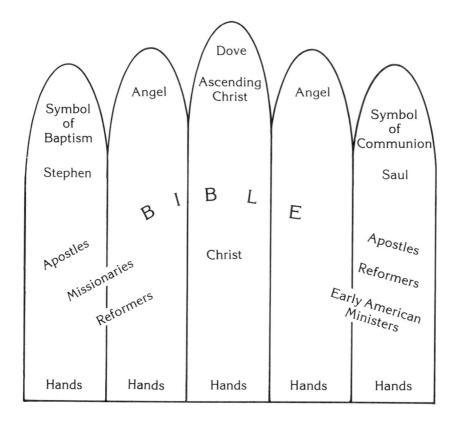

The lancet windows in the sanctuary were given by Mr. and Mrs. Ray Herrick. They were not members of LaGrave Church. As a boy, Ray Herrick often visited Macatawa Park, Holland, on the shores of Lake Michigan. As he played in the sand, he admired a particular house, vowing to own it someday if he could ever afford it. Becoming a wealthy man in his later life, he sought to realize his boyhood dream. By this time, Dr. and Mrs. H. Walkotten were the owners of the house he sought. They sold it to him through a realtor, never meeting in person. Sometime later, through a tax bill, Dr. Walkotten discovered that he still owned the lot between the house and the beach — the result of an oversight on the part of the realtor. He immediately sent a note to Mr. Herrick explaining the error and added, "Send me a dollar to make the transaction legal and the lot is yours." Ray Herrick, not accustomed to such gracious treatment, said, "Someday I'm going to do something nice for that man." Later they became acquainted. One day, Ray Herrick found Henry Walkotten poring over the La-Grave Church plans. Seeing his opportunity to return an earlier favor, Mr. Herrick volunteered to give one whole wall side of sanctuary windows. Henry Walkotten appeared at the next weekly meeting of the building committee with a check for $18,000 from Ray Herrick. At the next meeting, he came with a second Herrick check for $17,000. Mrs. Herrick had chided her husband: "What is that church going to look like with one side stained glass windows and the other side frosted glass!"

Mr. and Mrs. Ray Herrick

All the windows in their entirety would be used as a tool for telling visitors and groups (Boy Scouts, senior citizen tours, etc.) the story of the life of Jesus Christ.

In October of 1959, these lovely windows were not yet realities. Much more work needed to be done by the contractor, Mr. Bert Johnson of the Johnson Construction Company, before the windows could be put in place. It was remarkable that during the time of construction all the building supplies were left out in the open, undisturbed, and never subjected to theft although they were unguarded at night.

The contractor's goal in the summer of 1959 was to have the church entirely "roofed in" before cold weather interfered. Co-treasurers, G. Hartger and T. Kullgren, worried about the slack in giving during the summer months. The building committee met regularly every Monday noon in the parish house. They would spread plans and papers over half-a-dozen tables and ponder a myriad of details.

Gradually all things were coming together and taking shape in the form of steel, wood and stone arches, a laminated roof deck, and an eighty-six-foot open frame spire atop a seventy-four-foot masonry tower in the Gothic tradition. The spire being open (or pierced), was reminiscent of the fifteenth century spires in Germany's famous Cologne Cathedral.

Meanwhile, the congregation continued worshipping in strange surroundings. Mr. James Dice, who was chief usher, and his assistants worked out seating arrangements for three serv-

155

ices in two different locations. Mr. H. Isinga, custodian, had additional duties to perform. Not only did he keep the parish house neat and clean, but the Central Seventh Day Adventist and Westminster Presbyterian Churches as well. Alyce Lantinga and her assistants along with Seymour Swets and the choir were also involved in such maneuvers and adjustments as the new arrangements required. Every Sunday morning the choir processed in their robes from the parish house across the alley to the Central Seventh Day Adventist Church, through rain and storm, on their appointed mission.

The Rose Window, one of two "old sanctuary valuables" (the other being the organ), had been preserved. Its position had been over the pulpit on the front wall. The congregation felt a great affection for this beautiful window. Generations had contemplated the circular, colorful stained glass window showing Christ our Lord on His knees in prayer in the Garden of Gethsemane — a copy of the painting by Johann Heinrich Hofmann. By November, 1959, it had been safety re-installed high on the rear wall of the new sanctuary, a position exactly opposite of that which it held in the old sanctuary. Sunday worshippers went on their weekly tours of inspection to approve or disapprove of the progress made during the week. They breathed a sigh of relief when they beheld their beloved Rose Window safely housed once more.

On Thanksgiving Day, 1959, the service held in the Central Seventh Day Adventist Church was followed by the cornerstone laying. The sermon of that day, "Christ, the Sure Foundation," was placed inside the stone, with the following declaration:

Dearly Beloved:

For the erection of this public house of
   worship:
WE LAY THIS CORNERSTONE

In order that there may be a sanctuary to fill
   men's minds with greater reverence for
   His Glorious Majesty:
WE LAY THIS CORNERSTONE

Above all, that His Name may be more greatly
   magnified in a place of preaching and
   of prayer:
WE LAY THIS CORNERSTONE

Let us not doubt then that God will favorably approve our action here on this Thanksgiving Day in the year of our Lord, nineteen-hundred-and-fifty-nine.

To This Declaration We Add This Prayer:

We pray that the LaGrave Avenue Christian Reformed Church and the Dewey Battjes Memorial Chapel shall stand to serve the coming generations until that day when Christ shall appear again upon the day of days.

But if not: Should this structure be destroyed by natural or by mortal storm; God forbid, but should this house for God be demolished by Satan's forces of evil, then: be it known by whosoever finds this testimony, that God's work in this congregation shall far outlast and outlive these stones. For we, the members of the LaGrave Avenue Christian Reformed Church, who are toiling to erect this earthly house of praise, " . . . Having a building of God. A house not made with hands, Eternal in the heavens." II Corinthians 5:1.

Dr. Walkotten and Reverend Eppinga placed the following items into the cornerstone: The Declaration, Rev. Eppinga's Sermon of the Day, Letter of Presentation Relating to the Dewey Battjes Memorial Chapel, President Eisenhouwer's Thanksgiving Day Proclamation, The Pamphlet, "107 LaGrave," Describing the Church's Ministry to Its Members and the Community, The Church Directory of 1959, The Church Bulletin of Sunday, November 22, 1959, The First Page of the Grand Rapids Press, Thursday, November 26, and copies of Newspaper Stories Describing the Ceremony, and Photographs of the Ceremony

The sanctuary plans called for a divided chancel. In order to symbolize the historical fact that the Gospel travelled West, the plans placed the pulpit on the west side. Workmen mistakenly reversed this arrangement. The error was discovered too late and never corrected. Thus, the lectern with the baptismal font was installed where the pulpit was intended. The divided chancel occasioned a considerable debate which reached the pages of *The Banner*. Its editor, earnestly contending for the centrality of the Word, felt that it was a Calvinistic architectural principle to place the pulpit front and center so that the Bible became the focal point. Rev. Eppinga attempted to defend LaGrave's choice of a divided chancel by saying that the centrality of the Word was asserted by what the preacher *said,* not by where he stood. After a number of comments by readers, some for and some against, the issue faded.

By the late spring of 1960, Henry Walkotten, the capable building chairman, was bringing all things to an orchestrated climax: the Schulmerich Carillon including a Westminster Peal and Hour Strike, had been donated and was being installed; Ray Weidenaar was making good progress on the fresco project.

Reynold H. Weidenaar, a member of the congregation and a well-known and established artist, had spent some time in Italy studying frescoes — the art or method of painting over freshly spread plaster before it dries. This project was sponsored by Mr. William B. Eerdmans with a view to providing LaGrave's new sanctuary with a Weidenaar fresco of its very own. The artist's first effort — Christ framed by the pillars of the LaGrave sanctuary — resulted in failure, due to a lack of adhesive quality in the plaster mixture.

> *Mr. Weidenaar's first fresco attempt landed in the alley. When Rev. Eppinga discovered it, he had it brought to church. It is presently displayed in the chapel narthex. To deter further crumbling of the plaster, it was placed behind glass. All agreed that its artistic beauty far outweighed its material deficiency.*

His second fresco was placed in the narthex adjacent to the chapel. Mr. Weidenaar named it, "The Great Commission" and based it on Ecclesiastes 4:1 "So I . . . considered all the oppressions that are done under the sun: and behold the tears of such as were oppressed, and they had no comforter . . . " At its installation, Mr. Weidenaar provided the building committee with the following description:

> The fresco attempts to depict the undertones of this plight of mankind struggling under its burdens of futility, despair and evil, restlessly seeking out the meaning of it all, of life, of man's purpose and his destiny. With many devisings, massive incantations, millions of prayers, pilgrimages, stairways, idols, pagodas, towers, sacrifices, burnings, or with a super state religion, mankind strives to placate or equate, or even supplant the one true God of the universe.

> And out of this striving, milling meleé, there emerge toward the foreground many faces, wearing the garbs of all corners of the globe. It is the worldwide Macedonian cry of old, "Come over and help us!" Interspersed throughout the design, one comes upon a medallion-like portrait of a worker in this vast field; he may be within our denomination or from without, some are actually shown in their labors as they pioneered for Gospel work. But spread across and beyond, and transcending all, are the vertical and horizontal lines of the cross bearing the Great Sacrifice, as He redeems a believing and repentant mankind. It is the dominant motif: Christ between heaven and earth, soon to rise from the dead. It is the supreme event of all history: mankind lost is become mankind redeemed. "Go ye . . . "

Reynold Weidenaar working on one of the frescoes (See Addendum)

157

Eventually, Reynold Weidenaar completed two more frescoes which were placed in the narthex of the sanctuary. The subject matter of these two frescoes dealt with various aspects of church history.* These frescoes became famous and were written up and featured in publications of both popular and technical nature. Because of the tremendous value of these frescoes and the art glass produced by the Willet Studios in Philadelphia, the building committee took immediate and appropriate action to insure them all.

The Dewey Battjes Memorial Chapel, adjoining the sanctuary, also reflects the same solemn dignity and quiet meditation conveyed in the church proper. It imbues reverence with its contemporary form but traditional detail. An Italian marble reredos screen, highlighted with a wooden cross, accents the chancel. The spire above the chapel blends gracefully with the tall tower and gold cross atop the new church.

The chapel windows had been installed and drew the inspection and approval of all. The Rose or circular window, over the outside entrance of the chapel, depicts Jesus with arms outstretched to welcome the faithful. Along the east walls are four three-lancet windows. The first presents Christ's ministry to individuals; the second shows Christ in the role of preaching; the third illustrates various types of prayer, and the fourth portrays Christ as the Great Physician. Twelve square windows, showing the symbols of the twelve apostles, were installed on the west wall.*

The pipe organ in the Dewey Battjes Memorial Chapel was a two-manual and pedal instrument,

*For complete description, see color section of this book.

custom built by the Wicks Organ Company of Highland, Illinois. The pipes were located in the tower behind the chapel balcony.

The sanctuary organ, retained from the old church and enlarged to suit the needs of the new sanctuary, was housed in two chambers on either side of the chancel. The work was done by Casavant-Frères Co., Ltd. of St. Hyacinths, Quebec, Canada, organ builders since 1879.

JOHN 12:21

Mrs. Lee (Matilda) Huizenga wished to present the church with a gift in memory of her husband, but lacked the means. She sought the pastor's assistance in selecting something meaningful, yet modest in price. The following Sunday he told the story of a minister whose sermons were brilliant yet contained no Gospel. One day, entering his pulpit, he discovered an anonymous note referring him to John 12:21. It was the story of some Greeks who came to Philip saying, "Sir, we would see Jesus."

After the service, Mrs. Huizenga called the pastor and thanked him for his suggestion. When he expressed surprise and ignorance, she said that she would seek permission from the building committee to have a small brass plaque placed in the pulpit for everyone who stood there to read. Its message: "Sir, we would see Jesus."

The gift was as fine as any that was received and a fitting memorial to Dr. Lee S. Huizenga, LaGrave's first missionary, who in both his preaching and medical ministry showed Jesus to all.

The first service in the new sanctuary took place on June 19, 1960. In the first sermon preached from the new pulpit, Rev. Eppinga referred to certain features of the new church and their meanings:

The Spire — Heavenly aspirations; pointing to God

The Octagonal Base of the Spire — The eight attributes of God

The Square Base of the Octagonal Base — The City Foursquare

The Gothic Arches — Hands in prayer

The Sanctuary Pillars — The saints upholding the truth

He also said:

> Let the modern touches tell us that we live in a changing world. But let the lines of the tower and the arrangement of the chancel and nave — all basic and traditional — speak to us of that which endures throughout the ages; of Him who in a changing world is ever the same.

Early in the fall, dedicatory organ recitals took place in both the chapel and sanctuary with Alyce Lantinga at the organ consoles. A "Community Night," in which ministers of area churches and representatives of Classis Grand Rapids South participated, was well attended.

On October 12, 1960, the service of dedication took place. The chancel choir rendered two appropriate anthems: Carl Mueller's "God Himself Is with Us," and Johannes Brahm's "How Lovely Is Thy Dwelling Place." In moving words, Dr. Walkotten presented the "Keys" to the congregation. He quoted the poet Keats:

> A thing of beauty is a joy forever,
> Its loveliness increases,
> It will never pass into nothingness.

He quoted Winston Churchill:

> Architecturally, we shape our buildings,
> Thereafter, they shape us.

Dr. Walkotten ended by saying:

> In the name of the building committee, I surrender this key with the admonition that we look backward in gratitude, upward in reverence, and forward in confidence.

After the benediction, something wonderful happened —

THERE WAS SPONTANEOUS APPLAUSE!

Thus did LaGrave's new sanctuary come into being. It could not have been accomplished without the cooperation of all and, above everything —

The Grace of God.

The applause was in thanksgiving and praise to Him.

The Interior of the new LaGrave Avenue Christian Reformed Church

Chapter 22

A DIFFICULT DECADE

The LaGrave congregation entered the 1960s on a high note. Its services in the new sanctuary were well attended. Indeed, the crowds were viewed with a kind of joyful dismay. Chairs were carried in for the morning services, and overflow crowds were seated in the chapel. Evening services filled both the main floor and the balcony. There were those who wondered whether or not LaGrave's new facility had been built on too small a scale.

The country, too, met the 1960s with a wave of energy. President John F. Kennedy, addressing the nation said:

> We stand today on the edge of a new frontier — the frontier of the 1960s, a frontier of unknown opportunities and perils, a frontier of unfulfilled hopes and threats.

In the spirit of these remarks and similar sentiments, Americans shed their previous mood of apathy and self-content. A feeling of challenge and commitment surfaced on college campuses, in executive board rooms, and everywhere. There was a growing list of Peace Corps volunteers (19,000 the first year) who, following their new president's challenge, marched boldly and eagerly forward. Yet, before the decade was over, the feeling of a new and dawning day would change

from optimism to doubt and disenchantment.

The assassination of President Kennedy in November, 1963, proved a harbinger of similar tragedies to come. Churches, including LaGrave, filled with mourners for the president. Still, it was not over. Civil rights leader Martin Luther King was assassinated in April of 1968, and Senator Robert Kennedy was felled the following June. Richard Cardinal Cushing, Archbishop of Boston, cried: "Good Lord, what is this all about?"

Following President Kennedy, President Lyndon B. Johnson (LBJ) tried hard to move the country forward into "The Great Society." But the Vietnam War was beginning to divide the people into "doves" (those opposed) and "hawks" (those in favor of pursuing the war to final victory). War protests mushroomed; draft dodging became an art. A generation gap opened wide (don't trust anyone over thirty), and long hair for boys and miniskirts for girls became the fashion. "The Beatles," four mop-haired rock singers from Liverpool, England, made their profound impression. Haight-Ashbury, San Francisco, became the epicenter of the hippie world with its love-ins and flower children. Everywhere, young people in significant numbers were "dropping out of the straight society," causing Groucho Marx, a Hollywood comedian, to turn serious and observe, "Kids today are detestable."

In a decade begun in high hope but rapidly falling apart, the drug cult only added to the disarray of the nation. "Psychodelia" was formally described as the intensely pleasureful perception of the senses. The young, who were developing their own grammar, if not language, defined it as, "Something beautiful, man — like it blows your mind." From 1960 to 1970, the number of marijuana users rose from one hundred thousand to eight million. Like lemmings, embarking on an incredible march to their own destruction, many young people plunged themselves into an unknown chemical sea. Cults, too, multiplied, in a chaotic decade. Eastern religions allured. On the street corners of the great cities, the repetitive Hindu invocations were heard:

Hare Krishna, Hare Kirshna,
Krishna Kirshna, Hare Hare,
Hare Rama, Hare Rama,
Rama Rama, Hare Hare.

Actress Shirley McLaine, national idol, said incongruously, "Once the soul of India gets into you, it sits on your shoulder all the time." Meanwhile, at the other end of life's scale, sunset villages sprang up for those too old to work and too young to die. "Senior citizen" became a phrase. Some sought unsuccessfully to change it to "mature adults." Those among them who were dying of lung cancer were learning of a hazard previous decades had not divulged; but cigarette sales remained largely unaffected.

As the 1960s got underway, the nation's nineteen million blacks served notice that they would no longer endure their lot. Thus, there was violence. Non-violent Martin Luther King registered his famous "I Have a Dream" speech. The year 1965 brought the civil rights march in Montgomery, Alabama. Cities, as well as spirits, were inflamed. Between 1964 and 1967, fifty-eight cities exploded in riots, leaving 141 dead and 4,552 injured. Detroit burned. Spiro T. Agnew, running with Richard Nixon on the Republican ticket, visited the Motor City and said, "If you've seen one ghetto area, you've seen them all." Still, the end of the decade saw progress in race-relations.

In the realms of science, there were new frontiers and opportunities. Man reached the moon. Ten years before this event, a member of LaGrave had chided the ninth pastor for entertaining such

PRESIDENT KENNEDY IS SLAIN BY HIDDEN TEXAS SNIPER

DR. KING FATALLY SHOT BY ASSASSIN IN MEMPHIS

KENNEDY DIES
Succumbs to Assassin's Bullet

South Viets Forming Army To 'Liberate' North Vietnam

Pullout Irrevocable, Johnson Says

a possibility in a sermon. In laboratories, technicians were deciphering the genetic code. There was talk of laser beams and computers changing life as it was known.

Meanwhile, the turbulent sixties were constantly at work unalterably altering the land and its people. High-rise apartments and condominium living became the style of many. The ascendancy of television brought about talk of the "decay of the written word" and the demise of the *Saturday Evening Post.* The "single" life became a touted lifestyle. Through it all, American soldiers fought and suffered in Vietnam.

The churches of America, including LaGrave, were all deeply affected by and ill-prepared for the astonishing context of the revolutionary decade in which they found themselves. Some sought to climb aboard every bandwagon that came along. Some preachers vied with each other to see who could shout the loudest: "Black is beautiful!" Some churches actively encouraged draft dodging. Others turned their liturgies upside down in their efforts to appeal to an increas-

ing notion that what was old was bad and what was new was wonderful. LaGrave, too, felt the strain of a decade unlike any it had previously experienced in its three-quarters-of-a-century of existence. LaGrave, too, would be affected.

None of this was sensed when the congregation first entered its new gates with praise. The consistory and members generously gave its pastor a sabbatical leave as a reward for guiding the church through the preceding strenuous years which had included the building of a new sanctuary. Rev. and Mrs. Eppinga and their children, Richard, Jay, Susan, and Deanna spent the time in Richmond, Virginia, where LaGrave's pastor attended Union Seminary of the Southern Presbyterian Church.

Dr. Jacob Bruinooge, emeritus minister and member of LaGrave, did the pastoral calling while Rev. Eppinga was away. While in Richmond, Virginia, the pastor wrote the following song which appeared in the October, 1961, *LaGrave News* along with monthly letters.

A PASTOR'S SABBATICAL PRAYER

The ascendancy of television saw the demise of the Saturday Evening Post

Mr. and Mrs. Howard VerMerris were the new custodial team residing in the parish house apartment. LaGrave's missionaries, the Vroons (Africa), the Nyenhuises (Cuba), the Izquierdos (Cuba), and the Dykemas (New Mexico) continued their reports to the congregation. The Sunday Niters, from which the college age Young Adults had separated in 1958, was revitalized and reorganized. It was a very enthusiastic society with good sponsors, notably Wesley and Betty De-Young, Jerry and Jess VanderWall, and Al and Ruth Bosscher. Their first project was the purchase of flags for the sanctuary, manifesting a spirit and a patriotism which the decade in its latter half would challenge. Wisely, the consistory organized a youth council made up of representatives of the Young Adults, the Sunday Niters, the Campfire Girls, and the Boy Scouts, giving them a voice in the life of the congregation.

The new sanctuary encouraged new activities as did the parish house before it, in 1940. From time to time, special speakers and lecturers were brought in, and the meetings were well attended. Among the speakers were Dr. V. Raymond Ed-

MEMBER EXTRAORDINAIRE

Mr. Adrian C. Kett, retired supervisor of the Calvin College dormitory, self-styled theologian, chess expert, and widower was one of many very colorful characters enriching the life of the LaGrave family. He never missed a service, even though he was handicapped and suffered from severe headaches. His love for LaGrave Church knew no bounds. Being of limited means, Mr. Kett could give only modestly to the church. This brought him much sorrow. Accordingly, he applied by letter to the various television networks seeking to become a contestant on one of the many quiz shows. His category? The Bible. He was especially desirous of being accepted by the $64,000 show, a favorite at the time. His application was never accepted; yet, in the hope that it would happen, he studied Bible encyclopedias every night. One show did respond to his application, informing him that to remain qualified would necessitate his purchase of a set of books they were selling. Mr. Kett gleefully made the purchase, but nothing further was heard. To his dying day, it remained his goal to win $64,000 in the category of The Bible and to give it all to LaGrave.

man, President of Wheaton College, representatives of the National Association of Evangelicals (NAE), and various members of the clergy, from both home and abroad. Among the latter, there was a Dr. R. Schippers from the Netherlands, who wrote of his impressions in a Holland newspaper. The translation was made by Mr. A. C. Kett, member extraordinaire of the LaGrave Church:

I have in my possession a bulletin of the LaGrave Christian Reformed Church in Grand Rapids, Michigan. I consider it as valuable as a jewel, because it states that I was going to deliver a sermon that evening . . . In America, the pulpit is used to introduce the speaker. Its pastor, the Rev. J. D. Eppinga, opened the service with, "We welcome to the pulpit Dr. Reinier Schippers, Professor of New Testament at the Free University of Amsterdam."

LaGrave is a big church with many members. Its building is located in the old part of the city. Many of its members live in the suburbs of Grand Rapids; in some instances as far as six English miles . . . .

The cost of LaGrave's beautiful church and chapel amounts to approximately $750,000. Its chapel is used for prayer meetings and marriage. The church has many separate rooms. A separate room for its pastor, one for its assistant pastor, a business office with a lady secretary, rooms for the choir, Sunday school and catechism, and a banquet hall which can hold about 1,000 people, and kitchens. I must mention that I had the pleasure of being present at a wedding in that banquet hall after the ceremony was completed in the chapel.

The above description is rather businesslike, notwithstanding, it all made a tremendous impression on me. The church is beautiful, its glass-in-lead windows superb, fancy lumber, and an excellent organ. But that is not all. The entrance is something that when entering, you become impressed. It demands reverence and, consequently, the entering of the members is calm. There is a committee to welcome, also shake hands with you, and another committee to give you a place to sit. This is all something to make you feel at home in the LaGrave Church.

When all this was finished, Rev. Eppinga and myself walked in the central aisle towards the two pulpits, good sized lecterns, apart from each other, at the same height . . . .

Rev. Eppinga announces the number of the processional hymn and the choir marches forward with the choirmaster, who has a handsome gray head, leading. Their seats are located behind the lectern. They are all dressed in light blue robes . . . .

Then follows the votum and blessing which is pronounced while the congregation remains standing. The twelve articles are repeated while the congregation is seated. The choir sings Gloria Patri, as printed in the bulletin. Prayer is rendered after which the deacons take the collection, which after having finished, is brought forward while congregation and choir sing, "Praise God From Whom All Blessings Flow."

After the sermon and song glorifying God's name, there is a silent prayer.

Taking all this in consideration, I must state that I was deeply impressed with all that had taken place.

Donald Postema, a Calvin seminarian, completed his internship at LaGrave in 1961. He continued his theological studies at the Free University in Amsterdam. Another Calvin seminarian, William LaFleur, then served for two years as an assistant to Rev. Eppinga, after which time he left for Japan to serve as a missionary.

LaGrave Church began to advertise its services in the *Grand Rapids Press* identifying itself as "The Church of the Chimes and the Challenge."

Hymns were played twice each day from the carillon tower. This elicited favorable responses from the neighborhood residents and, particularly, from the patients at Ferguson Droste Ferguson Hospital, located just northwest of the church. Some of the patients who wrote came from various parts of the country.

October 6, 1963

Dear Friends:

This is just a note of appreciation for the lovely chime music I've been hearing while a patient at the Ferguson Clinic. When I checked in a week ago, I was a little depressed, and the hymns that were played just as I was having a meager supper were very comforting. Thank you for having made my stay here a little more pleasant.

Sincerely,
Mrs. M. Burke

November 1964

To the Minister and Congregation of the LaGrave Church:

Christians! I wish to let you know how much I enjoyed listening to the hymns as played on your church's electronic chimes from my hospital bed in Ferguson Droste Ferguson Hospital between January 8th and 19th. On some of my most miserable days, those hymns lifted my spirits. You have my deepest appreciation. Also, I wish to thank the secretary who at my telephoned request, sent the words of the hymns that were played. I feel those hymns, played periodically throughout the day, are a big Christian service to your hospital surrounded area. Thank you.

Sincerely,
Wrex D. Pierson

December 1963

To the LaGrave Church:

We would like to express our sincere gratitude and thanks to you for the refrigerator, gas stove, steam table, double coffee urn and table, and the other kitchen utensils you so thoughtfully donated to the Kent County Honor Camp for Youthful Offenders. Your thoughtfulness and generosity is certainly appreciated and we thank you again.

Arnold O. Pigorsh
Kent County sheriff

Other expressions of appreciation for various services rendered by LaGrave to the community-at-large were also received from the YMCA, YWCA, Kent County Cancer Society, Kent County Tuberculosis Society, and St. Mary's Hospital.

Throughout this period of LaGrave's history, its Young Adult and Sunday Niter organizations flourished as never before and, perhaps, never since. In 1961, the Henry Beets Mission Society sent thirteen young people away for summer mission assignments. That number increased to twenty the following year. A summer Bible school of approximately 100–150 neighborhood children also benefitted from the help given by La-Grave's young people. This effort was continued into the fall and winter season and was, accordingly, renamed the Saturday Bible School. But as the decade wore on, more and more dwellings disappeared, and fewer children were found in the neighborhood.

Accessibility to the LaGrave location, however, was enhanced by the appearance of an express-way snaking its way through the heart of the city. With no shopping malls in the suburbs, the traffic flow was towards downtown. Thus, more people went to LaGrave for midweek events, such as organ concerts in the LaGrave sanctuary by such well-known musicians as Gordon Young of Detroit, Michigan, and Marilyn Mason of the University of Michigan, Ann Arbor. Laymen's Institutes, sponsored by the mission committee of the consistory and the Henry Beets Mission Society, were also annual events well attended by people of various churches.

Continuing in a strong mission tradition, weekly meetings were begun at the Lafayette Nursing Home and the Christian Nursing Home. George and Sena Houtman, Adrian Slings, Peter VanHerp, and Gil and Connie VanSledright were much involved in these projects. Maxine Ohlmann, LaGrave member, volunteered for mission service and was sent by the Henry Beets Mission Society to Africa. A year later (1963), Sis Rozeboom, another member, went to Uganda with LaGrave's support. Meanwhile, the Henry Beets Auxiliary, made up of women, met regularly in order to supply our hospitals in Nigeria with many needed items.

In 1963, Sis Rozeboom sent an SOS to La-Grave. She needed all the eye glasses she could get. She found poor vision and blindness rampant. Spectacles might help those whose sight had only been impaired. Five hundred pairs would be

The Henry Beets Auxiliary, making bandages. Left to right: Ann Scherphorn, Theresa Vroon, Jennie Westveer, Jean Dice, and Deane Schuitema

---

In 1964, the Henry Beets Auxiliary provided our denomination's medical effort in Nigeria with:

Boxes of surgical dressings	25
Gauze sponges	26,088
Gauze rolls	100

In 1965:

Gauze sponges	24,744
Gauze rolls	431
Dressing pads	120
Plaster cast rolls	9
Terry towels	299
Knitted bandages	86
Operating room caps	144

from *LaGrave News*, Feb., 1966

---

a real blessing. LaGrave's Sunday Niters, anxious to help, translated Sis Rozeboom's SOS into a slogan: "So Others See." They advertised, collected, and mailed over 3,000 pairs of glasses to Uganda.

Mission interest was further evidenced by a yearly Palm Sunday canvass of all dwellings within an area bounded by Division, Wealthy, Madison and Fulton. These efforts demanded good organization and preparation. Some seventy to eighty canvassers spent their Palm Sunday afternoons extending invitations to our services and distributing Bibles and literature. Later in the decade, Rev. John Moes, a member, carried this work forward in a neighborhood door-to-door ministry and a follow-up on contacts made by way of the general canvass. In this way, many individuals were helped and the Gospel was spread. Still later, this work was apportioned among three seminarians, Jake Corvers, S. Edward Groot, and A. James Heynen. LaGrave also combined with four other downtown churches to support an ecumenical effort in reaching out to the increasing numbers of young people adrift and gravitating to the downtown area.

Meanwhile, as many as twenty-three of La-Grave's young people at one time were in the service of their country. Mrs. John Cook and Mrs. John Dekker served as service secretaries. The effect of the war in Vietnam and general unrest among the young people in the country moved the LaGrave consistory to approve a request for special young adult worship services. These highly informal meetings were held once a month, at 5 P.M., in fellowship hall. Initially, there were from three-to-four hundred in attendance. There were those who were polarized by this development — being either strongly for or against such meetings. It was a time of restlessness in which some became more emotional and less wise — truly a time of testing throughout the denomination.

Earlier in the decade, Andrew Templeman succeeded William LaFleur as assistant to the pastor. Templeman's participation in the ecumenical youth ministry was augmented by projects carried on exclusively by LaGrave's young people. A house was rented in a ghetto area to serve as headquarters for a mission outreach. Some of La-Grave's doctors, lawyers, and businessmen met

Young Hands Help

Christian Action Youth Group Paints Homes
As Community Project

neighborhood people there and gave them both the advice they sought as well as LaGrave's expression of Christian care. This project was highly effective but, in an explosive time, of short duration.

A Wednesday morning prayer breakfast was initiated. The LaGrave library was begun. A Saturday Bible School required supervision and coordination. A Women's Board was organized to coordinate all women's activities and serve as liaison between the women's organizations and the building (facilities) committee of the consistory. There were "Mr. and Mrs. Club" retreats. A Board of Trustees was organized to deal with such matters as insurance, mortgage payments, and the like. Rev. Eppinga founded the Benefactors Trust Fund which would receive monetary gifts to be used for the enhancement of LaGrave's programs, e.g., education, music, missions, young people. Half of the monies were liquid and could be used; the remaining half would enter a restricted fund from which only the interest could be used.

In May of 1963, Rev. Eppinga served as state chairman for Spiritual Foundations Day during Michigan Week. The job required promotional travel throughout the state. Considering this an opportunity for contribution to the community-at-large, the consistory graciously permitted the pastor to carry out the required duties. The following article appeared in the *Grand Rapids Press.*

SPIRITUAL OBSERVANCE
TO OPEN MICHIGAN WEEK

Highlighting the vital role of religion in the history — and in the future — of Michigan, Spiritual Foundations Day will open the Michigan Week celebration throughout the state Sunday, May 19.

CHAIRMAN OF DAY

Rev. Jacob D. Eppinga, pastor of La-Grave Avenue Christian Reformed Church, Grand Rapids, is chairman of the special Sunday observance.

"Spiritual Foundations Day this year will be not only an occasion to remember past blessings, but a day in which to pledge ourselves anew to the observance of the eternal truths without which Michigan cannot forge ahead," he said.

"The many spires and steeples which have been added to Michigan's silhouette since the first Spiritual Foundations Day of the first Michigan Week, ten years ago, prove that the faith of our founding fathers is still a significant factor in the life and health of our state."

The same year, Rev. Eppinga was invited to attend the World Congress on Evangelism in Berlin, Germany, as an observer. The consistory, feeling that such an opportunity would be spiritually and intellectually rewarding, also approved this trip. Mrs. Eppinga accompanied her husband.

Mr. Templeman was succeeded by Mr. Harold DeJong, Mr. Douglas Warners, and Mr. Henry Hoeks, in that order. Mr. Hoeks, in a second term, also served as director of education. In this capacity, he had direct access to and benefitted from Rev. William VanderHaak, who had joined La-Grave Church and who was serving as the Denominational Executive Secretary for Religious Education. Later, in December 1964, Rev. Wesley Smedes of the Denomination Home Missions Board joined LaGrave; the congregation was blessed by his presence.

In 1963, Seymour Swets who, by this time was "Mr. Music" for the entire Christian Reformed denomination, retired from his position as La-Grave's choir director. It was a position he had held for thirty-seven years. This was a wrench for

Amid all of these activities, the pastor's telephone rang as much at home as in the church study. Rev. Eppinga had an easy home phone number (CHerry 1-1122), He was not pleased when it was changed. He notified the congregation of the change via the LaGrave News.

I have had a beautiful telephone number. The exchange was "Cherry," which is one of my favorite fruits, and the numbers were 1-1122. The whole thing had personality. But times change — and not always for the better. The parsonage telephone number has now been reduced to the numbers 949-5338 which I deplore. I cannot take this dictation from the telephone company lying down. It serves only to make life more impersonal than it already is. Therefore, I hereby announce that I have done something about it. I have changed my telephone number from 949-5338 to WIgwaam 9-5338. This strikes me as easier to remember. Also, this change has personality and it is very American — early American.

the congregation, as well as for him. Professor J. G. VandenBosch wrote a moving "Appreciation" for him in the pages of the *LaGrave News.* On May 1, 1963, over 200 choir members gathered to pay Professor Swets tribute. Former pastors Rev. H. Bel and Dr. E. Masselink and their wives, along with others, came to honor Seymour Swets. Rev. William Swets, Seymour's brother, gave the invocation. Dr. Orren Bolt spoke appropriate words on behalf of the choir and congregation, and fitting remembrances were proffered. The evening marked the end of an era and reminded all present that even long tenures must end. La-Grave was fortunate to find an excellent replacement in the person of Mr. Albert Smith.

CHANCEL CHOIR
Annual
SPRING BANQUET

Honoring

Prof. and Mrs. SEYMOUR SWETS
for their 37 years of devoted Christian Service to the Chancel Choir.

In *The Story of Grand Rapids*, Z. Z. Lydens commented:

LaGrave Avenue Church was designed in somewhat contemporary style with traditional influence by the architectural firm of J. & G. Daverman of Grand Rapids. It was erected in 1961. Its effectiveness suffered from limited land area.

To help solve this problem, a Property Purchase Program (PPP) was initiated to acquire properties on both LaGrave and Sheldon Avenues. With $50,000 in cash and pledges received in an initial drive, the Maccabees Building on Sheldon Avenue, just southwest of LaGrave, was acquired, as approved by the congregation at its meeting of April 27, 1966. It was used for a time for church school classroom space. During weekdays it housed the I-Teach-Me Academy, a community effort in which LaGrave cooperated with Fountain Street Church in trying to help highschool dropouts. The students were supervised by two young men, one of whom — A. James Heynen — was a LaGrave member. The building was soon razed to make way for further parking. The Property Purchase Program added necessary parking space. Its efforts, however, were somewhat hampered by those who worried about the dangers of an edifice complex and a brick and mortar mentality. Even so, the three-year Property Purchase Program project netted almost $100,000.

Rev. Eppinga wrote the first article for his column "Of Cabbages and Kings" in the November 8, 1968 issue of *The Banner* entitled, "Always Something." In the same year, the Boy Scouts acquired some recreational property on the Muskegon River from the Consumers Power Company, under a lease of a dollar a year. Mr. Elmer Van-Beek, a member of LaGrave, initiated and finalized this arrangement. Rev. Wayne Gritter, pastor of the Cherry Hill Christian Reformed Church, Inkster, Michigan, accepted LaGrave's call to become assistant pastor in September 1968. Rev. Eppinga was granted a second sabbatical which he chose to spend at Cambridge University in England in the fall of 1969.

The 1960s were drawing to a close. They had brought a revolution to American culture. Long standing traditions and assumptions had been questioned, challenged, and frequently abandoned. A new morality found an increasing acceptance in the land. It was, in some ways, a trying decade for the churches. It was an even more trying time for the young people of that day — some of whom lost their way.

It was on a Sunday morning that one of them attended LaGrave Church. He was a young man who, by his appearance, was identifiable as breathing the spirit of the 60s. After the service, he introduced himself to the pastor. "My name," he said, "is Klaas Troon."

Through the years, the members of LaGrave have been faithful in their financial support of the church, its needs, and causes. The Property Purchase Program was no exception.

PROPERTY
URCHASE
ROGRAM

JULY 1, 1966 TO
DEC. 31, 1968

I WILL SUPPORT THIS PROGRAM WITH A:

☐ SEND ENVELOPES

CASH GIFT . . . $_____

PLEDGE . . . . $_____

TOTAL . . . . $_____

WORKER'S SIGNATURE   DONOR'S SIGNATURE

LA GRAVE AVE. CHRISTIAN REFORMED CHURCH

DONOR'S RECEIPT

CASH $_____

PLEDGE $_____

TOTAL $_____

LA GRAVE AVE.

PROPERTY
URCHASE
ROGRAM

WORKER'S SIGNATURE

The pastor had seen the name Troon in some old directories. He invited the young man into his study and found in him a ready conversationalist. Klaas said he was from California. He was named after his great-great-grandfather Klaas, who had lived a hundred years ago and emigrated to Grand Rapids. His great-grandfather was Pieter Troon, who had been a member of LaGrave — even an elder in the consistory. His grandfather, John, had been a physician. Before he moved to Ann Arbor, Michigan, he had been a member of LaGrave, too. Klaas's father, Jack, had gone to Oakdale Christian School before moving to Ann Arbor. Jack married and moved to California. How did this young Klaas know all this? He learned it from his Aunt Karen. He asked her because he was interested in his roots. That's why he had come to church that morning — to see where his father, grandfather, and great-grandfather had attended. Where did *he* go to church? He didn't. But he enjoyed the service. He might even come back some time if he was in town. But again, he might not. He said he was not a believer.

After Klaas left, the pastor looked in the record book. Pieter Troon had joined LaGrave in 1900. The pastor spoke to an aged member who remembered Pieter — a godly man who often spoke of his father Klaas who, though opposed to English services, had been quite a leader in his church. Too bad this second Klaas was rejecting the faith of his fathers! How many, mused the pastor, have left their moorings over the years and, especially, in this confusing decade? Would others follow in his steps? Recently, the church balcony had been closed for evening services. The morning attendance was good, but there were definitely fewer going to the second service. Had LaGrave seen its day?

Pastors sometimes worry over their flocks like parents over their children. Sometimes, like parents, they can fear the worst. So pastors, too, must sometimes be reminded to trust in the Lord. The gates of hell shall not prevail against the church. The young man he had just met might very well return, one day, to the Lord. Such miracles happened in every generation. He said a prayer for Klaas Troon and all those who had to find their way and who were getting lost in — a difficult decade.

Chapter 23

SIGNIFICANT HAPPENINGS

At the New Year's Eve service closing the 1960s, LaGrave's members wondered what the 1970s would bring. The end of the 20th century's sixth decade saw a different world from that which had existed ten years before. Indeed, 1960 was born in relative calm, but 1969 was ending in wild commotion. It would be nice if the 1970s, born in turbulence, would end in peace. Instead, as before, there were wars and rumors of wars.

The 1970s would bring significant happenings. Only four months into the new decade, four students at Ohio's Kent State University were slain by National Guardsmen at a demonstration protesting our country's incursion into Cambodia (May 4, 1970). The Vietnam War, raging abroad, was pitting citizen against citizen at home. The end of the conflict would arrive before the 1980s, but history, with its developments, would go on.

Racial desegregation by bussing (1971)
The recognition of China (1971-1972)
The Watergate scandal (1972)
The resignation of Vice President Spiro T. Agnew (1973)
The resignation of President Richard M. Nixon (1974)

Mr. Nixon's "full, free and absolute pardon" by his successor, Gerald R. Ford, Sept. 8, 1974

These were some of the developments the new decade would bring.

In 1977, the first woman Episcopal priest was ordained. That same year, draft dodgers were pardoned by President Jimmy Carter. In 1978, a baby girl was born from an egg fertilized outside the womb — a harbinger of an increasing number of ethical problems for theologians to ponder. Pope Paul VI died at age eighty (1978). He was followed by Pope John Paul who died after just thirty-four days in office. He, in turn, was succeeded by Karol Cardinal Wojtyla of Poland as Pope John Paul II. Another traditional religion, Islam, caught the public eye in the person of the Moslem leader Ayatolla Ruhollah Khomeini (1979).

There were many more happenings and significant developments. The Women's Liberation Movement abroad rejoiced in its flowering as Margaret Thatcher became the Prime Minister of England (1979). Americans worried about the nuclear power plant accident at Three Mile Island, Pennsylvania (1979). And in Nicaragua, where the LaGrave congregation built a church to replace the First Evangelical Church of Managua, which was destroyed by an earthquake, President General Anastasio Somoza Debayle resigned and fled to Miami (1979). The aftermath of this event would spell much trouble in the next decade in U.S. and Central American relations.

It was against the background of such a decade that the LaGrave Church would work and pray for the coming of God's kingdom and the doing of His will. Rev. Eppinga had just completed a term at Cambridge University in England. The congregation had given him a second sabbatical for study and rest. In his first sermon upon his return in January of 1970, he chose as his text God's words to His prophet Elijah that there were yet more than seven thousand who had not bowed the knee to Baal. This, he said, was true in the present day as well, despite the many empty churches he had seen abroad and the overthrowing of traditional standards on the part of many of the younger generation.

There was unrest in Grand Rapids as well, but LaGrave Church had prospered through the difficult decade of the 1960s. The congregation had witnessed 250 professions of faith and 244 baptisms. There were 126 members who had passed on to their eternal reward. LaGrave Church had become the largest congregation in the Christian Reformed denomination. The denominational *1960 Yearbook* reported that LaGrave had 285

families, 736 communicant members, and 1,161 souls. In 1969, the congregation had grown to 344 families, 1,011 communicants, and 1,529 souls. The church budget for the ten years totalled $1,460,000 within which mission giving had doubled. The Christian Education Society had raised large sums, and the Property Purchase Program (PPP) had met its considerable obligations.

But changes were underway. They were symbolized by Klaas Troon II who had surfaced a few years before 1970 at a LaGrave service. His ideas, reinforced by his dress, challenged all the traditionally accepted values. Campuses in the land were in turmoil. The Vietnam War seemed eternal. Draft dodging received a left-handed blessing in many churches. Homosexualism was emerging from the shadows. A new kind of music was filling the ear. Racism, sex, drugs — these and more were ingredients which made for the unrest that permeated everywhere and affected staid Christian Reformed circles as well. The founding fathers had sought to build their walls high. They had even tried to hold to their ancestral language as a barrier to keep the world out. The founders of LaGrave had removed that language barrier to keep the young people in. But all such issues were long gone, dead, and part of a far distant world when LaGrave approached the ninth decade of its existence. So much had happened that had LaGrave's founders returned in 1970 for a

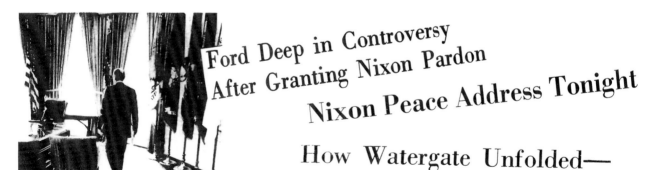

Ford Deep in Controversy After Granting Nixon Pardon

Nixon Peace Address Tonight

How Watergate Unfolded—

Fighting Precedes Hour of Truce

Cease-Fire Arrives in Vietnam

Supreme Court Strikes Out School Segregation As Against Constitution

Troops Kill Four Students in Antiwar Riot at Ohio College

Guards' Gunfire Wounds 11 at Kent University

Reverend Peter Winkle

brief visit, they would have thought themselves to be on another planet.

In June, 1971, the LaGrave consistory received a letter signed by a number of members requesting a third worship service, to be held, initially once a month in order to allow greater diversity in format and greater spontaneity of expression. At the same time, an overture appeared before synod requesting a study of the second service which, at LaGrave and elsewhere, had experienced a considerable decrease in attendance. In response to the request for a third service where the emphasis might not necessarily fall on a monologic sermon, the worship committee of the consistory sought the aid of the membership in "sorting out all present thoughts and impulses among us." Rev. Wayne Gritter, assistant pastor, had labored among the youth and sought to give guidance and leadership. Prior to joining the staff at LaGrave, Rev. Gritter had served Christian Reformed Churches in Austinville, Iowa, and Inkster, Michigan. His term of service came to an end in 1971, and Rev. Gritter moved to Canada to serve the Christian Reformed Church of Halifax, Nova Scotia.

Dr. William Kooistra had begun a weekly meeting in LaGrave's parish house for those seeking drug rehabilitation, an effort which would result in an independent organization known as "Project Rehab." "The Bridge," a home for teenage runaways, was supported by LaGrave. Mrs. Patricia DeHaan, a LaGrave member, served on its board of directors. "Food for Youth," an ecumenical effort, also received LaGrave's strong support. It provided another way for the congregation to show Christ's love and concern to the many adolescents who were disenchanted and drifting.

Meanwhile, seminarian Peter Winkle organized and directed the 1972 summer reach-out program which proved to be very successful. He also involved LaGrave in a chaplaincy effort at

Grand Rapids Junior College. Prior to coming to LaGrave, Peter had served as a teacher on the Nigerian Mission Field in Africa. While there, he felt God's call to the ministry and entered Calvin Seminary. He agreed to serve his internship at LaGrave, and it soon became apparent to the consistory that the congregation would be happy to have him serve as its assistant pastor. He accepted LaGrave's call. The congregation, and the neighborhood, benefitted greatly from Peter Winkle's ministry. At the end of 1976, Rev. Winkle and his wife Joy and their two children, Julie and Jeffrey, moved to New Mexico where he undertook a hospital chaplaincy ministry on the mission field in Rehoboth.

The LaGrave consistory had granted permission for a number of trial "third services" which initially drew a great attendance from among the young people of various churches and backgrounds. The services also attracted critics, particularly from members of a local Christian Reformed Laymens League, some of whom overreacted. Eventually, those who identified strongly with the nature of the third service formed a loosely organized group which met in an old school building. They called themselves "The Fellowship of the Acts." This group, too, drew much criticism as well as support. In retrospect, it was seen by many as the means of holding some

whose connections to the church were hanging by a thread. The challenge to the monologic sermon was so strong in the early seventies that Professor John Timmerman, a highly respected and articulate member of the faculty of Calvin College, was prompted to write the following in the April, 1972, issue of *The Reformed Journal*. The article appears here in order to convey the nuances of that day in the life of LaGrave and the entire denomination.

I grew up as a minister's son in what may now be called the golden age of the ministry in the Christian Reformed church. My father enjoyed respect, confidence, authority, and affection. He was a dignified man when the ministry enjoyed great dignity. He meticulously prepared his sermons, which possessed both art and insight. They were listened to by intelligent audiences, even though many had little formal education. He felt it his duty to proclaim what he considered the full counsel of God as far as his abilities permitted. The minister and audience constituted a harmonious unit. None felt the urge to muscle in, share rare wisdom and searing hang-ups or personal encounters with the Lord. The audience felt instructed, inspired, and cleansed. Audience participation would have been regarded as intrusive, unmannerly, and unprofitable as we would regard it in a good play, where no one but a fool would rise to reinterpret Macbeth. That day, to my deep personal regret, seems to be about finished.

Many people seem to relish the new day coming, the day of audience participation, the day when the worm will turn and ultimately devour the lark. Some want not only attenuation of the minister's role, but are ready to scrap every custom about worship. This, I suppose, includes the role of the clergyman, who will become some sort of moderator or facilitator.

He will be engaged in arranging the moveable seats so we can see each other better; he will be busy hustling about with hymnbooks and contemporary ballads, patiently tolerating seven rambling opinions on neighborhood projects, ordering the holding of hands and the letting go of hands, seeing to it that everyone is listening actively, while preparing the next spontaneous remark, plugging people into new programs, guiding the mass analysis of texts, and

summing up the consequences. Having done all this:

> *At last he rose, and twitched his mantle blue*
> *Tomorrow to fresh fields and pastures new.*

Audience participation is the sparkling word today, but I don't like audience participation in the exposition of texts in Sunday services. Some say the single voice in front is a bore and a drone, but are seventeen bores any better? The participators are as likely to be neurotic exhibitionists as mature and gifted saints. If a group wishes to discuss the sermon afterward, and the minister wishes to participate, that is another and, probably, a profitable matter, but to invite instant opinion on the meaning of texts seems absurd to me. A well-prepared and substantial sermon to which I actively listen, means infinitely more to me than comments even by gifted people, who can't be masters of everything.

The Sunday sermons are the most significant and often most pleasurable parts of the Sunday services to me. The poetic calibre of many hymns is slight; the responsive readings in uneven pace and frequent dissonance are not always an inspiration. Many are so intent on reading words that words is all they hear. I greatly prefer a trained and articulate reader. If the sermon disappears, a fine and rewarding experience will vanish, and I shall be poorer for it.

Discussion of Scripture on Sunday by many voices holds no attraction for me. There are suitable societies for such activity, where many of the severest critics of sermonic exposition never appear.

Finally, I fear that if the sermon goes, the audience will diminish too, but maybe that is what some members want — no organized church services, but little cells where congenial spirits meet to talk to each other about the religious life.

Throughout this period and reaching back into the late 1960s, the servicemen's secretaries, Mrs. John Cook and Mrs. John Dekker, had been maintaining contact with some twenty or more members in uniform who were scattered far and wide. Above the guest registry in the narthex hung a plaque bearing the names of those who gave their lives in service to their country in World War II. Those who saw that plaque each week breathed a prayer that no more names would appear. Weekly prayers for the safety of those in service ascended from the pulpit. Yet, in the deep and mysterious providence of God, David Ross Dekker gave his life on foreign soil. The news of his death was received in shock by his family and the entire congregation. Vietnam, so far away, became an even greater reality. David Dekker died April 16, 1971. His memorial service took place April 29, 1971, in the LaGrave sanctuary. In the *LaGrave News* of May, 1971, Pastor Eppinga wrote the following:

> Dave was a Christian, a son of the congregation, born November 7, 1948, baptized January 2, 1949. He grew up among us, a member of a loving family circle, together with whom he faithfully attended church services all his life. At the age of seventeen, and altogether on his own accord, he made known to me his desire to make profession of Jesus Christ as his Lord and Saviour in order that he might be a member in full communion in his church. His public profession of faith was made April 10, 1966, in the presence of us all.
>
> Dave was a quiet man. But the above-mentioned facts speak loudly and beautifully and so clearly about the Christian way of life that I need add nothing to them.
>
> Let us pray for peace. And let us remember the Dekker family: John and Vi, John, Jr., and Judy — and Dave; all of them living, even though one has died.

IN MEMORIAM

DAVID R. DEKKER

BORN NOV. 7, 1948

DIED APR. 16, 1971

THE TOWER ROOM

After the Vietnam conflict, a modern art display was placed in the tower room, designed in part by Douglas Pettinga. It depicts the dove of peace breaking through the wall man has built between himself and God. An accompanying plaque reads as follows:

> *Dedicated to the men who have given their lives in the service of their country.*
>
> *"In the tender compassion of our God the morning sun from Heaven will rise upon us, to shine on those who live in darkness, under the cloud of death, and to guide our feet into the way of peace."*
>
> Luke 1:78, 79

The plaque listing LaGrave's war dead was removed from the narthex to the tower room. In the center of this room was placed a circular bench and flower arrangement, given by John and Viola Dekker in memory of their son David and all those who gave their lives in answering their country's call.

Throughout the 1970s, treasurers succeeded one another yearly and, although all reported growing deficits as the years progressed, all could submit credit balances as each year ended. And the congregation was active!

Mr. A. James Heynen had been engaged in early 1970 as coordinator of church outreach, in an effort to help the congregation address itself to a growing community need.

Internally, the Campfire Girls, whose life would be limited, rivalled the Boy Scouts in healthy activity.

The shut-ins received the faithful and loving attention of the deaconesses.

An art show, in which the members had opportunity to display their talents, enjoyed a month-long showing.

Pre-marital courses were offered as good preventive medicine in the face of a growing divorce rate in the country.

And FISH (because the first letters of the words "Jesus Christ, of God the Son, Saviour" in Greek spell fish), a national organization offering help to those who needed assistance — mainly in the area of transportation — was supported by LaGrave Church.

There were other happenings. The pastor, J. D. Eppinga, produced a book on the life of Paul entitled, *For Sinners Only*. The consistory produced a

The Jellema House

new stewardship committee whose study would bring results — both immediate and in the succeeding decade — when its recommendation regarding a budget built on pledges would be adopted. There were those outside the congregation who were critical of this idea and called it an "American importation;" but the congregation was largely inured, having withstood not only *The Banner's* criticism of its divided chancel, but its condemnation of the wonderful frescoes by Reynold Weidenaar as "pictures in the church."

Amid the furor and concern which had arisen around narcotics and drug abuse, the continuing problems of alcoholism were being submerged from public view. In the 1950s and 1960s, Dr. John Jellema, M.D., member of LaGrave, had given this problem his almost undivided attention. On numerous occasions and at all hours of the night, he and Rev. Eppinga would call on some unfortunate soul ill with the disease to pray with him and administer "antibuse," the treatment of the day. Dr. Jellema rose to state-wide prominence in combatting this disease. He died in 1966, spent and worn. A few years later, a group of LaGrave members, under the leadership of Mr. Neal DeMey, carried forward Dr. Jellema's concern and initiated an organization which established the Jellema House, a treatment home for alcoholics. It became a lasting contribution to the community. Mr. Jack Swets, LaGrave member, served as its first president. Numerous other

LaGrave members served on its board, some as directors, such as Rev. Herman Teitsma and Mr. Joseph Schuitema. For many years, Mr. Neal De-Mey served as its assistant director, allowing him more time to work with individuals on a personal level. Since the opening of its doors in 1971, Jellema House has served over 1,500 individuals, a great many of whom have been helped to return to a life of sobriety. In all of its years, LaGrave continued to give strong financial and moral support to this effort born from within the congregation.

LaGrave's interest and cooperation was also given to "Key 73" — a nationwide effort to bring the message of the Gospel to every American. In addition to supporting a similar effort in Africa called "New Life For All," LaGrave joined "Key 73" by participating in "Evangelism Thrust" under the leadership of LaGrave members, Rev. Wesley Smedes of the denomination home missions office and Mr. Harold Witteveen, layman. Bible study and mission method courses were offered to the members, many of whom responded.

The Henry Beets Mission Society and its auxiliary were also continuous in their mission endeavors. Dr. C. Helmus, LaGrave member, made frequent visits to Guatemala to use his medical skills in the Lord's service. Mr. Charles Werner, LaGrave member, was instrumental in heightening LaGrave's interest, via the Henry Beets Mission Society, in that Central American country. LaGrave's prayers and material assistance spread to Nicaragua. Managua, its capitol city, sustained a devastating earthquake on December 23, 1972. Many LaGrave members had journeyed to these mission fields. In one special Sunday morning collection, the members of LaGrave contributed over $35,000 for Managuan needs, namely, to rebuild the First Evangelical Church which was completely destroyed by the earthquake. The dedication of that church was an occasion! Rev. Eppinga, who was welcomed as Reverendo Jacobo Springa, addressed the congregation with the words of Matthew 7:24–27 as his text. The local pastor responded as follows:

Distinguished visitors from the USA, missionaries, pastors, and all who are present: In this glorious afternoon at the dedication of this temple, the part given to me is the easiest — that of welcoming all of you, and especially to thank the brethren of the LaGrave Church who, with their gifts, made possible the construction of this beautiful building. For this temple to be built, it was necessary that gener-

ous hearts filled with the love of God send us their timely help. Not all has been suffering and tragedy. The generosity of the hearts beyond our boundaries have lifted our burdens.

When the catastrophe of December 23, last year, struck our city, razing it to the ground as if it were a city of cardboard, and the sorrow and desperation overcame us, certain brethren whom we knew not lent themselves to us to help us. While many people sent aid to our stricken areas, LaGrave Church helped us in a direct way, especially the Primera Iglesia Centroamerica in Managua. Our former Sala Evangelica has disappeared, with it times of great blessing, and we are left with precious memories of that old Lighthouse, that shone forth its light in the darkness. Losing that church was losing part of our life. How many anniversaries were celebrated there; how many Christmas programs and New Year's festivities, and how many souls were saved through the preaching of the Gospel in that church of our love. Now that place is covered with rubbish, like an abandoned holy camp where we can go and weep and bury our memories. It is no more the bestknown geographical site in Managua where our grandparents, we, and our sons met to worship God in spirit and in truth.

How many reconstruction plans died instantly. Now we cannot see that building on the corner that we loved and now we miss. But there is not a suffering that time does not heal. But the destruction of the oldest temple and most blessed does not destroy the Church of Christ, which one hundred earthquakes could never destroy, the spiritual church which was, and is, and will live on.

The bretheren of the LaGrave Church reached out their hands to us and sent us their help, and with their help, this temple was built, which will be the House of God, a new Lighthouse giving out the Light of the Lord Jesus Christ who said, "I am the Light of the world."

The interior of the First Evangelical Church of Managua, Nicaragua

LaGrave Members Rebuild Church in Nicaraguan Capital

By Scott Scholten

The LaGrave Christian Reformed Church gave a $16,500 Christmas present to Central America this year, and found what it was looking for.

"We went to Nicaragua (last winter) looking or a cause," says Rev. Jacob Eppinga, pastor of the church.

What the church found there was the city of Managua, capital of Nicaragua, demolished from the tremors of a giant earthquake which rent the town last Dec. 23.

BUT IN THE RUBBLE, LaGrave found its cause — the burned out shell of the First Evangelical Church (La Sala Evangelica) of Managua.

Now, almost one year later, LaGrave has completely rebuilt the church and given it to the Nicaraguan congregation as a combination christmas-anniversary gift.

"Even though they probably don't care to remember the anniversary very much," quips Rev. Eppinga.

Rev. Eppinga, along with three couples from the church — Dr. and Mrs. Clarence Beets, Mr. and Mrs. Kenneth Faber and Mr. and Mrs. John Jurries — all visited Nicaragua Nov. 25 for special dedication ceremonies of the gift they had built.

THEY WERE GREETED by a vast crowd which covered several city blocks, and by a speech given by a member of the Evangelical Church:

"As the old church was the first Evangelical temple built in the Managua of yesterday, so this modern temple is the first to be dedicated in this era of new beginnings."

The church member's words were more than fancy rhetoric.

The Evangelical Church, which had been one f the most familiar landmarks in downtown Managua, also was the first church, if not the first building of any kind to be rebuilt after the earthquake.

THE CHURCH WAS BUILT from the church's Henry Beets Society. That fund, which is named after a former pastor of the church and the first editor of the Christian Reformed denomination's weekly magazine The Banner, has funded several other projects in Central America, including construction of a medical clinic.

A single collection at LaGrave Church, aimed t paying off the new Nicaraguan church, netted virtually the entire cost, $15,400, and "it was easy to raise the rest," according to Rev. Eppinga.

The LaGrave Church work in Managua is "entirely separate" from the work of the Christian Reformed World Relief Committee, the denominational relief agency, Rev. Eppinga said.

The church actually decided on the building project after Rev. Eppinga and Rev. Harold VanBroekhoven of Outreach, Inc., a local evangelistic agency, toured the devasted city in April.

CENTRAL AMERICA is a heavily Roman Catholic area, but Rev. Eppinga was surprised that about 10 per cent of the Managuan population made up of Protestants. "Very active, ecumenical Protestants," is the way he likes to put it.

"Evangelicals make up about 10 per cent of the city," Rev. Eppinga said. "But their denomination doesn't really matter. Down there, out from the concentration of churches, doctrinal differences tend to fade in importance."

As the old church was the first evangelical temple built in the Managua of yesterday, so this modern temple is the first to be dedicated in this era of new beginnings. Now it is my pleasure to say in the name of our church to the representatives of La-Grave Church the significant two words:

MANY THANKS.

The greatest quality of a human being, that which makes us noble, is to be thankful. I desire that the members of LaGrave Church receive our profound and sincere gratitude. Will you kindly take back to the brethren of LaGrave Church this short message: "The House of the Lord has been built and that the Voice of God is heard in this Holy Place, saying: 'Now my eyes will be open and my ears attentive to the prayer that is made in this place. For now I have chosen and consecrated this house that my name may be there forever; my eyes and my heart will be there for all time.' "

In 1972, LaGrave formed a board of trustees and charged them with property, insurance, and other concerns pertaining to the outward business of the church. The new arrangement sought to relieve elders and deacons of an overload. Although it was a sound idea, the new venture did not succeed and the "trustees" experiment was shelved in favor of a new organizational study committee.

At the morning service of May 23, 1971, the congregation expressed its thanks to Alyce Lantinga for having served LaGrave so faithfully as organist for thirty-five years. Following the service, a reception in her honor was held in fellowship hall. As a token of appreciation, she was presented with a Weidenaar etching of the sanctuary chancel with the words: "We have heard a joyful sound." On November 14, 1978, the family of

177

Reynold Weidenaar's etching of the LaGrave Church sanctuary, presented to Alyce Lantinga as a token of appreciation for her 35 years as church organist

LaGrave gathered again to honor Alyce for forty-two years of loyal service. With Dr. W. Clarence Beets as the amiable master of ceremonies and the prime rib prepared by Leo Peters, it was an evening of fun and fellowship. Professor Harold Towers, Alyce's first teacher and former organist at St. Mark's Episcopal Church in Grand Rapids, and over ninety years of age, travelled *by bus* from Indiana to Grand Rapids to be present for the occasion. The choir rendered three of her favorite selections, and John Schurman, general chairman of the evening, presented a beautiful plaque to Alyce on behalf of the congregation. Along with Professor Seymour Swets, Alyce Lantinga had placed her stamp of musical excellence not only on the congregation and its services of worship, but on the denomination and the community-at-large. The November, 1978, issue of the *LaGrave News* contained the following letter to Alyce Lantinga, written by Rev. Eppinga:

THANK YOU, ALYCE,

For the sacred organ concert October 15. The evening was cold and wet, nevertheless, the attendance was not dampened. I sat in the balcony from where the sanctuary looked even lovelier as it was filled with your playing. From

that distance, I could not tell that there was a small spider crawling around on your music page. He didn't know, did he, that it takes much more than that to disturb your presence of mind?

The whole concert was a service of praise to God. It was a typical "Alyce" performance — keeping yourself in the background, and your music in the forefront for all. There were moments when you filled our souls with quietude, and others when you lifted our hearts on winged notes. When we all joined in the singing of "Praise to the Lord, the Almighty," it was an outburst of what had been building in our spirits throughout the preceding numbers.

And so we say, as we reflect upon your contributions to our worship these many years,

THANK YOU, ALYCE.

Soli Deo Gloria!

LaGrave was blessed not only with dedicated staff members but others who, like Dr. Henry Walkotten, building chairman, worked for their church as volunteers on an almost daily basis. Marie VanBeek, her husband Elmer, Dr. W. Clarence Beets, and others, served as archivists and in countless other capacities. They were representative of a spirit and support without which LaGrave Church would not have been LaGrave Church. Mr. George VanWesep who, until his retirement, was a leader in the world of education — Christian and public — was also ever present and on deck, serving quietly and efficiently. Having served so many terms as elder and considered indispensable, the consistory appointed him honorary elder with indefinite tenure. Years before, Mr. G. J. Rooks had served LaGrave in a similar capacity. Thus, Mr. VanWesep attended all consistory and elders

Wilma and George VanWesep

"LET GEORGE DO IT!"

On May 24, 1976, the consistory honored George VanWesep and his wife, Wilma, with a dinner. The program that followed made the evening complete. Norman DeGraaf told about his third grade deportment at Oakdale Christian School where George VanWesep could always distinguish wisely between a person and his pranks. Ted Vanderveen told some of his famous Yankee Dutch "Jan en Piet" stories. Rev. Eppinga directed a skit he had written entitled, "Let George Do It."

The consistory, it seems, had to decide whether or not to acquire a spiritual weather ball (a la Michigan National Bank) for the church steeple. Dewey Hoitenga Jr., was concerned whether this move was consistent with the Church Order. Rich DeVos, who "Believed" in many things, said:

"If the people want a weather ball, give them a weather ball!" Cornie Pape, given to philosophical analysis, wondered whether Dooyeweerd and Vollenhoven, leading Dutch thinkers in the Netherlands, would agree with the idea. Marvin De-Winter, the consistory's "volunteer," did just that in order to "get the ball rolling." Ted Vanderveen said that the whole idea reminded him of another "Jan en Piet" story. John Leegwater suggested that the whole thing could easily cost the church "a hundred thou." The whole discussion ended with all saying: "Let George do it."

At the end of a very pleasant evening, Mr. VanWesep expressed his thanks with characteristic humility and with his hopes for the church he loved and to which, with God's permission, he wished to give his continued efforts.

meetings, serving as advisor, parliamentarian, expert on *Church Order,* and assisting in family visitation and disciplinary matters. As chairman of the membership committee, he wrote letters endlessly to out-of-town members encouraging and assisting them in finding good church homes in their new locations.

In 1912, the LaGrave Church burned its first mortgage. Having survived a financial crisis of the worst kind only a little more than a dozen years before, its debt erasure was viewed as a miracle. On April 17, 1977, LaGrave had a second mortgage burning. Through the generosity of two of its members, the event took place long before it

LaGrave's Second Mortgage Burning, April 17, 1977.
From left to right: Rev. Eppinga, Seymour Swets, Herbert VanderMey, Norman DeGraaf, Theodore Vanderveen, John Spalink, George VanWesep, Dr. W. Clarence Beets, J. Gordon Hartger, Elias VanSweden

was anticipated. The "burning" was scheduled during the evening service after a sermon in which Rev. Eppinga had traced God's leading of the congregation for ninety years. Surviving members of the original building committee were called forward. Mr. George VanWesep and Mr. John Spalink took mortgage and matches in hand and, over a stainless steel bowl from the kitchen, made smoke and flames — reducing the mortgage paper to ashes. The congregation watched with thanksgiving. Appropriate displays were presented at the reception that followed. Dr. W. Clarence Beets gave a slide presentation on the construction of the church. Mrs. Henry Walkotten and Mrs. John Spalink, wives of the building chairman and deputy chairman, served as hostesses.

At the time of the mortgage burning, another project was coming to a successful conclusion. Early in 1974, Dr. Orren Bolt, Mr. Loren Dykstra, and Mrs. Alyce Lantinga, members of an organ study committee appointed a number of months before, brought their findings and recommendations to the consistory. Based on thorough research, including consultations with many experts, the committee recommended the installation of a new organ console, several additional stops, and a reconditioning and remodeling of some of the existing components of the present instrument at a cost of approximately $55,000. These recommendations were approved by the congregation upon the consistory's recommendation. A low-key drive was initiated before signing a contract with the Burger & Shafer Organ Company of Findlay, Ohio. The project proceeded under the watchful eye and able direction of the committee chairman, Orren Bolt, who made regular progress reports to the consistory and congregation. Careful planning insured the use of the organ until the latest possible date, at which time the congregation would be without the instrument for two or three weeks. In the process of rebuilding, it was unexpectedly discovered that the antiphonal organ also needed attention to the tune of $4,500 — a sum which the Benefactors Trust Fund supplied.

During Alyce Lantinga's periods of vacation, the organists ably serving the congregation at an organ console that was being rebuilt were Helen Bolt, Sondra Swets, and David VanderVliet. Prior to this time, Evelyn Brandt and Harold Witteveen also served as assistant organists. The organ rebuilding project was brought to a successful con-

clusion in the fall of 1977, due largely to the meticulous supervision of chairman Orren Bolt.

In 1973, the King James Bibles in LaGrave's pews and pulpits were replaced with the Revised Standard Version — to the regret of some and the approval of others. Donald Oppewal was appointed coordinator of church school education, a position in which he was succeeded by Donald and Sharon Verduin, David and Linda Male, and Robert Fry. This position was terminated in the fall of 1985. The firm of Norman Bouma & Company was hired to do LaGrave's bookkeeping.

The consistory decided to get out of the housing business and so, in 1973, offered Rev. and Mrs. Eppinga the parsonage at 2443 Oakwood S.E. at a very reasonable price.

Early in the decade of the seventies, Bingo was played on Friday mornings in the parish house. This was another attempt on the part of the congregation to show its concern for its neighbors. Area residents were invited for a social hour, followed by a time of devotions. Bingo was con-

---

In the LaGrave News *of February, 1973, Dr. Beets, in reviewing the previous year of La-Grave's activities, took sorrowful note of the death of Henry Walkotten who had participated in the founding of the Henry Beets Mission Society, led the congregation in the erection of a new house of worship, brought into existence the Benefactors Trust Fund and, who, at the time of his sudden death, was preparing to establish dental clinics in Barillas and Chichicostenanga, Guatemala. He was also preparing to serve as LaGrave's church manager for a dollar a year.*

Other observations of Dr. Beets regarding the year 1972, made on the occasion of La-Grave's 86th birthday, referred to the evening service attendance, the pastor's Sunday evening Hours of Sharing — inviting members by congregational districts to attend — the successful Fellowship Dinners, the huge Boy Scout rummage sale at the old Hoekstra Printing Plant on Wealthy that netted thousands of dollars, the agonies of making a pictorial directory, and LaGrave's building of a medical facility in Barillas, Guatemala, where all roads ended in an area serving upwards of 40,000 Guatemalans hidden in the surrounding hills.

ducted by the Friendship Club. Other members of the congregation helped by supplying suitable gifts as prizes for the Bingo winner. The neighbors looked forward with eager anticipation to Friday mornings and were saddened when this activity was terminated in 1985. There were those who questioned the propriety of Bingo at LaGrave until they were told the nature and purpose of the hour which was a part of an outreach effort adapted to LaGrave's surroundings.

Another such effort was the neighborhood Thanksgiving dinners offered on the Tuesday evening before Thanksgiving Day. This effort was begun before Rev. Peter Winkle came and was greatly enlarged through his efforts, drawing some 200 neighborhood people each year, some of whom were residents of the Morton House and Mertens Hotel, and many of whom were hungry street people coming in from the "highways and byways." Thus, LaGrave initiated the Pre-Thanksgiving Sunday evening service and designated it as a time in which members could bring their gifts of groceries and money to make possible not only the neighborhood Thanksgiving dinner but the making and distributing of many Thanksgiving baskets by the Esther Circle.

On September 22, 1974, John Ouwinga was ordained into the ministry of the Christian Reformed Church. LaGrave had been asked by the Grand Rapids Board of Evangelism to be the calling church for John Ouwinga to serve as chaplain at the Grand Rapids Junior College. An arrangement was made whereby he would also serve LaGrave Church on a part-time basis as a youth worker. Accordingly, LaGrave paid an appropriate portion of his salary to the Board of Evangelism. John and his wife, Beverly, found a ready entree into the life of the congregation. As the work at

---

BINGO!?

"Sorry, Sally, but I'll have to break our coffee date on Friday mornings. I'm scheduled to play Bingo at church that day."

"Bingo!? At LaGrave!?"

"Let me explain . . . our Friendship Club has a group of volunteers who spend Friday mornings playing Bingo with a group of neighborhood friends — people from the New Mertens Hotel, the Morton House, and Pleasant Street (that's an adult foster care home). These people have so little to do, few places to go, and almost no way to get around. One of our former ministers who knew these people suggested that a social hour at the church with devotions, games, and coffee might really fill a void in their lives and bring them to the church in a 'non-threatening' situation. Bingo was chosen because it was something they all knew, and it is uncomplicated."

"Do you play for money?"

*"No, we play for cosmetic samples, toothbrushes, combs, snacks, used clothing, and garage sale items. Anything we find that they might be able to use in their situation — you know, a hotel room with no stove or refrigeration. They really appreciate used clothing and white ele-*phants — and the Friendship Club will take donations from anyone!"*

"What about the devotions you mentioned?"

"Well, we keep them simple. Sometimes we cover topics like "What God Expects of Us," "How to Treat Our Fellowman," or "How Good God Is to Us." For a while, we used Sunday school material on various Bible characters. Now we're about to begin a short film series on the life of Christ. We play bingo for awhile, take a break for devotions, coffee and, oh, yes, our homemade goodies that the gals bring every week — those are special treats. Then back for more bingo. It's a most interesting morning.

Often someone needs something that we can arrange to pick up for them. At Thanksgiving and Christmas, each player is given a gift. They love being remembered. I come away from a morning of Bingo feeling especially aware of my blessings. I feel that this is one way I can express my own gratitude by sharing some time, some cookies, and showing an interest and concern for others who have less."

"That's the best reason for missing a coffee date I have ever heard."

from *LaGrave News,* February, 1977

Reverend John Ouwinga

LaGrave progressed, the arrangement was adjusted so that more of Rev. Ouwinga's time could be given to the work of the church.

Fieldtrips for LaGrave's young people were led by both Rev. Winkle and Rev. Ouwinga. A trip to Appalachia with twenty-two young people was an eye-opening experience for all of them and determinative for some in the choice of a work later in life. Rev. Ouwinga's activities at Junior College (8,000 souls, including students, faculty, and administrators) fell under three categories: teaching, counseling, and evangelism. His summer ministry work for the church included not only LaGrave's young people, but those from other Christian Reformed Churches as well, sent via the Young Calvinist office under a program called SWIM (Summer Workers in Missions). In 1978, Rev. John and Beverly Ouwinga moved to Holland, Michigan, where he undertook his ministry as pastor of the Niekerk Christian Reformed Church.

Before Rev. Ouwinga left LaGrave, Rev. John Steigenga arrived to join the ministerial staff. Rev. Steigenga was ordained in Inkster, Michigan, in 1968 and had served as pastor of the Cherry Hill Christian Reformed Church of that city, the same church that Rev. Wayne Gritter had served before him. In 1974, Rev. Steigenga had moved to Detroit to become pastor of the Nardin Park

Community Church (CRC). Four years later, he accepted LaGrave's invitation to join its ministerial team. He was installed as a LaGrave pastor, February 5, 1978. A reception took place afterwards and the congregation was able to meet the new pastor, his wife Judy, and children Timothy, Julie, and Michael. In the 1978 March issue of the *LaGrave News,* the editorship of which he assumed soon after his arrival, Rev. Steigenga shared his first impressions of LaGrave Church. (They were good; and so were the congregation's first impressions of him).

Contributing to the health of LaGrave, as Pastor Steigenga found it, were many factors — big and small. The congregation had a strong and dedicated "core" whose commitment to Christ was evident. Among the smaller signs of vitality, easily forgotten with the passage of time, were the purchase of a minibus for outreach and youth activities, and the beginning of a children's church for pre-school through the first grade and meeting during the second half of the morning service. LaGrave's ecumenical involvements were made evident in the ecumenical Pentecost service in the LaGrave sanctuary. Numerous retreats were sponsored for adults, youth, and consistory members. The *Trinity Hymnal* was carefully selected by the worship committee to supplement the *Psalter Hymnal.* Congregational district meetings were held at church or at various homes for faith and

Reverend John Steigenga

ticular. The article appeared in the Christmas issue of *Centraal Weekblad,* official weekly of De Gereformeerde Kerken In Nederland, and was written by Rev. G. VanHalsema.

I had the opportunity to worship in several churches in Grand Rapids. It was pleasant when arriving in the narthex of LaGrave Church to be greeted by several people, young and old, usually a different family each Sunday. They greeted you, and there were also ushers who showed you to your place. This was for visitors as well as for members of the congregation. After the service, there was a chance to meet each other while enjoying a cup of coffee. Sometimes, at the beginning of the service, the minister greeted the congregation with "Good Morning," and then gave the congregation the opportunity to greet each other in the pews. There was a lot of commotion, but it was pleasantly different. I was approached from different sides, and I must confess that it was pleasant.

"Overdone," I can hear a few members of my congregation say. But this is not so. Several times while visiting the United States, I felt embarrassed when I heard that someone visiting the Netherlands was coldly received, with little or no affection shown. Very often, no greetings or acknowledgement, no information or invitation for a cup of coffee was given. No time after the service for even a little chitchat. When I hear these stories — and how true they are — I cannot help but think that the connection between "right teaching" and "right living" for many seems to be a difficult, if not impossible task.

The services that I participated in in the United States were of a "joyful spirit." The congregation would sing with enthusiasm from the beautiful Psalter Hymnal *and, afterwards, the congregation would participate with reading responsively. This is a custom that I am not familiar with, but that seems to be enjoyed by young and old.*

Gracious and dignified was the communion service I celebrated in the LaGrave Avenue Christian Reformed Church in Grand Rapids. After a short introduction, everyone was offered a small piece of bread. After that, the minister spoke, and then the congregation took the bread. The wine was offered in small glasses that were placed in small holders in the pews. After the whole congregation had received a glass, the minister again spoke, and the congregation took the wine.

A printed liturgy with information about the congregation was issued upon entering the church. It gave everyone a positive impression and also heightened the involvement of the members in the church service.

fellowship. Careful attention was given to the instructions for ushers and greeters; flowers were regularly and carefully supplied for all services, giving visitors the impression of a church that paid attention to details, just as the keepers of God's House in the Old Testament. Peter Noorman, who assumed the janitorship in 1974, endeavored to keep the sanctuary clean. Such efforts as these cannot be ignored in recording and understanding the history of a church.

Foreign visitors are often impressed by church services in the United States. The following observations are representative, mentioning American churches in general, and LaGrave Church in par-

---

Early in this century, Rev. Eppinga's father, Dirk, immigrated to America at the age of seventeen in the company of his close friend, Pieter Steigenga, also seventeen, the brother of Rev. J. Steigenga's grandfather. What a small world! Travelling steerage, young Dirk and Pieter often talked about a future time when their names, Eppinga and Steigenga, would comprise a part of the LaGrave staff (ha! ha!).

LaGrave Church, despite the times, was not only healthy as Rev. Steigenga found upon his arrival, but throughout its history, tremendously talented. Many of its members occupied positions of trust and leadership in the community. Others were knowledgeable in other fields. Many were creative with brush, or pen, or skilled in countless crafts. Some such as Reynold Weidenaar and Alyce Lantinga found their skills to be in public focus. Frank Davidhazy, adherent, was another skilled craftsman — an artist specializing in Oriental lacquer decoration of fine furniture. There were simple souls like Jimmy Hall who adopted the whole church as their own. Although retarded, he could outshine most other people in congeniality. And there was Levi Perry, rheumy-eyed, aged, and feeble-minded, who could say with joy on Easter Sunday, "He got up again, didn't He?" Levi loved LaGrave so much, he willed it all his worldly goods — $27.56 and a small television set. These special souls were as dear in God's sight as the many other members who were so gifted and endowed.

Examples of other talents which the Lord distributed so liberally among LaGrave's members are too numerous to cite. Here are two examples: The first is a poem by Winifred Ernzer, written when she was dying of cancer. The second is a thoughtful essay on retirement, by Garritt E. Roelofs, former Iowa state senator and member of the United States State Department.

RELINQUISHMENT

Great and wonderful God,
I had not fully understood how kind you are, how loving
* and gracious*
Until I learned to trust you more, to trust you with my life,
Until I learned to surrender my will to yours.
Then you gave me joy and peace and contentment.

And you give me untold blessings in times of great
* suffering*
You cheer me each day with your Presence —
Often in the disguise of a thoughtful letter
Or a reassuring card,
Or the kindness of a friend . . .
You give me songs in the night.

You taught me, Lord, to thank you, to thank you
* in everything,*
And you keep reminding me because I am so prone
* to forget.*
You taught me to thank even when the way is difficult
* and obscure.*
For I know that this too is part of your Divine will
Which though so mysterious and past our
* understanding,*
Is wholly right and perfect.

O for a silver tongue to adequately praise your Name —
But, Lord, accept these halting words and this my
* paltry love*
In response to your Great Love.
And evermore may Jesus Christ be formed in me.

Winifred M. Ernzer
LaGrave News, April, 1975

"The light of day is sweet, and pleasant to the eye is the sight of the sun; if a man lives for many years, he should rejoice in all of them. But let him remember that the days of darkness will be many."

Ecclesiastes 11:7, 8 NET

When asked what I am doing now that I am retired, the answer, only half-facetiously, is: "I'm a full-time philosopher."

With greater leisure, this is my time to think and re-think; with undiminished curiosity, to read and re-read; with maturer judgment, to re-evaluate and re-sort priorities. Added years influence perspective on life and judgment of values. More importantly, age is the last chance to seek and find essentials. I may be on the countdown, but I'm not yet counted out. I'm still in quest of the final great discovery.

I've learned a lot lately by taking a long, cool look at life and times, especially, as I have been touched by them. For example, I'm surprised at how much I know — an amazing collection of facts, fancies, ideas, thoughts, and opinions! And then, to find out how much of what I know isn't so at all; how much is wrong or wrongly placed in the fragile structure of memory, attitudes, biases, preferences and preju-dices; how much to do, how little done; how much to know, how little learned.

It's a confusing world. Often I feel like

> *"The centipede who was happy quite
> Until a frog said, 'which leg comes after which?'
> This wrought its mind to such a pitch
> It lay distracted in the ditch
> Forgetting how to run."*

But then I take comfort from a Greek sage who learned that the secret of happiness is freedom, and the secret of freedom is a brave heart.

Despairing, soul-sick Hamlet said,

> *"The time is out of joint;
> Oh, cursed spite that ever I was born to set it right."*

Less poetic but more hopeful and courageous is to bless the day that I was born to such a time as this.

An advantage of age is the privilege of being autobi-ographical and to be indulged in when editorializing or talking of oneself. It is fortunate then to have interesting, adventurous, and hopefully, useful years to reflect upon. Such reflections can turn out to be an exercise in humility. Even so, I like to think that I may have touched for good the lives of many in ways no man can measure and only God can reward.

Garritt E. Roelofs, 1972
LaGrave News, February, 1972

In 1976, the LaGrave congregation celebrated two hundred years of America's existence in ways it deemed appropriate. In the beginning years of the decade, some churches had removed the American flag from their sanctuaries. The Viet-nam conflict had caused a reexamination of what had been routinely accepted in mainline churches nationwide. But, Vietnam aside, was it proper to display a national flag in a holy Catholic (univer-sal) church? The question was asked in the La-Grave Church as well. The American flag was not removed as in some churches. It was deemed honorable and appropriate for display. America was a place where men and women were free to worship. LaGrave prayed for a revival and forgive-ness of national sins, but it also gave thanks for a nation preserved for two hundred years and where the founders of the LaGrave Avenue Christian Re-formed Church had found a haven one hundred years before.

Besides having gone to England on a sabbati-cal leave in 1969—1970, Rev. Eppinga engaged in other activities beyond the local scene. There were journeys to Guatemala and Nicaragua for mission purposes. On January 15, 1974, at a "Family of LaGrave" fellowship dinner, the con-gregation, to the surprise of Rev. Eppinga, cele-brated his twentieth year as pastor of the church with a "This Is Your Life" program and presented him and his wife, Anne, with a trip to the Holy Land. In April of that same year, he travelled to Berchtesgaden, Germany, where he conducted a retreat for Reformed and Christian Reformed servicemen. In September of 1975, he served as a delegate from the Christian Reformed Church to the Synod of De Gereformeerde Kerken in the Netherlands, and in 1976, together with elder Al-bert Bel, he was delegated to attend the Reformed Ecumenical Synod in Capetown, South Africa. He also served as a delegate to the Christian Reformed Synod in Grand Rapids, Michigan, a number of times. The LaGrave consistory considered these tasks to be part of his job description which sought to have him involved in community and denominational, as well as congregational, activities.

Rev. Eppinga, in a sermon entitled, "Our Help," delivered on the occasion of his twenty-fifth year as pastor of LaGrave Church, sought to review the developments in church and world in the past quarter century. It appeared in the March, 1979, issue of the *LaGrave News*. The April issue described an evening of fellowship, sponsored by the congregation and held in observance of Rev. Eppinga's twenty-five years of service. Rev. Eppinga and his family expressed their deep appreciation for the special tribute.

Mr. Mark Draugelis

SHOW US A MAN

Show us a man

Who will not rake the flank of waywardness
with the sharp spur of scornfulness,
Who will not rankle the wound of regretfulness
with the galling goad of self-righteousness,
And he shall be acclaimed as counsellor.

Show us a man

Who will not bludgeon the head of reluctance
with the threatening cudgel of perdition,
Who will not gall the neck of conscience
with the man-made yoke of prohibition,
And he shall be a bearer of the Word.

Show us a man

Who will not tickle the ear of complacency
with the frail feather of platitude,
Who will not cram the craw of content
with the pre-digested pap of generality
And he shall be proclaimed a pulpiteer.

Show us a man

Who will not dull the edge of inquiry
with the blunt stone of dogmatism,
Who will not hawk the pearl of redemption
with the bungling palms of ineptitude,
And he shall be called an under-shepherd.

Donald Oppewal

written for the occasion celebrating
Rev. Eppinga's 25 years at LaGrave

With the appearance of Rev. Steigenga on the ministry team, there was a surge in new directions. It became necessary to seek a third staff member to engage in outreach activities. Such a person was found. Mark Draugelis had been working in the field of outreach for the Sun Valley Christian Reformed Church of Denver, Colorado, as an unordained seminary intern in a program sponsored jointly by Calvin Seminary and the Home Missions Board. He accepted LaGrave's invitation, arriving in the summer of 1979. The consistory assigned him to work with the mission, hospitality, and social concerns committees and gave him the further task of being involved with the young people with regard to service projects in the community. Rev. Steigenga was assigned to the education committee and Rev. Eppinga to the worship committee. All three staff members were asked to assist one another in his area of specialty, with pastoral concerns involving both of the ordained members of the team.

Rev. Steigenga's talents were soon sought by his brother-in-law, Dr. Joel Nederhood, radio minister of the Christian Reformed Church, in the writing of meditations for the monthly publication *Today*. Responses to Rev. Steigenga's efforts were highly affirmative. He also became interested in the Bethel Bible Series and persuaded the consistory, through its education committee, to adopt it as a project. This effort was an enormous challenge to Pastor Steigenga and required his studying in Madison, Wisconsin, in order to prepare himself for the work. On May 11, 1978, he scheduled a meeting to acquaint the members of LaGrave with the series — a widely successful

congregational Bible study. An explanatory letter was sent to all informing them that the first two years would be spent in training teachers to teach others — the key to its success. The program was initiated and carried forward and proved to be a blessing to all who participated.

In the fall of 1978, the mission committee recommended the acquisition of a building located at 25 Commerce S.W. (corner of Weston) to be used for outreach purposes. Mr. Robert A. Jeursema, a neighborhood resident befriended by the LaGrave Church and whom the congregation thought penniless, died and left a considerable sum of money to LaGrave. It was this money that was used for the purchase of the building on Commerce Street. It was another effort on LaGrave's part to address itself to ministry in the community. It was in that same spirit that LaGrave made a sizable donation to the building fund of the Grace Christian Reformed Church — nearest of all Christian Reformed churches to LaGrave — also engaged in inner city outreach. When the La-Grave congregation, in the middle 1950s, voted to remain downtown, it had no way of knowing that in twenty years downtown would move to the suburbs in the form of the many shopping malls.

Thus, with the core city greatly altered, La-Grave constantly searched for new effective ways in which to address its immediate environment with an effective outreach in a changing culture and neighborhood. In its eagerness, LaGrave

bought the building at 25 Commerce, deciding afterwards what to do with it. There was one immediate answer. The Guiding Light Mission on Division Avenue was in need of a new home and so moved into part of the building. Further study eventually led LaGrave church into what was called a landlord ministry in which it sought to house various organizations which addressed themselves to the needs of the community. Some of the tenants were GRACE (Grand Rapids Area Center for Ecumenism), Criminal Justice Chaplaincy, and Inter-Varsity Christian Fellowship. In 1986, the Guiding Light Mission moved out. That same year the building was sold. The experiment

---

LaGrave's feeling of responsibility to the downtown area was not unnoticed. In May of 1978, William A. Johnson, former police chief of Grand Rapids and Kent County Commissioner, wrote the following letter:

Dear Pastor Eppinga:

As a citizen of Grand Rapids, I would just like to take this opportunity to express my appreciation to you and the members of your very fine church for the contribution you have made to the city of Grand Rapids in not only remaining at your original location, but — and more importantly — demonstrating your faith in the future of our central city by the substantial and material investment in your religious home.

In an age when so many of our congregations have elected to depart for the suburbs, it is gratifying to note the examples which have been set by your church, as well as Westminster, St. Andrew's, and St. George's.

While there are still many problems to be solved in this location, the action taken by LaGrave and your sister churches is a source of hope and inspiration not only to the near southeast side but to the entire city as a whole.

May God bless you for all that you have done!

William A. Johnson
from LaGrave News, May, 1978

had proved only partially successful.

On September 16, 1979, a son of the congregation, Steven J. VanHeest, entered the Christian Reformed ministry, the first since Willis DeBoer, great-grandson of LaGrave's first minister. Another son, Roger Rozeboom, had entered the ministry of the Reformed Church. Two daughters of the congregation, Patricia E. DeJong and Marchiene Vroon Reinstra, would enter other ministries. Steven VanHeest became pastor of the Christian Reformed Church of Alamosa, Colorado. LaGrave sent a bouquet of flowers for the occasion with its thanksgiving to God. Other sons and daughters of the congregation entered into missions, education, counselling, and other fields of service to proclaim their Christian witness.

In 1978, the Synod of the Christian Reformed Church, in a historic decision, opened the office of deacon to women. In its meeting of February 12, 1979, the LaGrave consistory decided not to move in this direction because of great confusion and concern in the denomination and because of a stipulation that the office and work of the deacon be clearly distinguished from the office of elder. The consistory adopted a "wait and see" policy. In further actions, the consistory commended Dick VanOverbeek and Ronald Cook for

their faithful work in running the sound system. Later, Jim DeMull joined them. In addition to helping the congregation tune in to the sermons, they also taped them for the deaconesses to distribute to the shut-ins. They made tapes of the services for those who requested them. By this means, LaGrave's services received a wide distribution — including such distant places as Africa and China.

Between 1973 and 1980, "Of Cabbages and Kings" and "More Cabbages and Kings" appeared beside the earlier book, "For Sinners Only." All three volumes by Rev. Eppinga were promoted and sold by various LaGrave societies with profits going to the societies.

Towards the close of the decade, the LaGrave Benefactors Trust Fund reviewed its history since its inception. It was organized December 21, 1964, with assets totalling $1,000. During its relatively short history, it had disbursed more than $75,000.

With the 1980s coming into view, the disturbances of the late 1960s and early 1970s had been replaced by another mood. The country's campuses had changed from scenes of protest to places where young people were intent on preparing themselves for careers and profit. But a new morality had settled on the land. The Christian Reformed denomination had lost its unanimity and uniformity. Debates on women in office and other questions came down to the issue of scriptural interpretation. Through it all, LaGrave, always known as a progressive church, steered a moderate course.

The list of disbursements from the LaGrave Benefactors Trust Fund in the first fourteen years of existence is far too large to itemize. It included contributions to practically all of LaGrave's activities. Some of the gifts were:

LaGrave special fund for community
    improvement program $15,000
Parking lot and landscaping 10,000
Henry Beets Mission Society
    Project Outreach 2,500
Antiphonal Organ (additions
    and repair) 4,500
Church bus 5,800
Choir and clergy robes 2,200
Hymnals and Bibles 7,000
Contribution to air-
    conditioning system 10,000

Smaller contributions were made to the Sunday Niters, Boy Scouts, Adult Retreats, Church School, Service Guild, and the Christian Education Society.

Chapter 24

COMING FULL CIRCLE

Russia entered Afghanistan; Ronald Reagan entered the White House; the Pope entered Ireland, Germany, and the United States; and LaGrave entered the final phase of its first one hundred years of existence.

Founded in 1887 as the Fourth Holland Christian Reformed Church and the first English-speaking Christian Reformed Church, LaGrave had grown considerably from small beginnings. So had the denomination of which it was a part.

DENOMINATIONAL STATISTICS		
	1885	1986
Churches	65	859
Families	4,600	73,788
Communicants	6,942	189,239
Souls	21,156	306,309

The denomination had also altered in character. *De Wachter,* an official publication of the denomination written in the Holland language, was terminated at the end of 1985. But that is as close to the horrors of George Orwell's *1984* as those who deeply mourned its passing got. While Dutch, as a language, officially exited from the denomination, others entered. Here and there Christian Reformed services were conducted in Spanish, Vietnamese, Chinese, and in the great Southwest, in native American tongues.

We can always see change better in others than in ourselves. The LaGrave congregation, entering the eighties, bore small resemblance to the LaGrave of the turn of the century. Its pastors had gone from a horse feed allowance to a car allowance. Its members, who had been forbidden to attend movies, now watched them in their living

While calling in a local rest home, Rev. Eppinga discovered a former member from his first charge occupying a bed next to the person he was visiting. He barely recognized the man. He had lost his hair, hearing, teeth, and about a hundred pounds. He couldn't get over the change! Approaching the bed and rousing the man, he shouted, "Do you remember me? I'm Rev. Eppinga." The man looked up with uncomprehending eyes. Gradually, recognition dawned. He said, "Rev. Eppinga? Boy, did you ever get old!"

rooms. The church, in seeking to meet the needs of a "new society" expanded not only externally, but internally — from missions to enlarged staff. There were organizations and activities enough for everybody.

MUSIC

But although much had changed, much was also the same. Alyce Lantinga was retiring from her long tenure as chancel organist. Musical excellence, however, was an enduring tradition. The consistory, via a committee, sought a worthy successor. David VanderVliet, M.D., a psychiatrist at Pine Rest Christian Hospital, had been presiding at the organ console on an interim basis. He was appointed chancel organist in February of 1980. In December of 1981, almost two years later, he was reappointed chancel organist with indefinite tenure. Dr. VanderVliet had studied organ with Roger Rietberg at Hope College, and with John Hamersma and Trudy Faber at Calvin College. He had served as organist at Fourth Christian Reformed Church in Holland, Michigan, the Christian Reformed Church and Campus Chapel in Ann Arbor, Michigan, and as assistant organist at Our Shepherd Lutheran Church in Birmingham, Michigan. At the time of his appointment with indefinite tenure at LaGrave Church, he was the accompanist for the King's Choraliers Male Chorus as well. In October of 1980, David VanderVliet initiated his annual organ concerts for the benefit of the children at Pine Rest Christian Hospital.

Seymour Swets went to be with his Lord in 1981. For many years he had been "Mr. Music" in the denomination. His death marked the passing of an era. Rev. Eppinga said at his funeral, "I can't picture him singing in the heavenly choir, but I can picture him directing it." Another member, Suzanne Bos Muller, an excellent pianist, died in a tragic automobile accident. Through the efforts of her husband, Wayne Muller, a Suzanne Bos Muller Music Fund was established. The interest from this fund was designated to be used for the enhancement of LaGrave's music in the services of worship.

In June of 1982, the LaGrave Benefactors Trust Fund agreed to supplement a gift from the late Mr. and Mrs. Henry Highstone for the purchase of a set of Verdin Handbells. Mr. Steven Brook was appointed to direct the handbell choir. After a year, a second handbell choir comprised of young people was begun under the leadership of Linda Male. She was succeeded by Stephen Girod who also served as associate chancel organist. The handbell choir performed at special services and occasionally joined the chancel choir and organ, contributing significantly to the worship hour.

In the fall of 1980, Mr. VanWesep relinquished his position of honorary elder, having served twenty-one of the past twenty-seven years. With many talents and always willing to take assignments, he had provided wise counsel and good judgment and was a stabilizing influence in the ruling body whose membership altered yearly. A consistory party was held in his honor and the thanks of the congregation was expressed.

Dr. David VanderVliet, Organist

Children's and young people's choirs also took part in the worship services. They were successively led through the years by Kay Oosting, Kenneth Karsten, Kathryn Poel, and others. However, none contributed more than LaGrave's hard working chancel choir. Its members showed great loyalty and dedication; many of them sang for years. In a salute to them, their director, Albert P. Smith, wrote of their loyalty in the *LaGrave News.* The choir had been a regular part of the Sunday services long before it had won the denomination's approval to participate in the services of worship.

Official church services, according to Christian Reformed tradition, were to be composed of only two elements; *Acta aparte Dei* (Acts on the part of God), and *Acta aparte populi* (Acts on the part of the people). The first category contained the invocation, scripture reading, sermon, and benediction — acts on the part of God to His people. The second category consisted of prayer, song, and the offering — acts on the part of the people. In such a schema, it was felt that there was no room for solos and choirs. They were considered entertainment. Where choirs existed, they were permitted to sing only on week nights or, if on Sundays, only after the benediction had been pronounced.

Gradually, in the 1950s, other Christian Reformed churches altered their stance to one which was less rigid and more in the spirit of Psalm 150. Choirs, too, could be viewed as acts on the part of the people — singing to God's glory. Some Christian Reformed churches began to include more elements, abandoning the traditional schema. Still later, the liturgical dance was approved in the denomination. Through this reexamination of principles of liturgy, the LaGrave Church, maintaining its traditional patterns, lost its image in the eyes of some as being liberal or progressive.

In 1983, in an effort to further improve the sound of the choir, a hardwood floor replaced the carpeting in the chancel area. Many willing hands from the congregation and the choir did the work, with none doing more manual labor than the maestro himself — "Smitty." In 1985, the Benefactors Trust Fund made it possible for the choir to have new robes. The old ones were given to some smaller churches through the help of the denominational home missions office.

The dedicatory services of the new sanctuary had climaxed with a purposeful prayer, "To Build a House Unto My Name," and had been preserved, in part, by a recording. The carillon, or-

In the October 3, 1983, issue of the LaGrave News, *Albert Smith, chancel choir director, wished to recognize some of the choir members for their longevity of service.*

William Smits . . . . *47 years*
Ruth DeJong . . . . *42 years*
Ruth Yonkers . . . . *42 years*
Gilbert VanSledright . . . . *37 years*
Mary DeGraaf . . . . *36 years*
Barbara DeHaan . . . . *36 years*
Marie VanBeek . . . . *33 years*
Connie VanSledright . . . . *32 years*
Carol Steensma . . . . *31 years*
Robert Haan . . . . *23 years*
Wesley Westmaas . . . . *22 years*
Nancy Peters . . . . *20 years*
Mae Smith . . . . *20 years*
Daniel VanderVliet . . . . *17 years*
Kay Hoitenga . . . . *15 years*
Barbara Voshel . . . . *15 years*
Kenneth Karsten . . . . *13 years*
Marie Werner . . . . *12 years*
Gerald Kruyf . . . . *12 years*

These services totalled 505 years. In addition, Albert Smith paid tribute to all those who served less years but with equal love and devotion.

gan, and choir were featured in this record entitled, "Chancel Echoes." These sounds of the year 1960 enjoyed a wide distribution. In 1982, a lovely recording made by Alyce Lantinga entitled, "Sanctuary Pipes," appeared. In 1985, the Benefactors Trust Fund, having made new robes a reality, also assisted the choir in the production of another record called, "A Jubilant Song." It was made to mark the occasion of Albert Smith's retirement as director of the chancel choir and also the forthcoming LaGrave Centennial Celebration. "A Jubilant Song" contained selections by the chancel choir, junior choir, handbell choir, and renditions by organists David VanderVliet and Stephen Girod.

Albert P. Smith, Choir Director from 1963 — 1985

THE END OF AN ERA

In February, 1987, LaGrave Church will celebrate the end of an era spanning 100 years. In June of 1985, we observed the end of an era-within-an-era. Musically speaking, "The Smith Era" came to an end with the retirement of Albert P. Smith as chancel choir director. For twenty-two years, the shape and sound of choral music at LaGrave bore the inimitable stamp of Professor Al Smith. How blessed we were to have had the services of that indomitable and unquenchable spirit, that bundle of exuberance and superb talent known as "Smitty."

LaGrave's long history of inspiring and worshipful choral music was continued and abetted immeasurably by the devotion and skill of this delightful man. And so we say our thanks:

*Thank you, Lord, for your gifts in
Al Smith.
Thank you, Lord, for your gift to us:
Al Smith.
Thank you, Al Smith, for using your gifts
here at LaGrave for twenty-two years.*

God bless you!

from *LaGrave News*, May-June, 1985

After twenty-two years as LaGrave's choir director, Albert Smith's announcement that he was retiring was received with great regret. He was recognized and thanked in a Sunday morning service with a reception following in fellowship hall, and at a subsequent choir banquet. A search committee was appointed, and on September 22, 1985, the congregation welcomed Merle Mustert as Albert Smith's successor.

Merle Mustert graduated from Calvin College and Michigan State, receiving music degrees from each. Since 1960, he has taught and conducted in the Grand Rapids Christian schools and at Calvin College. In 1981, he was appointed to the faculty of Calvin. From 1970 to 1985, Merle was the Director of Music at Fuller Avenue Christian Reformed Church.

SUNDAY EVENING SERIES

With the encouragement of Rev. Herman Teitsma, one of LaGrave's associate ministers, the church became the sponsor of the Sunday Evening Series (SES). This was a privately funded program which presented Christian artists (musicians) in six concerts a year — free to the public. The purpose of the venture was to provide a place and program to which people might come together to end the Lord's Day in a spirit of praise. Controversial Christian rock music was offered as part of an admixture of musical styles, including the more traditional fare. Doris VanDellen, Albert Smith, Sue McCarthy, Gerald Kruyf, and Robert Noordeloos served on the initial committee. James Wieland offered good ongoing leadership. Most of the concerts were presented in DeVos

*Mr. Merle Mustert,
appointed new Choir Director in 1985*

THE GRAND RAPIDS PRESS □ SATURDAY, MARCH 9, 1985 □

SUNDAY EVENING SERIES
PRESENTS AN INSPIRATIONAL CONCERT FEATURING

Eternity

ADMISSION BY FREE TICKET

GROUP TICKETS: CALL 451-0717 OR WRITE S.E.S.
25 S. DIVISIONS AND ENCLOSE SELF ADDRESSED
5"x7" ENVELOPE WITH PROPER POSTAGE - 39¢;
LIMIT 25 TICKETS.

TICKETS
AVAILABLE
AT DOOR

SUNDAY, MARCH 10, 1985
8:00 P.M. - DEVOS HALL

SPONSORED BY LA GRAVE AVE. CHRISTIAN REFORMED CHURCH.

'Messiah' sing-along scheduled Sunday

Hall. In December, 1982, Robert Swets initiated the SES-sponsored December *Messiah* Sing-Alongs in the LaGrave sanctuary with a full orchestra and local soloists. These sing-alongs were open to anyone bringing a musical score. Local conductors participated, dividing their tasks. Many came to take part and, in the words of Handel, to "swell the chorus." Participants occupied the first floor; listeners were seated in the balcony where the sound was indeed magnificent.

The LaGrave Benefactors Trust Fund gave continuing support to the cause of music at LaGrave. In addition to the items reported, it supplemented a gift to the church for a Trumpet En Chamade, a horizontal series of beautiful trumpets to be installed between the antiphonal pipes in the balcony. The Benefactors Trust Fund paid the major share of the cost of purchase and installation.

MISSIONS

LaGrave's mission support continued unabated. Missionary letters regularly appeared in the pages of the *LaGrave News*. With the encouragement of the mission committee, a large number of members volunteered to correspond with those who were supported by LaGrave's prayers and gifts. The Henry Beets Mission Society extended help to many mission causes, its source of monies being two special annual offerings. Members of the church willingly gave of their time and

great personal effort in LaGrave-sponsored or other mission endeavors. In addition to countless young people, such individuals as Dr. Ralph Blocksma, Dr. Christian Helmus, and Dr. Austin Lamberts used their skills in the cause of Jesus Christ.

LaGrave's mission interest extended beyond the support of those who served on mission fields near or far. A surprising number of the members themselves were active on the local scene. The chairman of the 1982 mission committee, John Leegwater, scheduled a mission recognition dinner in order to acknowledge their efforts. There were over 150 members in attendance — all of whom were a part of the church's outreach. LaGrave's involvement with the community came to expression in many ways. Some of them had names.

HEARTSIDE NEIGHBORHOOD ASSOCIATION
LaGrave became a dues-paying member in 1980. Initial leadership came from Rev. John Ouwinga and Carol Landheer, with vigorous support from Mark Draugelis. Clifton Orlebeke served as its president for a time. Instead of retreating behind fortress walls, LaGrave, in cooperation with others, concerned itself with neighborhood planning, zoning, and efforts at general neighborhood improvement. There were results in the form of new business establishments, including a grocery store, street lighting improvements, less litter, and less crime. Financial support for this neighborhood effort, however, was weak.

193

MISSIONARY NEWS

The Church Herald *of October 4, 1985, contained an article entitled, "Docta Hea," written by our fellow member, Dr. Austin Lamberts. Dr. Lamberts served as a volunteer physician in Pakistan, Ethiopia, Nigeria, and Cameroon. The article describes how medical missionaries bring new hope to the hopeless.*

An article in the Saturday Evening Post *of March, 1986, entitled, "My Father and Other Good Guys: Plastic Surgeons Abroad," by Mary Blocksma, chronicled some of the work of her father, Dr. Ralph Blocksma.*

The letters from the missionaries were always interesting, and sometimes humorous. In August, 1985, Rev. Ren Broekhuizen in one of his letters from Liberia wrote:

> *Some of our supporting congregations send us tapes of the worship services. We got a package recently and on the customs' sticker where it asks "Contents," the person had written, "Pastor's Sermons." Where the sticker asks "Value," the person had written, "No Value."*

> *We won't tell.*

DWELLING PLACE

Governed by a board made up of representatives from downtown churches, hospitals, and other non-profit organizations, its goal was to enhance the quality of life for the residents of the city center area. Norman DeGraaf served ably as LaGrave's representative on this board and Mark Draugelis gave much of his time. Dwelling Place was located at 359 S. Division (presently at 343 S. Division). For a time, its progress prompted the *Grand Rapids Press* to label it the mushrooming giant of Heartside.

CENTER FOR CHRISTIAN HOPE

Through a committee comprised of John Leegwater, Richard Eppinga, Tom Stuit, Kenneth Mouw, Joe Schuitema, David Graf, and Mark Draugelis, the definition of the Center for Christian Hope was delineated as:

An expression of the LaGrave Avenue Christian Reformed Church in its commitment to serving its neighbors in Christ's name. The purpose of the Center for Christian Hope is to provide facilities for various Christian ministries and forms of outreach and to participate thereby in meaningful service to the residents of the community. These programs and ministries will be subject to the governing body of the LaGrave Church or other instituted body. Recognizing reconciliation between God and man as the greatest need, all programs and ministries, including those whose orientation are physical and/or emotional, will have the presentation of the Gospel of Jesus Christ as their primary objective.

DOWNTOWN MINISTRY

This was an effort, under the direction of Mark Draugelis, to form various ministry teams. One was the Morton House ministry with Neal DeMey as leader. Another was the Mertens Hotel ministry with Donna Oppewal having the charge. Area nursing homes had various people involved, and still others contributed time and effort to children and Bible Schools. The downtown nursing ministry was led by Judy Eppinga and Sharon Etheridge. Visits were made to such places as the Morton House. The nurses took blood pressures of the residents, answered their questions, and gave general health instructions. This unique outreach caught the attention of other churches who also sought to do the same.

LaGrave nurses who signed for service at the Morton House, as reported in the LaGrave News *issue of February, 1981, were:*

Betty Boerema	*Barb Orlebeke*
Pam DeGraaf	*Drynda Ritsema*
Pat DeKryger	*Lynn Rottschafer*
Judy Eppinga	*Mary Beth Schurman*
Sharon Etheridge	*Sue Swets*
Barb Leegwater	*Carolyn Vaandrager*
Kay Oosting	*Ellen VanArtsen*
Jess Oppewal	*Ellen Wierenga*

DEGAGÉ MINISTRIES

Degagé was an effective coffee house ministry reaching out to others for fellowship and Bible study (e.g., the YMCA). This ministry was not carried forward by LaGrave members but was sponsored by the LaGrave Church. The Grand Rapids

Board of Evangelism, of which LaGrave was a member, required all aspects of its ministry to have a sponsor. LaGrave served in this capacity for the Degagé — submitting its budget yearly to the Board of Evangelism, along with the budget of Degagé, for approval of the grant-in-aid for the Degagé ministries.

THANKSGIVING DINNERS AND BASKETS

Annually, at LaGrave's Sunday evening pre-Thanksgiving service, opportunity was given for the members to give groceries, as well as money, at the time the offering was received. These gifts were used by the Esther Circle for the distribution of food to the needy. The cash gifts received at the pre-Thanksgiving service varied in amounts of up to $3,000. The food gifts would stock a small grocery store. One year, fifty food baskets were distributed, thirty-six plants were delivered to shut-ins, and twelve fruit baskets were brought to nursing homes. These were average figures; the exact numbers varied from year to year. It was an effort coordinated by Esther Circle and involved the cooperation of great numbers of people, including thirty-five to forty delivery people. Individual baskets held approximately thirty-five dollars worth of food. Another effort made possible by the pre-Thanksgiving offering was the Thanksgiving dinner for the neighborhood, which drew from 160 to 200 people. Anna Day presided in the kitchen over donated turkeys. Servers were furnished by the Friendship Club and also gathered from among the young people. Warren and Angel DeHaan gave unstintingly to make this effort the success that it was. From time to time, expressions of appreciation came back to LaGrave from various sources and in many forms.

FISH

LaGrave's FISH program was organized in 1970 by Connie DeVries who served as coordinator until 1974 when Marge VanOverbeek replaced her. In the early '70s, the volunteers received *ten to thirty* calls a day for food, clothing, and transportation for the handicapped, ill, and elderly.

The February, 1982, issue of the LaGrave News *reported that FISH drivers included: Mary DeGraaf, Marie VanBeek, John Oole, Martin Engbers, Jess VanderWall, Anne Eppinga, June Minnaar, William Pastoor, Ray Pastoor, Gertrude and Henry Elsenbroek, Neal DeMey, Clazina Masselink, Cornie Pape, Bea DeVries, Helen VanVliet and Thelma Kemink. LaGrave is also indebted to the Jellema House for providing drivers and seven years of service to this fine organization.*

CAPITOL LUNCH

Capitol Lunch, located two blocks from LaGrave, was established as an ecumenical program to serve hungry people in the downtown area. LaGrave's young people and adults helped serve 300-400 people per day and, on occasion, helped prepare the food.

HUNGER WALK

Annually, many members of LaGrave participated in a community hunger walk — a twelve-mile route. The walkers were sponsored by other members with pledges of varying amounts for each mile. The funds amounted to sums as high as $280,000 in 1986 and were divided among causes dealing with the needs of the hungry, both locally and abroad. LaGrave's contributions were sizable — from $380 the first year to $4,500 in the year 1985.

SPONSORSHIP

Beginning with Cuban refugees in the 1950s, LaGrave maintained its interests in those made homeless by upheavals wrought by politics and war. LaGrave helped several refugees who had come to America from Hungary and, in the seventies and eighties, aided some families from Vietnam.

These efforts involved the cooperation of many in the renting and furnishing of apartments and in the matter of orienting "strangers in our midst" — not only to new surroundings, but to a different climate and culture.

After four-and-a-half years, Mr. Mark Draugelis resigned as Minister of Outreach. His services were recognized with thanksgiving to God at a special reception on Sunday, January 8, 1984. At a meeting on January 10, 1984, the consistory accepted the recommendation of pastors Eppinga and Steigenga to appoint Neal DeMey as a temporary part-time replacement for Mr. Draugelis. Already serving as chairman of LaGrave's mission committee and as an elder of the downtown congregational district, Mr. DeMey was well acquainted with the challenges and opportunities of the local neighborhood scene. In due time, the temporary nature of the appointment was altered to a more permanent one but remained a part-time position. Thus, Neal DeMey replaced Mr. Draugelis as a member of the ministry staff.

A week after Rev. and Mrs. Eppinga visited the Zuni mission field in New Mexico, in the company of Rev. Peter Winkle, a flood ravaged the area, doing severe damage to the church and school. Through its Henry Beets Mission Society, LaGrave made a generous contribution for repairs to the damaged property. The following summer, June 17, 1983, seventeen LaGrave young people, under the guidance of Rev. Steigenga, Keith and Hermine Winn, and Jack and Debbie Nuiver, left for Zuni to contribute manual labor as well as assistance in the Vacation Bible School. Long before the departure date, the young people did everything from raking leaves to baby-sitting in order to raise money which, supplemented by a grant from the Benefactors Trust Fund, financed the trip to the Southwest. Similar earlier ventures to the Appalachia region were typical, too, of the mission projects initiated and carried out by LaGrave's young people in the seventies and eighties.

LaGrave's youth group in Zuni, New Mexico, June, 1983

BUT, WAS IT WORTH IT?

In the October, 1983, issue of the LaGrave News, *Rev. Steigenga wrote the following concerning the trip to Zuni, New Mexico with seventeen young people and their guides:*

Anyone who has ever organized a trip for twenty-two people for eleven days knows how much work it takes. And how expensive it is! The Zuni trip cost approximately $7,000. It required countless hours in planning, training, and supervising. Was it worth the work and expense? Without a doubt!

Twenty-two people now have a first-hand knowledge of what it means to do mission work among the Zuni people.

Twenty-two people now have first-hand Zuni brothers and sisters in Christ.

Twenty-two people have had an experience probably never-to-be-duplicated in their lifetimes.

And who knows what the Holy Spirit may yet do with this experience in the hearts of LaGrave youth?

LAGRAVE ORGANIZATIONS

From 1887 until the 1940s, there was a total of about twelve organizations formed; seldom were more than eight active at any one time. From the 1940s through the 1980s, over three dozen new groups were organized; often, more than thirty of these were active simultaneously.

Nursery
Children's Church
Church School Classes
Adult Forum
Henry Beets Mission Society
Henry Beets Auxiliary
Men's Bible Study and Prayer Breakfast
Women's Board
Women's Bible Study
Women's Book Club
LaGrave Service Guild
Esther Circle
Missionary Society
Friendship Club
Stephens Series
FISH
Young Adults Fellowship
Senior High Youth Group
Junior High Youth Group
Boy Scouts
Junior Choir
Chancel Choir
Chancel Ringers
Handbell Choir
LaGrave Players
Christian Education Society
Benefactors Trust Fund
Sunday Evening Series
LaGrave Bowling League
Softball Teams

from LaGrave 1985 Church Directory

In 1985, LaGrave participated in a city-wide evangelistic campaign called "Alive '85." Ten years earlier, a similar venture, the "I Found It Campaign" also found LaGrave cooperative as did the already mentioned "Key 73" and "Evangelism Thrust" efforts. In 1986, a Missions Emphasis Week was begun, initiating what was hoped to become an annual event as part of LaGrave's continuing mission mentality.

CONGREGATIONAL LIFE

There were other aspects to LaGrave's congregational life besides music and missions. An excellent and aggressive church library committee, comprised of: Pieternella Faber, Nancy Glupker, Ruth Dommisse, Sharon Lantinga, Jean DeKryger, and Sharon Karsten, spent hours building and cataloging one of the best church libraries in the city. With an excellent selection of books available for all ages, the library facilities were enlarged and improved. By 1986, it received the name of LaGrave Centennial Library in anticipation of the church's one hundredth birthday. The Central Ladies Aid and the Mens Brotherhood no

longer existed, but there were thirty organizations in 1985 that were functioning. Church picnics came into vogue again in an age of nostalgia and were well attended. So were the Christmas Eve candlelight services. Ecumenical Tuesday morning Lenten services involved LaGrave Church, along with a number of other downtown churches. Scouts and young people's suppers, progressive dinners held in the fall in LaGrave members' homes, and other church dinners did much to encourage fellowship among the membership. Beginning in 1980, roses began to appear on the baptismal font announcing newborn arrivals into the membership. In 1984, LaGrave initiated an annual stewardship commitment week wherein telephone calls were made to all members for financial pledges and commitments of time and talent.

Beginning in January, 1981, Pastor Eppinga became a shut-in with an eight-week stay in the hospital because of a serious illness. During that time, Rev. Steigenga did double duty. The prayers of the congregation were heard, and by midyear Rev. Eppinga was grateful to be able to resume his duties once again — and did so with zeal. It was not his zeal, however, which set fire to the lounge. It was faulty wiring. Nero fiddled while Rome burned, but Rev. Eppinga, reviewing his sermon in the study an hour before an evening service early in 1982, was completely oblivious to the fact that just outside his study door firemen were battling — not the flames of hell — but the fire in the lounge. The evening service took place as scheduled despite the considerable damage done to another part of the building.

The March-April, 1982, issue of the *LaGrave News* paid tribute to LaGrave's former pastor, Dr. E. Masselink, who was retiring as editor of *The Cynosure.** Later that same year, LaGrave took note of the denomination's 125 years of existence.

In 1983, Rev. Eppinga was again delegated to synod where he served as president for the second time. In the fall, Mrs. Abe (Connie) DeVries was appointed LaGrave's representative of *The Banner,* the denominational weekly. It was also in 1983 that Rev. Eppinga stepped down from the presidency of the LaGrave consistory, having served in that capacity for twenty-nine years. Rev. Steigenga assumed that position while Rev. Eppinga remained the chairman of the elders.

In order to make the community more aware of the presence of LaGrave Church, the consistory appointed a promotions committee consisting of Richard Eppinga, chairman, Kenneth Faber, Erwin Johnson, and Pastor Steigenga.

The Christian Education Society, begun in the 1950s, was still functioning well, promoting the cause of Christian education, giving assistance where needed, receiving tuition payments for some 100 to 140 LaGrave children, and guaranteeing the area Christian schools full tuition payment for all.

On November 28, 1982, a new organization,

*Historic name for the North Star, a sign of certainty in all times; a guide to travellers.

the LaGrave Players, under the direction of Robert Haan, presented its first production entitled, "Forgive Us Our Chicken Coops." It was organized to aid and abet the proclamation of the Christian message in drama form.

FACILITIES

The facilities committee of the consistory (formerly the building committee), always active, became more so in the 1980s due to an increased work load caused by the aging of the premises. The parish house, finished in 1939, needed constant attention. The parish house apartment, no longer housing the custodian since the arrival of Mr. Peter Noorman, was occupied by seminarians from Calvin and students from the Grand Rapids School of the Bible and Music (GRSBM). Among them were Mr. and Mrs. John Visser, Mr. and Mrs. Bruce Persenaire, Mr. and Mrs. Mark Deckinga, Mr. and Mrs. Kenneth Paulson, and Mr. and Mrs. Carl Main. Their presence added security and afforded part-time janitorial service in return for free accommodations. The apartment occupants, Mr. Ed Stephan (a part-time janitor), and Mr. Noorman comprised the custodial staff, under the supervision of the facilities committee chairman. This work increased during the chairmanship of Mr. G. Tiesma and expanded still further with the appointment of Mr. Bruce Glupker as chairman — not only because of the increased need for maintaining the parish house, but also the sanctuary, chapel, and church offices which, after a period of over twenty years, were beginning to show wear and tear.

Increased energy costs rose to emergency proportions. Ceiling fans were considered but rejected for aesthetic reasons. Acid rain was causing irreparable damage to the leaded sanctuary windows. The energy and window problems were addressed by installing Lexan windows in the manner of storm windows. This addition was as attractive as it was protective. Painting, roof repairs, and air-conditioning needs were reviewed and met. Attention was also being given to make the church barrier free. A member had made a donation for this cause. It seemed an expensive venture, but by the mid-eighties, rest rooms accessible to the handicapped were installed in the porch area. An elevator, made possible by another gift, replaced the stairs in the southeast corner of the building, and spaces for wheelchairs were made in the sanctuary by shortening a number of pews along the outside aisles.

In September of 1983, a special edition of the *LaGrave News* presented an overview of all the needs of LaGrave's physical plant. This was followed by a forum, guided tours, pledge cards, and gifts — all leading to such capital improvements as were not optional, but essential. The LaGrave Benefactors Trust Fund, in early 1984, agreed to assist the facilities committee in financing a complete overhaul of the twenty-four-year-old sound system, including the replacing of the outdated speakers.* Thus, the whole facility, including the already referred to Centennial Library, was brought into such a renovated condition as bespoke loving care for God's House. Rev. Steigenga's study was moved from the upper level of the parish house to an area on the lower level adjacent to the Centennial Library. This project was ably directed by the facilities chairman, Mr. Bruce Glupker.

There were further needs. At the congregational meeting of April 20, 1986, the consistory submitted to the congregation a plan for additional remodeling needs at an estimated cost of $200,000. After considerable discussion, it was rejected because it was thought to be inadequate for LaGrave's long-range needs. There were those who spoke in terms of enlarging the vision for the future. And so, almost on the eve of LaGrave's Centennial, the congregation returned the matter of its housing needs to the consistory for further study and a new recommendation. A good spirit among the membership prevailed in all these procedings. So it ought to be among Christians. And so it was.

MINISTRATIONS

Beginning in the 1970s and continuing throughout the 1980s, the consistory, comprised of fifteen elders and twelve deacons, sought to streamline, improve, and make itself more efficient. The deacons and elders, in their separate meetings, sought to do the same. All minutes, committee reports, and recommendations were required to be in writing and in the hands of the office bearers prior to the consistory meeting on the second Monday of every month. Separate elders' and deacons' meetings were held on the fourth Monday of every month. The executive committee, made up of three elders (vice president, clerk, and elder-at-large) and three deacons (president of the diaconate, treasurer, and deacon-at-large), with staff members as advisors, met prior to all consistory meetings in order to prepare the consistory agenda and deal with such

*not the preachers

Increased costs for building repair required increased giving. To call attention to this need, the clerk of the consistory, Clarence Huizenga, in reporting "Consistory Happenings" in the May-June, 1982, issue of the LaGrave News, wrote:

> *We were visiting a church in another city recently. The senior pastor was making a pitch for the annual all-member canvass for the general fund and told about the call received in the church office from the Internal Revenue Service. The question was: "Is it true that John Doe gave the church $1,500?" The person in the office replied: "I can't answer that today, but if you will call tomorrow, I'm sure he did." It may be that some of us are not giving as much as we intended to give.*

matters as were referred to it by the consistory. The membership and worship committees reported to the elders' meetings, and all other committees reported to the consistory.

Beginning in 1984, the position descriptions of the pastors were refined and delineated — designating Rev. Eppinga as Minister of Preaching and Rev. Steigenga as Minister of Pastoral Care — with each assisting in the other's area. An organizational review committee was appointed in an ever ongoing attempt to improve the operations of the church and its governing body. Its members were: Gordon Buter, chairman, Richard Eppinga, Kenneth Horjus, John Leegwater, Gerald VanderWall, Pat Verduin, and Philip Versluis. The concept of a volunteer church manager, already thought about in the 1960s, kept resurfacing from time to time, but up to the mid-eighties was an idea whose time had not yet come — if ever it would. In all of these matters, the Spirit led and His leading was continuously sought.

The Holy Spirit did lead the church in the direction of seeking a youth leader. Upon the resignation of Mr. Draugelis, a committee of the consistory invited the members of the congregation to express their feelings and wishes regarding a successor. The many responses were invaluable and led to the creation of a search committee. After much work and prayer, the committee recommended the appointment of Mr. Robert Grussing who, at the time, held the position of youth pastor at the Brookside Christian Reformed Church of Grand Rapids. Upon receiv-

Mr. Robert Grussing, Minister of Youth, Education, and Hospitality

ing LaGrave's invitation, and after due consideration, Robert Grussing sent a letter of acceptance.

At a reception on February 10, 1985, the congregation met its new youth minister and his wife, Carol, and children, Sheri Lynn and Lora Beth. Mr. Grussing graduated from Dordt College. His experience included: counseling for two years at the Harmony Youth Home in Orange City, Iowa; acting as Director of Education and Evangelism for the First Christian Reformed Church of Zeeland, Michigan; and serving as Director of Church Education at Brookside Christian Reformed Church, Grand Rapids. At LaGrave, Mr. Grussing was commissioned to work with and develop programs for the youth and young adults, the education committee, and the hospitality committee. He brought experience, insight, and energy into his position.

With the coming of Robert Grussing, the part-time position of church school coordinator was no longer necessary and, therefore, was terminated. Robert Fry had ably filled this position as had his predecessors before him.

Neal DeMey and his wife, Dorothy, were also recognized at that February 10, 1985, reception. Mr. DeMey had been assistant director of Jellema House since 1973. In 1984, when Mark Draugelis resigned as Minister of Outreach, he filled that position on a part-time basis and continued to work part-time for the Jellema House. In January of 1985, he was appointed as LaGrave's official

Minister of Outreach. He retired from the staff at Jellema House in July of the same year but continued to serve on the board. Though his job description listed him as "part-time," Mr. DeMey devoted all of his time to LaGrave's neighbors in the Heartside district and touched numerous lives for good.

STEPHEN MINISTRY

In the spring of 1984, the consistory authorized Rev. Steigenga, Marian Smedes, and Jackie Fazekas to attend a two-week training course in Kansas City, Missouri, to learn about the Stephen Series — a program of lay caring ministry for the congregation. Upon their return, an interesting fifty-hour training program for this new ministry was offered to volunteers from the congregation. This venture was financed in part by a special offering. Seventeen LaGrave members volunteered and attended two-hour training sessions each Tuesday evening. In the fall of 1985, a second Stephen Series class was begun with thirteen LaGrave volunteers. By that time, the Stephen ministry was underway in the life of the congregation. Those receiving the care and help of these fellow church members in their needs testified to the blessing of this activity. In addition to pastoral care, elders' calls, the work of the deaconesses and deacons, LaGrave was as involved with in-

Mr. Neal DeMey, Minister of Outreach

reach as it was with outreach.

There were some activities or events that didn't fit into categories but nonetheless had impact on the life of the congregation.

CENTENNIAL

In March, 1982, the LaGrave historical committee, comprised of Elmer and Marie VanBeek and James and Marilyn DeMull, alerted the congregation to the fact that in five years the LaGrave Church would observe its centennial year. In preparation, it asked the members to turn in whatever pictures or documents of historical importance they could find that pertained to the church. Photographers were appointed to record forthcoming events. On October 26, 1983, at an area restaurant, Dr. Gerald VanderWall, at precisely 8:29 A.M., agreed to serve as general chairman for LaGrave's Centennial Celebration. The Service Guild had already allocated funds for the publishing of a centennial history book, and many sub-committees began to function — all in preparation for the great event. Other members of the centennial committee were: Gordon Buter, Rev. Eppinga, John Pool, Charles Strikwerda, Nancy Peters, and Barbara Leegwater.

Psalm 90:1 and 17

Lord, thou hast been our dwelling place in all generations.

And let the beauty of the Lord our God be upon us: and establish thou the work of our hands upon us; yea, the work of our hands establish thou it.

LaGrave's Centennial logo and texts

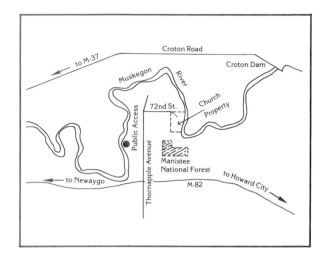

PROPERTY

At a congregational meeting held on April 28, 1985, approval was sought and granted to purchase an eleven-acre parcel of land on the Muskegon River in Newago County. The property was part of a larger section LaGrave had been leasing from the Consumers Power Company for a dollar a year. The eleven-acre parcel was purchased for the sum of $20,400. With 365 feet of river frontage, the property would be available for day use and overnight primitive camping by the LaGrave Boy Scout Troup 342 and other church groups. Mr. Harold VanDyk, scoutmaster, anticipated extensive use of the property.

WOMEN IN OFFICE

Because of confusion at the synodical level, the LaGrave consistory had withheld women's names from the lists of nominees for the office of deacon. Hearings were later held by the executive committee of the consistory and many members came to express their views as favoring or opposing this move. In April of 1986, the LaGrave congregation chose Grace Achterhof as the first woman to serve in the position of deacon.

SABBATICALS

In May, 1985, the consistory reinstituted the former arrangement of giving sabbatical leaves to the pastors after seven years of service. Accordingly, Rev. Steigenga made plans to study in Nottingham, England, for the fall term, leaving in August and returning in December of 1986.

CHURCH OFFICE

In 1983, Ruth Snoek completed twenty-five years of service as executive secretary in the church office. In appreciation, the congregation celebrated her years of efficiency and faithfulness with an evening in her honor and presented her with tokens of its gratitude. During her tenure, the office workload continually increased, making more secretarial help necessary. Eleanor Scholten, Marge Scripps, Lucille Buffinga, and Jessie Gritter served successively as assistants until RoseAnn Koning was employed full-time and later part-time. Subsequently, Jan Huisman was hired; Jan and Rose shared a full-time secretarial position as assistants to Ruth. LaGrave had gone from no secretarial help to a church office that was often referred to as Grand Central Sta-

Mrs. RoseAnn Koning

Mrs. Jan Huisman

tion. Unlike many church buildings which are quiet and uninhabited most of the week, the La-Grave Church at 107 LaGrave seemed not only occupied most days — but busy — and with the office as the hub.

From the days in the 1890s when LaGrave almost died, it had gone on to the eve of its centennial very much alive.

A GALA AFFAIR

Congratulations, LaGrave congregation, on having such an excellent secretary in RUTH SNOEK for the past 25 YEARS!

Congratulations, too, to all for keeping her surprise party a complete secret. That took everyone's cooperation. Ruth didn't suspect a thing. Really!

What a fine evening we had together! Thanks to all who had a part in making the party such a gala affair. Most of all, thanks to Ruth for her loyal and devoted service. We pray that God will bless her and hers. We hope, too, that she will continue in her present capacity with us.

As one who has worked with Ruth Snoek for a quarter of a century, I would like to say to all that she has been a tremendous help and blessing in the LaGrave Church. Her ability, discretion, and dedication to her work has made her a model for others. Viewing her occupation as a calling, she has never been a clock watcher; indeed, I can't count the times when she has gone the extra mile. She will continue to be good for us — as well as to us.

Acting out "The Ruth Snoek Story" at the party on Monday, January 31, were staff members RoseAnn Koning, Mark Draugelis, John Steigenga, Imposter Ruth Snoek (Bob Haan), the REAL Ruth Snoek, David VanderVliet, and J.D. Eppinga.

*Rev. Eppinga
from the LaGrave News, Feb.–Mar., 1983*

Chapter 25

ANOTHER CENTURY OF GRACE!

I t was February, 1987. LaGrave was celebrating its 100th birthday. A Century of Grace! The United States of America, in which it had been born and in which it had enjoyed freedom of worship for ten full decades, would soon be 211 years old. The Christian Reformed denomination, of which LaGrave was a part, was in its 130th year. Jesus Christ, the King of the Church, had not yet returned. That great event, still future, was, however, a hundred years closer than the day the first English-speaking Christian Reformed Church came into being.

LaGrave's ninth minister, having served for thirty-three years, one-third of the congregation's life span, was approaching retirement. A search committee, under the chairmanship of Mr. Norman DeGraaf, was seeking a successor who would carry forward with a staff which would include Rev. J. Steigenga, who had just returned from a sabbatical leave. The ending of a long ministerial tenure signalled changes ahead. LaGrave's entire history had been filled with them. No two of its decades of existence had been alike.

The changes had been brought about, in large degree, by the stage in world history in which La-Grave had been born and in which it had attained

its centennial year. If the history of the human race, from Adam to LaGrave's 100th birthday, could be compressed into the sixty minutes on the faces of all the clocks in LaGrave's many rooms, most of history's major changes and developments would be found in the last minute. It was in that particular 1/60th part, so filled with inventions and alterations — from bicycles to space travel, from traditional weapons to hydrogen bombs, from simple life-styles to complex, from old morality to new — that LaGrave had lived and endured from birth. The seeds of a Reformation (Luther, Calvin), exploration (Columbus, Magellan), revolution (political, scientific), sown in the previous minute, were ingredients for the next, in which all things changed, and only Jesus Christ — who was before Abraham — remained the same.

There were those who feared the changes time had brought. There were those who felt that the denomination was being loosed from its moorings. There were those who indeed were pushing panic buttons. Some were seeking reverse gear in order to bring the church back to where it had been.

Their fears were justified in the sense that they

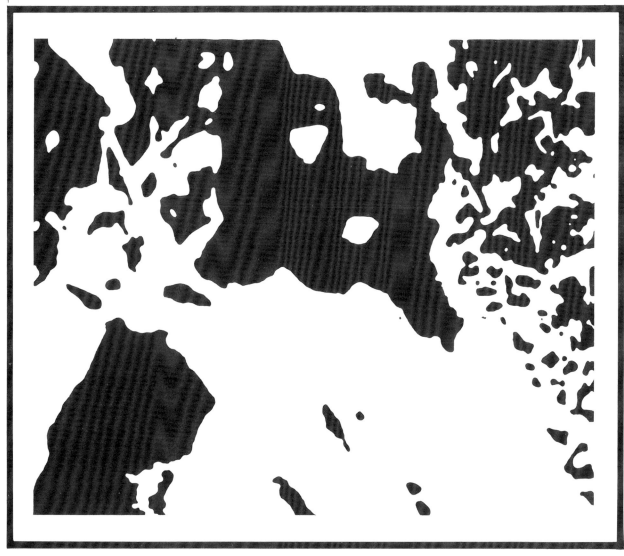

Sir, We Would See Jesus! Snow on a New England bush resulted in the above picture called, "The Hidden Christ." It hangs in Rev. Eppinga's study, and he has found it a useful teaching tool. Jesus should be seen in us more readily than many can trace His face in the above picture. Can you find Him?

always are — in whatever decade — for Satan never sleeps. For example, there had been a time when divorces were uncommon in society but, because of new ways of thinking, they were becoming almost common in the church. There were other alarming facts, for it was an age in which the church was often more acted upon, rather than acting — reflecting a world, rather than influencing it. Thus, there were those in the denomination who organized themselves into a society of "the concerned."

A centennial, however, in which a church still stood on the same rock — Jesus Christ — on which it was founded, was heartening. It was proof

of the fact that the gates of hell had not, as Christ promised, prevailed (Matthew 16:18). Indeed, the positive side of that promise in which the Lord had said that the Spirit would guide the church into the truth (John 16:13) was also evident on LaGrave's landmark birthday and was cause for great thanksgiving. Its centennial text, "Lord, thou hast been our dwelling place in all generations . . . " Psalm 90:1, was its heartfelt testimony and spoke of God's faithfulness to His little flock in an inner city which was fast becoming a metropolis. LaGrave had not only survived, but prospered. It had done so — not "because of" its members and pastors — for, alas, "in spite of" would be the more Biblical truth. It was God's grace alone that accounted for LaGrave's endurance in what some were calling a post-Christian age.

Whether "post-Christian age" was an accurate designation would be for future historians to assess. In any case, LaGrave had lived and moved and had its being in a century of history — linear, not circular. History was a continuum. It did not repeat itself, as the seasons did. Rather, it was something that unfolded and that went ever onward towards a final climax — Judgment Day. Thus, in its 100th year, in 1987, LaGrave was finding itself where it had never been before. Its "today" was wholly other from its "yesterday." It had new challenges, new problems, new possibilities, new perils, and new opportunities. Because of an acceleration of developments and a revolution in mores, 1887 seemed more like a thousand years removed rather than a hundred. In a turbulent century, however, LaGrave had not lost its compass. With that compass — the Word of God — the congregation could go confidently onward into the unknown. But before it did so, it paused in its 100th birthday to look back with thanksgiving, breathing a prayer that was the other part of its centennial text:

> Let the favor of the Lord our God be
> upon us, and establish thou the work
> of our hands, upon us, yea, the work
> of our hands, establish thou it.
> Psalm 90:17

On its 100th birthday, LaGrave received a number of greetings and congratulations. The denomination and community, both of which it had been a part, took note. Among the many pieces of mail, there was one that came from another church. It contained a transfer of membership to LaGrave, commending to its spiritual care Mr. and Mrs. Klaas Troon and their two children. Another letter was from Mr. Troon himself. Addressed to Rev. Eppinga, it read, in part, as follows:

> . . . I don't think you remember me. The only time we met was some years ago after a church service when I introduced myself to you. At the time, I was a rebel, turned off to society and, especially, the church. I came that morning, simply out of curiosity, to see where my father Jack, and grandfather John, and great-grandfather Pieter, had been members. Since then, I have experienced a great change in my

life. I accepted Jesus Christ as my Saviour and joined a church . . . My company is transferring me to Grand Rapids. We hope to be in LaGrave Church in a few weeks. I've already asked for our membership statement to be sent to you. I hope we will be accepted . . .

The pastor filed the letter, together with the statement of membership, for the forthcoming meeting of the elders — and reflected. He had been writing the history of LaGrave and recalled the name of Klaas Troon as one who, over a hundred years before, had not favored the formation of an English-speaking Christian Reformed Church. Yet his son, grandson, and great-grandson had been members, together with their families. And now his namesake would be coming — one who, for a time, had fallen away!

The pastor thought of those who, during his tenure, had left the church, and he said a prayer for them. He prayed to a covenant God; to One who had said, "I will be a God unto you, and to your children." He took Klaas Troon's letter out of the file again and looked at it. It was almost as if it were a message from heaven, along with those other messages from the denomination and the community. A birthday card from heaven! It said — between the lines — that He who had been faithful to LaGrave in the past, would carry His faithfulness forward into the future. The letter was a portent of what was ahead!

Another Century of Grace

Of continued Grace

Until Jesus would come again.

SOURCES

QUOTATIONS (Page numbers indicate pages in *A Century of Grace.*)

Pages 29, 42, 52, 66, 97, 117, 130

The Banner (Christian Reformed Board of Publications,
     Grand Rapids, MI.)

Pages 42, 84

Fifty Years of Music At Calvin College,
     by Professor Seymour Swets; ©1973.
Reprint permission, Wm. B. Eerdmans Pub. Co., Grand Rapids, MI.

Page 86

Not of This World, by R. B. Kuiper.
Reprint permission, Wm. B. Eerdmans Pub. Co., Grand Rapids, MI.

Pages 55, 87

Promises To Keep, by John J. Timmerman; ©1975.
Reprint permission, Wm. B. Eerdmans Pub. Co., Grand Rapids, MI.

Pages 29, 72, 173

The Reformed Journal.
Reprint permission, Wm. B. Eerdmans Pub. Co., Grand Rapids, MI.

Pages 5, 168

The Story of Grand Rapids, by Z. Z. Lydens; ©1966.
Reprint permission, Kregel Publications, Grand Rapids, MI.

Page 8, #355:4; p. 122, #309:1; p. 134, #470:2; p. 153, #479:2

The Psalter Hymnal (Christian Reformed Board of Publications,
     Grand Rapids, MI.).

Page 101

Time Capsule (Time/Life Books, New York, N.Y.)

ILLUSTRATIONS

Page 133

American Fads, by Richard A. Johnson; ©1984.
Reprint permission, Beech Tree Books, a division of William Morrow
     and Co., New York, N.Y.

Pages 51, 58, 78, 82, 102, 161, 171

America's Front Page News, by Emery, Smith, Schuneman, Emery;
     Vis-Com Inc., publishers.

Pages 51, 82, 124, 132, 133

Dynamic America, by General Dynamics Corp., St. Louis, MO.

Pages 26, 124

The Grand Rapids Public Library, Michigan Historical Room.

Page 6

Pictorial History of Grand Rapids, by Mapes & Travis; ©1976.
Reprint permission, Kregel Publications, Grand Rapids, MI.

Page 133

Remember Television, by Ron Lackman; ©1971.
Reprint permission, The Putnam Publishing Group, New York, N.Y.

Page 124

Zondervan, P. J. (picture of Billy Graham).

WORDS, *THE WORD,* AND THE WORLD — AN APPRECIATION

Dr. Dewey J. Hoitenga, Jr.

THANKING OUR PASTOR

How can we thank our pastor for
   His tireless labors, eager zeal?
That which we give is not enough,
   Nor can words show just how we feel.
There is but one sure way to prove
   Our great esteem, our tender love,
It is to take to heart his words,
   A gift through him from God above.

How can we show how much they mean,
   His sympathy, his ready smile,
Except by showing in our lives
   That all his efforts are worthwhile?
His sermons from the Word of God
   Strike home with force, prod us anew,
They comfort, strengthen, build, maintain.
   May our walk show him that they do.

Josie Pangborn, 1902-1976
Written in honor of Rev. Eppinga's
44th birthday

WORDS, *THE WORD,* AND THE WORLD — AN APPRECIATION

What does German measles have to do with Adam and Eve? A famous triple-play combination in baseball with Christian education? A pedigreed dog with St. Paul? Few of us would know, had it not been for our pastor, Rev. Eppinga. For thirty-three years, with his wonderful use of words, he has brought together for us, in pulpit, print, classroom, and hospital, God's Word and God's world.

Jacob D. Eppinga. Who is this man who has ministered to the LaGrave Christian Reformed Church these many years — one-third of its Century of Grace — and whose unique history of our congregation we now have in our hands? Pastor, preacher, counselor, writer, churchman — he is indeed a man of words, of the Word, and of the world.

His love of language, his faithfulness to the Word of God, and his interest in the world began at home. In addition to their native Frisian, his parents spoke both Dutch and English; they were deeply committed to the Reformed faith; and they were adventurously involved in the world.

We, his congregation, will long remember his eloquence; but he remembers how he stuttered as a lad, and how his father sent him to a specialist at Wayne College who made him struggle for the syllables that would not come, even by accenting the wrong ones: "won-der-ful." It was a progressive step for his father to take, long before the day of a speech therapist in every school.

But then, his father, Dirk Eppinga, was no ordinary man. Having grown up in the Netherlands, he graduated from the Harlingen trade school in 1905 at the age of seventeen. On borrowed money, he left his parents, nine brothers and sisters, and his fiancée and sailed for America to find his way in the New World. He came first to Grand Rapids, but, not liking it, in two weeks was on a train for Detroit where he heard there was work in the building trades. There, with his suitcase in one hand and his toolbox in the other, he was literally hired right off the street.

Several years later, having established himself, he returned to his native land to marry Sjoerdina Brölman, the girl he had left behind, and to take her back to Detroit with him. She did not like America with its strange language and foreign ways. This led Dirk to make a promise that one day they would move back; but until then he would take her every three years for an extended visit to the Netherlands and home. Though young Jacob had to take his school work with him, he remembers the exciting world which opened up for him on these regular trips abroad. Among the many relatives visited, he especially remembers the Reverend Dirk Zoete, his great uncle and namesake, one of the leading ministers in the Hervormde Kerk. Rev. Eppinga still speaks fondly of the early impression and lasting inspiration of the Reverend Dirk Zoete for his own calling to the ministry.

It was on June 7, 1917, that Jacob Dirk, the first son of Dirk and Sjoerdina, was born. He remembers a happy childhood, even though when he was just eight years old his mother died while giving birth to his brother Stuart. He remembers her fondly, a woman who, though she longed for her native land, was both a devout and a fun-loving person. She early recognized Jacob's gifts and said, "Jacob, je word en dominie." His last memory of her alive was the morning of the day of her death when he knelt at her bedside before leaving for school. He and his brother Stuart have been close ever since.

It was one year later that his father married Johanna Geverink, who had come in as nurse to help the family during Sjoerdina's illness. Jacob remembers how his father asked his permission to marry her, even though "he surely had decided what he was going to do." Thus Johanna became the dear mother of the two brothers, and gave them two more — twins — Pieter and Johan. In these new circumstances, his father felt released from his promise to Sjoerdina to move back to the Netherlands.

La Grave News

APRIL—MAY 1981   VOL. XXII - 208

PUBLISHED BY THE LAGRAVE AVENUE CHRISTIAN REFORMED CHURCH
107 LaGrave Ave. S. E. Grand Rapids, Michigan

Dear Boys and Girls:

Who am I?

My middle name is Dirk—after my father who had no middle
name. He was named Dirk, after his uncle, his mother's
brother, Dirk Zoete. Dirk Zoete was a minister in the
state church in the Netherlands. He was president of the
synod three times for which he was knighted by the Queen.

In a Dutch book on the history of preaching, there are
several references to Dirk Zoete. This makes me feel
pretty good—not only to have the honor of bearing my
father's name, but also the name of his famous uncle.

One day Dirk Zoete fell seriously ill. He was out of his
pulpit a whole year. God answered the many prayers that
were offered, and restored him. The first Sunday that
Dirk Zoete was in his pulpit, he announced in Dutch Psalm
118 as the opening song.

> I shall not die, but I shall live
> And recount the deeds of the Lord,
> The Lord has chastened me sore,
> But He has not given me over to death.

Dirk Zoete could hardly sing the words himself because he
was so grateful that he had been spared to preach the gospel again. It was what he loved doing best of all.

I have been ill, too. Not as long as my father's uncle,
but long enough. When I get into the pulpit again, I, too,
will be grateful to be able to preach the gospel again. It
is what I love doing best of all. When it happens, I would
like to announce Psalm 118 as the first song too. God answered the many prayers of the congregation and restored me—
just like my father's uncle.

> He has not given my soul to death,
> But chastened and restored.

Psalm 118
232 Psalter Hymnal

Who am I?

_____?_____ Dirk _____?_____

210

DAY OF ALL THE WEEK THE BEST

Those Sundays of long ago were wonderful. Father was home; my favorite toy, an electric train, could be brought out of the closet on no other day; the meal was the best of the week; and all those Sunday clothes gave the day a festive air. Of course, church attendance was mandatory. Twice. Also, there were things you could not do — like listen to the radio or go "joy-riding" in the family car. Yet those strictures, rather than detracting, somehow added to the dimension of the day.

This is not to say that there were no real sacrifices to be made. For example, I had to put out of my mind any thought of ever becoming Charlie Gehringer's successor as second baseman for the Detroit Tigers. This was, indeed, a burden. I had a friend in catechism class who was equally sad because of similar yearnings he thought would be forever unfulfilled. I recall a twitch of envy when, sometime later, it was suddenly all right for him to go to Sunday games because he had turned Lutheran. Yet, all in all, those Sundays, including those repeated countings of the organ pipes in church when my mind wandered from the sermons, constituted a

real head start for me. I would not trade them for anything. It follows from this that I view today's growing permissiveness in respect to Sabbath observance with some thoughtfulness. Far be it from me to impose such a regimen as I witnessed on a preaching engagement one weekend when the children of my hosts could only sing hymns, read the Sunday school papers, or take a walk around the block. I couldn't blame them for labeling Sunday — day of all the week the worst. But the pendulum can swing too far in the other direction too.

There is something healthy in our learning that man was not made for the Sabbath (Mark 2:27). At the same time, however, we must remember that the Sabbath was not made for stadium turnstiles, lying abed, endless homework, and evening TV services conducted by comedians.

from "The Captain of the Azolla" in
Cabbages and Kings (Zondervan Corp.,
Grand Rapids, MI., 1974), pp. 123f.

Among Jacob's happy childhood days, Sundays were the best. The family would begin them with a hymn sing in the morning, led by father Dirk at the pump organ, and end them in the evening with storytime, again with father presiding, telling the tales of Aesop or recounting the great deeds of the heroes of Dutch history. For Dirk was a many-sided man. In addition to becoming a successful carpenter, cabinetmaker, and contractor, he wrote essays for his own amusement (e.g. "Famous Last Words"), painted (e.g. the cows and canals of his native Friesland), played organ and piano (he bought Jacob a piano of his own when he was seven), and kept all kinds of animals (he always missed racing his homing pigeons in the finals, which were on Sundays). But the center of Jacob's father's life was the First Christian Reformed Church of Detroit, which he had helped to found and organize in 1914. Later, he was one of the founders and builders of the Grosse Pointe Day School. In his retirement, he helped to develop land in Lake Worth, Florida, a central parcel of which was reserved for the site of the Lake Worth Christian Reformed Church and of the Christian School.

Jacob was first sent to St. Paul's Lutheran School, where the instruction was still in German. "Such had been the convictions of my parents that they preferred Christian teachers in another language to uncommitted ones in familiar English."[1] It was one more experience of a world beyond — another people, another language, and another Christian tradition. When he could finally attend the new Christian school, it was the

teaching and influence of Dewey Westra, the poet and musician, that left its mark on him. "Every week we had to learn five new words." Jacob would occasionally be an accompanist for Mr. Westra who played the trumpet and helped Jacob buy his own first horn for twelve dollars from a pawn shop. He went on to play first trumpet in the Southeastern High School Orchestra and at once resolved to learn every other instrument in the orchestra. He played second chair trumpet in the Detroit All-City Band and was delighted when he got to keep one of the brand new horns donated by the Hudson Department Store for a major concert. He could even play it for Billy Sunday, whose staff had chosen him, along with some others, to play in those great tent revivals during the early Depression years. Jacob did well in his studies. He received special attention and encouragement from his high school English teacher, Mr. William Bedell, because he alone of all his classmates, with his knowledge of Frisian, could translate *Beowulf*. He graduated valedictorian of his class.

There were also the lessons of the city streets and vacant lots. His boyhood neighborhood — Drexel Avenue — was an American melting pot of "Dagos," "Polacks," and "Buffaloes." Stanley White, his best friend, a Roman Catholic, could buy licorice on Sunday. Clarence Shoenborn's dad was a member of the lodge.[2] But Jacob was the champion at marbles — until he was put up by his friends against the hero of the neighboring Anderdon gang. He lost all the marbles he had ever won (stored in his father's cigar boxes) and even "Greenie," his shooter. That is when he learned never again to play for keeps.[3] There were, of course, other Christian students in the public high school; nevertheless, he was not allowed to date a certain pretty girl, even though she was the daughter of a Lutheran minister. "Jacob, je bent Gereformeerd," his father would say. Though it had many windows and even doors to the great big world outside, the wall formed by his father's commitment to the Reformed way of life was both strong and high.

Now on his own and attending Calvin College, Jacob continued to absorb and test the Reformed way of life and learning. Here he was taught by distinguished professors such as Jacob VandenBosch, Henry VanAndel, and Albert Rooks. Later, Jacob would become pastor to these men, for they were all members of LaGrave. It was at Calvin that he met Albert P. Smith, who would join him again at LaGrave, years later in 1963, as the director of the chancel choir. He and "Smitty," who was from Paterson, New Jersey, both hailed from points far outside the "Grand Rapids circle." Both were "pre-sem" and both loved music (although the legend grew that it was Smith the pre-sem who was becoming a musician, and Eppinga the music major who was becoming a minister). "Eppinga," recalls Smith, "fascinated the musicians, for he could play jazz on the piano." Jacob graduated from Calvin in 1939, having been active in Thespians, editor of the *Prism,* and president of the senior class.

After a summer stint with Sutherland and Avery Lumberyard in Detroit, Jacob enrolled at Westminster Seminary in Philadelphia, feeling the need for a Reformed world different from the familiar setting of the Calvin campus. But when he got there, he found another world as well, the world of "the East." He spent as much time exploring *that* world as he did exploring the world of Hebrew verbs in class. At the end of one semester, he returned home to work again at Sutherland and Avery and to marry Anne Batts.

Anne had grown up with Jacob in the Detroit Church. Her parents were Gertrude Dykstra and Herman Batts. A builder like Dirk Eppinga, and his friendly competitor, Mr. Batts became his partner in the Lake Worth development project mentioned earlier. Not pleased that Anne would have to attend the public high school, her parents sent her to Grand Rapids where she lived with her aunt and attended Grand Rapids Christian High School. When she returned to Detroit, she was a "new girl" there; and the pleasant consequence was the beginning of Anne and Jacob's seven-year courtship. This included her contralto solo performances with Jacob as her accompanist, dates with him in Theodosia — the model-T Ford he had bought with a friend for five dollars — and many separations. While Jacob was at Calvin, Anne studied at Wayne College to become a dental assistant. The separations continued even after they were married, for he returned to Westminster in the fall. They met every month in Pittsburgh and, of course, were together summer vacations in Detroit. Finally, during his last year at Westminster, Anne found work in Philadelphia, and joined him there.

At Westminster for the second time, Eppinga now thrived in his studies, coming under the influence, among others, of R.B. Kuiper, Professor of Homiletics (a former pastor of LaGrave Church). "R.B." was a model rhetorician; his advice to students, however, was to read and study the sermons of the great Christian preachers of the past. By this time, Jacob's reputation for getting the most out of life was firmly established. Anne remembers how his fellow seminary students would say, "Nothing happens to Eppinga that does not happen to the rest of us; but he always makes something special of it."

He graduated from Westminster in 1943 and instead of considering calls received from Orthodox Presbyterian and Reformed Church of America congregations, he enrolled for a year at Calvin Seminary, a requirement for ordination in the Christian Reformed Church. But on his way to synod the following June to be declared a candidate, he turned back, went home, and took a job with Nichols and Cox, a Grand Rapids lumberyard. "I knew lumber," he says on looking back today, "but as yet did not quite know my calling to the ministry." In December, however, he accepted a position as "stated supply" for the Dearborn Christian Reformed Church, where he was ordained an elder so that he could attend the consistory meetings. His ordination to the ministry followed in September 1945, and he was now officially a man of the Word; his mother's words, "Jacob, je word en dominie," had come true at last.

It was in Dearborn that three of Jacob and Anne's four children were born: Richard — born the day before Jacob's classical examination by Classis Grand Rapids East — Jay, and Susan Jean. Deanna, their fourth, was born in Grand Rapids, while they were at Highland Hills, his second church.

Reflecting on his years as husband, father, and pastor, Anne is impressed by her husband's deep devotion to his work. "He always gave his family quality time; and we are very close; but sometimes," she adds, "I think he should have been a priest." We to whom he has ministered, however, would not have had it thus; we have always appreciated the fact that our pastor was a family man, for his sake and ours. It has helped him to be even more a man of the world — our world, too — a world of family joys, responsibilities, and heartbreaks. He is one who knows what it is like to have two young sons, late one winter's night, start a neighbor's bush on fire.[4] Only a family man could tell us, as he once did, what fun it was to have his grandchildren fishing from the sofa in the living room while he played a fish on the floor.

It was while serving the Highland Hills Church that the Eppingas enjoyed their first television set, a parting gift from the Dearborn congregation. It was also the first TV aerial on a Christian Reformed parsonage roof, and it led to a special consistory meeting to debate the subject. Rev. Eppinga has often reflected on movies and television, those alluring windows to the world. He had seen his first movie aboard ship, during one of those trips in his youth which his family took to the Netherlands — long before the year 1966 when the Christian Reformed Synod officially opened the "Film Arts" to its members. For a generation or more, what one said about movies, not to mention what one did, became a shibboleth for Christian Reformed piety.

Now it was the mid-fifties, a turning point in the denomination's relationship to the world. It was also a turning point for downtown Grand Rapids (as it was for the downtown of many an American city) and in the history of the LaGrave Church — the only really "downtown church" in Grand Rapids of the Christian Reformed denomination. Finally, it was a turning point for Rev. Eppinga, who accepted the call to LaGrave in 1954.

It was an excellent match from the start: an imaginative leader and a congregation whose vision awaited discovery, definition, and development. Though an old

congregation (he had more funerals than baptisms during his first year), it had the talent to meet the many challenges and opportunities that lay ahead.

In the first five years, Rev. Eppinga tapped a bundle of energy that has kept us an active church ever since. In those years — and the record bears repetition — we established a Christian Education Society (different from the Booster Clubs of the day), the Sunday Niters, Young Adults, Lenten Luncheons, Summer Youth Projects in Missions (years before SWIM), and a Boy Scout Troop. To these ideas that arose within the congregation, Rev. Eppinga added his own: The first church office with a secretary, the *LaGrave News*, deaconesses, women voting in congregational meetings (which he had introduced already in the Dearborn church long before it was officially encouraged by synod in 1956), the neighborhood canvass, the student pastoral internship (which has evolved through an era of ordained assistant ministers into the team ministry concept that prevails today), and the Cuban Missionary venture. By 1959, the congregation, under his leadership, was poised to make one of the major decisions of its one-hundred years: to build a new edifice and to build it

---

THE MOVIES

I saw some "Christians" the other day emerging from a filthy movie. The sight triggered a meandering train of thought: . . . I never used to go to the movies. That was a long time ago . . .

A short time ago, Charlie Chaplin died. As a lad, I was never allowed to see Charlie Chaplin. We used to play "Tom Mix — cowboy," but I could never see him either. There had been just one exception. I saw a movie aboard a ship. It was called Sonny Boy and it starred a kid named Jackie Coogan. In the film, he held his toothbrush under the faucet when he went to bed, but he didn't brush his teeth. Later, when his mother checked the brush, she was satisfied to discover that it was wet. It was a neat trick! I started doing the same thing, proving that the minister was right when he said that people learn bad things at the movies . . .

A block from our church was the Aloma theater. I looked inside one day, at noon, when the doors were open. I didn't see the devil because it was too dark. But I did smell a kind of burnt odor, more reminiscent of overdone popcorn, however, than of Lucifer. Inevitably, being both curious and something less than a saint, I secretly went to see Frank Buck in Bring 'Em Back Alive. It was all about catching wild animals in Africa — which was what I was going to do when I grew up. I didn't see the devil, but I did see some missionaries on the screen. Feeling guilty, I couldn't sleep that night.

My next trip to the movies, when I was grown, was the fault of James Fenimore Cooper. Having read all his books, I couldn't stay away from the filmed version of The Last of the Mohicans, starring Henry Fonda. Fearing discovery under the blazing lights of the marquee, I turned up the collar of my coat and turned down the brim of my hat and with correct change in hand, charged the ticket window, looking for all the world like Humphrey Bogart. I had a friend who took even greater precautions against being recognized. But he fainted in the balcony, and the ushers laid him out on the front sidewalk — downtown.

So what am I trying to say with all of this? First, I wish to pay my respects to a generation now mostly gone. There was something wrong about making an eleventh commandment regarding movies. At the same time, there was also something good about a prohibitive mentality as opposed to our present permissive one . . .

. . . So much around us, including the movies, is getting worse. Perhaps I am an alarmist. But I would rather be a Calvinist who reminds fellow Christians that we are chosen to serve, to build the kingdom, and to bring redemption to all spheres of life. To be sure, this involves a whole lot more than merely being careful about the films we see. But if we do not the latter, can we catch the vision of the former? New people do not build a new society without maintaining the old sensitivities in a new age. Therefore, a gentle reminder seems in order. An ecclesiastical prohibition, emanating from our synod in 1928, has been retracted. Good. But Romans 12 has not.

from *More Cabbages & Kings*
(Christian Reformed Board of Publications, Grand Rapids, MI., 1972-78), Chapter 15.

downtown where the church was born.

It was a decision which had its sincere and articulate opponents, one of whom was Eppinga's college mentor himself, now become his parishioner, Jacob Vanden Bosch. But the decision was reached, and Rev. Eppinga won the cooperation and even the support of those who had opposed the idea. He was just the man to do it. Born and reared in the city — a city boy — he had learned to love it. Now a city man, he had learned much more: to *listen* to the city and to *speak* to it in turn — all of which he had just related in his first book, *The Soul of the City*, published in 1954, the year of his coming to LaGrave. The voice of the city is "more subdued at four in the morning than at four in the after-

noon. But even then the city is awake. And that kind of reminds me of God. For the Bible says that He, too, never slumbers, never sleeps." The voice of the city spoke to him of its pain (the wailing of a siren), of its hurry (the screeching of brakes), of its growth (the noise of wrecking balls and building hammers), of its fun and hope (children laughing in its playgrounds), of its products (the smudge and din of its factories), of its wisdom (by its proverbs — "Look out for number one," and many more), and of its fences (between black and white, rich and poor, Protestant and Catholic, and more).

Could he ever speak to such a big complex and noisy thing? Yes . . . for he had known what it was as a ten-

WHY WE STAYED DOWNTOWN

It is an unfortunate fact of life — of city life — that the advent of suburbia, and the suburban mentality, has as its counterpart that which has come to be known as "inner city blight." Consequently, the La-Grave Church finds itself today in an environment totally different from the surroundings which existed at the time of its organization. Whereas, in days gone by it was the geographical center of its membership, it is today bordered on one side by a downtown area which is in trouble, and bordered on the other side by a neighborhood which, though it represents only 15 percent of the land area of the city, nevertheless contains 30 percent of its dwelling units, 55 percent of its adult crime, 75 percent of its delinquency, and 75 percent of its multiple family problems. It is an area which costs the city eight dollars for every dollar it gives . . .

In this setting, the congregation faced a problem quite apart from the problem of its neighborhood. It felt itself to be inadequately housed. Because this sanctuary could seat little more than half of the membership of over 1100, overflow crowds had to be seated elsewhere on the premises. This was discouraging to attendance. Some came early to assure themselves a place, while others who came later had to be content with being ushered elsewhere. For many children, Sunday after Sunday, the minister was no more than a speaker-box hanging on the wall. Furthermore, the building was in bad repair, therefore expendable . . .

Of the possibilities open to the congregation, . . . that of building anew on its present site seemed the most foolish of them all. Why invest a great sum of money in a piece of unsalable real estate in a run-down neighborhood? Yet, this alternative was chosen. What seemed on the surface to be an unwise decision, after much thought, prayer, and reflection, appeared to be the move that God might want, and the decision which God might bless . . .

May I say that we stayed because there is value in continuing to be known as a downtown church. American society has given increased recognition to the church as a significant factor in the community-at-large. This was not so true even

twenty-five years ago. Whatever the reasons may be, churches today have been clothed with a new dignity. This does not necessarily mean that America has turned to God. It does mean that in the present context it is important that there be not only neighborhood churches, but also downtown churches of evangelical persuasion to capitalize on present opportunities. Downtown churches today often have opportunities for witness presented to them which neighborhood churches do not . . .

Did you ever hear the story of the drunk who was crawling on his hands and knees downtown beneath a street light? An officer came up to him and said, "What are you doing?" He replied, "I'm looking for my ring." "Well," said the officer, "where did you lose it?" "Two blocks down," replied the drunk. "Then why are you looking for it here?" asked the policeman. "Well," said the inebriated one, "it's so dark two blocks down. The light is better here."

Maybe this is a parable. So often we build our churches not where souls are lost and where the houses of God are needed most, but where the light is best, where the lawns are wide, and where the parking space is adequate.

Let me say that I realize that the story does not hold up as an illustration all the way. Souls are lost everywhere. Therefore, we need churches in all places. But surely, also in the less desirable areas. When on our recent canvass to which I alluded earlier, a lady asked, "But why are you building here?" the answer was, among other reasons, "For you!"

. . . And so we will make our difficult neighborhood our parish. We are confident that if we will remain loyal to the gospel, and diligent in presenting it to the lost who live within the shadow of our spire, as well as to the community-at-large, God will keep us as a congregation and make us to be vital and to be strong.

by Rev. Jacob D. Eppinga
from *The Reformed Journal*,
June, 1960, pp. 9-11.

year-old to be lost in the city, *and* to be found by a wonderfully good Samaritan who took hold of his hand and led him home. Yes, he could speak . . . for he also had become a man of the Word: "Now I am a preacher. Not a very big one, perhaps. But a preacher, all the same. And with God's Word in my hand, I have something to say — of Christ, the Saviour of the world, and that includes the city."[5]

The decision to stay downtown has determined a significant part of our congregational character and mission ever since. Again, the record of many new beginnings will bear repetition: The Benefactor's Trust Fund (the first, and perhaps still the only, congregational endowment program in the denomination), downtown nursing home ministries, Property Purchase Program, Sabbatical leaves for the pastor (another denominational first), the Managua church rebuilding project, the stewardship committee, Project Rehab, the Jellema House, the downtown Reach-out ministry, Children's Church, the *Trinity Hymnal* (responding to the growing need to supplement the *Psalter Hymnal),* the Sunday Evening Series downtown, the Heartside Neighborhood Project, the Center of Christian Hope, the volunteer nurses, Thanksgiving dinners for the inner city residents, and the LaGrave Players.

If Rev. Eppinga has released our congregational energies over these thirty-three years, he has also, with his instinct for appropriate limits, kept them under control. It was a tumultuous world, and our creative energies might well have gotten out of hand. It is no secret that LaGrave has lost its reputation as the "liberal" church of the denomination. If LaGrave no longer stands out as the "liberal" church, it is partly because, under Eppinga's leadership, we have (as he himself puts it well[6]) "steered a moderate course" through two of the most trying decades of the twentieth century.

It is also partly because, as some have observed, other CRC congregations have "caught up" with LaGrave. One important aspect of its progressive character is the tolerance of diversity. If Rev. Eppinga has fostered the use of a great diversity of congregational gifts to meet a great diversity of congregational and neighborhood needs, he has also nurtured an expression of Christian tolerance and understanding among us, who are so very different from one another in so many different ways. Perhaps there will always be the more or less homogeneous, traditional Christian Reformed congregation. Ever since our founding as the first "English-speaking" church, LaGrave has not been one of that kind. Many other congregations have also learned, over the years, to be open to people of different backgrounds, interests, income, education, and lifestyles. Rev. Eppinga fervently hopes that the denomination itself will be moved by the same ideal, as it enters a period of increased diversity across the individual congregations themselves.

His leadership in our congregation has spilled over into leadership in both the denomination and the com-

---

ONCE MORE, WITH FEELING

From the start, synod knew exactly whom it wanted for its president. By a lopsided first-ballot vote, it chose Rev. Jacob D. Eppinga, 69, a two-time veteran of the synodical presidency (1980, 1983) — a tried and true leader whom delegates could not resist tapping for just one more presidency before his retirement next year.

For Eppinga, pastor of LaGrave Avenue Christian Reformed Church, Grand Rapids, Michigan, Synod 1986 was definitely a case of "once more, with feeling." . . .

Eppinga's zest was obvious to anyone spending even a few minutes watching synod this year. He appeared totally at ease in his demanding role, impeccably courteous, unpatronizingly kind, keeping things light and upbeat, gently prodding when delegates took verbal side trips. "Masterful," said Calvin Theological Seminary President, James A. De Jong, of Eppinga's performance.

He could get away with things that other synod presidents wouldn't even have thought of trying. "When I wave my arm like this (a slow, pushing motion away from the body with the left hand), it means we're tangled up and we are going backward in time," Eppinga told the delegates early on. Another wave, and time would miraculously be re-turned to present. Synod 1986 might have gone home hours later without that gesture . . .

Delegates from all over the United States and Canada have returned home. They remember that for nine frantically busy days in June, 1986, Rev. Jacob D. Eppinga was very, very good for them, for his church, and for his Lord.

They will not forget the bright vision of the man who told them in his farewell comments that they and their church are marching to Zion, that together they've already travelled a great distance, that they stand today where the church has never been before, and that they are meeting the future before it meets them.

As for Eppinga, on this last night he will go home from what he calls his last synod and get some much needed rest. In the next day or two, he hopes to conduct a wedding and beat the deadline for the next installment of his *Banner* column, "Of Cabbages and Kings." Next year, the Lord willing, he will officially retire from the ministry, but certainly not from preaching, writing, story-telling, joking — and just being the gentle and wise clergyman so many in the Christian Reformed Church have come to know and love.

from *The Banner,* June 30, 1986, p. 28.

munity. Having served on many classical and synodical committees and boards, he has had his greatest exposure to the denomination as author of "Of Cabbages and Kings" in *The Banner,* and as delegate to synod, which he served as president three times (like his namesake, Dirk Zoete, before him, who did the same for the Hervormde Kerk in the Netherlands), most recently in June, 1986.

Rev. Eppinga has also served many community organizations, including the Grand Rapids Ministerial Association and the Evangelical Ministerial Union. Breaking down the mutual stereotypes that have been built up between our denomination and others over the years, he has stimulated both our cooperation with other denominations and theirs with us. So he has not only been our pastor and preacher, but also a presence in the larger church and community around us. For all of this, he was honored by Calvin College, his Alma Mater, with its Distinguished Alumni Award, in these words:

> At this 1983 Commencement, Calvin College honors you, the Reverend Jacob D. Eppinga of the Class of 1939, as a distinguished alumnus.
>
> For your Christian service to your community and your commitment to a Reformed, Christian witness in downtown Grand Rapids;
>
> For your writing that has entertained, enlightened, and comforted so many;
>
> For your ecumenical leadership and your support of the missionary efforts of Christ's church;
>
> For your dedication to the parish ministry;
>
> And for your eloquent and faithful proclamation of the Gospel of Jesus Christ;
>
> In gratitude to God for what He has enabled you to do for the kingdom of Christ, we hereby present you the Calvin Alumni Association Distinguished Alumni Award.

There are those who find Rev. Eppinga somewhat distant and even aloof. It is true, he can be detached and scholarly, and often keeps his own counsel. No glad-hander, he has resisted deferring to special interests and influential people. Still, he is often open, engaging, and down to earth, and even the life of the party. We shall never forget those occasions on which he entertained us, for example, with his own great masterpiece composed for the piano entitled, "Three Blind Mice," or with his humorous historical musical sketch, "From LaCradle to LaGrave." He is a complex man, and such entertainment we have also acknowledged as part of his ministry to a complex church.

If he laughed with us, and helped us to laugh, he also worried, suffered, and grieved with us. Not always evident to everyone, his pastoral work has taken a large portion of his time and effort, as those who have been in hospital beds or at the side of their dying loved ones will testify. As Rev. Steigenga, himself also devoted to our care and counseling, observed for us on the occasion of Rev. Eppinga's 25th anniversary as our pastor: "Every line in his face has a name." Then, too, there were the youth, some of whom — like the young Klaas Troon — drifted or even bolted out of the church. Not all of them, like young Klaas, later returned; but there were those who did, whose parents have said, "If it were not for Rev. Eppinga, our son(daughter) might not have been a Christian today."

What is the life of a Christian? The life of a Christian fellowship? In good times and bad, it is always "a life made up in every part with praise." Yet there is a chief part among the many parts, a center from which those other parts may radiate. That Center is public worship. With Rev. Eppinga's lead, LaGrave has maintained a dignified service, with music as a large and integral part, so that we have always been able to worship the Lord "in the beauty of holiness." Divided chancel notwithstanding (see Chapter 21), he has singlemindedly focused our minds and hearts on the Word of God, in words of human eloquence (St. Paul in I Corinthians 1:17 notwithstanding), in a way that, from Sunday to Sunday, connected that Word with the world in which we live.

And so, the German measles, though they are as "American as apple pie," remind us of Adam and Eve and our tendency to blame our ills upon others.[7] "Tinkers to Evers to Chance," a famous Chicago Cubs triple-play combination, represents a picturesque reminder of the importance of Christian education (Lois to Eunice to Timothy).[8] If we pride ourselves on pedigree, as did even St. Paul, let St. Paul tell us that pedigree is not what counts (Philippians 3:3-11).[9] In this way, for thirty-three years, with his wonderful use of words, Rev. Eppinga has brought together for us, in pulpit, print, classroom, and hospital, God's Word and God's world. John Kromminga, then president of Calvin Seminary, summed it up nicely in these lines taken from an affectionate poem he read to help us celebrate the 25th anniversary of Eppinga's coming to LaGrave:

> He takes life's little cabbages and turns them into kings.
> He finds great significance in ordinary things . . .
> He brings us closer to ourselves, to God and our neighbor.
> What man could ask more abiding fruit upon his labor?

Many are the blessings which God in His grace has granted to us at LaGrave, to the Christian Reformed denomination, and to the church-at-large, through Rev. Eppinga's ministry. One of these clearly shines out among the others: The power of preaching. For he has kept the Christian sermon truly inspiring and alive, through an era when the nobility of language, the splendor of human speech, and the regenerating power of the Divine Word, have been eclipsed in home, church, school, and society alike. Among the great preachers Rev. Eppinga studied under Professor R.B. Kuiper at Westminster were the two nineteenth century English "divines": Joseph Parker and Charles Haddon Spurgeon. He remembers, however, the classic story about them, that those who heard Parker would leave saying, "What a mind!" while those who heard Spurgeon would say, "What a Saviour!"

Rev. Eppinga's favorite story on this theme is about another of his preacher-heroes, Thomas Chalmers, the Scot. His telling this story once during the building of the new church prompted the giving of that "gift as fine as any that was received": the small brass plaque in the pulpit for everyone who stands there to read, "Sir, we would see Jesus."[10] Rev. Eppinga, for one-third of our Century of Grace, has made us willing and eager hearers of the Word and, thereby, also faithful and happy followers of the Word Incarnate, Jesus Christ, our Saviour and Lord. That is what matters most.

NOTES

[1]*Cabbages and Kings* (Zondervan Corp., Grand Rapids, MI., 1974), p.43.

[2]*Ibid.,* pp. 123, 103.

[3]*More Cabbages & Kings* (Christian Reformed Board of Publications, Grand Rapids, MI., 1972-78), ch. 10.

[4]*Ibid.,* ch. 12.

[5]*The Soul of the City* (Wm. B. Eerdmans, Grand Rapids, MI., 1954), p. 11 *et passim.*

[6]*A Century of Grace,* ch. 23, above.

[7]*Cabbages and Kings,* p. 11.

[8]A Christian Education Sermon on 2 Timothy 1:5.

[9]*For Sinners Only* (Wm. B. Eerdmans, Grand Rapids, MI., 1970), ch. 2. This book, written on his second sabbatical in Cambridge, England, offers just the right advice to those anticipating their first communion (and to those perhaps no longer anticipating their hundredth), in the context of an inspiring account of the life of St. Paul.

[10]*A Century of Grace,* ch. 21, above.

ADDENDUM

Addendum researched and compiled by Mary Romence.

Addendum A — Chris Overvoorde

Chris Stoffel Overvoorde was born in 1934 in the Netherlands and immigrated to the United States in 1957 as a diesel mechanic. He received an M.F.A. degree in 1966 from the University of Michigan and was appointed to the faculty of the Calvin College Art Department where he holds the rank of Professor of Art. Overvoorde has been active as a graphic designer, stage designer, muralist, printmaker, and painter. He has been involved in more than 90 group shows, received more than 25 awards, and has presented over 40 solo exhibits in the U.S., Canada, and the Netherlands. He married Greta Duifhuis from Vancouver, B.C., Canada. They have four children and are members of Grace Christian Reformed Church in Grand Rapids.

Mr. Overvoorde was commissioned by the Centennial Committee of LaGrave Avenue Christian Reformed Church to paint portraits of LaGrave's pastors, past and present. When viewing the colored photos of Mr. Overvoorde's portraits, which appear throughout the book, observe the following:

The purple line running horizontally through each painting represents the constancy of grace; the shades of purple represent our changing perceptions of that grace.

Background colors change from blue to orange. These colors from the Dutch flag are reversed as LaGrave reverses the Dutch influence on the church.

The wallpaper in each painting is typical of the period.

On the following pages are the explanations of the details in each portrait.

Addendum B — Key to Portraits

REVEREND JOHN YEURY DEBAUN 1887–1892

1. Rev. DeBaun
2. Mrs. (Margaret Iserman) DeBaun
3. The DeBauns come to LaGrave from New Jersey (N.J.)
4. President Grover Cleveland, 1885-1889 and 1893-1897
5. President Benjamin Harrison, 1889-1893
6. A locomotive which ran between Grand Rapids and other cities
7. The first choir
8. Books/pamphlets common to ministerial studies in this period: *Pilgrim's Progress, The True Reformed Dutch Church, Lion in Tears, Lamentations, God's Marvelous Thunder, Plain Truth*
9. Rev. DeBaun was the first contributor to the Calvin College Library (emblem of 1900)
10. The purple line of grace, which runs through all the portraits
11. A furniture leg and the GRM (Grand Rapids Made) logo
12. LaGrave was a street before it was an avenue
13. The Dutch national emblem
14. The American national emblem
15. The first church building on LaGrave Street
16. Luce Hall was the first meeting place of the new congregation
17. Commemorative stamp of the Statue of Liberty and its creator
18. *The Banner of Truth* was first published by Rev. DeBaun in 1866
19. Medicine bottles and quarantine sign signify frequent epidemics
20. LaGrave was formed as the Fourth Holland Christian Reformed Church
21. Bicycle (c. 1890s)
22. Rev. DeBaun belonged to the True Reformed Protestant Dutch Church before coming to LaGrave

REVEREND SAMUEL I. VANDERBEEK 1892–1898

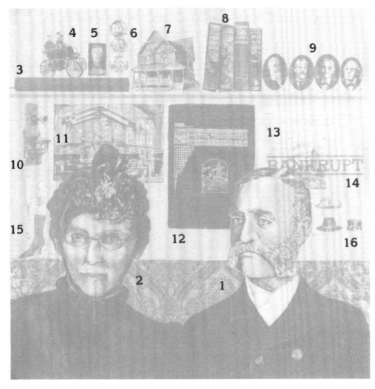

1. Rev. VanderBeek
2. Mrs. VanderBeek
3. LaGrave congregation initially used the United Presbyterian "Psalter"
4. A horseless carriage
5. Thomas Edison invents the "glow lamp"
6. Medallions honoring Presidents William Harrison (1889-1893), Grover Cleveland (1893-1897), and William McKinley (1897-1901)
7. The first official parsonage; later the parish house
8. Books reflect the period: *Songs of the Household, Coleridge's Poems, Curiosities of the Bible, The Life of Jesus Christ*
9. Some of the first elders: Benjamin DeGraaf, John Benjamin, C. VerBruggen, J. Gelock
10. An early telephone (c. 1900)
11. Church interior
12. *The Spiritual Thermometer,* sermons by Rev. VanderBeek sold to raise money
13. *The Church Chronicle* published by LaGrave
14. The "crash" of 1894 forced many businesses and churches into bankruptcy
15. Shoe lace hook, a lady's shoe boot: feminine accessories of the day
16. The Spanish American War saw hats worn by Army and Navy troops during Cuban conflict

REVEREND HENRY BEETS 1899–1915

1. Rev. Beets
2. Mrs. (Clara Poel) Beets
3. LaGrave youth pledged a nickel a week to raise funds for an organ; J. Benjamin, first lead singer and choir director is followed by a quartet of lead singers
4. The Christian Psychopathic Hospital (Pine Rest) is established on a farm plot following an organizational meeting at LaGrave; Dr. Gerrit Stuart, the first doctor at Pine Rest, was a member of LaGrave
5. The first airplane flight
6. The denomination establishes Christian Reformed Indian Missions, and LaGrave sends Dr. Lee S. Huizenga to New Mexico
7. Austin automobiles were manufactured in Grand Rapids in the early 1900s
8. U.S. Presidents of the period: William McKinley (1897-1901), William H. Taft (1909-1913), and Theodore Roosevelt (1901-1909)
9. World War I photo
10. The Church Council, 1912
11. Church publications include *De Wachter* and *The Banner* which was edited by Dr. H. Beets from 1904 to 1929.
12. The Interurban first ran between Holland and Saugatauk and then to Grand Rapids
13. A few of the books published by Rev. Beets while at LaGrave: *Het Leven Van Wm. McKinley, Johanna of Nigeria, Triumfen van het Kruis, Van Het Groote Goed, Doliantie*
14. Ellis Island: Dutch immigrants colored by the Dutch flag
15. Rev. Beets relished political activity and was an active participant

REVEREND WILLIAM STUART 1915-1925

1. Rev. Stuart
2. Mrs. (Helena Knook) Stuart
3. Radios and silent movies starring Charlie Chaplin come to Grand Rapids
4. The Model T Ford
5. Dr. Lee S. Huizenga and family travel to the Far East; a Chinese advertisement for the Christian Reformed mission; ministering to lepers in China
6. Unions organize and strikes become more common
7. The dissenters Bultema, Janssen, and Hoeksema divide the denomination
8. World War I brings air warfare and new helmets; the Germans sink the Lusitania; stamps show support for servicemen
9. Women's suffrage gains steady support, corn-flakes are consumed, prohibition is often evaded, and Sinclair Lewis' *Main Street* is debated
10. Raccoon coats are deemed stylish, sewing circles start in the church and, with coffee, facilitate women's mission efforts
11. Three Presidents of the time: Woodrow Wilson (1913-1921), Warren Harding (1921-1923), and Calvin Coolidge (1923-1929)
12. Stamps honor the teachers of America and underscore Rev. Stuart's concern for education
13. A new parsonage at 616 College
14. The first airport in Grand Rapids served by the Furniture Capital Air Service
15. Emblem of Grand Rapids Christian High School, founded in 1920; Rev. Stuart begins teaching there in 1925

REVEREND R. B. KUIPER 1925-1929

1. Rev. Kuiper
2. Mrs. (Marie Jansen) Kuiper
3. Lindberg and the Spirit of St. Louis
4. The editor of *De Wachter* notes that the initials "R.B." stand for "Rijk Begaafd" (richly talented)
5. The age of Al Capone, the Monkey Trial, and Babe Ruth
6. Benny Goodman and Duke Ellington are popular, a senator does the Charleston on the steps of the Capitol, the 1928 Synod discusses worldly amusements, and B. K. Kuiper suffers after being seen exiting a movie house
7. Seymour Swets becomes choir director of LaGrave
8. President Coolidge poses with members of the D.A.R.
9. The 1922 Chevrolet overtakes the Model T in sales
10. A trumpet "Heralds the Truth"
11. A five-cent soda is a popular treat
12. Mrs. Kuiper was principal of West Side Christian School before marriage
13. Publications of Rev. Kuiper: *The Glorious Body of Christ, For Whom Did Christ Die, As to Being Reformed, Not of the World, While the Bridegroom Tarries;* the 1924 *Psalter Hymnal* is published
14. The "Crash" of 1929
15. Calvin College campus; Rev. Kuiper becomes its president (1930-1933)

REVEREND HERMAN BEL 1932–1939

1. Rev. Bel
2. Mrs. (Tena Dykstra) Bel
3. The seven-passenger 1931 Buick was favored by the Bels — and mobsters
4. The era of Father Coughlin, collective bargaining, labor organizer John L. Lewis
5. A soup kitchen
6. The unemployed sell apples, and President Franklin Roosevelt promises a New Deal
7. Adolf Hitler invades Poland and World War II begins.
8. William Harry Jellema begins a distinguished teaching career as a philosopher
9. Bastian Kruithof preaches frequently during the years of pulpit vacancy; a gift of a gold watch reminds him not to preach too long
10. Rev. W. D. VanderWerp becomes LaGrave's first assistant pastor
11. The north wall of the church collapses during the construction of a parish house
12. Good church music becomes a hallmark of LaGrave.
13. Abraham Kuyper and "Kuyperianism" are discussed in *The Calvin Forum*
14. The parsonage often rings with "two Bels and eight chimes"

DR. EDWARD J. MASSELINK 1940–1944

1. Dr. Masselink
2. Mrs. (Clazina Baker) Masselink
3. Dr. Masselink often travelled on denominational business; ministers received special rail rates.
4. Gas pumps fuel the growing number of automobiles; wartime C ration cards distinguish ministers from other citizens; civil defense helmets mingle with those of the air force, army and navy
5. Dr. Masselink's calling card pictures the new stained glass window
6. Events and items of World War II include the meeting of Allied leaders at Teheran, the establishment of a Department of Defense, B-24 bombing, a GM truck, army jeep, Mail Call, remembrance of Donald E. Dice killed in action, an American and German helmet
7. The 1940s also bring the juke box, a 1939 Plymouth convertible, and FDR campaign buttons
8. LaGrave is proud of its new Parish House, and Mrs. Karsies caters from the church kitchen
9. James Dice serves as head usher; Jacob Vanden Bosch is "Mr. Hospitality"
10. J. G. Rooks and H. Daane become honorary elders with lifetime appointment
11. Mrs. Anne Maris purchases a new organ, played by Alyce Lantinga

DR. GEORGE GORIS 1945–1952

1. Dr. Goris
2. Mrs. (Jennie Brink) Goris
3. World War II ends, but few forget Anne Frank, VE Day, General Eisenhower
4. The explosion of the atomic bomb brings a new age of anxiety
5. LaGrave members are familiar with President Harry Truman, General Douglas MacArthur, Japanese wartime leader Tojo, the deaths of members Roger J. Niewold and John Spalink, Jr., the victory logo, and Iwo Jima
6. Senator Arthur VandenBerg of Grand Rapids promises bipartisan support for the new United Nations and NATO
7. Americans are fond of television, Jackie Robinson, Frank Sinatra, instant coffee, cokes and hamburgers, new telephones; modern medicine attempts to wipe out polio
8. The Korean War breaks out in June, 1950
9. The Volkswagen Bug is introduced to Americans
10. Drs. Ralph Blocksma and John Vroon establish a medical ministry in India and Pakistan; the Henry Beets Society supports missions
11. *The Reformed Journal* and *The Torch and Trumpet* begin publication
12. Dr. Goris's M.A. and Ph.D. theses focussed on *Puritan Legalism as a Method of Moral Reform,* and *The Relation of Youth to Organized Christianity*

REVEREND JACOB D. EPPINGA 1953–1987

1. Rev. Eppinga
2. Mrs. (Anne Batts) Eppinga
3. The 1950s see Cadillacs, "Ike" for President, the Army-MacCarthy hearings, statehood for Alaska and Hawaii, and the Cuban revolution
4. In 1957 the Christian Reformed Church celebrates its centennial
5. LaGrave establishes a Boy Scout troop
6. A SWIM team logo celebrates this new mission
7. 1960's America divided by Vietnam War and domestic protest, but enthused with the Beatles
8. The Mackinac Bridge is built
9. During the 1960s and 70s, Americans witness a moon walk, the resignation of President Nixon, Grand Rapids resident Gerald Ford assuming the presidency, and the U.S. Bicentennial
10. LaGrave commits itself to a downtown ministry
11. George VanWesep serves as an honorary elder
12. Albert Smith directs the Chancel Choir
13. Henry Walkotten and committee oversee construction of a new sanctuary
14. LaGrave supports a dental clinic in Nicaragua
15. Church Secretary Ruth Snoek (1958-)
16. The 1970s and '80s bring Presidents Carter and Reagan, the space shuttle, computer cables and chips, pop cans, Japanese imports; the thread of grace continues to the future
17. The United States and the Netherlands celebrate 200 years of amity in 1982
18. LaGrave contributes to rebuilding the Managua Church after the earthquake
19. Rev. John Steigenga becomes assistant pastor at LaGrave in 1978
20. Rev. Eppinga's publications
21. Rev. Eppinga serves three times as president of the Christian Reformed Synod

THE CHRONICLE,

Rev. S. I. VANDERBEEK, - Editor.

JOHN BENJAMIN - - Manager.

Our Talents.

Our Lord's parables have sometimes been indicative of existing circumstances and sometimes of circumstances relating to future events. In his first allegories he s'ws by practical figures the Kingdom of God to come and then he presents an awful exhibition of their fitness or unfitness for that everlasting Kingdom, in which he unfolds what their condition shall be when all mystery, all instruction, all preparation shall be at an end, when the actions of every being shall be laid bare before the eyes of the whole assembled world.

The conclusion to be drawn from the parable of the talents is, that we have nothing that is properly our own, nothing that is underived from God. Every talent is a deposit placed in our hands, not for own exclusive benefit, but also for the good of others. Whatever we have which may either be improved for God's glory or perverted to his dishonor comes within the description of a talent. To use our possessions, time and influence as if we had an independent right to the disposal of them, is to usurp the prerogative of the giver. Many, it is feared, will wait until that great disclosing day, which will throw a blaze of light on all of our motives, as well as deeds, before they will be convinced of the fallacy of the popular maxim "that a man may do with his own as he will." He has indeed a full right to his proprietorship with respect to other men, but with respect to God he will learn that he possesses no exclusive property.

God proportions his requisitions to his gifts. Paul urged this important truth upon his hearers that God was the giver of every good gift ; he admonished them not to err in this matter, not to think they proceeded from great wisdom on their part. Again we read of him that had much, of him shall much be required, so we perceive that one is commensurate with the other. His duties and obligations are peculiar and personal ; we must each render an account of our own talent when the Master shall come as cited in God's word.

Deficiency and excess are the two great rocks which tend to the destruction of the multitudes ; if our talents are splendid we are tempted to err on the side of dis-

play, if small to suppress their exercise, apologizing for our indolence by their insignificance, but the smallness of our talents is as insufficient an excuse for sloth as the superior talent is for vanity. The true requirement of each is to exercise the brightest faculties with humility and the most inconsiderate with fidelity. The faithful and highly gifted servants in the parable, it is apparent, was far from being lifted up with pride or reduced into negligence by the great importance of the riches entrusted to them. They considered their responsibily increased by the largeness of their talents, they did the will of the Lord without debating ; their slothful associate, instead of doing the will of the Master, contented himself with arguing about it—he who had disputed much had done nothing. He should have known that true Christianity is not simply a matter of debate, but of true obedience—"if ye love me, keep my commandments."

There is not one doctrine of Holy Scripture, either insignificant or merely theoretical; that which the parable teaches is highly special as respecting persons, and practical as it respects the performance of duty. The instruction to be deduced from it is as extensive as the gifts of God to his creatures. It is especially practical as it designates this world to be a scene of action, exertion and diligence ; our talents, such as riches, power influence, wisdom, learning and time are the instruments, the wants, helplessness and ignorance of mankind are the objects upon which these instruments are to be used. God has not given the command to work without furnishing the instruments with which to perform the work and the materials to work on. Hence the important inquiry: "why stand ye here idle all the day long ?" We do not hear them say, "there is nothing to do, no place to work, but no man has given us work," and we see the Master giving each a work and his wages until the eleventh hour.

The parable further informs us, after a long time, that the Lord required the accounting so long that the careless and ungodly think it will never come, and even the good are apt to persuade themselves that it will not come soon. Let not those who are sitting at ease in their possessions, whether of nature or fortune, fancy that the reckoning is forgotten—the more protracted the account the larger will be the sum total, and

of course the more severe the requisition.

All delay indeed is an act of mercy, but many neglected or abused mercies will enhance punishment in proportion as it aggravates guilt.

Again it is apparent that the servants in the parable had been in the habit or attending to their mercies—they seem to have appreciated the exact value of what had been committed to them, "Lord, thou gavest to me five talents." If we do not frequently enumerate the mercies given us of God we shall be in danger of losing sight of the giver while we are revelling in the gift—neglecting its application and forgetting our responsibility.

See the expostulation with the unprofitable servant—what a lesson against distrust in God, and false views of his perfect and glorious character ! Common prudence might have taught this servant that with such a master, as he portrayed God, that his only security was in assiduous duty ; the want of love to God was the root of his sin.

Many of us, dear readers, are ready to condemn the unprofitable servant, while, like him, we conceal our self love under the cloak of modesty and indulge our sloth under the humble pretence that we have no talent to exercise.

Let us all be assured it is the deadness of our spiritual affections and not the mean opinion of ourserves, which is the real cause of our luke warmness in the service of God. The service of God is irksome because the commands interfere with self indulgence.

Let us each examine ourselves and remember in proportion to our mercies and blessings we shall be required to render our account in the day the Lord shall visit us and our talents will be inquired of, whether improved or neglected : let none imagine an excuse will be sufficient. Even the least given is to be improved to the glory and honour of God, thus proclaims the greatest of all teachers in his parable of the talents.

In reading my attention was called to a small extract referring to the trials of the early Christians, a number of whom had been banished for their obstinate refusal to deny their faith. One standing by, and seeing the procession of condemned Christians on their way to exile, said that it was a very sad condition these poor people were in, to be hurried from the society of men and made companions of the beasts of the

field. "True," said another, "it were a sad condition indeed if they were carried to a place where they should not find their God. But let them be of good cheer. God goes along with them and will exhibit the comfort of his presence withersoever they go."

During the great exhibition of the World's Fair, in which the country commemorates the discovery of America, I have thought of the many who have lef- their native land and home to come to this blessed country, where they have erected an altar to their God. How true. Let them be of good cheer, God goes along with them. That which was once a wilderness has been made to blossom as the rose. Its population has increased and extended over the length and breadth of our domains until the name of the United States possesses in it a charm to the downtrodden of the earth, where they may find an asylum from their woes, and the privilege of a citizen. But this can alone continue and our land prosper as God is pleased to abide with us. We are glad that the directors of the great Fair at Chicago, who ignored both the law of God and the Congress of this great country, have met with such a wholesome rebuke from the populace of this great land. They frankly admit the closing of the Fair grounds on the Sabbath is from no religious views on their part, but from a lack of patronage from the masses. We rejoice that God is with us still, and if there is no other way to head off the floods which threaten our Christian Sabbath the aggressors will be denied the wages they seek, as in the case of the Sabbath opening of the Fair. Closed from lack of patronage is a much greater glory for our blessed Republic than if it had been closed by the mandate of a King, or a standing army. Be of good cheer; God is still with us. "*The Fair is closed on the Sabbath from lack of patronage.*" This speaks volumes! What a blessed thing it would be if the same might be said with respect to the Sabbath resorts in our own beautiful city. "Closed from lack of Patronage."

Died.

Miss Jennie Brummel, at the residence of her Uncle, corner of Bartlett and Finney streets, July 28th, in the 19th year of her age.

While in the bloom of youth and a life full of expectation, the golden cords are loosened, all that the world holds dear is left, lovers, relatives and friends, at the solemn call. Ought such lessons not to teach us the uncertainty of life and the certainty of death. Pause my young friends, and consider that when the time will come to you, ye may be ready.

Personal.

Mrs. Peter Reynders is still confined to her bed, with little or no improvement.

Mrs. L. Semeyn is still confined to her home through illness. We hope soon to see her again in her place in the church.

Miss Anna A. Vanderbeek, the daughter of Rev. S. I. Vanderbeek, has been confined to her bed for three weeks with a severe attack of bilious fever. We are glad to mention she is gradually improving in health.

Mr. and Mrs. A. DeBaun, of Hackensack, N. J., have been visiting relatives and friends at Grand Rapids, on their return from Chicago for two weeks, by the way of Meadville, Penn., last Tuesday. We were pleased to see them.

The Sabbath School outing of the Church on Lagrave street, which was deferred for two weeks on account of the death of Arend Ooms, who was one of the teachers, was spent Thursday, the 20th of July, at Reeds Lake. The day was very pleasant and the children returned to their homes in health and safety, having enjoyed the day.

Bible Questions.

11. Who was the first Negro converted to Christianity mentioned in the Bible?

12. Where was the ferry-boat first used and by whom?

13. Where have we an account of the first Missionary meeting?

14. What was the text of our Saviour's first sermon?

15. Who first took an oath or affidavit?

16. Where is the first mention of beggars?

17. Who was the first Jew to marry a Gentile?

18. What was the first miracle performed by Christ?

19. What were the first words spoken to man?

20. Who was the first shepardess?

What We Should Have.

Have a hope in thy sorrow,
A calm in thy joy;
Have a work that is worthy
Thy life to employ;
And Oh! above all things,
On this side the sod,
Have peace with thy conscience
And peace with thy God.
—Selected.

We, the Consistory of the English Christian Reformed Church of Lagrave street, Grand Rapids, Mich., acknowledge the dispensation of God in His alwise providence, in which he has seen fit to remove our esteemed brother and Elder by the afflicting hand of death from our midst after a short and severe illness, Arend Ooms, in the 36th year of his age, on the 29th of June, while young and a life so full of promise, cut down in the midst of his years and usefulness to his family and church. We bow with sorrowful, yet believing hearts, that the death of His saints are precious in the sight of the Lord, and that death with all its solemn attendants will not effect the happiness of those who love and serve God.

It was enacted that we extend our heartfelt sympathy to the bereaved family, widow and children, and commend them to God and the love of the congregation in this their hour of death and sore affliction, That this action shall be spread upon our minutes and a copy of which shall be presented to the widow and printed in the Church organs.

(Signed)
S. I. Vanderbeek, Pastor.

D. Kruidenier,
C. Verburg,
A. T. Welmers,
            Elders.
J. L. Benjamin,
G. Haan,
Jas. C. Van Heulen,
J. Van Dinen,
            Deacons.

Death Bed Repentance.

A minister who frequently visited the sick kept a diary with some account of the various people that he visited; and, when summing up in after years, he found that some two thousand, under the fear of death, gave some evidence of repentance, yet, when they recovered, all but two returned to the world, showing that God had never given them that repentance which needs not to be repented of. How much more satisfactory is a real change of heart when in health, than a socalled death bed repentance, which is frequently only the alarm of a guilty conscience. —[Selected.

CHILDREN'S COLUMN.

Samuel, or the Pious Mother.

You have heard, my dear children, how the Israelites came into the land of Canaan. I shall now tell you what happened to them in Canaan, after Joshua was dead. Do you know who was their King? God was their King. Joshua was not their king, though he used to tell them what God wished them to do. After Joshua was dead there were other men who told them what God wished them to do; but God was their King.

Do you remember that the tabernacle was placed in Shiloh? The high-priest lived in Shiloh, that he might offer sacrifices in the tabernacle.

I am now going to tell you of a high-priest called Eli. Eli was a very good old man. A great many people used to come up every year to Shiloh to worship God at the tabernacle. There was a man who had two wives. You know that people might have two wives a long time ago, though they must not have two now. One of these wives was a very good woman, and she was called Hannah; but she had no little child.

The other wife was unkind and wicked, but she had a great many children. The unkind wife laughed at Hannah and said that God gave Hannah no child because he did not love her. This was not true, for God loved Hannah very much. Poor Hannah used sometimes to cry when the other wife spake so unkindly to her. Once when Hannah had come to Shiloh, and the other wife had been laughing at her, poor Hannah went to the tabernacle to pray to God. Eli was in the court of the tabernacle. He was sitting upon a high seat, and he saw Hannah was praying to God in a very low voice, and her eyes were red with weeping. When Eli saw Hannah he thought she had been drinking wine, and he spoke roughly to her, and said, Why do you not leave off drinking wine? How much ashamed poor Hannah must have been when Eli said this to her before all the people. But she answered very meekly, and said, I have not been drinking wine; I have been praying to God, for I am very unhappy. When Eli heard this, he spake kindly to her, and said, May God give you what you have been asking for. What had poor Hannah been praying for? She had been praying for a little child, and she had been promising God to bring him up to serve God, and to teach people about God. Hannah was very glad when Eli spoke so kindly to her, and she wiped away her tears, and she went home looking quite happy.

You see, dear children, that it is a good thing to pray to the Lord when you are sick, or when you are in disgrace, or when people are unkind to you. Hannah went away from Shiloh to the place where she lived in Canaan, and God gave her a little babe, and she called his name Samuel. While Samuel was a babe Hanna not go to Shiloh; but when he was a little child about three or four years old she took him to Shiloh with her. Hannah did not forget her promise to bring up her child to teach people about God, and she did not mean to keep him always at home with her, though she loved him very much, for she wished the good old high-priest Eli to bring him up, and to teach him. So she brought the child to Eli, and said to him, I am the woman that you once saw in the court of the tabernacle, praying to God; I was praying for this child and God has heard my prayer, and I wish the child to be brought up to serve God. Eli took the little boy to live with him. Hannah sang a beautiful song of praise to God for his goodness in hearing her prayer, and then she left her dear litte Samuel, and she went home again with her husband.

Do you think she ever came to see her child? Yes, every year, and she always brought him a present of a dress such as the people wore in those days. It was a linen dress down to his feet, and it had long sleeves. Samuel used to wear a linen ephod also, such as the priests wore, though Samuel was not a priest himself. God had put his spirit into Samuel's heart, so that he liked serving the Lord in the tabernacle, and seeing the sacrifices offered, and hearing the Lord praised by the priests and the people. As he grew older he pleased God more and more, and a great many people loved him. How glad Hannah must have been when she came to see him, to hear that he was a good child.

It makes your parents, dear children, very happy to hear that you are good. And the angels are pleased when you are good, and Jesus your Saviour is pleased. I hope you will be like little Samuel, and be God's children while you are very young.

We are pleased to inform the friends of the church on Broadway that July 16th its consistory was ordained, and at the last classis Rev. P. Exter was appointed their counselant.

Addendum D — Organists and Choir Directors of LaGrave

Organists:

1887-1893	Mrs. A. M. Maris	1926-1927	Misses Alida Vanden Berge and Hilda Vanden Bosch
1893-1904	Mr. A. J. Englewood		
1905-1914 (?)	Mr. J. S. Jeltes	1928-1936	Miss Alida Vanden Berge
1914-1918 (?)	Miss Edith Winsemius	1936	Miss Ethel Leestma
1918	Miss Anna Mulder	1937-1979	Mrs. Garret Lantinga
1918-1925	No record	1979-	Dr. David Vander Vliet

Choir Directors:

1887-1910 — Mr. John L. Benjamin founded and maintained the music program of LaGrave for nearly a quarter of a century. If there was no choir, he organized a vocal quartet as in 1892. If there was no quartet, he led the congregational singing as precentor. Mr. Benjamin did not hesitate to use the talents of others to lead the choir from time to time.

1910-1916 — Mr. Jeltes, the organist, directed a quartet during part of this period. Mr. P. Henry Sluyter / Mr. P. A. Beneker

1916-1920 — The choir was a male chorus. Mr. Cornelius Benjamin is mentioned as the president. There was a mixed choir, but they performed for special occasions only.

1920-1922 — A vocal quartet performed. No director is mentioned.

1922-1924 — Mr. Henry Dice

1925-1964 — Professor Seymour Swets

1964-1985 — Professor Albert P. Smith

1985 — Professor Merle Mustert

Addendum E — Missionaries Supported by LaGrave

1912-1950
Dr. and Mrs. Ralph Blocksma, Pakistan
Dr. and Mrs. Lee S. Huizenga, China
Miss Rosbeck, Rehoboth, New Mexico
Rev. and Mrs. John O. Schuring, Ceylon (Sri Lanka)
Dr. and Mrs. Everett Van Reken, China

1950's
Rev. and Mrs. Earl Dykema, New Mexico
Miss Marjorie Feenstra, Pakistan
Miss Betty Heerema, Pakistan
Miss Eunice Huizenga, Pakistan
Rev. Vicente Izquierdo, Cuba
Rev. Clarence Nyenhuis, Cuba
Miss Marian Postema, Pakistan
Dr. and Mrs. John Vroon, Pakistan and Nigeria

1960's
Miss Marilyn Baker, Alaska
Dr. and Mrs. Paul Groen, Nigeria

Miss Betty Huizenga, Mexico
Mrs. Alex Johnston, Uganda
Rev. and Mrs. W. R. La Fleur, Japan
Miss Maxine Ohlman, Nigeria
Dr. Keith Plate, Nigeria
Miss Gertrude Rozeboom, Uganda
Dr. Andrew D. Tempelman, Grand Rapids Inter-racial Ministry
Mr. Verlyn Verbrugge, Nigeria

1970's
Miss Joanne Boomsma, Inez, Kentucky
Miss Jan Camburn, Mexico
Miss Pat De Jong, Utah
Rev. and Mrs. Gary De Velder, New Mexico
Mr. Arnold Duban, Guatemala
Mr. and Mrs. John Gezon, Liberia
Dr. and Mrs. Paul Gezon, Nigeria
Mr. Robert Haan, Jordan
Miss Johanna Hoftyzer, West Africa

Miss Betty Huizenga, Texas and Mexico
Mr. Peter Kuiper, Ionia, Michigan
Mr. Oscar Mazariegos, Guatemala
Mr. and Mrs. Alex Munro, Philippines
Mr. and Mrs. Bernard Oldenkamp, Brazil
Rev. James Oosterhouse, Onalaska, Wisconsin
Dr. and Mrs. Dale Peerbolte, Jos Plateau State
Dr. Keith Plate, Nigeria
Miss Pam Potter, Campus Crusade for Christ
Mr. Fred Rajaratnum, India
Rev. Earl Schipper, Columbus, Ohio
Rev. James Sloane, Jamaica
Miss Ruth Snider, Guatemala
Rev. Ronald Spoelman, Ann Arbor, Michigan
Rev. and Mrs. Harvey Stob, Argentina
Mr. and Mrs. Larry Vanderaa, Liberia
Mr. and Mrs. Dan Vander Vliet, Jordan
Rev. Roger Van Harn, Columbus, Ohio
Mr. Steve Van Heest, Jellema House, Grand Rapids
Rev. and Mrs. Stanley Verheul, Boulder, Colorado
Mr. Anton Vroon, Ethiopia
Mr. and Mrs. Thomas Weeda, Rehoboth, New Mexico
Mr. Jack Wiechertjes, Alaska

Rev. and Mrs. Peter Winkle, Rehoboth, New Mexico
Mr. and Mrs. John Witte, Honolulu, Hawaii

1980's
Mrs. Ruth Snider Aju, Guatemala
Miss Joanne Boomsma, Inez, Kentucky
Rev. and Mrs. Ren Broekhuizen, Liberia, West Africa
Miss Jan Camburn, Wycliffe Translators
Mr. and Mrs. Mark Deckinga, Denver, Colorado
Miss Joyce Gordon, Young Life, California
Miss Betty Huizenga, Tucson, Arizona
Mr. and Mrs. John Miller, Mission Aviation Fellowship
Rev. and Mrs. John Moes, Helena, Montana (later Seattle, Washington)
Mr. and Mrs. Alex Munro, Philippines
Mr. and Mrs. Bill Redondo, Mexico
Miss Janne Ritskes, Philippines
Mr. and Mrs. John Paul Roberts, Mexico
Rev. Gary Roest, Hong Kong (later Taipei, Taiwan)
Mr. and Mrs. Larry Vanderaa, Mali, West Africa
Rev. and Mrs. Stanley VerHeul, Los Angeles, California
Dr. and Mrs. Hendrick Visser, Nigeria
Mr. and Mrs. Thomas Weeda, Rehoboth, New Mexico
Rev. and Mrs. Peter Winkle, Rehoboth, New Mexico

Addendum F — Sunday School Superintendents

Mr. Jacob Trompen (1887) - total enrollment March 1887 - 54 pupils
Rev. J. Y. DeBaun (1888)
Mr. J. Scheffer (1892)
Mr. John Benjamin
Mr. G. G. Haan
Mr. J. L. Benjamin
Mr. G. J. Haan
Mr. Lambertus Lamberts
Mr. J. VanDuinen
Mr. J. C. VanHeulen
Mr. C. J. Brouwer - total enrollment 1910 - 253 pupils
Mr. H. Hubert Daane
Mr. Rhine Oosting (1913)
Mr. J. G. VandenBosch (1918)
Mr. Charles DeLeeuw
Mr. G. J. Stuart (1925)
Mrs. S. Hazenburg - "Cradle Roll" Superintendent
Mr. C. E. Pratt (1926)
Mr. D. Blocksma (1928)
Mr. Al Bishop
Mr. Paul Gezon (1929)

Mr. J. H. Spalink (1936)
Mr. C. Scherphorn (1940) - total enrollment 1940 - 230 pupils
Mr. Reynolds Brander (1941)
Mr. Henry Slings (1957)
Mr. Cornelius Bishop (1957)
Mr. Chris Walstra (1962)
Mr. Gil VanSledright (1964, 1966 and on)
Mr. Jake Corvers (1965)

In 1973, the consistory approved the position of Church School Coordinator

Mr. Donald Oppewal (1973)
Mr. and Mrs. Donald Verduin (1977)
Mr. and Mrs. David Male (1979)
Mr. Robert Fry (1983)

Minister of Youth, Education, and Hospitality
Mr. Robert Grussing (1985) - total enrollment 1986 - 175 pupils

Addendum G — Organizations at LaGrave, 1887-1986

1887   May 22 — *Catechism* organized

Rev. DeBaun — A class for married people, and a class for young people.
Elders C. Verburg and B. DeGraaf — Classes for school children (held on Saturday afternoons).

1888   *Ladies Sewing Circle* — initially distinct from *Ladies Aid*, but later seemed to be the same group.

1889   March 14 — *Central Ladies Aid Society*

Charter Members: Mrs. J. Y. DeBaun (Pres.)   Mrs. L. Semeyn
   Mrs. L. Johnson   Mrs. A. Benjamin   Mrs. J. Volten
   Mrs. H. Kievit   Mrs. B. DeVlieger   Mrs. J. VanWyck
   Mrs. L. Quartell   Mrs. DeBoer   Mrs. C. VanderBre
   Mrs. L. Smitter   Mrs. H. Gezon   Mrs. J. Benjamin
   Mrs. L. Schuitema   Mrs. J. Johnson   Mrs. C. Borrendamme, Sr.
   Mrs. R. VanderWerp   Mrs. Karman   Mrs. C. Borrendamme, Jr.
   Mrs. C. VanDam   Mrs. C. Koetsier   Mrs. J. DeVlieger
   Mrs. Jacob Wierenga   Mrs. C. Scherphorn   Mrs. L. Drukker
   Mrs. C. Verburg   Mrs. J. Scheffer   Mrs. J. Gezon
Entrance fee — 50 cents
Purchased choir benches for first sanctuary and later for present sanctuary.
Merged with *Ladies Missionary Society* in 1969.

1890?   *Young Peoples Literary Society*

First Executive Committee: John L. Benjamin (Pres.)   Jennie Quartell (Treas.)
   G. J. Haan   Gelmer Kuiper (V. Pres.)   C. A. Benjamin
   John Brummeler   Lizzie Quartell (Secy.)
Purpose was literary and musical entertainment.
Original membership of 30 soon grew to over 90 young people
Monthly mid-week meetings in lecture room of the church.

1892   *Young Peoples Society*

Met before the evening service on Sundays.
Generally for those age 16 and over.

1894   *Young Misses Sewing Circle* — (*Young Ladies Sewing Circle* and in the 1920, *Young Ladies Missionary Society*)

Early Member: Alberta VanVelzel

1895   *South End Ladies Aid* — "For benevolent and charitable purposes" (See *Service Guild* — 1957)

Charter Members: Mrs. R. Blocksma (Pres. for first 16 years)
   Mrs. A. Dooge   Mrs. H. Houtman   Mrs. G. J. Haan
   Mrs. J. VanWyck   Mrs. H. Daane

1908   October 2 — *Ladies Missionary Society* — "For the development and growth of missionary zeal by educational and inspirational programs," for the purpose of "aiding mission work along educational and philanthropic lines".

First President: Mrs. Gelmer Kuiper (followed by Mrs. John Rooks, Mrs. J. G. VandenBosch, and Mrs. G. J. Stuart)
Its Christmas Tea became an annual event, a tradition carried on today by the *Womens Board*.

Addendum G — cont'd.

1908?   *(LaGrave Street Chr. Ref.) Literary Society*

First Officers:

Gelmer Kuiper (Pres.)	G. L. Daane (Secy.)
N. H. Battjes (Treas.)	J. S. Pleune (V. Pres.)

Possibly later became *Mens Bible Club*

1914   *Esther Circle* — "To work for charity"

Early Active Members: Mrs. Henry Beets, Mrs. Jay Oom, Mrs. W. Karsies
"Aim of giving material assistance to needy families and individuals and at the same time to spread the influence
of Christian love and sympathy".
Helped fund new kitchen; packs Thanksgiving baskets for neighborhood needy; offers benevolent services to
church members.

1919   *Brotherhood* — organized on October 20 to promote Christian fellowship and to stimulate interest in Christ's
Kingdom

First Leaders:		
	Dr. G. J. Stuart (Pres.)	Mr. Adrian Dooge (Secy.)
Mr. J. Vandenberg (Treas.)	Mr. Charles DeLeeuw (V. Pres.)	Mr. Dewey Blocksma (Secy. Pro-tem)

First year organized a young mens *Basketball* team.
Discontinued in 1967.

1923   (approx.) — *Marathon Club*

Young men, age 16 and older, who met every other Monday night.
Early Leaders: Mr. H. Fred Oltman and Mr. Dewey Blocksma
Proceeds from a group-sponsored concert purchased the sign which was placed in front of first church building.
Responsible for ushering.
Reorganized in February 1932 as the *Young Mens Society*.
Early Leaders: Al and Tennyson Bel and Ralph Blocksma
Discontinued in early 1950s.

1930   *Junior Choir*

Ann Scherphorn, director
Florence Stuart, accompanist
Became *Girls Choir* in 1940 — led by Mrs. Donald DeLoof

1930s   *Mens Forum* (additional information unknown)

1930s   (1938?) — *The Girls Society* — for young women age 16 and over; grew out of the *Young Ladies Missionary
Society* (member of Christian Reformed Federation of Girls Societies)

Early Sponsor: Mrs. W. Karsies
Early Members: Helen and Stella Bel

1937   *Business Girls Club*

Organized for women who were employed during the day (see *Friendship Club* — 1946).
Many early members had formerly been members of the *Girls Society*.

1940   *Mr. and Mrs. Club*

Began Sunday, October 6, 1940 as a "Young Married Peoples Bible Class" with such enthusiasm that soon mid-
week meetings were scheduled.

Addendum G — cont'd.

First President: Mrs. Ed Hekman
1944 — Sponsored the monthly publication *Mail Call*, which contained church news and information and was sent to all the service men and women.
Editor-in-Chief: M. J. Wyngarden
Business Manager: Jerry Timmer
Publication Committee Chairman: Ted Vanderveen
News Editor: Marion DeJonge
Art Work: Ilse and Ray Weidenaar

1941 *Senior Fellowship* — organized October 14, 1941 for older men and women (a senior Mr. and Mrs. Club) — age 40 and above

Early Leaders:
Mr. W. B. Eerdmans (Pres.)   Mrs. S. Hazenberg (V. Pres.)   Mrs. J. Borgman (Secy./Treas.)
In 1954, this became simply *Fellowship Club* and later evolved into *Family of LaGrave*, holding once-a-month dinners on Tuesday evenings — potluck, open to the whole congregation regardless of age.

1940s *Boys Club* — organized for boys under the age of 16

Early Leaders: Mr. A. Kinkema, Mr. Howard VerMerris, and Mr. Reynolds Brander
Donated new collection plates
Members of Calvinist Cadet Corp for short time in 1950s

1941 Bulletin announcement for December 21 said, "It has been suggested we again have a *nursery* during the morning services. May we ask parents who might be interested to get in touch with one of the members of the consistory."

1944 *Young Mens Forward Club*

Organized January 12 for young men over age 16
Leader: Mr. A. C. Bishop

1944 *Christian Co-ed Club* — first meeting February 29, 1944 — another form of the *Young Peoples Society*

1946 *Friendship Club*

New name for *Business Girls Club* to reflect changing membership
Became responsible for nursery and eventually Friday morning Bingo; organizes community Thanksgiving dinner.
Charter Member: Mrs. C. VandenBerge

1946 *Fidelis Club* — another regrouping of the young people

First President: Miss Barbara Bishop
First Sponsor: Mrs. Paul Gezon

1948 October 26 — *Mens Mission Society* organized and soon officially named *Henry Beets Mission Society*

Forty-five men were present at first meeting
Officers:
Dr. W. C. Beets (Pres.)   Mr. Robert Twyning (V. Pres.)   Dr. Henry Walkotten (Secy.)
Mr. Milo DeVries (Treas.)   Prof. Don Bouma (Corres. Secy.)   Mr. Ralph DeBoer (Asst. Secy./Teas.)
Dr. Guy DeBoer, Mr. John Dolfin, and Mr. W. B. Eerdmans (Additional Directors)
Specific purpose — to awaken an interest in missions and to guarantee the support of Dr. Ralph Blocksma.
In 1956 women were invited to attend the meetings.

1951   January — The *Bandaging Class* began to make bandages for medical missionaries, sponsored by several church guilds

Later became the *Henry Beets Mission Auxiliary*, sponsored by the *Henry Beets Mission Society*.
Organizer and leader for 25 years — Mrs. Marinus Scherphorn

1950s   *Junior Choir* — directed by Prof. Seymour Swets

For high school age young people — met every Wednesday at 7:45 p.m. before the *Senior Choir*.

1951   *Sunday Nighters* — soon to be *Niters* — held their first meeting on October 21, 1951 with 18 high school and college-age young people present (also see *Young Adults* — 1957)

First Sponsors:	Mr. and Mrs. Fred Baker	
First Officers:	Charles Vandenberg (Pres.)	Roger Boerema (V. Pres.)
	Wilma Beets (Secy.)	John Pastoor (Treas.)

1960s Influential Leaders:

Dr. and Mrs. Wes DeYoung	Dr. and Mrs. Jerry VanderWal	Mr. and Mrs. Al Bosscher

1954   *LaGrave Christian Education Society* — organized September 21, the first group of its kind in the Grand Rapids area

Purpose — "forwarding the cause of Christian education among the youth of this church"
First Officers:

Mr. Gordon Buter (Pres.)	Mr. William Eerdmans, Sr. (V. Pres.)
Mrs. Richard Boelkins (Secy.)	Mr. George Scherphorn (Treas.)
Mr. John Peterson (Finance Chairman)	Dr. Orren Bolt (Membership and Program Chairman)
Mr. A. J. Bosscher (Public Relations Chairman)	

1954   *Adult Discussion Group* — formed by the Education Committee of the consistory, held its first meeting Sunday, October 24, in the Assembly Room.

Initiated by Leo Peters
First Moderator: Dr. Richard Boelkins

1956   *Adult Athletic Club* — organized to stimulate healthy athletic program

First President: Mr. George Scherphorn
Other athletic groups at various times:

Baseball Team	*Bowling League*	*Volleyball Team*
Softball Teams	*Basketball Team*	

1956   *Deaconesses* — were organized by congregational vote in December 1955

The first Board: (two from each of the women's organizations)

Central Ladies Aid	Mrs. Ralph Vandenberg
	Mrs. Martin VerMerris
Esther Circle	Mrs. Wesley Karsies
	Mrs. John Stuit, Sr. (V. Pres.)
Friendship Club	Mrs. Harold J. VanVliet
	Mrs. Gerald Prins (Secy.)
Ladies Missionary Society	Mrs. John R. Huizinga
	Mrs. William Stuart (Pres.)
South End Circle	Mrs. Cornelius Troost
	Mrs. Marinus Scherphorn

1956   *Girls Junior Choir*

     First Sponsors: Judy and Lynn Hoekzema
     Thirty girls from the 7th, 8th and 9th grades met on Sunday afternoons
     Later, under Marion DeVries and Marie Houtman, it became *Girls Club*

1957/1958 — *Young Adults* separates from the *Sunday Niters* to form a separate group for college age students

     Early Leaders: Marie Houtman, Art Brown, Marian DeVries, Bill Jellema
     Early Sponsors: Mr. and Mrs. C. Pape, Mr. and Mrs. J. Jurries and Mr. and Mrs. F. Davidhazy
     Newsletter called "Glow and Blow" and later "The Forward"
     Held weekend retreats in fall and spring (at first with "Forthcomers" of the Fourth Presbyterian Church in
       Chicago)
     Sponsored Saturday Bible School
     Met for supper before the evening service

1957   LaGrave *Boy Scout Troup* #342 organized; first official meeting — January 1958

     First Scoutmaster: Mr. Reynolds Brander
     First Troup Committee:

Mr. John Dekker	Mr. Reynolds Brander	Mr. James Koert (Scout Council Liaison)
Mr. Dick Pettinga	Mr. Thomas Kullgren, Sr.	Mr. Daane Ethridge

     Scoutmasters:

Mr. Dale Korthuis (1959-1973)	Mr. Clare DeGraaf	Mr. Bill Swets
Mr. Doug Bouma	Mr. Gary DeGraaf	Mr. Russ Rykse
Mr. Harold VanDyk		

     Thirty-four scouts in the troup have earned the Eagle Award
       First Eagle Scout — Bob Kullgren — December 24, 1961
     Many scouts have also earned the God and Country Award

1957   *LaGrave Service Guild* — reorganization of *South End Ladies Circle* with a new constitution and name

Officers during change:	Mrs. T. S. Vanderveen (Pres.)	Mrs. D. VandenBerg (V. Pres.)
	Mrs. R. Weidenaar (Secy.)	Miss A. VanVelzel (Treas.)

     Continued "to serve" the church by funding a large part of kitchen in new church and refurbishing the lounge
       and Womens Guild Room in the 1960s.
     Provides flowers for Sunday services; annual Christmas dinner for congregation

1958   *Bible Study and Prayer Hour* — began on October 7, met bi-weekly

     Organized by Rev. J. D. Eppinga

1958   *Building Project Committee*

Dr. Henry Walkotten (General Chairman)	Mr. Donald Battjes (Chapel Coordinator)
Mr. John Spalink (Deputy Chairman)	Dr. Richard Boelkins (Design and Plans)
Mr. Edward Hekman (Finance)	Mr. Seymour Swets (Interior Appointments Chairman)
Mr. Bert VandenBerg (Survey Chairman)	Mr. Elias VanSweden (Construction Chairman)
Mr. Herbert VanderMey (Special Gifts Chairman)	Mr. Gordon Hartger and Mr. Thomas Kullgren (Treasurers)
Rev. Jacob Eppinga (Consultant)	

1959   *Campfire Girls*

Early Leaders:	Mrs. Betty Boerema	Mrs. Esther Michmerhuizen
Mrs. Gay Peterson	Mrs. Judy VandeGuchte	Mrs. Helen VanVliet

Addendum G — cont'd.

Other Helpers: Miss Julia Baker Mrs. Helen Bonzelaar
  Mrs. Jen Browning Mrs. Thelma Kemink Mrs. Betty VanHeest
Later Influential Leader: Julie Korthuis

1960 *Youth Council* — organized by consistory to coordinate and promote the work among our youth

First Members: Mr. J. G. Rooks Mr. G. DeGraaf
  Rev. J. D. Eppinga Dr. E. Sevensma Mrs. J. Boerema
  Mr. W. Lafleur Mr. C. Bishop Mrs. D. Ethridge
  Mr. A. Bosscher Miss M. DeVries

1960 February 28 — First *Youth Church Service*

1962 *Young Adult — Sunday Niter Choir*, sometimes called *Youth Choir*

Directors: Mr. Bob Haan Mr. Dale Bonge
  Mr. Brad Bloom Mrs. Carl Huisman Miss Barb Crounse

1960s, 1970s, 1980s — *Youth* and *Childrens Choirs*

Directors:
  Miss Kathy Block Miss Kathy Poel Mr. Ken Karsten
  Mrs. Connie Scripps Miss Kay Oosting Mr. Wes Westmaas

1964 *Womens Board* — organized in 1964 with the first annual meeting held May 24, 1965

Organizers: Mr. Henry Hoeks and Mrs. Richard Boelkins
First Elected Members:
  Mrs. A. Bel (Treas.) Mrs. R. C. Boelkins (Pres.) Mrs. R. Brander
  Mrs. E. Brown Mrs. J. Browning Mrs. E. Gaikema
  Mrs. D. Goris Mrs. C. Pape Mrs. C. Riddering (V. Pres.)
  Mrs. E. Rodenhouse, Sr. Mrs. M. Scherphorn Mrs. W. Stehower (Secy.)
  Mrs. W. Sterk Mrs. W. Stuart Mrs. J. Stuit, Sr.
  Mrs. G. VanSledright Miss A. VanVelzel Mrs. M. VerMerris
Formed to coordinate services and needs of women's organizations in the church and to serve as a channel
  between them and the consistory.

1964 December 21 — *Benefactors Trust Fund*

Organized by Rev. J. D. Eppinga and Dr. H. Walkotten
Purpose — to enlarge, enhance, augment, and encourage the activities of the LaGrave congregation, and (later)
  the services of the church to its members, to the community, and to all persons, with consistorial approval,
  through the gifts of financial stewardship.
Original Trustees: Dr. Oren A. Bolt Mr. John D. Fles
  Mr. John H. Spalink Mr. John F. Stuit, Jr. Mr. John a. Swets
  Dr. Henry J. Walkotten Rev. Jacob D. Eppinga (Consultant)

1964 *LaGrave Library*

Began with installation of bookshelves in southeast corner of the Parish House Lounge.
Library Committee:
  Mrs. William Eerdmans Mr. Ronald Jacobs Mrs. Alden Walters
  Mr. Henry Hoeks Mrs. Henry Zylstra Rev. Jacob D. Eppinga (Consultant)

Addendum G — cont'd.

1965   *Womens Bible Study* — organized in April

Leader: Dr. W. Jellema
Organizer: Mrs. R. Weidenaar

1970   *FISH* — organized at LaGrave as a part of a community-wide effort to minister to the practical needs of others

Local Leaders: Mrs. Abe DeVries and Mr. Jim Heynen
Organizer for Grand Rapids Area: Mrs. John Rienstra

1970s *Celebration* — (began in 1960s as *The Fellowship*)

A special vesper service held in Fellowship Hall before the evening service.
The Candlelight Christmas Eve Service and Pre-Thanksgiving Day Donation Service are partially the result of
this activity.

1970   *Jellema House* organized

Named for LaGrave member Dr. John Jellema (worked to rehabilitate alcoholics)
Organized by Mr. Neal DeMey
Facility opened July 1, 1971
First Board:

Mr. Jack Swets (Pres.)	Mr. Neal DeMey	Mr. Dick VanderWal
Mr. John Leegwater (V. Pres.)	Dr. W. C. Beets	Mr. A. James Heynen

1970   *Young Couples*

Organized by Rev. Peter Winkle as a result of "Thrust" activity.

1971   *Reach-Out*

Ministry and service project for young adults
Began as summer project, continued through winter for several years
Volunteers went to Lake Michigan beaches, city housing projects, etc.

1972   November — *Historical Committee*

Mr. Loren Dykstra (Chairman)	Rev. J. D. Eppinga	Dr. W. C. Beets
Mr. and Mrs. Jim DeMull	Mr. and Mrs. Elmer VanBeek	

1973   *Senior Mixer*, or *Over 55s*

Leader: Mrs. Alta Tanis
Members: LaGrave members and neighborhood seniors

1978   *The Group*

Organized for post-high-school singles
Started again in 1981 as *Young Singles*

1978   *Bethel Bible Study Program* instituted

Director: Rev. John Steigenga
First Teachers:

Dr. and Mrs. James Benthem	Mr. Clarence Botting	Mrs. Mary Jo DeJong
Mrs. Susan Draugelis	Mr. Charles Dykstra	Mrs. Jackie Fazekas
Miss Alice Oosterhouse	Mrs. Judy Steigenga	Mrs. Marilyn Stob

1979   September — *Progressive Dinner* (not an organization, but an annual activity)

Began as a substitute for fall *Fellowship Dinner*.

First Committee:

Mary Romence (Chairman)	Barb DeVries	
Nancy Glupker	Mary Jo DeJong	

1980   October — *LaGrave Nursing Ministry*

Organizers: Sharon Ethridge and Judy Eppinga
Purpose — to offer basic health counseling and blood pressure screening to Morton House residents.
Volunteer participation by LaGrave nurses

1979-1980 — *LaGrave Young Marrieds*

Organized by pastors
First Leaders:

Dick and Judy Eppinga	Bruce and Joyce Persenaire	Jack and Debbie Nuiver

1982   Fall — *Sunday Evening Series* (Downtown)

Purpose: to provide a place and a program to which people may come together to end Sunday in a spirit of praise.
Privately-funded, once-a-month musical program in downtown Grand Rapids, offered free to the public.
First Producer: Rev. Herman Teitsma
First Business Manager: Mr. Richard VanVliet
First Committee:

Miss Doris VanDellen (Chairman)	Mr. Jerry Kruyf	Mr. Al Smith
Mr. Hans Altena	Mrs. Sue McCarthy	Mr. Robert Swets
Mr. Mark Draugelis	Mr. Bob Noordeloos	Mrs. Betty Teitsma

Annual "*Messiah* Sing-A-Long" is result of this organization.

1982   *LaGrave Hand Bell Choir*

First Director: Mr. Steve Brook

1982   *Junior High Youth Group*

Organizer: Mrs. Lynn Dykman
First Committee:

	Mr. and Mrs. Charles Dykstra	Mr. and Mrs. Thomas Riewald

1982   *The LaGrave Players*

Organized to provide dramatic presentations by volunteer church members.
Director: Mr. Robert Haan

1983   *The Centennial Committee*

Dr. Gerald VanderWall (Chairman)	Mrs. Nancy Peters	Mr. Charles Strikwerda
Mr. Gordon Buter	Dr. John Pool	Rev. J. D. Eppinga
Mrs. Barbara Leegwater		

1984   *Womens Bible Study*

Small group Bible study led by Rev. John Steigenga
Organized by Mrs. Ken Faber

Addendum G — cont'd.

1984 *Young Adults* organized

Sponsors: Mr. and Mrs. Dan VanEerden

1984 *Stephen Series* — organized in the fall

Director: Rev. John Steigenga
First Ministers:

Mr. and Mrs. Marlan Arnoys	Mr. Neal DeMey	Mrs. Lee Mulder
Mrs. Grace Brouwer	Mrs. Ann Mary Dykstra	Mrs. Nancy Peters
Mrs. Katie Danhof	Mr. Rick Eisen	Mrs. Marian Smedes
Mr. Les DeJong	Mrs. Jackie Fazekas	Mrs. Lynne Swets
Mrs. Mary Jo DeJong	Mrs. Marge Maliepaard	Mrs. and Mrs. Elmer VanBeek

Addendum H — "What Is Truth?"   A Sermon by Professor R. B. Kuiper

(Reprinted in abridged form from the magazine *Christianity Today*, March, 1931)

Pilate saith unto him, "What Is Truth?" John 18:38.

Just what did Pilate mean when he asked, What Is Truth? What was he driving at? In what tone of voice did he put the questions? Did he ask it seriously or sneeringly?

He was a Roman, an educated Roman of the first century of the Christian era. The Roman eagle had flapped its wings over the whole of the then known world. The marching Romans had come into contact with all kinds of peoples, philosophies, religions; all kinds of answers to the question What is Truth? They had made the discovery that they, the Romans, did not know it all; other people knew something too. It had even occurred to them that the gods of the Egyptians, the Babylonians, and the Greeks might be just as great as their own. They had begun to question whether the traditional Roman definition of the truth was quite correct. The Roman mind had lost its moorings. Agnosticism was the philosophy of the day. And no doubt it was in the spirit of agnosticism that Pilate put the question What Is Truth? He meant to say: "What is it anyhow? Nobody knows."

Let us face a concrete question here. There are several religions in America, each of which gives its answer to our question. To mention just a few, there are Christianity, Liberalism, Humanism, Mormonism, Christian Science, Spiritism, and Buddhism. How do you know that the traditional Christian answer to the question "What Is Truth?" is correct and that all other answers are essentially false? *Do* you know it?

So extremely difficult is this question that all men everywhere, if left to themselves, would never be able to answer it. The reply is far beyond the reach of the finite and sin-darkened mind of men. The only reason why we can answer it is that God has seen fit to reveal the truth to us. Apart from revelation, agnosticism is reasonable. If divine revelation be left out of consideration, it must be granted that Pilate was right.

Pilate sneered at the Galilean and His preposterous claim: "To this end was I born, and for this cause came I into the world, that I should bear witness unto the truth."

Would that the Roman had been willing to listen to the Jew! Would that the judge had come from his throne, and invited the defendant to take his place, and then had humbly seated himself at His feet to listen to His words! Then Pontius Pilate would have learned the answer to the question What Is Truth? and would have been delivered from the bondage of error into the glorious liberty of the children of God. But alas! he was too proud for that.

Let not us be so proud. Let us even now very humbly, as little boys and girls, mere school children, sit down at the feet of the Divine Teacher to hear from His lips the answer to our question.

God is truth. About that there can be no reasonable doubt. It is a truism. To be sure the gods of ancient mythology rather frequently committed dishonesties, but that very fact is proof that they were no gods. If there is a God, if God is God, He must be truth.

It follows that the truth does not change. As God is the unchangeable, with whom is no variableness or shadow of turning, so also the truth is the same yesterday, today, and forever. It is often suggested that the holy men who wrote the Scriptures did indeed write the truth for their day, but that the truth has changed so radically since that by this time the Bible is hopelessly out of date. The fact is that if the Bible ever was true it is true today.

God's revelation is truth. That is another truism. If God Himself is truth, then His revelation cannot but be truth.

Addendum H — cont'd.

God has revealed Himself in His Word. By His Word we mean both the inscripturated Word, the Bible, and the personal Word, Jesus Christ. The two are inseparable. The authors of the various books constitution the Bible were controlled by the Spirit of Christ, the great Prophet. And all the light of Scripture gathers round the sublime person of Christ. Both are truth. Said Jesus: "Thy Word is truth," and "I am the way, the truth, and the life."

We shall not weary you at this time with the traditional dozen or more proofs that the Bible is the Word of God. But allow us to shed a little light by means of an illustration on what has been called the most conclusive reason why Christians honor the Bible as the very Word of the living God. We refer to the testimony of the Holy Spirit within the Christian.

Let us assume that my father is in an adjoining room, the door to which is closed. I know him. I *know* him. Some of you have perhaps a superficial acquaintance with him, but not one of you *knows* him as do I. Now he speaks in his natural voice. At once i say: "That's my father speaking." If you ask me how I know my simple reply is: "Don't I know my own father?" You, however, do not recognize his voice because to you it is the voice of a stranger.

Listen! The Christian is a regenerated person. And every one who is born of the Spirit knows God. Consequently he recognizes God's voice as a matter of course, let us say intuitively. When he opens his Bible he knows at once that God, his heavenly Father, is speaking.

Not all truth is contained in the Bible. Don't let that statement alarm you. The whole Bible is true, but there is much truth not recorded in Holy Writ. That Columbus discovered America in 1492 and that George Washington was the first President of these United States are facts about which the Bible says nothing. There is a general revelation of God in nature and history as well as a special one unto salvation in the Bible. The former is as true as the latter. Surely, it behooves us Christians to study the one as well as they other. And let us never worry that the proper study of nature may lead our young people away from God. Let us be on our guard against science falsely so called and at the same time remember that the truly scientific pursuit of any branch of learning must of necessity lead the student Godward.

We come to a most interesting though difficult problem. Those who accept the Bible as the Word of God frequently differ among each other in its interpretation. This accounts in large measure for the rise of the various denominations. There are Roman Catholics and Protestants, Calvinists and Arminians. Pedobaptists and those who would baptize only adults, Premillenarians, Postmillenarians, and Amillenarians. Now how are we going to decide which of various interpretations is correct, which has the best claim to being truth?

The problem is not altogether so bewildering as some would have us think. One frequently hears the remark that there is hopeless confusion regarding the interpretation of Holy Writ. That is by no means the case. All those churches which hold unqualifiedly to the Bible as the truth have a common confession. We refer of course to the Apostles' Creed. It is a concise statement of certain fundamentals of the Christian faith, all of which are obviously taught in the Bible. It may well be called the norm of a church's Christianity. All Christian churches honor it. The church which rejects such doctrines as the Trinity, the Deity of Christ, the Virgin Birth of Jesus, and so on, forfeits its claim to the Christian name.

But we may go a step farther. Christ promised that the Holy Spirit would lead the church into the truth throughout the centuries. It goes without saying that this promise has been kept. Consequently, there runs through the history of the Christian church a stream of orthodoxy, a line of truth. In the days of the apostles the church stood on the solid foundation of the truth. Almost at once error crept into the church. It began to prevail. The King and Head of the church at the right hand of God, mindful of His promise, filled a certain man, or perhaps certain men, with the Spirit of truth. They reasserted the truth and called the church back to it. The church gave heed. Again error crept in. Again it began to prevail. Again Christ filled a certain man with the Spirit of truth. Again the church gave heed to His message. Such has been the history of course of its history will continue until Jesus comes again. The line of orthodoxy runs from paul to Augustine, to the great reformers of the sixteenth century as Luther and Calvin, to the recent scholarly defenders of the faith, such men as Orr in Scotland, Kuyper and Bavinck in the Netherlands, Hodge and Warfield in our own America. All these men interpreted the Bible in essentially the same way. In essence they all reasserted the doctrines of the apostle Paul. Every one of them was an apostle of the truth.

It was one truth which each of these teachers stressed with all the powers at his command. It is the doctrine of salvation, not by words or by character, but by the sovereign grace of God in Jesus Christ. The Bible has been rightly called the Book of Salvation, and on this point in their interpretation of the Book they were an absolute unit. And do not all Christians in all denominations agree on this all-important point? Every sincere Christian, no matter what his theoretical theology may be, in his heart of heart is convinced that the one way to be saved is by sovereign grace.

To put the matter somewhat differently, the truth is expressed in the great historic creeds of Christendom, most precisely in such monumental expressions of the Reformed faith as the Westminster Confession.

It seems hardly necessary to add that the creeds are not of equal value or authority with the Bible. The holy men who wrote the Bible were guided infallibly by the Spirit. That claim cannot justly be made for the church in its interpretation of the Bible.

The history of the Christian church is evidence that the Spirit leads the church in the truth progressively. To be sure, this progress is by no means uninterrupted. It may best be pictured by a zigzag line, rather than by a straight line angling upward. But the zigzag line too tends upward. And so it may well become the church's duty from time to time to add to its creed by virtue of additional light shed by the Holy Spirit on the truths of Scripture.

Let us suppose that all of us are agreed on the answer which we gave to the question "What Is Truth?" Does it follow that we are Christians? No! It does follow that we are orthodox. But orthodoxy is not synonymous with Christianity. Orthodoxy is indeed essential to Christianity, but it does not constitute the very essence of Christianity.

What the bones are to the human body that orthodoxy is to Christianity. Imagine a body without bones. Is it really a body? Hardly. It is just a lump of flesh. So Christianity without orthodoxy is not really Christianity. On the other hand a body consisting solely of bones is not a body either, It is a skeleton, and skeletons are wont to be dead.

There is such a thing as the orthodoxy of demons.

James tells us that they believe that there is but one God. About that they are absolutely right. But he adds that they tremble. For all our orthodoxy you and I might conceivably be demons trembling on the brink of hell.

What then constitutes one a Christian? Not merely to know about the truth, but to know the truth. Not just to know some, or for that matter many, things about God, but to know God personally. We must be able to say with the psalmist of old: "I love the Lord." We must sing from the heart:

"My Jesus, I love thee, I know thou art mine;
For thee all the follies of sin I resign.
My gracious Redeemer, my Savior, art thou;
If ever I loved thee, my Jesus, 'tis now.

I love thee because thou hast first loved me
And purchased my pardon on Calvary's tree;
I love thee for wearing the thorns on thy brow;
If ever I loved thee, my Jesus, 'tis now."
from *The Psalter Hymnal*, p. 440

That constitutes Christianity.

And to such knowledge Christ referred when He spoke those mysteriously deep words: "This is life eternal, that they might know thee, the only true God, and Jesus Christ, whom thou hast sent."

Addendum I — LaGrave Servicemen and Women — World War II

William Alberta	Donald E. Broene	Gerald Dykstra
T. R. Battema	Florence Brummel	William Eerdmans, Jr.
N. Battjes	Jack B. Bursey	Rudy Elwell
Clyde D. Battjes	Evelyn Cooper	Donald H. Ernzer
Gerald Bazan	G. Warren Daane	R. Etheridge
W. C. Beets	Marie G. Danhof	T. F. Frieling
G. Beasecker	Guy De Boer	Russell Gelders
Albert A. Bel	Willis De Boer	Jack Gelders
John H. Bel	Harold C. De Boer	Kenneth Gelders
T. R. Bel	Neal De Mey	Horace Gezon
D. D. Blocksma	John M. Dekker	R. A. Granstra
R. Blocksma	Howard R. Dekker	Erwin Haan
R. Boelkins	Elmer De Jong	P. Haan
O. A. Bolt	Donald De Loof	H. Hartger
Don Bomers	Peter De Visser	E. Hekman
John F. Bosma	Wesley De Young	Floyd Hendricks
Jordan Bosma	Evelyn Dice	Henry P. Hendricks
Kenneth Bosscher	Norman Dice	David G. Hertel
Clarence Botting	Robert Dice	Jacqueline Heyns
Donald H. Bouma	Chester Dykgraaf	Roger Heyns
Lewis G. Bouwman	Wilma Dyk	S. Hollander

Addendum I — cont'd.

A. F. Hylkema
Lyman I. Jellema
A. C. Kinkema
Adrian H. Koert
James H. Koert
K. V. Kuiper
A. H. Langereis
T. A. Langereis
Peter Lugtigheid
William H. Medema
M. Michmershuizen
R. Michmershuizen
R. H. Morgenstern
Ivan A. Nichols
R. J. Niewold
Theodore T. Newhof
Eugene Peters
W. J. Pylman
Peter Rickers
R. Roelofs

Kenneth Rodenhouse
J. G. Rooks
R. Dale Rooks
George Scherphorn
Howard J. Schuitema
E. S. Sevensma
J. S. Sluyter
J. Spalink
R. Spanninga
Lawrence Spoelstra
Jack Stuit
F. G. Timmer, Jr.
James Tornga
Elmer Van Beek
James G. Van Beek
Roy E. Vanden Berg
Charles Vanden Berg
Grace Vander Galien
R. Vander Wilt
John Van Domelen

Wynerd A. Van Dyke
Jacob Van Loo
Gilbert A. Van Sledright
W. D. Van Velzel
Robert Van Zytveld
Eugene Ver Merris
Virginia R. Vermerris
W. M. Waalkes
Peal Wierenga
H. Warren Wierenga
E. J. Woltjer
P. Woltjer
James Wyngaarden
Leo Yonkers
Earl A. Zuidema
H. Zylstra

Gold Star:
Donald E. Dice
September, 1944

Addendum J — LaGrave Servicemen — Korean War

Carl Battjes
John K. Boerema
Donald J. Brouwer
Leon Daane
Lawrence H. Franken
William B. Johnson
William W. Johnson
Dale Korthuis

Edward J. Rodenhouse
John G. Rooks
Marius Rooks
L. P. Smith
Jack Smitter
James B. Timmer
L. Vanden Berg
Charles Vanden Berge

Roger G. Vander Kooy
Ronald G. Vander Wilt
John Van Dommelen
Clarence Van Dyke
Roger Van Malsen
Henry Van Reken
Ted G. Wierenga
Warren Wierenga

Addendum K — LaGrave Servicemen and Women — Vietnam War

Calvin Aukeman
Fred Baker, Jr.
Douglas Battjes
Scott M. Bishop
James M. Botting*
Jack Coulter
L. Carl De Jongh
David R. Dekker**
John M. Dekker*
Douglas W. DeMey*
James DenBraber
John C. DenBraber

Phillip Dommisse
Charles Emory*
Richard D. Ernzer
Robert D. Etheridge
Robert J. Frazee
Bernard Geisel
Robert Granstra*
Mark Haeck
Thomas Hartger
H. C. Hekman
R. J. Hekman
H. C. Henshaw

George M. Houtman*
David Kemmink
Robert Kullgren
Thomas Kullgren
Thomas R. Larsen*
Garry J. Moes
Mark C. Newhouse*
Terrell Plantinga
R. W. Poel
Dick Riekse*
Thomas Riewald*
Robert O. Roskam

Addendum K — cont'd.

Gary J. Rypma
William Smits
Sally Roorda Tilley
Chester Van Dellen*
Richard A. Vanden Berg
Karl Van Dyke*

H. Roy Van Vliet
Robert E. Van Vossen
Dennis Vennema
David A. Verduin
David D. Westmas*

Jack B. Yonker
Jack L. Yonkers

*   Denotes service in Vietnam
**   Died in Vietnam

Addendum L — Reynold H. Weidenaar — 1915-1985

Reynold H. Weidenaar was born and raised in Grand Rapids and lived there throughout his life. He traveled widely and received honors as one of America's most distinguished artists. Mr. Weidenaar's work has been displayed in more than 100 museums across the country. The Metropolitican Museum, The Wadsworth Athenum, The Library of Congress, The Smithsonian, The Boston Museum of Fine Arts, and the major museums of Philadelphia, San Francisco, and Kansas City are a notable few. He was 27 years old when he had a one man show in the Smithsonian. In 1974 when the Kennedy Gallery in New York celebrated its 100th anniversary, he was one of seven living artists represented. He was a remarkable figure in American art.

In reviewing his 1981 New York show, Theodore Wolff in the *Christian Science Monitor* compared his work to Bruegel, John Taylor Arms, Martin Lewis, and Grant Wood. He called Weidenaar "...a virtuoso with the etching needle, a master craftsman with extraordinary skills." He also noted "...a rare ability to reach deep into the unique identity of an object or an individual and to bring it forcefully to the surface in a few lines."

He was a Guggenheim Fellow, a Tiffany Scholar, received the Rothschild Prize, and the John Taylor Arms Award. His etchings, "Home from the Forest," "It Was a Terrible Day," and "The Great Society" are masterpieces. His oils, watercolors, and sketches show his many strengths. He was a man in love with drawing and a passion for life. His work reached out to all who will look.

Reynold Weidenaar provided the following explanation of fresco art: Fresco is said to be the oldest kind of painting known to man; some art historians claim it still to be the best. Frescoes have been found which are more than 3000 years old. Most frescoes are painted directly on walls. When properly made, they do not fade, darken, or crumble; are washable, durable to the touch, and outlast most other forms of painting. They do require much hard work. The artist begins with slaked quicklime which has soaked many months in water - in this instance over a year, to provide later strength against dampness, and for solidity and permanence. After this prolonged soaking, it is sieved and mixed with marble chips which were washed clean, dried, and sifted to various sizes. This "roughcast" mixture is then plastered to a wall or, in the case of "The Great Commission" to a metal framed plaster-bearing screen. Successive coats are added later, using the lime aged fresco lime putty with marble meal and marble dust, until the upper layers are thinner and smoother, but with an over depth of at least 1-1/2 inches. In Pompeii, walls exist that are actually three inches thick. (A thick wall carries moisture longer, hence is desirable for richer color later) The final coat is applied thinly, troweled very smooth, and kept moist. Colors are painted directly upon the wet surface - if it dries too soon, the colors will not "set" permanently. Therefore, the artist plasters the top "intonaco" layer only over that part he can finish at a sitting - with a thick moist wall and damp weather, he can work most of a day. Sometimes only a few square inches are plastered, sometimes several square feet, depending upon the kind of detail to be painted. Dry powdered clays, metallic salts, or oxides (some of which are dug right out of the ground - Italy has many such color sources) are used for colors. They are mixed with wet lime (or in this case, plain distilled water) and applied with a brush right onto the wet plaster. (Colors for this fresco were tested for six months in lime water in test tubes, to insure permanence, as some colors bleach in lime, causing eventual fading in the wall). The plaster then undergoes a chemical reaction with air. It takes up carbon dioxide, causing it to "set" to marble-like hardness which increases with age; the colors are held fast. If the work has been done well, they should not wash off, chip, flake, or fade. Because of the physical demands, and because in the past many frescoes have failed through technical inexpertness or attempted shortcuts, not many frescoes are in existence, especially in the North Americas. "The Great Commission" is the only known Fresco in this part of the United States with the exception of the gargantuan work by Rivera in the Detroit Institute of Arts. It required several years work, (almost five) in testing and research, and involved a trip to Italy. Fresco is unpredictable and has many contradictions unless thoroughly understood, but to this day many fresco techniques have mysteriously disappeared into the dim historical past.

Addendum M — Last Sermon Preached in the Original LaGrave Sanctuary
Rev. J. D. Eppinga

"Build A Church To His Name" — I Kings 5:5

It was on June 14, in the year of our Lord 1888, that the present sanctuary of the LaGrave Avenue Christian Reformed Church was dedicated. Songs of praise and prayers of thanksgiving were uttered by the congregation. An appropriate message was delivered. Tonight, exactly 71 years later, lacking two weeks, the congregation is meeting within these selfsame, long-standing walls for the last time. It is a strange sensation.

We know that the Church of God is not a building. We know that the body of the Lord Jesus Christ is not brick, stone, mortar, walls and windows. Nevertheless, God has created us in such a way that we grow fond of things, places, houses, and church buildings, too. Some call this sentiment. If it is, then we may point out that Christianity is not opposed to proper sentiment. We find such sentiment in the Psalms. In Psalm 48—which the choir shall presently render—we read:

"Beautiful for situation is Mt. Zion.
Walk about Zion; go round about her;
Tell the towers thereof.
Mark ye well her bulwarks.
Consider her palaces."

If we think that these words were authored by the Holy Spirit—which they were—then we realize that God not only has feelings of sentiment, but further brings them to expression. And so it was also with the Lord Jesus Christ when He walked among men. And so we have feelings too about this building.

Most of you have worshipped here for a number of years. Many of you have worshipped here for a number of decades. And so, through the years, this has become a place of meaning, a place of beauty, and a place of holiness. And in five years of preaching within these walls, I, too, have come to associate these physical surroundings with the hallowed and ongoing presence of God through the generations. Therefore, to know that we have assembled here for the last time makes not only for a strange sensation, but even a painful one.

Why then do we leave this place? Why then do we close these doors?

The answer, I think, is found in I Kings 5:5 which was chosen as our theme at the beginning of our present building project and which appears on today's bulletin as the title of this message. King David had grown as fond of the Old Testament tabernacle as any of us have of this building. However, as much as he loved it, he knew that it was no longer adequate. Therefore, because that tabernacle could no more serve the needs of his people and of the generations yet unborn, he desired to build a more adequate edifice. This never became his privilege.

It was an honor reserved for his son. Nevertheless, in placing the needs of the present and the future ahead of sentiment for the past, David was to be commended. And God did commend him.

Similarly, I would say that this congregation is to be commended. What you do this evening is not an easy thing. This is a hallowed place. These walls are associated with 71 years of unfailing divine faithfulness. In the history of God's church, in our hearts, these walls shall stand forever. However dear as these walls have grown, it is also true that if this congregation is to continue to advance and grow and continue to be vital, if this congregation is to reach forward increasingly to what, I am convinced, are almost limitless opportunities and breathtaking challenges, more adequate facilities are desirable. We know that facilities do not make a church. The most commodious structure is not necessarily the place where the Spirit shows His power. Nevertheless, facilities help and can be a strong aid in the work to which the church has its calling. Therefore, for all these reasons, we do a difficult thing tonight—but also a good thing. A thing that is right. We close these doors to open more adequate doors to the tomorrows that lie ahead.

Before we close them, however, it is proper to remember June 14, 1888—the date of this building's dedication—and to consider what was dedicated in that hour threescore and eleven years ago.

I was not present on that occasion. Nor have I been able to obtain an eyewitness report of that event. But though I was not there, the following items were definitely there. A Bible—it lay open before all those present; it represented God speaking to man. And hymnbooks (Psalm books). A choir. And a pulpit, testifying to the fact that there was a Gospel in this world. There was also a baptismal font, signifying the covenant; and the communion table, signifying the ever-present Christ who died and lived again, and lives forevermore. Besides all this, there was present the real church—the organized body of believers. Not just the temple, but the soul within the temple. And it was all this that was dedicated on that date of long ago—June 14, 1888.

Today we do not undedicate all this. Instead, we take it all along.

The question has been asked: "What is there of the present sanctuary that we can take with us into the new?" Motivated by a sentiment that is not wrong, many asked what is there here that we can take with us, incorporating it into the new? It seems to me that there are two ways in which we can answer that question. First of all, there is the usual answer that I have given myself to many these past few months. We are taking with us into the new sanctuary the Maris Memorial Organ. We are taking with us the cornerstone. We are further taking with us the stained glass window that you see above me, depicting the Master in the Garden of Gethsemane. These three features we are incorporating into the new sanctuary whose outline is even now taking form.

But there is another way to answer the question. What are we taking with us into the new house of worship? All that was dedicated for use to the glory of God on June 14, 1888.

As we go from the old into the new, as we go through these doors which then shall close for good, and enter the new doors by and by, we take with us God's Word. We take with us hymnbooks and our voices, wherewith to praise Him unceasingly. We take with us a pulpit, signifying that there is still a Gospel in this soul-sick world to proclaim. We take with us a baptismal font—the seal of God—and a table of communion, signifying the living Christ who died for our sins. Yes, and we take with us ourselves—the real church—the body of the living Lord. All that was dedicated then—right here on June 14, 1888—we take with us to the new church. And, indeed, if we didn't, how could be continue

"to build unto His Name?" Tonight, therefore, we do not deconsecrate a building, but rather reconsecrate ourselves. Tonight marks not the ending, but only a chapter division in a story that has no ending—the story of the church. We have said that tonight we shall close these doors. It isn't true. They shall only be widened. We have said that we shall take down these walls. It isn't true. They shall only be made sturdier. The faith of our fathers—of 1888—is living still, for as they built unto His Name, so do we in 1959.

Therefore,

What shall we say that may mark the last words here as we continue from here onward and forward? Many words have been spoken in this place. Many wondrous texts have been sounded, proclaimed, preached, from this place. What shall be the last? As we look back here on 71 years of mercies, as we look forward to further challenges and opportunities, we close—we cap all the words from this spot with these words of the Psalmist: "Great is the Lord and greatly to be praised—in the city of our God—in the mountain of His holiness."

Excerpts of the last sermon preached by Rev. Eppinga in the first sanctuary of the LaGrave Church, May 31, 1959.

Addendum N — First Sermon Preached In the New LaGrave Sanctuary
Rev. J. D. Eppinga

"The Same Christ" — I Corinthians 13, Hebrews 13:8

Everything in this world is constantly changing. All things are always in a state of flux. Man goes from infancy to childhood; the youth matures and grows old, and dies. All of this is change.

Moods change. We go from sadness to joy, from the grip of indolence to industrious zest. A man, they say, is never the same man twice.

Customs change, and ideas too; and the seasons. We go from summer to fall, to winter, and to glorious spring. The word the weatherman uses most is "change."

But there is not only constant change in the natural climate, for political climates also vary from place to place, and in those places, from time to time. I have on my shelf a book on economics entitled *The Big Change*. I received another book this past week labeled *The Historic Faith and a Changing World*. It is true indeed—our fathers wouldn't recognize the earth they left for a better one so short a time ago.

I wonder. How old would you say the world is? How long ago was it that God formed the earth and flung it into space? Was it 6,000 years, as some maintain? Or

10,000? Was it 100,000? I am not interested in involving you in all the complexities of this difficult yet fascinating debate. I ask the question in order that I may confront you with an illustration.

Suppose that it was 100,000 years ago that this world was made by God. I do not say it was 100,000 years. I only say "suppose". Then, support furthermore that those 100,000 years could be telescoped into a period of twelve hours, beginning at 12 midnight. Then we would have to say that nothing amounting to any progress happened this past night from 12 midnight to 8 a.m. Or from 12 midnight to 9 a.m. Or from 12 midnight to 10 o'clock. On this basis, all the big changes have happened only in this last half hour—from Christ to the printing press to the discovery of atomic energy. Astounding! More has happened to change this world in that last forty years than has happened in he previous 2,000 years. More than our parents and more than our forefathers, we are sensitive to change and the changes our world has been undergoing—with accelerating speed. It is no wonder then that people are talking about space travel tomorrow when only a little while ago people were laughing at Edison, Ford and brother Wright. It's kind of an uneasy feeling, isn't it, "when change is all around we see?"

It was also an uneasy feeling once upon a time for the ancient Hebrews to whom the Epistle to the Hebrews was written. They were told that those things which in their minds they had invested with ideas of permanence, were, in essence, not permanent but transitory. The temple. The law. Mosaic ritual and ceremony. Time-honored customs and ancient notions of family and face. They were told that these things had all passed away. That was kind of unnerving, to say the least, when "change in all around" they saw. So the writer to the Hebrews comforted them. He told them of something, nay, of *Someone* who did not change, who was the same. "Jesus Christ," he said, "is the same yesterday, today, and forever." (Hebrews 13:8).

I hope it is easy for you to see why we speak as we do in this introduction to the first sermon preached in this new sanctuary. This is a Sunday, and this is a season of great changes for this congregation. Not only does our newspaper confront us with a changed world almost daily but even our own small world, as a congregation, has metamorphosed so completely today. We are in our new sanctuary this morning, and it's all so different. It's all so strange! It's all so changed!

Remember the old sanctuary? There was a section of pews way in the back fondly referred to as the lecture room. To the minister's left sat the organist and the choir, while to his right there was a little section known as the elders' benches. And overhead, high on the chancel wall, was Hofmann's picture of Christ in Gethsemane in glass. The windows on the north wall were always open, allowing at least some of those who were seated in the parish house to look in. For years the congregation worshipped in that sanctuary, with many of the parishioners always seated in their favorite places. And .then came the last Sunday in May of last year, 1959—the last service in the old sanctuary. The choir recessed to the back of the sanctuary and sang the "Sevenfold Amen." That was the last of a pattern and a place that had existed for so long a time. The next Sunday it was all changed for us.

The next Sunday we met in multiple morning services in the Central Seventh Day Adventist Church and in the evenings in the Westminster Presbyterian Church. We did that for a year and a month. And then, just about the time we were growing accustomed to the new arrangement, last Sunday dawned. We had communion. In the prayer we thanked our Lord for having blessed us and guided us during that interim period in our history. When the congregation retired from the sanctuary last Sunday evening I ascended the pulpit once more, in an empty church, and thought: "This was the last time. Next Sunday it will all be changed again."

And here we are. What a change! Of the old sanctuary only the Gethsemane Window, the organ and the former cornerstone remain; but even these are not as they were. The old cornerstone inhabits a new place; the organ has been remodeled and enlarged; and the Gethsemane Window has been moved from the chancel wall to the balcony wall. The church is changed. The time of worship is changed. The order of worship is changed. 1 The hymnbooks have changed. And the congregation—?

Dear friends, the congregation, too, has changed. In my period of six-and-a-half years as the minister here, there are those who have left and there are others who have come. Seventy-nine members who were here when I arrived have since transferred to the church that is above—an average of one a month. And as these died, so others were born. And so the congregation, too, is not the same.

Therefore, we may well inquire: What is the same? What has not changed, if anything? We do well, I think, with a constantly changing congregation, with a new order of worship, and with a new and different sanctuary, to ask: "Is there anything that abides? Is there anything that changes not? The congregation changes. every once in a while we have a change in ministers; our house of worship has changed. Is there anything here that is not subject to change? Is there anything here that was here when this congregation was organized in 1887?" We answer: YES!

Thank God!

For one thing, there is the Bible. "Heaven and earth shall pass away, but my word shall not pass away" (Matthew 24:35). God's Word endures. It changes not. It is ever the same. It was here before this church was founded. It stands eternal. It has survived all the changes this congregation has seen—both from without and from within. Our church today stands upon a new foundation. I saw it poured. But that is only in the outward sense. Actually, it still stands upon the old foundation—the Word of God. Church buildings can get aged. We can outgrow them. But God's Word is ever new and we never grow beyond it. Yes, there is something here this morning that hasn't changed at all—God's Word. We have changed buildings, but not Bibles. I pray God that we never will. There are those who have sought to remodel the Bible as one would remodel a church. There are those who have sought to replace the Word as one would replace a sanctuary. But when we replace the Word, then the sanctuary—however lovely it may be—is not longer a sanctuary. Is there anything here that is the same? We answer: YES! It is the Word of God.

There is something else too. "Change in all around" we see this morning, but the faith is the same. As the Apostle Paul said, "... Now abideth faith ..." (I Cor. 13:13).

In faith this church was founded. By faith it grew. With faith it faced the future. Through faith the congregation undertook the building of a "House unto His Name." "Faith is the substance of things hoped for; the evidence of things unseen" (Heb. 11:1). It has ever blossomed as a rose in he wilderness of history. It has survived the great mortal storms of the pages of the past. By faith, Christians have survived persecution, peril and sword. It is this faith that is with us still.

It was hard to select the psalms and hymns for the service this morning. There are so many that are fitting for such an occasion as this; among them that grand and glorious hymn, "Faith of Our Fathers." We shall not sing it today, but we shall later, D.V., in our services of dedication. Yet, because I must, let me quote the first line now: "Faith of our father, living still ..." And it is still living. There is much that has changed among us today, but the faith of our fathers has not changed. It is still here. it is living still.

The Bible. Faith. Is there anything else that remains the same? Yes, there is hope. For Paul speaks again and says, "And now abideth ... hope ..." (I Cor. 13:13).

Strange, isn't it? You would think that hope would have died a long, long time ago. What with man's inhumanity to man, with never-ending wars and world conflagrations, with sin, it seems, more in evidence than ever in days gone by, with the spreading of atheistic communism to staggering lengths and breadths in a world presumably civilized, you would think that hope had not only died long ago but that it had been dead, buried, and forgotten. With many that is so, but not with us. Our fathers were full of hope, and though many things have changed for us today, hope yet abides. We look for His coming as ever we did in days gone by.

Yes, hope abides, and likewise love. In a world of hate, in a world of selfishness, in a world that chokes out love, it abides. It is here. The communion of the saints at LaGrave has ever been not only tinctured but thoroughly colored by the spirit of Christian love. By its programs, by its support of missionary work, by the collection which shall be received in a little while for mission causes, and by a service with a missions emphasis this evening, we would continue to say: "Although much is new here this morning and changed, our love for God and the love we bear our fellow man has not changed."

But now, let us ask: "How can we summarize, how can we put into one word the Word that abides, and the faith that abides, and the hope that abides, and the love that abides?" We answer by naming the Name of Christ who is the Summary of the Word, who is the object of our faith and our hope, and who is the object of our love. the Word abides, for He is the Word. Faith, hope and love abide, for "Jesus Christ is the same yesterday, today and forever" (Heb. 13:8).

So there is one thing we want to say this morning—only one thing—and we say it from the pulpit.

We have placed it on the bulletin for today. We articulate with the best diction we possess, and say for one and all to hear: "THE SAME CHRIST." See the new church, hear the new organ, admire the new appointments, take in all the changes all around, but hear this: "THE SAME CHRIST! THE SAME GOSPEL!

On a Sunday evening last fall in the Westminster Church, I had occasion to tell the story of a minister who was most learned and who preached deep and penetrating sermons. All from the surrounding countryside came to hear the brilliant orations that fell from his silver tongue. But gradually, with all his learning, he was beginning to preach more and more of the wisdom of man instead of the Gospel of God. One morning as he made his way to church where an hour before great throngs had already gathered to hear his brilliance and his learning, he ascended the pulpit. There on the open Bible someone had placed a note which simply said, "Sir, we would see Jesus" (John 12:21).

Someone in the congregation that evening who heard that story, had the idea of taking those words and placing them in the pulpit as a plaque, so that whoever occupies this pulpit may always be mindful of his prime task and function. Because it is not yet fastened into place, I hold it up and show it to you now. If you cannot read it from where you are seated, let me tell you again what it say: "Sir, we would see Jesus." So we will show Him. We will proclaim Him, for He is here. Amid all the changes, He is the same.

Dear congregation, we have a new pulpit. Isn't it wonderful? But here is something even more wonderful—although we have a new pulpit, we have THE SAME CHRIST. He who said, "Come unto Me, all ye who are weary and heavy laden," says it still. He who said, "Cast all your cares on Me," says it still. A new church, but the same voice, and the same words, and the same compassion, and the same invitation: "Believe on the Lord Jesus Christ and thou shalt be saved."

It is sad, but true, that today, and all through history, there have been those who have sought to change Him. It can't be done, of course, yet there are those who try and who have tried. We shall not try it here. We don't want to try it. John Ruskin, on his visit to the Alps, fell on his knees and thanked God for creating those solid mountains in this fleeting world. But we know of one who remains the same, even when those mountains are removed and cast into the sea—Jesus Christ. And we are happy that it is so.

Dear friends, after the service this morning, you will no doubt wish to explore the premises. Indeed, you have already been able to engage in somewhat of an inspection from time to time. Note again, then, as you leave this morning, the basic lines of architecture. They are traditional. There is something here and there that is modern and contemporary. But the basic lines are traditional, and I am rather pleased that it is so. As you

Addendum N — cont'd.

view the building then, let the modern touches tell you that we live in a changing world. But let the basic lines of architecture in this sanctuary, and the basic arrangement of the chancel, and the basic lines of our tower and of our spire—which are traditional—speak to you of that which endures throughout the ages; speak to you of Him who is changeless—Jesus Christ—the same yesterday, and tomorrow, and in a changing world—the same today.

Excerpts of first sermon preached in the new sanctuary by Rev. J. D. Eppinga, June 19, 1960

Addendum O — Chapel Dedication Sermon — Rev. J. D. Eppinga

Last Sunday morning the LaGrave Avenue Christian Reformed Church congregation met in its new sanctuary for the first time. The message for that first service was entitled "The Same Christ" for we read in God's Word that He is the same yesterday, today and forever." Let us ask then, in these moments of consecration, who is this same Christ to whom we would dedicate this chapel in this hour. The Bible gives the answer—an answer which is reflected here in all we see.

The Rose Window

As the Son of God, He said, "Come unto Me." Because He is the same, He still says, "Come unto Me"—a glorious fact which is reflected in the Rose Window over the entranceway of this chapel.

The First Three-Lancet Window

However, not only did He extend His invitation to the thousands and millions, He came to individual people, to share their problems and to lighten their burdens. As He came to the many with a general invitation as depicted in the Rose Window of this chapel, so He also came to individuals, as depicted in the first three-lancet window which stands immediately to my left and which portrays Christ's intimate ministry. He dealt with the woman at the well as a person. He dealt with Nicodemus as an individual. He was mindful of children in an age when children did not count. As Hannah gave her child to God, so Christ gives Himself to children by saying, "Let the little ones come unto Me." He dealt with Zaccheus and with the sisters in Bethany. He was altogether mindful of individuals by name. This same Christ who practiced an intimate ministry to individuals as reflected in the first three-lancet window to my left, still practices this intimate ministry today.

May all those who use this chapel be comforted in this—that Christ deals with them as individuals—as persons.

The Second Three-Lancet Window

This Christ, who is the same, also exercised a preaching ministry; a fact which is reflected in the second three-lancet window. As a preacher, He told the wonderful story of the prodigal son. And as a preacher, he pointed to Himself as the Good Shepherd. He said, "Consider the lilies of the field, how they grow." The predella of the center lancet of the second section depicts the parable of the house on the rock and the house on the sand. And in the next lancet there is shown the parable of the Good Samaritan and the parable of the sower. Here then is Christ the preacher. And because He spoke so marvelously, therefore, the common people heard Him gladly. This Christ who spoke such living words when He was on this earth, still speaks today.

May all those who use this chapel be comforted in this—that Christ still speaks to them. And His words are the wonderful words of life.

The Third Three-Lancet Window

The next chapel window of three lancets illustrates various types of prayer. There is Moses' intercessory prayer for thechildren of Israel who had worshipped the golden calf during his absence on Mt. Sinai. Below is Daniel who bravely continued his habit of prayer to God int he face of threat and violence. At the top of the right lancet is Cornelius the centurion praying and being guided to seek out Peter. And at the bottom of the right lancet is David's prayer of confession derived from the 51st Psalm. And then there is the center depicting that great prayer which Christ taught us all to pray, namely The Lord's Prayer. Beneath this we see the praying Christ in Gethsemane.

How wonderful that we may pray and that God hears us when we pray. Yet, it is a privilege we could not enjoy without the Christ in whose name we pray. See here, then, the Master in His ministry of prayer; the Master who still prays for and makes intercession for us at the throne of God. This Christ who taught us to pray and who encouraged men to pray because He is the same, still invites us to come to God with our petitions.

May all who use this chapel use it also for prayer—here drawing nigh to the throne of God.

The Fourth Three-Lancet Window

The last three-lancet window portrays Christ in His ministry of mercy. At the top of the left lancet is the woman with an issue of blood touching the hem of Christ's garment. Below this is the one thankful leper out of the ten Christ healed who returned to thank and worship Him. The center lancet shows Christ healing blind Bartimaeus. The predella, which is an inset, shows Christ casting out a devil from the child who was brought to Him immediately after His transfiguration. The right lancet shows Christ speaking to the centurion whose faith was so great. The boom of the right lancet shows the scene at the Pool of Bethesda.

Christ the physician in His ministry of mercy. And, because He is the same, He is merciful still.

May all those who use this chapel find this same Christ—who can heal all their soul's diseases.

Thus we have Christ, the same Christ, in His intimate ministry, His teaching ministry, His praying ministry, His healing ministry, and in the Rose Window over the entranceway, the Christ of the great invitation. To Him we dedicate this chapel.

****

Let us now direct our attention to the west, high on which we find twelve clerestory windows presenting symbols of the twelve apostles.

Peter

Beginning at the rear there is the symbol of Peter. Here we have the crossed keys recalling Peter's confession and our Lord's statement regarding the office of the keys which he commited to the church on earth.

James

Next there is James whose symbol is the staff, wallet and hat, signifying his pilgrimages. The scriptural reference upon the scroll indicates the incarnate Christ whom he proclaimed.

John

Next there is John whose symbol is the eagle. The eagle is one of the four beasts mentiond in the fourth chapter of Revelation. John's Gospel, from the first to the last, soars on eagles' wings to the very throne of heaven.

Andrew

The next window depicts St. Andrew's symbol. The crossed fish recall his original occupation and his call to become a fisher of men.

Bartholenew

The fifth window represents St. Bartholemew. When Philip sought out Bartholemew to tell him about Christ, he found him under a fig tree, hence the fruit and leaves of the fig. The folded hands before an open book refer to the fact that Bartholemew seems to have been a withdrawn man who spent much time in meditation.

Philip

The sixth window represents St. Philip, a basket, two loaves of bread and a Tau cross, recalling his remark when our Lord fed the multitude.

Thomas

The seventh window is the symbol of St. Thomas. Thomas reached out to feel the wounds of Christ's outstreatched palms, whereupon he made his great confession of faith: "My Lord and my God."

Matthew

The eighth window shows the symbol of St. Matthew, the winged man, because that evangelist began his gospel by tracing the human descent of our Lord.

James the Less

The ninth window symbolizes James the Less. He is characterized by the lily of the valley, that frgrant but modest flower which is the symbol of humility.

Thaddeus

The tenth window represents St. Thaddeus. This apostle sailed far on missionary journeys, hence his symbol is a sailing vessel.

Simon

The eleventh clerestory signifies St. Simon. Simon was a zealous man and thus his symbol is the symbol of Christian zeal, which is a cross with flame-like edges.

Matthias

And then there is the last window representing St. Matthias, the apostle who was chosen by lot to take the place of Judas. His symbol is the paper bearing his name which decided his fate and the Easter lily referring to the fact that he witnessed the resurrection.

****

These are the twelve apostles whose windows have been so arranged that they face the windows signifying Christ in His various ministries. While He was with them, the disciples always had their faces to Him, while in their ministries they always proclaimed this same Christ—of the intimate ministry, the teaching ministry, the ministry of prayer, the healing ministry, and the Christ of the great invitation. In short, they proclaimed the Gospel, which is also signified here through symbols carved in wood at the ends of the pews, and the cross

Addendum O — cont'd.

which is mounted on marble for all to see.

On behalf of the consistory and congregation of LaGrave, I take this opportunity to express appreciation to Mrs. Dewey Battjes for this chapel erected in memory of her late husband. We give thanks and gratitude to God who is the lover of hearts, the giver of ever good and perfect gift, the author and finisher of our faith, and the God of grace who bestows salvation through Jesus Christ His Son, our Lord.

Excerpts of the chapel dedication sermon preached by Rev. Eppinga, June 24, 1960

Addendum P — Special and Memorial Gifts to the LaGrave Building Fund

Mrs. D. Battjes	Chapel and Chapel Organ
D. Battjes	Hi-fi Equipment
Dr. and Mrs. C. Beets	Kitchen Dishes
Dr. and Mrs. D. Blocksma	Lord's Supper Carving
Dr. and Mrs. R. Blocksma	Lord's Supper Carving
Dr. and Mrs. R. Boelkins	Lord's Supper Carving
G. Boer	Desk Set
A. Boot	Equpiment for Air Conditioner
Borgman Estate	Office Drapes and Carpeting
Bosma Estate	Oriental Rug
Botting Family	Communion Table
Mrs. A. Botting	Kitchen Silverware
Choir	Robe Room
Central Ladies Aid	Choir Pews
Mrs. G. L. Daane	Lectern and Baptismal Font
F. Davidhazy	Gold Leaf on Communion Table
J. De Boer	Furniture for Assistant Pastor's Office
John and Howard Dekker	Gold Lettering on Bibles
DeVlieger Estate	Sheltered Narthex Entrance
Mrs. C. De Vries	Pulpit Furniture
J. Door	Piano
Mrs. J. Door	Lamps and Chairs in Waiting Room
Mr. and Mrs. Wm. Eerdmans	Antiphonel Organ and New Pedal Section
Mrs. and Mrs. D. Ernzer	Cloth for Communion Table
Esther Circle	Kitchen
Dan and Daane Etheridge	Printing Service
Friendship Club	Reredos Screen, Steam Table, Coffee Spouts, Mobile Warmer Unit
Mrs. N. Haan	Planter
Mr. and Mrs. Herrick	Nave Windows
J. Hoekzema	Punch Bowls and Cups
H. Hondorp	Tile Work
Dr. Ann Huizenga	Chandeliers
Mrs. L. S. Huizenga	Pulpit Sign
Mrs. B. Hunderman	Kitchenette
P. Hyma	Furniture for Assistant Pastor's Office
Johnson Construction	Tile for Banquet Hall
Mrs. Phes Kieft	Bibles
Mr. and Mrs. B. Kuiper	Bulletin Board, Carillon Bells, and Auto-Bell Player
Bert Kuiper	Paint for Yellow Parking Lines
Mrs. E. Kuiper	Chancel Window
Maris Estate	Kern's Contract

Addendum P — cont'd.

Meerman Sisters	Guest Register
John Oole	Furniture for Assistant Pastor's Office
Mrs. E. Rodenhouse	Bibles
M. Rooks	Photo Work
D. Roskam	Two Typewriters
Mr. and Mrs. Milton Roskam	Music Storage
Service Guild	Kitchen
Mr. and Mrs. E. S. Sevensma	Bibles
Wm. Sterk	Refinish Organ
Mrs. Wm. Stuart	Bibles
Sunday Niters	Flags
Mrs. F. Timmer	Collection Plates
Mr. and Mrs. B. VandenBerg	Clocks
Don VandenBerg	Art Work
J. VandenBerg	Furniture for Pastor's Office
A. VanDongen	Punch Bowl and Cups
Mrs. A. VerMerris	Fill Planter
Mr. and Mrs. G. VanSledright	Drapes—Organ Pipes
E. VanSweden	The "I-Beam" Move
H. Walkotten	Furniture
Mr. and Mrs. C. Werner	Public Address System
Mr. and Mrs. W. Zweedyk	Flood Lights

Anonymous donors also provided a substantial amount of money.

Not only at the time of the building of a new church, but throughout the history of LaGrave, many individuals and organizations have donated a variety of gifts. Some have been of a practical nature, some decorative, but all have been appreciated.

Addendum Q — Special Funds at LaGrave

Through the years there have been many memorial funds established. The following funds are those which were active at the time of the Centennial.

Alida Geerlings Fund
    Established in 1981

Geerlings Flower Fund
    Established in 1970

DeVlieger Needy Medical Student Fund
    Established in 1970

Oosterveer Neighborhood Mission Fund
    Established in 1976

Ernzer Youth Education Fund
    Established in 1977

Sue Bos Muller Special Music Fund
    Established in 1981

Addendum R — LaGrave Church Organizations and Officers — 1986-1987

BENEFACTORS TRUST FUND
Ken Faber, President
Howard Goris, Vice President
Harold Knoor, Secretary
Robert VanderWal, Treasurer

BOY SCOUTS
Harold VanDyk, Scoutmaster
Bob Dykstra, Troup Committee Chairman

CHANCEL CHOIR
Kerrie Doezema, President
Dan VanderVliet, Vice President
Mary DeGraaf, Secretary

CHRISTIAN EDUCATION SOCIETY
Mary Jo DeJong, President
Julia Hoekstra, Secretary
Sue Ernzer, Treasurer
Ann VanEerden, Promotions

DEACONCESSES
Irene Cook, President
(After January 1, Marie VanBeek)

ESTHER CIRCLE
Linda Male, President
Marie VanBeek, Vice President
Mary Lois Gunther, Secretary
Jeanne DeVries, Treasurer
Rena Dozeman, Assistant Secretary-Treasurer

F.I.S.H.
Marge VanOverBeek, Coordinator

FRIENDSHIP CLUB
Susan Verwys, President
Susan Kruyf and Leesa Schram, Co-Vice-Presidents
Kathy Poel, Secretary
Carol Grussing, Treasurer
Karen DeVries, Assistant Secretary-Treasurer

HENRY BEETS AUXILIARY
Marge VanderMeulen, President

HENRY BEETS MISSION SOCIETY
Phil Versluis, Past President
Andy DeVries, President
Kay Oosting, Secretary
Phil Huizenga, Treasurer

JUNIOR HIGH YOUTH GROUP SPONSORS
Tom and Sharon Etheridge
Ron and Marsha Kooistra
Leo and Robin Mulder

LA GRAVE PLAYERS
Robert Haan, Director

MISSIONARY SOCIETY
Lois Knoor, President
Jean Clelland, Vice President
Sadie Gaikema, Secretary
Gertrude Brander, Treasurer
Jeanette Davidhazy, Assistant Secretary-Treasurer

SERVICE GUILD
Flora Horjus, President
Mary Romence, Vice President
Mary Boerema, Secretary
Joyce Thomasma, Treasurer
Ruth Roelofs, Vice Secretary-Treasurer

SENIOR HIGH YOUTH GROUP SPONSORS
Steve and Deb DeHaan
Dave and Sheryl Livingston
Bob and Karen DeVries

STEPHEN MINISTRY
Rev. J. Steigenga, Director
Jackie Fazekas and Marian Smedes, Assistants

SUNDAY EVENING SERIES
James Wieland, Chairman
Phil Huizenga, Treasurer

WOMEN'S BOARD
Lois Knoor, Convener

YOUNG ADULTS SPONSORS
Dan and Ann VanEerden

Addendum S — Membership List of Those Attending LaGrave 50 Years or More

(Some volunteered the
number of years)

Saralyn Andree — 77
W. Clarence Beets — 56
Anne Beets — 55
Albert Bel
Esther Bielema
Ralph Blocksma — 72
Alice Bloom
Gordon Boer — 56
John Boerema
Roger Boerema
Simon Boerema
Gertrude Brander
Reynold Brander — 61
Arthur Boot
Barbara Boot
Clarence Botting — 72

Ethel DeBoer

Marguerite DeBoer — 93
Barbara DeHaan
Pat DeHaan
Stanley DeHaan
Mary DeGraaf
Ruth DeJong
Lois DeNeut
Howard Dekker
John Dekker
Lois DeLoof
Louise DeYoung — 74
Fannie DeVries
Jean Dice — 86

Paula Eerdmans — 74
Daane Etheridge

Bertha Franken — 92
Theodore Frieling

Ed Gaikema
Sadie Gaikema

Earl Goudzwaard

Leone Harkema
Gordon Hartger — 75
Faith Hondorp

Lucille Jurries — 72

Alyce Lantinga
Garret Lantinga
Agatha Langereis

Bea Pape — 69
Theresa Pastoor
Bert Posthumus — 81

Edward Rodenhouse
Marius Rooks
Anne Sluyter
Marian Spoelstra — 71
Watson Spoelstra — 60
William Stehouwer

Henrietta Stuit — 64
David Swets
Jack Swets

Helen Timmer

Elmer VanBeek — 65
Louise VandenBerge
Dorothy Vandenberg
Roy Vandenberg
Ruth VandenBerg
Gertrude VanDongen
Shirley VanNoord
Tena VerMerris — 87
Jess VanderWall
Eli VanSweden
Helen VanVliet

Virginia Walstra
Betty Wierenga
Chester Woltjer
Dorothy Woltjer

Ruth Yonkers

Addendum T — Sermon on Psalm 90 (Centennial Psalm) — Rev. J. D. Eppinga

"The Hiding Place"

Younger people can't remember. Older people might. Years ago, passing from one year to the next, our forefathers invariably read and/or sang Psalm 90.

It was a tradition!

On the last day of every year, my father read Psalm 90 at the dinner table. Then we went to church to attend Old Year's Service, as it was called. There I heard Psalm 90 again—read by the minister.

Tonight we have followed that tradition. You have listened to a reading of this Psalm. You have also sung it. Having heard and sung it, let us now meditate upon it.

In doing so, let us first ask who wrote it? Moses wrote it. It's not the only song he wrote. For all we know, he might have written many. What we know, for sure, is that he wrote at least three. The first recorded song of Moses is found in Exodus chapter 15. It is referred to sometimes as the oldest recorded song in human history—a song of victory over Pharaoh who drowned in the Red Sea.

The next recorded song of Moses was composed some forty years later. It is found in Deuteronomy chapter 32. There is one more song of Moses. It is Psalm 90.

Psalm 90 have lived—and lives on in the hearts of God's people. It is a great favorite. With the exception of Psalm 23 and 103 it is the most quoted of all the 150 Psalms.

That is because it is so human.

People can identify with it.

It is surprising that it is so human, considering its source. Michelangelo carved a statue of Moses. He looks like the god Zeus. He looked like a god of mythology. Michelangelo depicted him as a superman; a powerful figure—which he was in more ways than one. All agree that Michelangelo's statue of Moses captures something of what and who Moses was; the leader of a nation; the great emancipator; the world's earliest and still greatest historian. The man from Mt. Sinai. A figure of greatness, and lonely and grand in his greatness. But in

252

Psalm 90 he doesn't sing of his greatness. He doesn't sing about his Mt. Sinai adventure where God wrote ten commandments on stone with his fingers of lightning. He doesn't sing of his experience at the burning bush whose flames would not diminish and where he heard the voice of God. He doesn't sing about great battles waged and won. Instead, he, great and mighty, chosen of God, wrote a very human prayer.

Psalm 90!

The song of Moses!

In this prayer, he dwells on man's misery, man's mortality, and man's sinfulness. He sings, first of all, about man's misery. He cries: "Have pity on Thy servants" (v.12). He writes about the days wherein we have seen evil (v.15). He had seen a lot of it in Egypt and in the wilderness.

We have seen a lot of misery, too, in the days of our years. Consider the year now closing. Earthquakes, eruptions, hurricanes. Even worse! Mortal storms, hunger, war, and racial strife. Terrorism. Crime. Loneliness. Disease. What a vale of tears! It gets us "down" sometimes.

It got Moses "down" too—great man though he was. "We are consumed by Thine anger," he wrote, "and by Thy wrath we are overwhelmed."

Moses also wrote about man's mortality. He said, "Our years fly by (v.10), like a tale that is told. We flourish like morning grass, but also like grass, soon fade." Moses lived a long time. During his unusual span of years, he saw the generations come and go. It made him melancholy. "For most," he said, "life was threescore and ten. For some, stronger, fourscore. Yet in the end, all were swept away."

Our mortality can make us melancholy too.

Moses also wrote in his song of man's sinfulness. "Thou hast set our iniquities before Thee, our secret sins in the light of Thy countenance" (v.8). Here, too, we can identify with this great man; identify—not with his tallness, but smallness. This, too, makes Moses' song—our song. No wonder our ancestors invariably turned to it at year's end, in penitence and weakness.

But are these (man's misery, man's mortality, man's sinfulness) the factors that make this song so popular? Great and necessary as these themes are, the greatness of this Song of Moses lies elsewhere.

Where?

The uniqueness of this Song of Moses lies in its beginning.

And in its ending.

Consider its beginning. "Lord, Thou hast been our dwelling place in all generations!"

What a statement! The Dutch word is "toevlucht." The German is the same. As a boy I heard my parents sing it:

"Een toevlucht in gevaren."

A "toevlucht" is a refuge. A hiding place! Remember Corrie TenBoom's book, *The Hiding Place*? She got the title from Psalm 90's beginning.

Moses lived in an Egyptian palace—but it wasn't home. He lived in exile in Midian for forty years and married there—but it wasn't home. He wandered in the desert for forty years but it, too—wasn't home. In all those years—and there were many of them—he never had a home!

And yet he did. God was his home—Psalm 90:1. The Christian can relate to that. The Christian has a dwelling place, a refuge, a hiding place, a home. His dwelling is his God.

The other reason for this Psalm's uniqueness is its ending.

"Establish Thou the work of our hands!" Moses, shading his eyes, looked to the horizon and saw the promised land. He would never enter it. But would his people reach and enter it? After all his toil and trouble, aching back and aching bones and aching head for all the years—would his people perish at the last and all his work be lost? Wasted? In vain? Thus Moses prayed. May my life not be wasted, Lord. Make it count for you! Establish Thou the work of my hands!

Who of us cannot relate to that? We were going to do so much this past year and now it is gone. Where did it go! I was going to do so much in my ministry and now forty years of it is gone! Retirement looms on the horizon but I have barely begun! There's so much I haven't done! Finish it, Lord. Establish it—the little there is of it to establish.

Who of you cannot relate to my words?

And so, the Song of Moses. He sang it, and died—the only human being buried by God himself; a God who stood at the foot of his grave and said, "Moses, I will establish your work." Years later, Moses himself saw it established. On the Mount of Transfiguration. There, together with Elijah, he saw a son of the tribe of Judah—

Jesus!

Moses still sings his song today. We know this because the Bible tells us so. We read in Revelation 15:2 and 3: "And I saw what appeared to be a sea of glass and those who had conquered standing beside it, with harps of God in their hands. And they sing the Song of Moses."

Can you see them? Your loved ones who have died? Peter, Paul, Calvin, Luther—Moses?

As they sing it up there, let us sing it down here.

"Lord, Thou hast been our dwelling place in all generations ... Establish Thou the work of our hands."

Excerpts of sermon preached at LaGrave Church, New Years Eve, 1985, by Rev. J. D. Eppinga.

Addendum U — Centennial Hymn — Kenneth Sweetman

Thy Hand, O God, Has Guided

LaGrave 7•6•7•6•D

Unison Voices

©Kenneth Sweetman 1986

1. Thy hand, O God, has guid - ed Thy flock from age to age;
3. When sha - dows thick were fall - ing, And all seemed sunk in night,
5. And we, shall we be faith - less? Shall hearts fail, hands hang down?
6. Thy mer - cy will not fail us, Nor leave thy work un - done;

The won - drous tale is writ - ten Full clear on ev - 'ry page;
Thou, Lord, didst send thy ser - vants, Thy chos - en sons of light.
Shall we e - vade the con - flict, And cast a - way our crown?
With thy right hand to help us, The vic - t'ry shall be won;

Our fa - thers owned thy good - ness, And we their deeds re - cord;
On them and on thy peo - ple Thy plen-teous grace was poured,
Not so, in God's deep coun - sels Some bet - ter thing is stored:
And then by men and an - gels Thy name shall be a - dored,

And both of this bear wit - ness: One Church, one Faith, one Lord.
And this was still their mes - sage: One Church, one Faith, one Lord.
We will main - tain, un - flinch - ing, One Church, one Faith, one Lord.
And this shall be their an - them, One Church, one Faith, one Lord.

254

Harmony

2. Thy her - alds brought glad tid - ings To great-est as to least;
4. Through man - y a day of dark - ness, Through man - y a scene of strife,

They bade men rise and has - ten To share the great King's feast;
The faith - ful few fought brave - ly To guard the Chur - ch's life.

And this was all their teach - ing, In ev - 'ry deed and word,
Their Gos - pel of re - demp - tion, Sin par-don'd, man re - stored,

To all a - like pro - claim - ing One Church, one Faith, one Lord.
Was all in this en - fold - ed, One Church, one Faith, one Lord.

255

ACKNOWLEDGMENTS

The author and editors are grateful to many individuals and organizations for assistance in finding and obtaining information. We especially thank Professor James J. DeJonge, College and Seminary Archivist, Heritage Hall, Calvin College; and Connie VanSledright, librarian, Calvin College; the Grand Rapids Public Library; Dr. W. Clarence Beets, a lifelong member of LaGrave, who provided much useful information; Ruth Snoek, LaGrave Church secretary for all the many questions she answered; and those LaGrave members who generously shared information and pictures with us and also offered financial support. The initial concept of this book and the funding to begin the production came from the LaGrave Service Guild. We thank the people listed below for making *A Century of Grace* a reality.

Centennial Committee

Gerald VanderWall, Chairman
Gordon Buter
Reverend Jacob D. Eppinga
Barbara Leegwater
Nancy W. Peters
Dr. John Pool
Dr. Charles Strikwerda

Centennial Book Committee

(Research and Editorial)

Nancy W. Peters, Chairman
Wilfred Clelland
Constance DeVries
Agnes Gezon
Philip and Marie Huizenga
Clazina Masselink
Mary Romence
Elmer and Marie VanBeek
Gerald and Jessica VanderWall
Wilma Walkotten

Photography

Marius Rooks
   (sanctuary and chapel windows,
      frescoes, and Dekker memorial)
Kenneth Porter (portraits)
Thelma Kemink
Joe Schuitema

Portraits

Chris Overvoorde

Production

James V. Hoekstra
   Hoekstra Printing Company
The Type Source, Typesetting
Edgar P. Stanard, Jr., Artist
Howard Dekker
   John H. Dekker and Sons,
      Bookbinders

Special Assignments

Sharon Etheridge
Dr. Dewey J. Hoitenga, Jr.
Mary Romence
Dr. Charles Strikwerda
Ellen VanArtsen
Marie VanBeek
Jessica VanderWall

Typists

Ruth Snoek, Church Secretary
Jean Garehan
Rachel Granstra
Nell Tjapkes
Ellen VanArtsen
Winnie Wulbrecht